Latin America since Independence

What is Latin America, after all? While histories of the "other" Americas often link disparate histories through revolutionary or tragic narratives, *Latin America since Independence* begins with the assumption that our efforts to imagine a common past for nearly thirty countries are deeply problematic. Without losing sight of chronology or regional trends, this text offers glimpses of the Latin American past through eleven carefully selected stories. Each chapter introduces students to a specific historical issue, which in turn raises questions about the history of the Americas as a whole. Key themes include:

- Race and Citizenship
- Inequality and Economic Development
- Politics and Rights
- Social and Cultural Movements
- Globalization
- Violence and Civil Society

The short, thematic chapters are bolstered by the inclusion of relevant primary documents—many translated for the first time—including advertisements and posters, song lyrics, political speeches, government documents, and more. Each chapter also includes timelines highlighting important dates and suggestions for further reading. A highly interactive companion website contains the full text of key excerpted documents, additional images, film clips, and student review materials as well as instructor resources designed to save instructors time, such as an instructor's manual, an abridged testbank, PowerPoint outlines, and more. Richly informative and highly readable, *Latin America since Independence* provides compelling accounts of this region's past and present.

For additional information and classroom resources please visit the *Latin America since Independence* companion website at www.routledge.com/textbooks/dawson.

Alexander Dawson is Associate Professor of Latin American History at Simon Fraser University, in British Columbia, Canada. He is the author of *First World Dreams: Mexico since 1989* and *Indian and Nation in Revolutionary Mexico*.

Latin America since Independence

A History with Primary Sources

ALEXANDER DAWSON

Routledge
Taylor & Francis Group

NEW YORK AND LONDON

Acquisitions Editor: Kimberly Guinta
Senior Development Editor: Nicole Solano
Editorial Assistant: Jenna Grady
Production Editor: Siân Findlay
Marketing Manager: Cheryl Vawdrey
Text Design: Karl Hunt at Keystroke
Copyeditor: Graeme Leonard
Proofreader: Samantha Green
Indexer: Perry Stein

First published 2011
by Routledge
270 Madison Avenue, New York, NY 10016

Simultaneously published in the UK
by Routledge
2 Park Square, Milton Park, Abingdon, Oxon OX14 4RN

Routledge is an imprint of the Taylor & Francis Group, an informa business

© 2011 Taylor & Francis

Designed and typeset in Dante by
Keystroke, Tettenhall, Wolverhampton
Printed and bound in the United States of America on acid-free paper by
Sheridan Books, Inc.

Library of Congress Cataloging in Publication Data
Latin America since independence: a history with primary sources / edited by Alexander Dawson.
    p. cm.
Includes bibliographical references and index.
1. Latin America—History—1830—Textbooks. 2. Latin America—History—1830—Sources.
I. Dawson, Alexander S. (Alexander Scott), 1967-
F1413.L38 2010
980.03—dc22   2010009503

ISBN13: 978–0–415–99195–7 (hbk)
ISBN13: 978–0–415–99196–4 (pbk)
ISBN13: 978–0–203–84535–6 (ebk)

Contents

Illustrations

Figures

Document

Tables

Acknowledgments

The ideas that ultimately became this book began percolating a very long time ago, when as a student of Latin American History, I had the good fortune to be taught by Christon Archer, Paul Gootenberg, Brooke Larson, Barbara Weinstein, Fred Weinstein, and Gene Lebovics, teachers who never failed to insist that however much I strived to understand this region, there was always more work to do. As a teacher of Latin America's past, I am similarly indebted to my students, who over the years collectively pushed me to provide them with access to the best that my field has to offer, and deliver that knowledge in a way that they find relevant and compelling. I have done my best here to meet all your expectations.

I received specific help in this project from Mónica Amaré, Santiago Anria, Dain Borges, Gaston Gordillo, José Gordillo, Adrian López Denis, Martín Monsalve, Timo Schaeffer, Richard Slatta, Perry Stein, Hannah Wittman, and Wendy Wolford. Even more critical was the patient and constant advice I received from Alejandra Bronfman and Jon Beasley-Murray, who suggested many of the documents and offered valuable critiques of every aspect of the book. Alejandra also read the entire manuscript, improving it considerably in the process. At Routledge, Kimberly Guinta and Nicole Solano were delightful editors. Angela Chnapko ably steered the book through a complicated permissions process, and Patricia Rosas and Diane Grosklaus Whitty provided excellent translations of several texts.

And of course, my warmest thanks are to Maia, Nina, and Alejandra, for giving me a reason to turn off the computer.

I would also like to thank the following academic reviewers whose anonymous suggestions during the reviewing process helped me greatly as I prepared the book:

Millagros Denis, Hunter College
John J. Dwyer, Duquesne University
Mary Karasch, Oakland University
Andrew Kirkendall, Texas A&M University
Peter Klaren, George Washington University
Kris Lane, College of William & Mary
Mollie Lewis, University of South Alabama

Jocelyn Olcott, Duke University
Rosa Maria Pegueros-Lev, University of Rhode Island
Charles F. Walker, University of California–Davis
Elliott Young, Lewis & Clark College

Abbreviations

ABI: Bolivian Information Agency (*Agencia Boliviana de Información*)—Bolivia

AJR: Association of Rebel Youth (*Asociación de Juventud Rebelde*)—Cuba

ALBA: Bolivarian Alternative for Latin America and the Caribbean (*Alternativa Bolivariana para America Latina y El Caribe*)

ANAP: National Small Farmers Association (*Asociación Nacional de Agricultores Pequeños*)—Cuba

APRA: American Popular Revolutionary Alliance (*Alianza Popular Revolucionaria Americana*)—Peru

CDR: Committees for the Defense of the Revolution (*Comités de Defensa de la Revolución*)—Cuba

CGT: General Confederation of Labor (*Confederación General del Trabajo*)—Argentina

CIA: Central Intelligence Agency—United States of America

CONADEP: National Commission on the Disappearance of Persons (*Comisión Nacional sobre la Desaparición de Personas*)—Argentina

CPBs: Pro-Bolivia Councils (*Consejos Pro-Bolivianos*)—Bolivians residing in Europe

CSUTCB: Bolivian Confederation of Rural Workers (*Confederación Sindical Unica de Trabajadores Campesinos de Bolivia*)—Bolivia

CTC: Cuban Workers Confederation (*Central de Trabajadores de Cuba*)—Cuba

FAO: Food and Agriculture Organization of the United Nations

FDR: Franklin Delano Roosevelt—United States of America

FEP: Eva Perón Foundation (*Fundación Eva Perón*)—Argentina

FORA: Argentine Regional Worker's Federation (*Federación Obrera Regional Argentina*)—Argentina

FMC: Cuban Federation of Women (*Federación de Mujeres Cubanas*)—Cuba

FTAA: Free Trade Area of the Americas

GDP: Gross Domestic Product

HDI: Human Development Index

IMF: International Monetary Fund

IRCA: International Railroads of Central America

ISI: Import Substitution Industrialization

MAS: Movement Towards Socialism (*Movimiento al Socialismo*)—Bolivia

MCAS: Consular Identification Cards (*Matriculas Consulares de Alta Seguridad*)—Mexico

MERCOSUR: Southern Common Market (*Mercado Común del Sur; Mercado Comum do Sul*)—
   Argentina, Brazil, Paraguay, Uruguay

MFI: Multilateral Financial Institution

MIR: Revolutionary Left Movement (*Movimiento de la Izquierda Revolucionaria*)—Bolivia

MNR: Nationalist Revolutionary Movement (*Movimiento Nacionalista Revolucionario*)—Bolivia

NAFTA: North American Free Trade Agreement—Canada, Mexico, US

NIC: Newly Industrialized Country

NGO: Non-Governmental Organization

OAS: Organization of American States

PCS: Political Constitution of the State—Bolivia

PDVSA: *Petróleos de Venezuela*—Venezuela

PEMEX: *Petróleos Mexicanos*—Mexico

PIC: Independent Party of Color (*Partido Independiente de Color*)—Cuba

PRI: Institutional Revolutionary Party (*Partido Revolucionario Institucional*)—Mexico

SIN: National Intelligence Service (*Servicio Nacional de Inteligencia*)—Peru

UCR: Radical Civic Union (*Unión Cívica Radical*)—Argentina

UDP: Democratic and Popular Unity (*Unidad Democrática y Popular*)—Bolivia

UFCO: United Fruit Company—United States of America

UN: United Nations

USAID: United States Agency for International Development—United States of America

YPFB: *Yacimientos Petrolíferos Fiscales Bolivianos*

Introduction

Latin America's Useable Past

Strolling through Mexico City's Parque Lincoln on any given Sunday, it is easy to forget the world beyond this small bit of paradise. Motorized toy boats meander around the small pond, the water clean and inviting. Children run around and laugh inside the high fences of a public playground that puts most North American parks to shame. The mouth-watering smells of Argentine and Italian bistros waft through the air, reminding you that you are in the heart of Polanco, one of the nicest neighborhoods in the city. Surrounding art deco apartment buildings provide a sense of safe and comfortable living, while the *belle époque* grandeur of the nearby Ford Foundation mansion evokes both a wealthy past and a beneficent present. People are out and about, seemingly unafraid. Bicycles abound, evidence that some of those eating lunch by the park took advantage of the relatively new practice of closing down the Paseo de la Reforma (this city's great nineteenth-century boulevard) on Sunday mornings so that people may ride, run, or walk from Chapultepec Park to the Zocalo.[1] No one here seems to mind that the greening of Sunday mornings has brought an end to the tradition of holding protest marches at this same time, along this same route.

Sundays tell a different story in Ecatepec, just a few short miles away. Many residents here are at work, in locations across the metropolis, selling in the informal and formal sector, driving busses and taxis, cleaning, working in shops, earning the few pesos upon which they depend for their survival. Open-air stalls sell tacos, *dulces* (sweets), and any number of treats, but the table-clothes are made of plastic, not linen. Children play in largely neglected parks, many of them decades old, where instead of falling to rubberized mat the unlucky toddler hits the pavement with a thud when they fall from a swing. Here and there one also sees the tragic signs of a discarded childhood, youths splayed out on cardboard mats, their minds lost in a haze produced by thinners or cement, homeless, desperate. The smell of diesel fuel is stronger here, the dust in the air more present, the result of untended roads, construction sites and the paucity of trees and grass. Few people here rode bicycles on the Paseo de la Reforma this morning.

At times these two versions of Mexico City seem unknown to one other. This is a survival strategy on the part of both. While the crossings are continual (poor people sustain communities like Polanco through their labor and consumption, and the wages paid by Polcano residents allow the poor in Ecatepec to survive), a certain amount of blindness allows residents of both communities some peace of mind. Poor people stay out of rich neighborhoods for the most part when they are not at work, as life is easier and the violence and powerlessness of everyday life less jarring when one stays closer to home or in more welcoming locales. They know their neighbors, often look out for one another, and feel somehow safer in their own community. The wealthy, for their part, are just as jarred by their adventures into the slums. They are not welcome there, and are more content when they can imagine that the world beyond their own neighborhoods does not really exist. One might describe this as a kind of fragmentary consciousness, in which residents of both Ecatepec and Polanco carefully shape their view of the world to make daily life in the city viable. Whenever possible, phenomena that are too difficult to confront must be made invisible.

The fragmentary nature of life in the metropolis reminds us that we need to go beyond the lines drawn on a map to understand the boundaries that we use to make sense of the world around us. In North America we might call a person Mexican, perhaps Latin American or even *Latino* or *Chicano*[2] if they come from Mexico City, but do these designations really tell us much about a person or the place from which they came? Do they even tell us if a person identifies with a common community, or what that community might be? Residents of Polanco and Ecatepec may all be Mexicans to the wider world, and *chilangos*[3] in the eyes of other Mexicans, and may even be mutually dependent on one another, but it is not at all clear that they imagine themselves as residents of a common city or that they share common interests. It is even more difficult to weave them into a common history.

A Common Past

History found itself in the curriculum of public schools in the nineteenth century precisely because it seemed like an ideal tool for producing communities. Historians were charged with writing national histories, stories that explained who *we* are through reference to where *we* came from. Nationalist histories proliferated in the former colonies of the Americas during this era, as local intellectuals endeavored to give shape to their nations through reference to the ancient indigenous past, colonial society, and the glorious quest for independence. Often written by prominent politicians, these histories served as foundational narratives for the post-colonial states of the Americas, proof that they had every right to stand apart from their former rulers.

Latin America was also invented in the process, although to somewhat different ends. The term was first proposed by the Colombian José María Caicedo in the mid-nineteenth century to describe former colonies in the Americas whose languages shared a common origin, grouping French, Spanish, and Portuguese speaking regions in the hemisphere together.[4] Others adopted the term soon thereafter, sometimes in an effort to simplify a collection of nearly 30 countries for outsiders, and sometimes because the idea of Latin America offered a vision of strength through unity. Reformers and revolutionaries have long embraced the ideal of a united Latin America that could stand up to the power of both Europe and the United States. In order to make their case, they almost invariably turned to history, producing narratives that create a common Latin American past as precursor to a single future.

There is real power in the story. In crafting a Latin American past we have the opportunity to justify or critique existing power structures, to offer a vision of greater or lesser unity, and to help shape the region's relationship to the outside world. This indeed is the reason that local elites began writing national and regional histories in the eighteenth century. The nations they described were then mostly an illusion, conjured up from the ancient Indian past and their own sense of personal injustice. Still, they offered a compelling vision of a common past that could in turn presage a common future.

Today the same impulse remains. Because we want to describe something we call Latin America, we produce narratives that somehow connect a vast number of peoples to a common community. We choose a specific place, incident, or person, and somehow describe them in ways that suggest that they speak for some larger Latin American experience—a part standing in for the whole. Alternately, we rely on other narrative devices, making sense of Latin America through dramas about good versus evil, stories of backwardness and progress or the primitive and the modern[5], or equally odd narratives of cultural sameness (they are really no different than us). Latin America thus becomes legible because we tell its history through reference to other familiar stories.

We might for instance introduce the wealthy residents of Polanco as models of civilization or capitalist fat cats. Residents of Ecatepec then become ignorant drug-abusers who re-inscribe their own poverty through their lifestyles, or oppressed revolutionaries in waiting. Linked to nationalist narratives, romantic or tragic stories about these individuals remind us that all Mexicans, as Octavio Paz once suggested, are *children of la Malinche*.[6] And if we want to suggest even grander commonalities, we might mention the Dora and Spiderman backpacks that one sees in both places in order to convince the reader that, as participants in global mass cultural phenomena, children are the same, wherever you go. The narrative is yours to choose, and reveals little more than your own ideological preferences.

It may be that the very project of trying to tell the story of the Latin American past forces these types of short-hand, as efforts to keep this vast region (Figure I.1) in the frame seem to invariably require a series of intellectual tricks. This is why this book turns instead to the idea of the fragment as a means of exploring the Latin American past. This concept informs this text in two ways. We begin by acknowledging that experience in this part of the world is fragmentary, as different communities and individuals may live in close proximity to one another, but often do not share a common sense of either the past or the present, let alone the future. Secondly, the concept of the fragment informs the way we approach the past itself. In writing history we take small bits and pieces of experience and transform them into a narrative. No history can be an exhaustive rendering of the past, so we must decide which fragments we will privilege and which story we will tell. In doing so we also reveal the extent to which history is a story about the past told in order to justify the present or make a claim on the future, and not simply a naïve arrangement of facts, an unvarnished truth.

Fragmentation does not speak to an absence of nations or nationalism. Latin Americans embrace their national soccer teams, join together in the veneration of national symbols, and celebrate national holidays. Yet these practices do not erase the deep divisions found here, divisions that are rooted in centuries of experience. When celebrating the victories of their national soccer teams, poor Latin Americans sometimes turn against their more wealthy compatriots. They might venerate some of the same heroes, but often do so in highly particularized ways. If we were to ask ten Venezuelans to describe Simón Bolívar's values,

Figure I.1   Map of contemporary Latin America

Source: Courtesy of: http://www.lib.utexas.edu/maps/americas/latin_america.gif

we might receive several radically different answers. The same would be true were we to ask ten Mexicans about their great national hero, Emiliano Zapata. Even Roman Catholicism, which was once thought to be the cultural practice that linked all people of the region, is practiced in highly particular ways from one region to the next. Every time we offer a single rendering of Catholicism, Zapata or Bolívar, we tell one version of the past as *the* Latin American past. In doing so we privilege one set of voices while silencing others.

This text seeks a way out of that dilemma by proposing a fragmentary history of Latin America. The following chapters do not purport to render a single Latin American past. They are instead offered merely as a collection of eleven stories from that past. While chronologically ordered, and chosen because they are among the stories that Latin American historians generally consider important, they were also selected because each story defies easy narration. They do not offer authoritative ways of understanding an episode from the Latin American past so much as they suggest that each could be told in multiple ways. Neither do they connect seamlessly or easily into a single narrative about Latin America. It would seem that many of these accounts are connected. We leave it to the reader to decide the nature and significance of these linkages.

We begin by confronting the difficulties we face when we attempt to describe Independence in the early nineteenth century (Chapter 1). This is in some ways an arbitrary choice, as Independence was a political act that did not dramatically change the lives of most people in the region. It was however significant in the creation of an idea of Latin America, and its meanings and implications for the Latin American future remain the subject of debate even today. Chapter 2 introduces the *caudillo*, a mythical military figure who is sometimes blamed for centuries of political strife in the region, but whom others have always seen as a complex, even heroic defender of common people. Even if we describe *caudillos* generally, they are best understood on very specific terms.

Chapter 3 again begins with a general concern; it introduces us to the question of what individual freedom meant in societies that had long relied on the forced labor of slaves and indigenous peoples for their prosperity. Independence promised a series of freedoms, and during the nineteenth century those freedoms gradually expanded to include all male citizens across the region. Nonetheless, lingering colonial attitudes and scientific racism also conditioned the rights and privileges that non-whites enjoyed. We see here a variety of struggles, not the least of which were the efforts of the newly free to defend their citizenship rights.

Chapters 4 and 5 explore two ways of narrating a single period in the Latin American past. The export boom of the late nineteenth and early twentieth centuries saw similar efforts across the region to create communities predicated on common values, in this instance shared faith in the nineteenth-century version of progress. Electric trams, railways, and booming exports came to signify a *modern* Latin America, even as millions of rural and poor people experienced modernity as the violent loss of their freedom and well-being. Through these chapters we see the possibility of narrating this period simultaneously as triumph and tragedy.

Latin America's twentieth-century history was similarly framed by global phenomena that played out in distinctly local ways. The United States cast a long shadow on the internal affairs of many societies in the region during the past century, but in ways that defy easy characterization (Chapter 6). Some viewed the United States as an imperial hegemon, living off the blood and sweat of the Latin American poor. Others admired the United States for its technological innovations, economic progress, and capacity to trade globally. At various points American-made products were avidly consumed across the region, often desired both for their quality and for the ways they suggested good taste on the part of the consumer. Then as now, Latin Americans have an unsettled relationship with the United States. The United States is easily the most commonly mentioned enemy of the Latin American people, and the destination of choice for the vast majority of migrants from the region.

Our other episodes from the twentieth-century history of Latin America consider the rise of mass politics in the 1930s and 1940s (Chapter 7), the Cuban revolution (Chapter 8), the dirty wars (Chapter 9), and the emergence of a new lexicon of rights at the end of the century (Chapter 10). Many of these phenomena were transnational. The rise of broadcast media, the intensification of cold-war hostilities after 1959, and the growing influence of rights-based non government organizations (NGOs) beginning in the 1980s were all global phenomena. This might in turn lead us to propose a common Latin American (or even larger) experience. And then again, it is also possible that the connections we see are imposed from the outside, that it is more important that we understand the specific local ways that each of these developments played out.

We conclude with an eye to the future in present day Bolivia (Chapter 11). Contemporary Bolivia lies at the center of many storms. The political left, reborn after decades of repression, has one of its most colorful representatives in Bolivia's current president, Evo Morales. Like other twenty-first-century socialists, Morales must contend both with a demand that he improve the lot of the poor, and with the expectation on the part of indigenous and other groups that their right to self-determination be respected. He also faces a vocal and mobilized opposition, and a regional movement that intends to secede from the country. It is altogether possible that his regime will not knit together a fragmented society, but preside over its dissolution.

It is easy to make sense of these sorts of dissonances by making them into stories of good versus evil. Today this is common in Bolivia, as opposing groups demonize one another in order to justify their demands for reform or autonomy. Interestingly, the power of their antipathies (if not their specific demands) resonates with the ways that residents of Polanco and Ecatepec often view one another (when they view one another at all), each with a hostility that imagines the other as the cause of their problems. At various points in the Latin American past any number of individuals and communities have been the subject of this kind of scorn.

My hope is that the stories contained in this text make it more difficult to demonize the people lunching in Polanco, the marginalized poor of Ecatepec, or for that matter, anyone whose story is told here. The text aims to instead offer some insight into the complexities of daily life in this part of the world as we enter a challenging period in the early twenty-first century. Latin Americans live in a fragmentary present, which is a product of their fragmentary past.

The Documents

The chapters in this book represent one type of story about the past. The documents that accompany these chapters are another. Traces of a specific moment in time, they offer readers the voices of witnesses to history, individuals who record their views because they want to shape the way we understand the past and present.

The chapters and the documents are complementary, though imperfectly so. Both the documents and the essays provide information, though they are not intended primarily as that. They are interpretations, and as such readers are encouraged to examine them critically. As much as possible, they are not excerpted (where they are, the entire text generally can be found on the website). Excerpting is a form of editing, in which someone other than the creator of a text determines what is significant about that text before it reaches the reader. Access to the entire text, changed only by the act of translation, offers readers the opportunity to develop their own interpretations, allowing them to more fully participate in the process of making history.

Some of the documents are widely regarded as classics. José Martí's *Our America*, Emiliano Zapata's *Plan de Ayala*, and Augusto Sandino's *Political Manifesto* have been read by generations of students as important historical texts. Others are less well known, familiar to regional specialists and not widely read. Drawn from letters, short stories, speeches, manifestos, personal memoirs, newspaper editorials, newsreels, and films, the documents introduce readers to a multitude of ways to understand the past, a range of story-telling techniques, and a significant number of interpretive dilemmas. In the end, they remind readers that history is not simply culled from documents, but is an act of interpretation built upon an act of interpretation.

Some years ago, my students became increasingly interested in the concept of *bias*.[7] Driven by a larger public debate on objectivity in journalism, they came into the classroom with a desire to distinguish the unvarnished truth from what was somehow tainted by the values and beliefs of the interlocutor. Many left my classroom disappointed when I agreed with them that historians were biased, though I disagreed with them when they asserted that the absence of bias (as they conceived it) was possible. I told them that these texts, like all texts, were written from a perspective, and that one of the things that historians do is examine the ways that our narratives about the past are influenced by the perspective we and our historical subjects bring to the text. I insisted that there were many potential truths to be found in the Latin America past, and not one unbiased truth waiting to be discovered. I then encouraged them to take this insight about the past and apply it to their understandings of the Latin American present. It is my hope that the present text contributes to that endeavor.

1717–1790s	1780–1781	1791–1804	1807–1808	April 19, 1810	May 1810
Bourbon reforms	Túpac Amaru rebellion in Andes	Haitian revolution	Napoleon invades Iberian peninsula, installs brother Joseph on Spanish throne	Cabildo of Caracas deposes Spanish governor, establishes Caracas Junta	Revolution in Argentina

August 24, 1821	September 7, 1822	August 6, 1825	1829–30
Treaty of Córdoba recognizes Mexican independence	Pedro, son of Portuguese King, declares Brazilian independence and is crowned Emperor of Brazil on December 1	Bolivian independence	Dissolution of Gran Colombia

Independence Narratives, Past and Present

1

September 16, 1810	December 15, 1812	1815	July 9, 1816	February–July, 1819	July 28, 1821
Grito de Dolores by Father Miguel Hidalgo (Mexico)	Simón Bolívar announces support of independence in Cartagena manifesto	Brazil made Co-kingdom with Portugal	Congress of Tucumán declares Argentine independence	Congress of Angostura leads to creation of Gran Colombia	Peruvian declaration of independence. Struggles with royalist forces continue until 1824

The Shot Heard Round the World
Was the Start of the Revolution
The Minutemen were Ready
On the Move.[1]

In what seems like the stone age of television, millions of North American schoolchildren once spent their bleary-eyed Saturday mornings watching a variety of public service announcements interspersed with their cartoons. They learned about grammar, math, civics, and science from *Schoolhouse Rock*, along with a series of lessons about a seminal moment in the national past. The best among those history lessons, the "Shot Heard Round the World," was a delightfully entertaining rendering of Paul Revere's ride, in which they were told that "we" kicked out the British Redcoats in order to "let freedom reign." It was a clever work of propaganda, in which independence was narrated not as the birth of the United States (there were, after all, already a "we" and a "British," and a pre-existing history covered in another *Schoolhouse Rock* episode called "No More Kings"), but as a moment in which Americans acted out their core values through the violent expulsion of tyrants.

Outsiders might find it difficult to imagine that a series of wars in thirteen distinct colonies could be defined as a single battle for independence through this cartoon. Still, it was possible to do this largely because in the aftermath of independence, those colonies created a common government, which in turn successfully promoted the belief that North Americans shared a common national history. That national government also endeavored to promote a vision of independence that held that this war was right and just, that the English colonists living here were more American than European, that they were being oppressed by people with whom they shared few common values, and that having escaped religious persecution in Europe more than a century before, it was their destiny to demand political freedom. There were, of course, silences in this narrative. It ignored the fact that women, indigenous, and African peoples did not gain their freedom, that not all colonists came to the colonies because of religious discrimination, that many atrocities were committed in the name of independence, and that tens of thousands of people who were born in the colonies and no less American than their neighbors lost their property and community standing after the war because they supported the losing side.

Still, what is remarkable about the narrative reproduced in the *Schoolhouse Rock* cartoons is its capacity to persist as the dominant view of U.S. independence, even after a violent civil war cost over 600,000 lives less than a century later. This power is instructive of the challenge that confronts us when we try to produce a similarly straightforward understanding of independence in the Spanish, Portuguese, and French colonies that lay to the south of the thirteen British colonies that formed the United States of America. What would a *Schoolhouse Rock* version of Latin American independence look like? Where would it begin? Would it even be possible?

The Problem of Beginnings

There was no "shot heard round the world" to signal a struggle for Latin American independence, in part because there was no single war for Latin American independence. Indeed, it is astoundingly difficult to even narrate the history of the French, Spanish, English, Dutch, and Portuguese colonies that comprised this part of the world in a way that sets up independence as the logical or inevitable culmination of a national destiny—a story of freedom or otherwise. Rather, when we look at the histories that preceded and followed independence in this part of the world we are struck by the fundamental challenges that undermine efforts to tell this as one story.

The first problem we confront lies on the national level. Mexicans, Argentines, Brazilians, Chileans, and residents of other societies in the region all have their own national independence narratives, and they often differ a great deal, not just in the military heroes they venerate, but in the underlying values these stories inculcate. Mexicans for instance, revere a liberal priest (Father Miguel Hidalgo). Brazilians claim a slave owning aristocrat (Dom Pedro I). Venezuelans, Colombians, and Peruvians revere a liberal autocrat (Simón Bolívar) as the "Great Liberator," a reference to the fact that he led the military coalition that ultimately drove the Spanish out of their last footholds in South America. Some Bolivians (whose country is named for the Great Liberator) also celebrate Bolívar, but millions of people in this country instead venerate Túpac Katari, an Ayamara leader who died in a rebellion against the Spanish more than forty years before independence. Their divided loyalties offer entirely different perspectives on where we should begin and end the story of this era.

As the Bolivian case suggests, the type of independence narrative we choose depends upon what sorts of actors we privilege. Told from the perspective of European descended elite males (*criollos*), independence was often a story of bravery and sacrifice in the name of ideals (national independence, freedom, self-determination). Told from the perspective of elite women it was often a much more ambivalent story of frustrated ambitions (see the story of Manuela Sáenz, Bolívar's lover and savior, on this account[2]). Indigenous peoples often opposed these local leaders, fearing that self-determination for colonial elites would signal ruin for themselves, as those same colonial elites were their worst exploiters. African descended slaves had similarly complex views, supporting a variety of sides in the conflicts depending on where individual and collective opportunities for emancipation seemed to lie.

These challenges might lead us to abandon both the idea of a common independence narrative and a sense that there can be a common story of Latin America. Yet if we do this we risk losing sight of what seems like a significant fact: between 1790 and 1830 almost every colony in the Americas (excepting Canada, Cuba, and a small number of other colonies in or bordering the Caribbean) violently dispossessed their European rulers. A shared history of colonial rule marked all of these societies, and left common legacies and challenges for most. Moreover, the battles for independence connected societies across the region. News of rebellions in one colony spread to others, as did rebel and imperial armies. The fact that different parts of the region were under the control of different empires also facilitated the process, as rebel leaders could flee from their home to the colony of another European Empire (thus Bolívar's *Letter from Jamaica*, excerpted below), and could at times enlist the support of the European enemies of their colonial overlords. This, of course, was possible because during the late eighteenth and early nineteenth centuries Europe was consumed by the Napoleonic Wars, leaving the governments of the old world without the wherewithal to fully dominate their colonies (Figure 1.1).

These phenomena leave us with a series of uncomfortable choices. If we choose one independence narrative, we offer the opportunity of imagining a common Latin American past, but silence other, equally valid ways of understanding this history. If we choose too many narratives we might do greater justice to a series of personal and local stories, but we risk losing a larger view of Latin America in the cacophony. My approach to this dilemma is two-fold. Below I will not tell one story of independence, but three. And rather than con-

Figure 1.1 Map of European possessions in the New World

Source: Courtesy of: http://history.howstuffworks.com/south-american-history/history-of-south-america2. htm

A larger version of this map can be found on the companion website at www.routledge.com/textbooks/dawson.

sidering independence as a series of personages and events that need to be remembered and venerated, the sections that follow focus on the ways that independence is narrated—the morals and messages that are usually invoked through the story of Latin American independence.

Stories of Freedom

On November 4, 1780 in the Andean town of Tinta, Túpac Amaru II (José Gabriel Candorcanqui) seized the local Spanish Governor, Antonio de Arriaga, and ordered that he be put on trial. Executing de Arriaga a week later, he declared a rebellion against the Spanish Empire. His rebellion failed, leading to his death and the deaths of thousands of his compatriots, but the cathartic (or alternately, frightening) power of his rebellion resonates in parts of Latin America to this day.

Colonial Latin Americans lived in unfree and unequal societies, and while most struggled against the injustices they faced only in limited quotidian ways, the region saw its share of spectacularly violent uprisings. Indigenous peoples, locked in a caste system that offered limited rights and made many demands, and slaves, were the most unfree and led the most impressive struggles. The Caste War in the Yucatán in 1712, millenarian revolts in the Andes, and the creation of vast communities of escaped slaves (the largest, Palmares, survived in Brazil from 1605 to 1694) reflected this. At their extreme these movements envisioned a world without Spaniards. They banished Europeans, their languages, and their food in their effort to return to a distant, utopian past. Nonetheless, as they were fighting against colonial states that were much stronger than them, most struggles for freedom in colonial Latin America were ultimately defeated—that is, until Haitian slaves took on the most powerful European nation of the day.

If we narrate independence as a story about freedom, Haiti (St. Domingue) is a good place to begin. During the 1780s St. Domingue accounted for 40 percent of France's foreign trade, and was arguably the richest colony in Latin America, producing two-fifths of the world's sugar and half the world's coffee. A half million slaves lay at the heart of that prosperity, and would also be its undoing. A glimpse of the island in 1791 would reveal hundreds of thousands of recently enslaved Africans, subjects who had been born free and longed for emancipation. One would also see a small but significant number of free people of color (some of whom supported slavery), important economic players on the island who chafed at the fact that even the revolutionary Estates General denied them political rights.

It was in this context that a slave revolt in 1791 metastasized into a civil war, and then a colonial war, leaving the island's white planters unable to defend their possessions. Slave emancipation came in 1793, when a French appointed governor (Léger-Félicité Sonthonax) used the promise of freedom to build alliances with newly-freed slaves and regain control over the island. Eleven years later, after a decade more of civil strife, occupations by British, French, and Spanish armies, and numerous attempts to re-establish slavery on the island, Haitians won their independence. Theirs was the first republic to ban slavery in the Americas.

Events in St. Domingue had an impact elsewhere. Slave uprisings in the Spanish colonies (e.g. Coro, Venezuela, in 1795) followed news of St. Domingue. Planters around the

Caribbean responded in kind, increasing discipline on their estates and mercilessly punishing even the hint of slave resistance. When war broke out in the Spanish colonies just a few years later, slavery was on many people's minds. Some slaves, like Juan Izaguirre in the Valle de Onato in Venezuela, appropriated the language of *criollo* (American born Spaniards) liberators to claim their own freedom. Others opted for loyalty to Spain when this seemed a likelier route to freedom. Slaves defended Buenos Aires against the British Invasion in 1806–7, and supported the royalist forces in large numbers in return for promises of rights and freedoms (commonly the right to be treated as a Spaniard). Not to be outdone, several rebel governments (*juntas*) outlawed the slave trade and passed (post-dated) free womb laws[3] (Santiago in 1811, Buenos Aires in April 1812, and Lima in 1821). The Venezuelan rebel Francisco Miranda, who was personally opposed to slavery, offered freedom in return for 10 years military service. Bolívar, who followed Miranda as a leading figure in Venezuelan revolutionary circles (and who was a member of the group that arrested Miranda and turned him over to the Spanish), actively recruited slaves beginning in 1816, and would not have succeeded without drawing them away from the royalist cause.

Miranda, Bolívar, and the other rebel leaders who openly opposed slavery have come to be known as Latin America's early liberals. This term was bandied about constantly during the nineteenth century, used to describe any number of political movements that identified with progress and against tradition. Liberals called for greater freedom, sometimes individual freedom and equality before the law, sometimes the elimination of government imposed trade restrictions, and often an end to the power of the corporate entities that characterized colonial society—the Church, the nobility, and the communal Indian village (the latter because liberals believed that communal land tenure restricted the free circulation of private property and thus limited their nations' potential for economic growth). Liberalism could thus be used to argue simultaneously for the freedom of urban elites from their colonial masters and for their right to gobble up the property of rural peasants, to in effect enhance their freedom at the expense of other people's interests.

Other stories of freedom in the region are similarly complex. In Mexico, Father Miguel Hidalgo's followers responded to his *Grito de Dolores* by raising a rag-tag army that swept through the Bajío in late 1810. Unlike earlier movements in the Andes, Hidalgo's armies were multiethnic, composed mainly of people who were already, to a certain extent free, but who, after years of drought and declining wages, viewed wealthy Spaniards (particularly grain merchants) as enemies, and at the very least wanted the king's intercession in their favor. "Death to Spaniards"—the popular slogan shouted as they marched—did not refer to the king, but his venal surrogates.

More complex still, it appears that beyond economic concerns, many of their grievances were the product of eighteenth-century religious reforms, which undermined their traditional religious practices in an attempt to enforce Catholic orthodoxy. They demanded a return to the colonial system as they had known it in the past, and restoration of the *old* Spanish King. Freedom then, was invoked to justify many different things. It could speak to a desire to escape human bondage, the demand that the avarice of your social betters be contained, or even be framed as the right worship according to the dictates of one's ancestors.

Stories of Tradition

Most modern individuals chafe at the idea of corporate privilege. It seems wrong that members of the nobility and clergy should enjoy special privileges, or that rights be apportioned differently based on one's place of birth. We see those who might defend these privileges as backwards at best, and antidemocratic at worst. We can easily understand villagers in the Mexican Bajío revolting because elites were treating them particularly harshly in the context of a famine (1808–10). It is easy to imagine slaves demanding the right to be free. It makes less sense that indigenous people might in fact support colonial rule, defending a system of corporate privileges that seemed to place them at the bottom of the social hierarchy. Nonetheless, this too is an important story of independence.

Indians in colonial Latin America owed service and tribute to the state. They also possessed rights to self-rule, to land, water, timber, and the practice of customary law. Though not always perfectly respected, these rights represented the most powerful currency that most indigenous peoples possessed within colonial society, claims that could be invoked in order to defend individual and community interests against otherwise more powerful outsiders, many of whom were politically connected *criollos*. A significant number of indigenous rebellions during the colonial period were efforts to preserve and expand these rights—rebellions, in effect, in defense of village autonomy. In fact, the Andean rebellions of 1780 were not invariably tied to demands for freedom or equality. They were often efforts to defend local village rights and ensure that royal officials respected local prerogatives. It was not just military repression that brought peace to the Andes in the aftermath of the 1780 rebellion, but a concerted effort by the Spanish state to deal more effectively with local grievances. In part due to their efforts to forge a new colonial pact of domination, Spanish officials did not see renewed rebellion in this region during the wars for independence. Liberal ideals generally fell on deaf ears here.

Tradition carried a great deal of weight elsewhere in Latin America. Lacking democratic institutions and a history of individual rights, state and society across the region were framed by and made sense of through tradition. Honorable families could trace their propriety back generations. Access to political privilege was decided by lineage. The Catholic Church acted as the social glue, operating schools, hospitals, orphanages, charities, and cemeteries, and dominating social and ecclesiastical life through its calendar. Agents of the Spanish Inquisition policed spiritual life in the colony. If change was in the air— and it was, as more and more Latin Americans read enlightenment thinkers, called themselves liberals, and questioned tradition—the backlash against new ideas was just as strong.

In Mexico, struggles between liberals and traditionalists (conservatives) spawned a decade of civil war and then a compromise at independence. The royalist Agustín de Iturbide turned on his superiors and joined the struggle for independence in 1821 in a bargain that saw the primacy of the Catholic Church and the unity of the nation preserved. In the Andes, the pull of tradition (and a fear of the power of the masses) would keep many on the royalist side until the region was liberated from the outside in the 1820s.

More powerful still was the claim to tradition in the parts of Latin America where slavery remained a dominant mode of economic production. In order to function, slave societies relied on a series of myths about stability, the power and virtue of the planter, and the natural order of things. Cuban elites—their terror stoked by race war in Haiti—never seriously considered independence in the early nineteenth century. In Brazil, the weight of tradition and the power of aristocracy were critical to the illusion that slavery was anything but an abomination. The Portuguese emperor was a father to the people of Brazil in the same way that the planter was a father to the slave.

This logic explains Brazil's unusual path to independence. Like other regions in the Americas, Brazil experienced its share of late eighteenth-century rebellions (the most famous led by Tiradentes in 1789), but by a particular turn of fate, these rebellions never became part of a national independence narrative, in which Brazilians freed themselves from oppressive and distant colonial rulers. Instead, the distant colonial state came to Brazil, and indirectly set off a series of events that would ultimately lead to independence. Fleeing the Napoleonic invasion of Portugal, Emperor João VI and 15,000 Portuguese relocated to Rio de Janeiro in 1808. The city quickly became the official center of the Empire, with concomitant increases in trade and investment, and Brazil itself was formally elevated to the status of co-kingdom in 1815. Still, this newfound prestige did not preclude mounting calls for independence from Portugal. Rebellions in Pernambuco and elsewhere repeatedly threatened royal authority during these years.

It is difficult to underestimate the role slavery played in Brazilian independence, even if slavery was rarely discussed and never seriously contested. Free Brazilians understood that their society depended on slavery for its economic well-being. This severely limited the appeal of liberalism in Brazil, as slavery acted to unite Brazilian elites (and many in the middle sectors), and made more authoritarian social systems more appealing. For most Brazilians, independence did not seem inherently logical until 1820, when liberal army officers in Portugal rebelled, formed a *Cortes*, and called the king home. The liberals in Lisbon then demanded that João bow down before their new constitution and that Brazil bow down before Portugal, and seemed poised to abolish slavery. When, in 1822, the *Cortes* called Pedro, the king's son and interim ruler in Brazil home, to *further his political education*, Pedro balked, declaring Brazil independent on September 7, 1822. A series of military skirmishes followed, but Pedro rapidly established a constitutional monarchy under the banner of the Brazilian Empire. Slavery was saved.

Stories of Nationhood

MEXICANS AS SPANISH COLONISTS?

When did Latin Americans begin to think of themselves as members of national communities, and not as colonial subjects? There are a number of interesting signs from this era. When they rallied behind the flag of rebellion, Mexicans followed the image of the Virgin of Guadalupe, a markedly local patron saint. Local publishing and literary communities flourished during these years, producing a sense of local specificity through the written word. Across the region intellectuals actively condemned the evils of Spanish colonialism and celebrated incipient national cultures, defining themselves as fundamentally distinct from their colonial overlords. Some even excavated local Indian pasts in order to paradoxically claim an ancient history for themselves that pre-dated the arrival of Europeans, and to argue that the presence of the Spanish crown in the Americas was pernicious, destructive; that they, like their fictive ancestors, were enslaved.

It was not so much that they had no desire to be connected to Europe. Europeans in the

Americas remained powerfully linked to their origins. They returned to Spain or Portugal to be educated. They actively looked for opportunities to marry their daughters to recent arrivals. They followed the fashions and attitudes of the Iberian Peninsula. Nonetheless, by the early nineteenth century *criollo* elites also increasingly saw themselves as rooted in the Americas. This sentiment—that they were Americans rather than Europeans—was both the product of their long history in the region and of recent developments, most notably a series of political and economic changes that historians have come to call the Bourbon Reforms. After the Bourbon's ascended to the Spanish throne in the early eighteenth century, they gradually implemented a series of new and often unwelcome policies in their American colonies. While local merchants benefited from some of the reforms (such as Bourbon efforts to create more legal avenues for trade), the new royal family collected taxes more aggressively and effectively, increasingly substituted peninsular Spanish officials for local ones, reserved many of the new economic opportunities in the colonies for Spaniards, and disrupted traditional governance in the colonies over time. *Criollo* grievances erupted into rebellion as early as the 1740s, and steadily mounted through the century.

It is not clear that these grievances were destined to lead to independence. Even if they were increasingly taken by liberal values during this era, *criollos* remained deeply bound to the mother country. Latin American liberalism was hierarchical, favoring individual equality for males of Spanish descent, but these same liberals rarely imagined that these same rights ought to be extended to the lower castes or women. Moreover, even in the 1810s there was very little of what one might call nationalist sentiment in the region, and certainly little communion between elite *criollo* liberals and the peasants, Indians, slaves, and *castas* (individuals of a variety of racial mixtures) who labored in the colonies.

History intervened in this story in the form of a diminutive Frenchman. Napoleon's invasion of Spain in 1808 threw the Iberian peninsula into turmoil, and had the effect of bringing the distinction between *criollo* and peninsular Spaniard to the fore in several colonies. Spain did not formally relinquish control of her Latin American colonies, but when Charles IV (the Spanish King) was forced from the throne and replaced by Napoleon's brother, Joseph, it was unclear to whom power in the colonies devolved. In capital cities across the region local elites clashed with vice-regal authorities, and what seemed like a vacuum at the very top of the state offered disaffected liberals the opportunity to conspire for more power at the very least, and independence at most. When residents of Buenos Aires learned that Iberia was almost entirely under French rule from sailors aboard a British frigate on May 13, 1810, they quickly deposed the Spanish Viceroy and formed a *junta*, initiating La Plata's May revolution. Though the *junta* leaders (among them, Argentine national heroes Cornelio Saavedra, Mariano Moreno, and Manuel Belgrano) declared their loyalty to the authentic Spanish King, they also demanded the right to choose their own Viceroy.

La Plata *criollos* clearly wanted to promote their own material interests (to trade more directly with England for instance), but their desires were not limited to financial matters. Members of the First Junta already demonstrated an incipient sense of nationhood, which hardened into an unrelenting desire for freedom from Spain through the course of several brutal military campaigns. It was following these battles, and not before (as in the case of the United States) that the rebels made a formal Declaration of Independence from Spain on July 9, 1816. With independence won in the core of the old colony of La Plata, their chief military leader José de San Martín expanded his battle against Spanish forces across the continent, fighting into the 1820s.

The ease of initial victory was deceptive. As *criollo* nationalists would quickly discover, there was a profound distance between imagining nations and seeing them come into existence. Elite liberals often shared little more than a desire to be free of the constraints of colonial rule, and turned on one another in internal struggles that resulted in the dissolution of their new nations even as the wars for independence raged around them. Still more complex was their relationship to the popular groups that formed the core of their armies. We lack comprehensive understandings of why poor and marginalized people joined the independence armies, but what we know suggests that their understandings of the struggle and the nations that would come out of it often differed from the views held by elites. Efforts to knit together these disparate passions into unified nations would not yield rapid returns.

The Documents: Bolivarian Dreams

No single figure is more associated with independence in Latin America than Simón Bolívar. His statue can be found in any major city in the region, and his image is iconic to school-children everywhere in Latin America. In part his fame is tied to his exploits, especially his role in leading victorious rebel armies across the Andes. More than this though, Bolívar has had an enduring place in the pantheon of Latin American idols because he matched his military victories with visionary ideals, with a dream that Latin America should stand united and strong against all enemies, that through unity would come strength, prosperity and freedom. Independence in Latin America left many dreams unfulfilled—dreams that in many ways have gone unfulfilled to this day—and the longing that Bolívar articulated has been a reference point for that sense of incompleteness for nearly two centuries.

Below are three examples of this practice. Each evokes the Bolivarian vision in its own particular way. Document 1.1, an excerpt from Bolívar's *Letter from Jamaica*,[4] offers us an opportunity to consider the Bolivarian dream on its own terms. Born into an aristocratic family in Caracas, Bolívar was simultaneously privileged and disadvantaged, a person of wealth and status and a second-class citizen next to the *peninsulares*. For these and other reasons Bolívar was drawn to both liberalism and to intellectual currents that envisioned Latin Americans as distinct from their Spanish rulers. He and his counterparts were *Americans*. Unsurprisingly then, Bolívar played an active part in the conspiracies that followed the Napoleonic invasion of Spain, leading several campaigns in Venezuela and Colombia, and establishing himself as an important intellectual author of independence through public speeches and his writings (see, for example, his Manifesto of Cartagena, in 1813, and his Address to the Congress of Angostura, in 1819, both on the website). It was during a brief exile in Jamaica that he wrote the letter included here. Shortly afterwards he returned to Caracas, and gradually assumed leadership of the rebel cause.

Over time he refined his vision, which was always a complex combination of liberal republicanism and authoritarian values. Bolívar opposed slavery and proposed the distribution of land to those who fought for independence, but also favored heavy restrictions on suffrage and believed in a strong, almost dictatorial presidency. He attempted to fulfill this vision with the creation of Gran Colombia (modern Venezuela, Colombia, Panama, and

Ecuador), over which he became president in September 1821. The country would dissolve even before his death in 1830, and Bolívar himself would die in disgrace, either the victim of his own ambitions or his follower's failures, depending on who told the tale. Whether or not these contradictions are tied to his enduring appeal, it is clear that his vision of a strong and united Latin America—an effective bulwark against an ascendant United States and imperial Europe—has always had the power to inspire political leaders in the region.

The second document (1.2) is a speech given in 2002 by Guyanese diplomat Odeen Ishmael (b. 1948), interpreting Bolívar's legacies. Ishmael has had a long career as both a teacher and a diplomat, the latter including an appointment as Ambassador to the United States and Guyanese Permanent Representative to the Organization of American States (OAS) from 1993 to 2003. He was appointed Guyanese Ambassador to Venezuela in 2003.

His long service at the OAS (he was twice the Chairman of its Permanent Council) might make Ishmael an easy target for critics on the left, who sometimes argue that this organization simply acts as a front for U.S. ambitions in the region. The OAS is based in Washington, DC, and between 1962 and 2009 actively excluded Cuba, in spite of protests from many member states. That said, it is not clear that member states and individuals like Ishmael were willing lackeys of U.S. imperialism so much as that they viewed the OAS as an (admittedly imperfect) forum for hemispheric dialogue. The Permanent Council meets in the Simón Bolívar Room at its Washington headquarters, and visitors pass a statue of Simón Bolívar on their way into the building. Indeed, the OAS' vision of a united and strong region lays a legitimate claim on his legacy.

The last document in this chapter (1.3) is a speech by Venezuelan President Hugo Chávez (b. 1954) made in 2004, invoking both Bolívar and the Chilean poet Pablo Neruda. During the early years of the twenty-first century Chávez has been one of the most polarizing figures in all of Latin America. Elected president of Venezuela in 1998, he actively lays claim to Bolívar's legacy, calling his movement a Bolivarian revolution. He renamed his country the *Bolivarian Republic of Venezuela*. His vision of the dream calls for radical internal reforms (an egalitarian social project that distributes wealth to the poor) and an expansive geo-political project that unites Latin America through military and economic alliances such as the *Alternativa Bolivariana para América Latina y El Caribe* (Bolivarian Alternative for Latin America and the Caribbean—ALBA). The project is complex, fueled by a mix of anti-imperial and socialist sentiments, along with a healthy dose of petro-dollar assistance from Venezuela, and has inspired powerful passions from all parts of the political spectrum. His admirers believe he represents the best hope for a more equitable Latin American future. His detractors call him a tin-pot dictator. His political style, characterized by long, often rambling, speeches, crude references to foreign heads of state, and mesmerizing political theater, likewise arouses intense passions, ranging from devotion to mockery.

Chávez, Ishmael and Bolívar each offer distinct visions for the Latin American future, and each also does it based upon a claim on the past. Indeed, Bolívar inserts himself into the struggles over history of his day as much as Chávez and Ishmael today insert themselves into struggles over the right to claim Bolívar's legacy. What is particularly interesting in these documents is each person's desire (including Bolívar's) to invoke a certain version of the past in order to dictate the future course of events. The subtle turns of phrase and the differing meanings of the struggle dictate significantly different paths.

Document 1.1 Simón Bolívar, the Letter from Jamaica: Kingston, Jamaica, September 6, 1815[5]

Source: Trans.: Lewis Bertrand, *Selected Writings of Bolívar*, New York: The Colonial Press, 1951.

My Dear Sir:

With what a feeling of gratitude I read that passage in your letter in which you say to me: "I hope that the success which then followed Spanish arms may now turn in favor of their adversaries, the badly oppressed people of South America." I take this hope as a prediction, if it is justice that determines man's contests. Success will crown our efforts, because the destiny of America has been irrevocably decided; the tie that bound her to Spain has been severed. Only a concept maintained that tie and kept the parts of that immense monarchy together. That which formerly bound them now divides them. The hatred that the Peninsula has inspired in us is greater than the ocean between us. It would be easier to have the two continents meet than to reconcile the spirits of the two countries. The habit of obedience; a community of interest, of understanding, of religion; mutual goodwill; a tender regard for the birthplace and good name of our forefathers; in short, all that gave rise to our hopes, came to us from Spain. As a result there was born [the] principle of affinity that seemed eternal, notwithstanding the misbehavior of our rulers which weakened that sympathy, or, rather, that bond enforced by the domination of their rule. At present the contrary attitude persists: we are threatened with the fear of death, dishonor, and every harm; there is nothing we have not suffered at the hands of that unnatural stepmother—Spain. The veil has been torn asunder. We have already seen the light, and it is not our desire to be thrust back into darkness . . .

The role of the inhabitants of the American hemisphere has for centuries been purely passive. Politically they were nonexistent. We are still in a position lower than slavery, and therefore it is more difficult for us to rise to the enjoyment of freedom . . . States are slaves because of either the nature or the misuse of their constitutions; a people is therefore enslaved when the government, by its nature or its vices, infringes on and usurps the rights of the citizen or subject. Applying these principles, we find that America was denied not only its freedom but even an active and effective tyranny. Let me explain. Under absolutism there are no recognized limits to the exercise of governmental powers. The will of the great sultan, khan, bey, and other despotic rulers is the supreme law, carried out more or less arbitrarily by the lesser pashas, khans, and satraps of Turkey and Persia, who have an organized system of oppression in which inferiors participate according to the authority vested in them. To them is entrusted the administration of civil, military, political, religious, and tax matters. But, after all is said and done, the rulers of Isfahan are Persians; the viziers of the Grand Turk are Turks; and the sultans of Tartary are Tartars.

How different is our situation! We have been harassed by a conduct which has not only deprived us of our rights but has kept us in a sort of permanent infancy with regard to public affairs. If we could at least have managed our domestic affairs and our internal administration, we could have acquainted ourselves with the processes and mechanics of public affairs. We should also have enjoyed a personal consideration, thereby commanding a certain unconscious respect from the people, which is so necessary to preserve amidst revolutions. That is why I say we have even been deprived of an active tyranny, since we have not been permitted to exercise its functions.

Americans today, and perhaps to a greater extent than ever before, who live within the Spanish system occupy a position in society no better than that of serfs destined for labor, or at best they have no more status than that of mere consumers. Yet even this status is surrounded with galling restrictions, such as being forbidden to grow European crops, or to store products which are royal monopolies, or to establish factories of a type the Peninsula itself does not possess. To this add the exclusive trading privileges, even in articles of prime necessity, and the barriers between American provinces, designed to prevent all exchange of trade, traffic, and understanding. In short, do you wish to know what our future held?—simply the cultivation of the fields of indigo, grain, coffee, sugar cane, cacao, and cotton; cattle raising on the broad plains; hunting wild game in the jungles; digging in the earth to mine its gold—but even these limitations could never satisfy the greed of Spain.

So negative was our existence that I can find nothing comparable in any other civilized society, examine as I may the entire history of time and the politics of all nations. Is it not an outrage and a violation of human rights to expect a land so splendidly endowed, so vast, rich, and populous, to remain merely passive?

As I have just explained, we were cut off and, as it were, removed from the world in relation to the science of government and administration of the state. We were never viceroys or governors, save in the rarest of instances; seldom archbishops and bishops; diplomats never; as military men, only subordinates; as nobles, without royal privileges. In brief, we were neither magistrates nor financiers and seldom merchants—all in flagrant contradiction to our institutions.

It is harder, Montesquieu has written, to release a nation from servitude than to enslave a free nation. This truth is proven by the annals of all times, which reveal that most free nations have been put under the yoke, but very few enslaved nations have recovered their liberty. Despite the convictions of history, South Americans have made efforts to obtain liberal, even perfect, institutions, doubtless out of that instinct to aspire to the greatest possible happiness, which, common to all men, is bound to follow in civil societies founded on the principles of justice, liberty, and equality. But are we capable of maintaining in proper balance the difficult charge of a republic? Is it conceivable that a newly emancipated people can soar to the heights of liberty, and, unlike Icarus, neither have its wings melt nor fall into an abyss? Such a marvel is inconceivable and without precedent. There is no reasonable probability to bolster our hopes.

More than anyone, I desire to see America fashioned into the greatest nation in the world, greatest not so much by virtue of her area and wealth as by her freedom and glory. Although I seek perfection for the government of my country, I cannot persuade myself that the New World can, at the moment, be organized as a great republic. Since it is impossible, I dare not desire it; yet much less do I desire to have all America a monarchy because this plan is not only impracticable but also impossible. Wrongs now existing could not be righted, and our emancipation would be fruitless. The American states need the care of paternal governments to heal the sores and wounds of despotism and war . . .

From the foregoing, we can draw these conclusions: The American provinces are fighting for their freedom, and they will ultimately succeed. Some provinces as a matter of course will form federal and some central republics; the larger areas will inevitably establish monarchies, some of which will fare so badly that they will disintegrate in either present or future revolutions. To consolidate a great monarchy will be no easy task, but it will be utterly impossible to consolidate a great republic.

When success is not assured, when the state is weak, and when results are distantly seen, all men hesitate; opinion is divided, passions rage, and the enemy fans these passions in order to win an easy victory because of them. As soon as we are strong and under the guidance of a liberal nation which will lend us her protection, we will achieve accord in cultivating the virtues and talents that lead to glory. Then will we march majestically toward that great prosperity for which South America is destined.

I am, Sir, etc., etc.

Simón Bolívar

Document 1.2 Ambassador Odeen Ishmael, "Influencing the Democratic Process in the Americas: A Tribute to Simón Bolívar"[6]

Source: http://www.guyana.org/Speeches/ishmael_bolivar.html.

Mr. Chairman, Secretary General, Assistant Secretary General, Ambassadors, Members of Delegations, Ladies and Gentlemen . . .

Today we honor the memory of the Liberator, the great Venezuelan and South American patriot, Simón Bolívar. Much has been written and said about this great citizen of the Americas over the years, and I believe that what I am stating is already well known. In paying this tribute to Simón Bolívar, I want to touch on two main areas. I will review the influence of the Caribbean region on the career of this legendary leader who led the independence struggles of the peoples of Venezuela, Colombia, Ecuador, Peru, and Bolivia, and whose military exploits influenced those who aspired for independence in other lands on the South American continent in the early nineteenth century. After this, I will examine, in the light of the Bolivarian experience, some current issues as they affect the growth of economic and political unity and democracy in this hemisphere.

By the time he was 25 years old, Simón Bolívar had traveled extensively in Italy and France. During this period, he studied the philosophies of Rousseau, Locke, and Voltaire and was particularly impressed with the military achievements of Napoleon I. On his way home to South America, he took the opportunity to visit some areas of the United States, which had won its independence from Great Britain just more than two decades before. He had also followed the victorious independence struggle of the Haitian people, and by the time he arrived back in Venezuela, he was convinced that the time had arrived for the territories ruled by Spain in the Americas to become independent. He had also decided to take the leadership in the independence struggle that he knew had to be waged against Spanish domination.

That was to come around 1810, when as a 27-year-old military officer, he inspired uprisings against Spanish rule. He led his loyal forces in spectacular military victories, and soon the battle cry for independence resounded from the flat *llanos* of eastern Venezuela and down the Andean backbone of South America.

But there were early setbacks. In 1814, the Spanish forces recaptured Caracas and the revolutionaries were in disarray. Bolívar escaped to Jamaica, and during his sojourn in Kingston, he wrote his famous *Letter from Jamaica* on September 6, 1815. In this profound political document he advocated a system of republican government throughout Spanish America with checks and balances modeled after the British system of government.

In the *Letter from Jamaica*, Bolívar did not confine his view of freedom to a continent free of colonialism and the imperialist oppressions. He outlined the main problems of the Latin American people and predicted how the nations he would liberate could move toward the ambitious aim of freedom and order, along with prosperity and peace for everyone.

He also expressed belief in a united and flourishing hemisphere, with opportunity for everyone to progress and to participate in national development. His call for the unity of the Spanish American nations went beyond formulas or political systems. Actually, he declared that it was not possible for the people to develop a perfect and complete form of government; as a result, he advocated reaching a compromise on a system of government to prevent any form of tyranny. He stated: "Do not adopt the best system of government, but the one that is most likely to succeed."

Departing from Jamaica in 1815, Bolívar went to the southern city of Cayes, Haiti, where he and his companions were well received by the people of the first Black independent nation of the Americas. He later traveled to the capital, Port-au-Prince, where he met with President Alexandre Pétion, who was well aware of Bolívar's cause and he offered him total support. It was Pétion who first called him "the author for independence in South America."

In the city of Cayes, Bolívar received a supply of weapons and ammunition and was granted permission by the Haitian Government to enlist Haitian volunteers who wanted to join in the struggle against Spanish rule in South America. The only condition President Petion requested in providing assistance was for Bolívar to free the slaves in all the countries that he would set free from Spanish domination.

In early 1816, with the backing of the Republic of Haiti which supported him with men and weapons, Bolívar launched an invasion on the Venezuelan coast. After making some military inroads, he immediately put his pledge to Pétion into action and began by liberating his own African slaves on a plantation he owned. However when he proclaimed general freedom for all slaves, all slave-owners, and even some of his own military commanders, turned against him. He was forced to escape again to Haiti, and spent six months in the south-eastern city of Jacmel. In 1817, he returned to South America, and after many struggles and fierce battles, he and his army made up in part of Haitian freedom fighters, defeated the Spanish Imperial army in Colombia and won that country's independence in 1819.

Bolívar's army also included many British and Irish mercenaries who were veterans of the Napoleonic wars. With respect to this, a further Caribbean connection must be noted. These British and Irish recruits occasionally used Georgetown, the capital of Guyana, as their staging post for organizing their supplies. From there, they arranged with Guyanese boat owners to transport them up the Orinoco River where they joined up with the army of *llaneros* led by the José Antonio Páez, Bolívar's able commander in the east. It was not unusual for some Guyanese at that period to team up with the British and Irish recruits and join the independence forces in the Orinoco province.

As President of Venezuela and Gran Colombia, Bolívar in 1826 expanded his vision of a united Spanish America by convening representatives of the new South American and Central American republics at the Congress of Panama. Although little was accomplished, it marked the beginning of Pan-Americanism. That Congress drafted the Treaty of Perpetual Union, League and Confederation, which was signed by the delegates but ratified later only by Gran Colombia (which today comprises Colombia, Ecuador, Panama, and Venezuela).

As we have seen, Bolívar overthrew the rule of the Spanish monarchy in South America and oversaw the formation of a number of new Republics. In the English-speaking Caribbean region, the struggle for independence was more evolutionary in nature. However, from time to time the British colonial masters put down with bullets, police suppression, and imprisonment, a number of efforts by political independence movements which agitated for more freedom and for improved rights for the people. Despite the evolutionary nature of the Caribbean independence struggle, the process was nevertheless influenced by the ideals, heroism, courage, and sacrifice of history's freedom fighters, including Simón Bolívar himself.

Bolívar's vision of a united American continent, even though it has dimmed from time to time, continues to be gradually illuminated more brightly today. The Congress of Panama planted the seed which was to later germinate into the Organization of American States. This body expanded particularly from the period after the decade of the 1970s with the entry of English-speaking Caribbean nations, and its influence is touching the lives of all peoples in all corners of this hemisphere.

We now see steady progress toward the formation of the Free Trade Area of the Americas, which will be the start of a firm economic union of all the countries of the Americas. As the peoples of the Americas draw fundamental benefits from this economic union, they will demand more closeness, and I predict that before the next decade the leaders of regions of the hemisphere will be seriously planning regional political unions. It is easy to predict that not too long after, the political leadership of the various regions will surely begin talking seriously about what can be termed the Union of the Americas.

But the expansion of hemispheric unity, economic or political, can only come about with expanding democracy. Our leaders and our peoples realize this fact, and that is why the leaders of the Americas established a mandate on democracy which resulted in the development of an Inter-American Democratic Charter.

Democracy has to be enriched based on the experience of our history. Today we talk about expanding democracy. Democracy itself, as a pattern of government and a system of belief, has been going through an evolution ever since the idea emerged out of Greek political economy and culture nearly three thousand years ago. In this hemisphere, we have reached a stage when we now boast of achieving representative democracy, as expressed in the OAS Charter of 1948. It is now necessary for our elected representatives to move representative democracy a number of steps further to make it more qualitative. They must apply consultative and participatory democracy by involving minorities and women in the process. In so doing a purer form of democracy will further evolve. We must remind ourselves that everything is always changing. This doctrine that everything is in a state of change was debated even as far back as during the era of the classical Greek philosophers. The process of change will have its pitfalls, and there will be times when it may be necessary for us to take one step forward and two steps backward. Plato summed up this doctrine very clearly when he wrote: "You cannot step twice into the same river; the fresh waters are ever flowing in upon you."

Today, despite the onward march of democracy in this hemisphere, it is still seriously challenged by forces that do not respect free elections, and others that promote violent crime and terrorism.

We must stress that the responsibility for maintaining democracy rests not only with the Governments, but with the opposition parties and civil society as well. While we agree that Governments have a greater responsibility, they cannot alone guarantee democracy, particularly if opposition political parties make unfair demands and do not want to dialogue in order to reach a compromise.

Despite the limitations of elections, there should never be attempts to discard elections and try to arrive at Governments by non-constitutional means. Such attempts are very dangerous and destabilizing. Our citizens must defend democracy, but to do so our societies have to develop a democratic culture to allow democracy to grow, and for citizens to want to defend it.

Furthermore, we cannot have sustained democracy if we do not tackle the problem of poverty. How long can the poor people of our hemisphere continue to listen to our political leaders and international policy-makers debating countless suggested pro-posals to ease poverty? We must be reminded that when people have a perception that action is of slow, they will want to carry out their own actions, which can lead to destablization and changes in the pattern of democratic development. Shakespeare summed of the feeling of the poor when in his historical play, *Henry IV, Part II*, one of his characters, addressing the Chief Justice, declared, "I am as poor as Job, my lord, but not as patient."

At the same time, the multilateral financial institutions have a moral duty also to pro-tect democratic governments. They must also have a democratic charter and mandate.

Many poor countries became heavily indebted because the multilateral financial institutions (MFIs) granted large loans years ago to the then despotic regimes which had no interest in promoting democracy. In reality, the MFIs propped up these non-democratic regimes which, after periods of long struggle by democratic forces, were replaced by democratic governments. Today, these democratic governments are being pressured to repay the heavy debt. Those which are negotiating debt relief are also constrained because of the unreasonable conditionalities by the MFIs, conditionalities which put pressures on their economic and social programs. By not being able to deliver quick development for the benefit of their people, the entire fabric of democracy becomes threatened, because impatient people may turn against the very democratic governments which sympathize with their problems. Thus, we are left to wonder if the MFIs are really fulfilling their mandates because their slow process concerning debt relief for poor countries is not really helping to bring quick relief to those fledgling democracies.

As we commemorate the life and achievements of Simón Bolívar, we also have to reflect on the high regard in which he is held, not only in Venezuela, Bolivia, Colombia, and Ecuador, but also in other countries of the hemisphere. The times of Bolívar were much different from today, but what remains common from those days to this day is the underlying problem of poverty. Countries of the Americas won political independence in different ways, but winning economic independence still poses a challenge. Due to historical circumstances of his day, Bolívar had to utilize the military option to win independence. In gaining the desired objective for a large part of South America, he brought a sense of dignity and pride to the peoples of those lands. By chasing away the colonial oppressor, he set the stage for the generations that succeeded him to organize and develop a popular system of government to protect their political independence and improve the conditions of life for all. It is a challenge that still confronts the Americas.

And so today we express words of admiration for Simón Bolívar. Even though we may not agree with all the political methods he applied, he deserves glory for being a visionary and for taking the decisive giant step to win and influence political independence for so many nations in South America. I paraphrase Shakespeare, who in his play, *Much Ado About Nothing*, wrote the following words which fit the qualities of Simón Bolívar most aptly: "He has borne himself beyond the promise of his age, doing . . . the feats of a lion."

Document 1.3 Speech by President Hugo Chávez at the opening of XII G-15 Summit, Monday, March 1, 2004

. . . Ladies and Gentlemen.

Welcome to this land washed by the waters of the Atlantic Ocean and the Caribbean Sea, crossed by the magnificent Orinoco River. A land crowned by the perpetual snow of the Andean mountains. . .!

A land overwhelmed by the never-ending magic of the Amazon forest and its millenary chants. . .!

Welcome to Venezuela, the land where a patriotic people has again taken over the banners of Simón Bolívar, its Liberator, whose name is well known beyond these frontiers!

As Pablo Neruda said in his "Chant to Bolívar":
Our Father thou art in Heaven,
in water, in air
in all our silent and broad latitude
everything bears your name, Father in our dwelling:

your name raises sweetness in sugar cane
Bolívar tin has a Bolívar gleam
the Bolívar bird flies over the Bolívar volcano
the potato, the saltpeter, the special shadows,
the brooks, the phosphorous stone veins
everything comes from your extinguished life
your legacy was rivers, plains, bell towers
your legacy is our daily bread, oh Father.

Yes, ladies and gentlemen: Bolívar, another "Quixote but not mad" (as Napoleon Bonaparte had already called Francisco de Miranda, the universal man from Caracas), who on this very same South American soil tried to unite the emerging republics into a single, strong and free republic.

In his letter from Jamaica in 1815, Bolívar spoke of convening an Amphictyonic Congress in the Isthmus of Panama:

"I wish one day we would have the opportunity to install there an august congress with the representatives of the Republics, Kingdoms and Empires to debate and discuss the highest interests of Peace and War with the countries of the other three parts of the world."

Bolívar reveals himself as an anti-imperialist leader, sharing the same ideals that materialized in the Bandung Conference in April 1955, 140 years after that insightful letter from Kingston. Inspired by Nehru, Tito, and Nasser, a group of important leaders gathered at this conference to confront their great challenges, and expressed their desire to not be involved in the East-West Conflict, but rather to work together toward national development. This was the first key milestone: It was the first Afro-Asian conference, the immediate precedent of the Non-Aligned Countries, which gathered 29 Heads of State and gave birth to the "Conscience of the South."

Two events of great political significance occurred in the 60's: the creation of the Non-Aligned Movement in Belgrade in 1961 and the Group of the 77 in 1964: Two milestones and a clear historic trend: the need of the South to be self-aware and to act in concert in a world characterized by imbalance and unequal exchange.

In the 70's a proposal from the IV Summit of Heads of State of the Non-Aligned Countries in Algiers in 1973 becomes important: the need to create a new international economic order. In 1974 the UN Assembly ratified this proposal, and while it remains in effect to this day, it has ended up becoming a mere historical footnote.

Two events that were very important for the struggles in the South occurred during the 80's: the creation of the Commission of the South in Kuala Lumpur in 1987 under the leadership of Julius Nyerere, the unforgettable fighter of Tanzania and the world.

Two years later, in September 1989, the Group of the 15 is created out of a meeting of the Non-Aligned Countries, with the purpose of strengthening South-South cooperation.

In 1990, the South-Commission submitted its strategic proposal: "A Challenge for the South." And later on . . . later on came the flood that followed the fall of the Berlin Wall and the implosion of the Soviet Union. As Joseph Stiglitz said, this brought unipolarity and the arrival of the "happy 90's."

All those struggles, ideas and proposals sank in the neo-liberal flood. The world experienced the so-called "end of History," accompanied by the triumphant chant of (those who advocated) neo-liberal globalization, which today, besides being an objective reality, is a weapon they use to manipulate us into passivity in the face of an economic world order that excludes our countries of the South and condemns us to perpetually play the role of producers of wealth and recipients of leftovers.

Never before had the world such tremendous scientific-technical potential, such a capacity to generate wealth and well-being. Authentic technological wonders that have eliminated the distances between places. Still, (these innovations) have helped only a very few people, the 15% of the global population that lives in the countries of the North.

Globalization has not brought so-called interdependence, but an increase in dependency. Instead of wealth being globalized, it is poverty that is increasingly widespread. We have not seen general or shared development. Instead, the abyss between the North and South is so enormous that it is obviously unsustainable—those who try and justify their opulence and waste are simply blind.

The faces of the neo-liberal world economic order are not only the Internet, virtual reality, or the exploration of outer-space, but they can also be seen—and more dramatically—in the countries of the South, where 790 million people are starving, where 800 million adults are illiterate, and where 654 million human beings alive today will not grow older than 40 years of age. This is the harsh and hard face of a world economic order dominated by neo-liberalism, and it is seen every year in the South, where every year 11 million boys and girls below 5 years of age die as a result of illnesses that are practically always preventable and curable. They die at the appalling rate of over 30 thousand every day, 21 every minute, 10 each 30 seconds. In the South, the proportion of children suffering from malnutrition reaches 50 percent in quite a few countries, while according to the FAO (Food and Agriculture Organization of the United Nations), a child who lives in the First World will consume the equivalent of what 50 children consume in an underdeveloped country during his or her lifetime.

The great hope that a globalization based in solidarity and true cooperation would bring scientific-technical wonders to all people in the world has been reduced to this grotesque caricature, full of exploitation and social injustice, by the Neo-liberal model.

Our countries of the South were told a thousand times that the only and true "science" capable of ensuring development and well-being for everybody dictated that we let the markets operate without regulation, privatize everything, create the conditions for transnational capital investment, and ban the State from intervening the economy.

Almost the magical and wonderful philosopher's stone!!

Neo-liberal thought and politics were created in the North to serve their interests, but it should be highlighted that they have never been truly applied there. They have instead been spread throughout the South in the past two decades and have now come to be become the only acceptable way of thinking, with disastrous results.

As a result of the application of (neo-liberal) thinking, the world economy as a whole has grown less than in the three decades between 1945 and 1975, when the Keynesian theories, which promoted market regulation through State intervention, were applied. The gap separating the North and the South continued to grow, not only in terms of economic indicators, but also with regards to access to knowledge, the strategic sector that creates the fundamental possibility of integral development in our times.

With only 15 percent of the world population, the countries of the North count over 85 percent of Internet users and control 97 percent of the patents. These countries have an average of over 10 years of schooling, while in the countries of the South schooling barely reaches 3.7 years and in many countries it is even lower. The tragedy of under-development and poverty in Africa, with its historic roots in colonialism and the enslavement of millions of its children, is now reinforced by neo-liberalism imposed from the North. In this region, the rate of infant mortality in children under 1 year of age is 107 per each thousand children born alive, while in developed countries this rate is 6 per each thousand children born alive. Also, life expectancy is 48 years, thirty years less than in the countries of the North.

In Asia, economic growth in some countries has been remarkable, but the region as a whole is still lagging behind the North in basic economic and social development indicators.

We are, dear friends, in Latin America, the favorite testing-ground of the neo-liberal model in the recent decades. Here, neo-liberalism reached the status of a dogma and was applied with greatest severity. Its catastrophic results can be easily seen, and explain the growing and uncontrollable social protests unleashed by the poor and excluded people of Latin America for some years now, and which every day grow stronger. They claim their right to life, to education, to health, to culture, to a decent living as human beings.

Dear friends:

I witnessed this with my own eyes, on a day like today but exactly 15 years ago, the 27th of February 1989, an intense day of protest that erupted on the streets of Caracas against the neo-liberal reforms of the International Monetary Fund and ended in a very real massacre known as "The Caracazo."

The neoliberal model promised Latin Americans greater economic growth, but during the neo-liberal years growth has not even reached half the rate achieved in the 1945–1975 period under different policies.

The model recommended the most strict financial and trade liberalization in order to achieve a greater influx of foreign capital and greater stability. But during the neo-liberal years the financial crises have been more intense and frequent than ever before. The external regional debt was non-existent at the end of the Second World War, and today amounts to 750 billion dollars, the per capita highest debt in the world and in several countries equal to more than half the GDP. Between 1990 and the year 2002 alone, Latin America made external debt payments amounting to 1 trillion 528 billion dollars, which is twice the amount of the current debt and represented an annual average payment of 118 billion. That is, we pay the debt every 6.3 years, but this evil burden continues to be there, unchanging and inextinguishable.

¡¡It is a never-ending debt!!

Obviously, this debt has exceeded the normal and reasonable payment commitments of any debtor and has turned into an instrument to undercapitalize our countries. It has additionally forced the imposition of socially adverse measures that in turn politically destabilize those governments that implement them.

We were asked to be ultraliberal, to lift all trade barriers to imports coming from the North, but those oral champions of trade have in practice been champions of protectionism. The North spends 1 billion dollars per day practicing what it has banned us from doing, that is, subsidizing inefficient products. I want to tell you—and this is true and verifiable—that each cow grazing in the European Union receives in its four stomachs 2.20 dollars a day in subsidies, thus having a better situation than the 2.5 billion poor people in the South who barely survive on incomes of less than 2 dollars a day.

With the FTAA (Free Trade Agreement of the Americas), the government of the United States wants us to reduce our tariffs to zero for their benefit and wants us to give away our markets, our oil, our water resources and biodiversity, in addition to our sovereignty, whereas walls of subsidies for agriculture keep access closed to that country's market. It seems a peculiar way to reduce the huge commercial deficit of the United States; to do exactly the opposite of what they claims is a sacred principle in economic policy.

Neo-liberalism promised Latin Americans that if they accepted the demands of multinational capital, investments would flood the region. Indeed, the in-flow of capital increased. Some portion (came) to buy state-owned companies, sometimes at bargain prices, another portion was speculative capital that seized opportunities arising from financial liberalization.

The neo-liberal model promised that after the painful adjustment period, which was necessary to deprive the State of its regulatory power over the economy and liberalize trade and finance, wealth would spread across Latin America and the region's long history of poverty and underdevelopment would be left in the past. But the painful and temporary adjustment became permanent and appears to be becoming everlasting. The results cannot be concealed.

If we look at 1980, the year we conventionally denote as the start of the neo-liberal cycle, we see that at that time around 35 percent of Latin Americans were poor. Two decades later, 44 percent of Latin American men and women are poor. Poverty is particularly cruel to children. It is a sad reality that in Latin America most of the poor people are children and most children are poor. In the late 90's, the Economic Commission for Latin America reported that 58 percent of children under 5 were poor, along with 57 percent of children between 6 and 12. Poverty among children and teenagers tends to reinforce and perpetuate unequal access to education, as was shown by a 15 country survey conducted by the Inter-American Development Bank. Among households in the 10 percent of the population with the highest income average schooling was 11 years, whereas among households in the bottom 30 percent of income the average was 4 years.

Neo-liberalism promised wealth. And poverty has spread, thus making Latin America the most unequal region in the world in terms of income distribution. The wealthiest 10 percent of the population In the region—those who are satisfied with neo-liberalism and feel enthusiastic about the FTAA—receive nearly 50 percent of the total income, while the poorest 10 percent—those who never appear in the society pages of the oligarchic mass media—barely receive 1.5 percent of total income.

This model based on exploitation has turned Latin America and the Caribbean into a social time-bomb; ready to explode, should anti-development, unemployment and poverty keep increasing.

Even though the social struggles are growing sharp and even some governments have been overthrown in uprisings, we are told by the North that neo-liberal reforms have not yielded good results because they have not been implemented in full. So, they now intend to recommend a formula for suicide. But we know, brothers and sisters, that countries do not commit suicide. The people of our countries will awaken, stand up and fight!

As a conclusion, Your Excellencies, (I say that) because of its injustice and inequality, the economic and social order of neo-liberal globalization appears to be a dead-end street for the South.

Therefore, the Heads of State and governments who are responsible for the well being of our peoples cannot passively accept the exclusionary rules imposed by this economic and social order.

The history of our countries tells us that without doubt, passivity and grieving are useless. Instead, the only conduct that will enable the South to raise itself from its miserable role as backwards, exploited, and humiliated is concerted and firm action.

Thanks to the heroic struggle against colonialism, the developing countries destroyed an economic and social order that condemned them to the status of exploited colonies. Colonialism was not defeated by the accumulation of tears of sorrow, or by the repentance of colonialists, but by centuries of heroic battles for independence and sovereignty in which the resistance, tenacity and sacrifices of our peoples worked wonders.

Here in South America, we commemorate this very year the 180th anniversary of the Battle of Ayacucho, where people united in a liberating army after almost 20 years of revolutionary wars under the inspired leadership of José de San Martín, Bernardo O'Higgins, José Inacio de Abreu e Lima, Simón Bolívar and Antonio José de Sucre, expelling a Spanish empire that had hitherto extended from the warm beaches of the Caribbean to the cold lands of Patagonia, and thus ending 300 years of colonialism.

Today, in the face of the obvious failure of neo-liberalism and the great threat that the international economic order represents for our countries, it is necessary to reclaim the Spirit of the South.

That is where this Summit in Caracas is heading.

I propose to re-launch the G-15 as a South Integration Movement rather than a group. A movement for the promotion of all possible trends, to work with the Non-aligned Movement, the Group of 77, China...The entire South!!

I propose that we reiterate the proposals of the 1990 South Commission:

Why not focus our attention and political actions to the proposal that we offer several thousand "Grants of the South" per year to students from under- developed countries so that they can continue their studies in the South; or (the proposal that we) dramatically increase our cooperation in health in order to decrease infant mortality, provide basic medical care, fight AIDS?

We must develop these and many other programs with solidarity in order to ease the deep suffering that characterizes the South, and confront the costly and ineffective results of our dependence on the North.

Why not create the Debtor's Fund as an elemental defense tool? It could have consultations and coordinate collective action policies to confront the ways creditor's forum protect their interests.

Why not transform our symbolic system of trade preferences among developing countries into something more advanced, that can counteract the protectionism of the North, which excludes our countries from their markets?

Why not promote trade and investment flows within the South instead of competing in a suicidal fashion to offer concessions to the multinationals of the North?

Why not establish the University of the South?

Why not create the Bank of the South?

These and other proposals will retain their value. They await our political will to turn them into reality.

But finally, dear friends, I would like to mention a particular proposal, which, in my opinion, has great significance:

In the South we are victims of the media monopoly of the North, which acts as a power system that disseminates in our countries and plants in the minds of our citizens information, values and consumption patterns that are basically alien to our realities and that have become the most powerful and effective tools of domination. Never is domination more perfect than when the dominated people think like the dominators do.

To face and begin to change this reality, I dare to propose the creation of a TV channel that could be seen throughout the world, showing information and pictures from the South. This would be the first and fundamental step in crushing the media monopoly.

In a very short time this TV channel of the South could broadcast our values and our roots throughout the world. It could tell the people in the world, in the words of the great poet Mario Benedetti, a man from the deep South, Uruguay, where the La Plata River opens so much that it looks like a silver sea, and washes my dear Buenos Aires and bluish Montevideo:

"The South Also Exists"

With its French horn
and its Swedish academy
its American sauce
and its English wrenches
with all its missiles
and its encyclopedias
its star wars
and its opulent viciousness
with all its laurels
the North commands,

but down here, down
close to the roots
is where memory
no memory omits
and there are those
who defy death for
and die for

and thus together achieve
what was impossible
that the whole world
would know
that the South,
that the South also exists

Ladies and Gentlemen, thank you very much

For Further Reading

Blanchard, Peter. "The Language of Liberation: Slave Voices in the Wars of Independence," *Hispanic American Historical Review* 82:3, 499–523.

Bolívar, Simón. *El Libertador: Writings of Simón Bolívar*. Oxford: Oxford University Press, 2007.

Brading, David. *The First America: The Spanish Monarchy, Creole Patriots and the Liberal State 1492–1867*. Cambridge: Cambridge University Press, 1993.

Canizares-Esguerra, Jorge. *How to Write the History of the New World: Histories, Epistemologies, and Identities in the Eighteenth-Century Atlantic World*. Palo Alto: Stanford University Press, 2001.

Earle, Rebeca. *The Return of the Native: Indians and Myth-Making in Spanish America, 1810–1930*. Durham, NC: Duke University Press, 2008.

Fernandez De Lizardi, Jose Joaquin. *The Mangy Parrot: The Life and Times of Periquillo Sarniento Written by Himself for His Children*. Cambridge, MA: Hackett, 2005.

James, C. L. R. *Black Jacobins: Toussaint L'Ouverture and the San Domingo Revolutions*. New York: Vintage, 1989.

Lynch, John. *Simón Bolívar: A Life*. New Haven: Yale University Press, 2007.

Rama, Angel. *The Lettered City*. Durham, NC: Duke University Press, 1996.

Scott, David. *Conscripts of Modernity: The Tragedy of Colonial Enlightenment*. Durham, NC: Duke University Press, 2004.

Stein, Stanley J. and Barbara H. Stein. *The Colonial Heritage of Latin America: Essays on Economic Dependence in Perspective*. Oxford: Oxford University Press, 1970.

Trouillot, Michel-Rolph. *Silencing the Past: Power and the Production of History*. Boston: Beacon, 1997.

Van Young, Eric. *The Other Rebellion: Popular Violence, Ideology, and the Mexican Struggle for Independence, 1810–1821*. Palo Alto: Stanford University Press, 2001.

Walker, Charles F. *Smoldering Ashes: Cuzco and the Creation of Republican Peru, 1780–1840*. Durham, NC: Duke University Press, 1999.

White, Hayden. *Metahistory: The Historical Imagination in Nineteenth-Century Europe*. Baltimore: Johns Hopkins University Press, 1975.

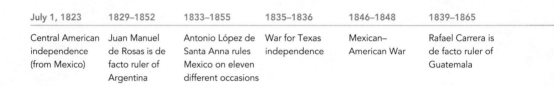

July 1, 1823	1829–1852	1833–1855	1835–1836	1846–1848	1839–1865
Central American independence (from Mexico)	Juan Manuel de Rosas is de facto ruler of Argentina	Antonio López de Santa Anna rules Mexico on eleven different occasions	War for Texas independence	Mexican–American War	Rafael Carrera is de facto ruler of Guatemala

Caudillos versus the Nation State

2

For the rare visitor who wanders through the Museum of the Illinois National Guard in Springfield, the oddest part of the adventure likely comes when they encounter the regiment's most famous trophy, a wooden leg encased in glass, which once belonged to a nineteenth-century Mexican president, General Antonio López de Santa Anna (Figure 2.1). It seems that in 1847 a group of Illinois National Guardsmen took it from him as he was eating his lunch (allegedly it was roast chicken) during a lull in the fighting of what Mexicans refer to as the North American Invasion. Santa Anna removed the leg (his left) so he could eat comfortably, unaware of the Illinoisans lurking in the nearby bushes, who quickly pounced and made off with the leg. As far as macabre symbolism goes, it ranks pretty high. American soldiers steal the prosthesis of a Mexican general, making his disability their booty.

The story of Santa Anna's leg grows even stranger. The sometime president and sometime rebel Santa Anna marked the history of post-independence Mexico more than any other public figure. He was a hero of independence and the civil strife that followed, and first elected president in 1833. He lost his actual leg in the Pastry War (named this because one of the grievances that prompted the war was a demand for reparations from a French baker whose shop had been destroyed in a riot) with France in 1838. The leg was initially buried on his estate at Manga de Clavo in Veracruz, but was disinterred and given a state funeral in Mexico City in 1842, when Santa Anna was again president. Some years later, his political enemies removed the leg from its tomb and dragged it through the streets of the city until it disintegrated.

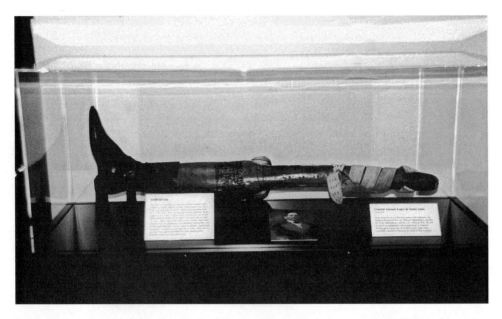

Figure 2.1 Picture of wooden leg belonging to the Mexican President, General Antonio López de Santa Anna

Source: Reprinted with permission from Dr. Antonio de la Cova

The story of the leg, like the story of Santa Anna, and even more broadly the century after independence in Latin America, can seem pretty confusing at first glance. Santa Anna assumed the Mexican presidency eleven times, often for short periods, and often ended his presidency in disgrace. Mexicans nonetheless turned to him time and time again to defend their country or take on its internal enemies, and each time he seems to have willingly assumed the role of national savior. He oversaw many national disasters, the loss of Texas (1836), the loss of the Mexican–American War (1846–8), and ultimately the Gadsden Purchase (1853), when he sold a sliver of Northern Mexico to the United States for ten million dollars. This signaled the end for Santa Anna. Driven into exile in 1855, he did not return to Mexico until 1874, and died in relative obscurity two years later.

Modern readers may be struck by the macabre quality of the story of Santa Anna's leg, but that is perhaps the point. Santa Anna reminds us that, as the novelist Leslie Poles Hartley famously noted, "the past is a foreign country"[1]—that the ways that people lived, thought, and made sense of the world in the past were often profoundly different than they are today. We need some signposts, some sort of explanatory key that will allow us to get beyond the farce and start to understand something of this past. We might consider the deeply Catholic quality of Mexican society during this era, where a fascination with the relic was deeply engrained, and where the relic itself (sometimes simply the hair of a saint, or a drop of Jesus' blood) was often invested with a special kind of power. Mexico's baroque Catholicism mixed a reverence for the relic with the sense that the representative object (in this case, his leg) embodied the properties of the thing it represented, a cultural practice that dated to Mexico's pre-Colombian past. Santa Anna's leg thus held special significance as a sacred object from a secular saint (or demon).

For visitors to the Illinois National Guard Museum, Santa Anna's leg, much like Latin America (and in particular Mexico's North), is a kind of prize, symbolized by a wooden leg never returned to its owner. Taken to its extreme, North Americans use the leg to symbolize a region that lacks a capacity to control itself and its own destiny (after all, the Mexican president was too fuzzy-headed to even pay attention to his own wooden leg). Mexicans, on the other hand, can view the display as representative of both a national tragedy and a reminder of how cruel their northern neighbors are. And yet, there is much more to the story. Santa Anna's leg forms part of a larger story of the turmoil that engulfed Latin America during the nineteenth century, which is sometimes referred to as the *caudillo* age.

The *Caudillo*

How was it that Santa Anna ruled Mexico eleven times? His story can seem idiosyncratic, about Mexico at a certain time and place, except for the fact that the term we use to describe him—*caudillo*—links him to the type of political leader that dominated the nineteenth-century history of Latin America. *Caudillos* were critical figures in societies torn by conflict, where citizens could not turn to civic institutions or processes to defend their interests. They were strongmen, literally, charismatic figures who could defend their interests and the interests of their supporters by unleashing violence against their enemies. Inasmuch as *caudillos* oversaw their share of national disasters, they were also formed by those disasters, figures who entered the vacuum of power left by the collapse of the Spanish colonial state and who offered hope for some type of stability through the force of their will and their capacity to vanquish their enemies.

Independence in the Americas left the new nations of the region with a number of critical challenges. Many members of the political and cultural elites were suddenly unwelcome, viewed as foreigners loyal to an imagined enemy who had not quite given up the dream of re-colonizing their nations. The Church too was suspect—long a servant of the colonial state and a possessor of great wealth, the Church promised the hope of stability to some and offered the threat of a return of the Spanish crown to others. More than this, the elites who remained in the former colonies generally took a fairly dim view of the populace, which was generally poor, uneducated, and either indigenous, African, or of mixed racial origin. They could not imagine their new nations as national folks, united through language, culture, and blood, as was increasingly common in Europe during this era. In the Americas the ethnic and cultural divides were vast.

Just as daunting were efforts to physically control national territories. England, then the emerging great power of Europe, was a tiny country. France was not much larger, and Spain was a country in name only. The United States were substantial, but mostly comprised of settlements along the eastern seaboard, easily traversed and relatively unobstructed by geography. Latin Americans faced an entirely different set of challenges. Most Latin American nations were, when first imagined, vast territories. In comparison to their Anglo-American cousins, the colonies had been far flung, often characterized by long distances between mining centers, administrative and commercial capitals, and the ports, linked by narrow and sometimes impassable trails. Consider a country like Mexico, which spanned from contemporary Oregon to Costa Rica, or the United Provinces of La Plata (modern Argentina), which spanned from the Tierra del Fuego to contemporary Bolivia. Even when these countries were sparsely populated, vast distances and geography put the lie to all illusions of central control.

What is more, these territories had been linked more loosely under colonial rule than the map of the colonial world suggested. Brazil's vast Amazonian interior remained largely outside the purview of the state. In many regions, colonial officials lived exclusively in cities, towns, and mining camps, relying on a vast network of indigenous and mixed-raced intermediaries to maintain colonial rule beyond these locales. In the countryside the colonial state was a shadowy presence, and the illusion of centralized authority collapsed quickly when local interests were threatened. The long history of rebellions in the colonies, in which not just the poor, but sometimes even colonial elites challenged the state and ensured a great deal of autonomy for themselves, revealed a state that was quite weak, and relied more on negotiation than coercion to rule.

The size of the territories and the physical obstacles to travel (mountain ranges, gorges, nearly impassible jungles) produced the logic by which the colonial state functioned, as they would for independent nations. Local officials acted mostly autonomously, only loosely controlled from the outside. To this, however, was added a new problem. With the collapse of colonial rule the citizens of the new republics had few compelling reasons to maintain the types of erstwhile loyalty central government that had informed three centuries of colonial rule. Cities and institutions that had once embodied royal authority now symbolized a recently vanquished enemy, and regional and local elites did not need to bow down to the centralized authority of the capital. With neither king nor Church to justify their position in the nation, the capital cities were likely to become shadows of their former selves.

This again, takes us back to one of the important features of colonial life. The Emperor and the Church played powerful symbolic roles as the social glue of colonial rule. The king did not represent the imposition of foreign authority, but a kind of paternal mediator, who sometimes intervened against the interests of the venal local aristocracy. Church and state were consciously positioned that way in the colonies, defending local peoples against their enemies—enemies who were often installed in colonial capitals. The king might intervene in local land or political disputes, might remove corrupt officials, or confer a pardon for crimes committed. Likewise the Church played a critical role in ministering to the poor and shaping ceremonial life across the colonies. With these two institutions gone or severely weakened, only the long-standing enemies of local interests were left in their place in the capital cities. The *caudillo* emerged in the midst of this divide.

In some ways *caudillos* provided a link to the colonial past. The types of loyalty they commanded was reminiscent of the devotion once paid to the Spanish crown. *Caudillos* were physically strong, carried an air of invincibility, but were closely connected to their followers, intervening on their behalf to settle grievances, defending them (as the king had once done) against outsiders who might oppress them. But the fact that *caudillos* generally relied on narrow regional power-bases also reminds us of just how fractured—by region, ethnicity, and class—post-colonial societies were. Those cleavages meant that *caudillos* had to rule through a number of distinct mechanisms. The first was the force of arms, their armies being largely local and tied together by personal connections and fictive kinship. The second was through the creation of informal patronage networks that promoted stability beyond the local level.

In the most basic sense, these networks involved a constant process of negotiation between different regional strongmen in order to maintain a minimum level of political peace and the appearance of functioning states. Successful *caudillos* might produce some political stability through their alliances with other regional strongmen, but those pacts were always in danger of collapsing as new internal and external threats emerged. These were therefore governments characterized by the absence of powerful or relatively autonomous bureaucracies, of regularly occurring elections, or of the markers of a robust civil society (independent newspapers, political parties, and the like). Perhaps best described as weak states, the governments ensconced in the capital cities lacked the power to enforce laws, collect taxes, or impose their will outside of regions militarily controlled by the ruling *caudillo*.

The Mexican case is poignant, as a nation in turmoil lost half its territory to the ascendant United States, and at other times saw secession in the south (Central America in 1823, which in turn dissolved in 1838), but perhaps the most powerful example of the dissolution produced through *caudillismo* comes from the Andes. At independence, Chile was a relatively peripheral nation in the South, while Peru and Bolivia represented two of the crown jewels of the Spanish Empire. Nonetheless, in the aftermath of independence Chilean elites bound themselves together to produce a stable oligarchy² empowered by mining exports, a formidable merchant marine, and a state that was capable of investing in economic development. Chile was hardly democratic—civil society was dominated by the Church and military, and most land in the country remained locked in a semi-feudal system characterized by huge agricultural estates known as *latifundio*—but the Chilean state had the resources to invest in education, a modern military, and public services.

Chile was well situated to gain control of the nitrate deposits of the northern Atacama Desert that became increasingly valuable as fertilizer by the 1870s. Though many of the deposits were on Bolivian soil, Chilean and British companies were better situated to exploit them than the Bolivians, and gained concessions to work these deposits in the 1870s. When the Bolivian government decided to raise the taxes charged in these concessions in 1878, Chilean merchants protested that these increases were illegal, and the conflict quickly spiraled into a much more serious dispute over the border. Bolivia declared war on Chile in February 1879, pulling Peru into the conflict because of a secret treaty between the two countries. In the war a relatively small and previously poor country took on two much larger neighbors, and defeated both conclusively.

The figure of the *caudillo* looms large over both Bolivia's and Peru's disasters in the war. Bolivian elites did not manage to consolidate under a stable national state after independence. Over time, peace between the cities and the countryside was maintained only through a phenomena known as the Andean Pact, in which indigenous *ayllus* (clans) essentially acted as independent states, paying tribute to the Bolivian government in return for autonomy. This left a series of *caudillos* in control of an extremely weak central state, unable to build a modern infrastructure, develop the national economy, or create a modern military. Peru's story was even more desultory. After banning Indian tribute in the country's first constitution, Peruvian elites rapidly retreated from their image of a modern nation. An impoverished Peruvian state reinstated tribute as early as 1826, and even when the country experienced a boom in *guano* exports in the 1840s, most of the revenues from *guano* were lost to ill considered development efforts, civil war, and graft. Peru's dominant *caudillo* of the era, Ramón

Castilla, who ruled 1845–51 and 1855–62, left behind an empty treasury and growing foreign debt in spite of his country's export boom. When Chile invaded, Peruvians had little capacity to mount a spirited resistance, a problem made worse by the fact that Andean elites refused to arm Andean peasants, for fear that the arms might be ultimately turned on them. Peru lost territory and the lingering traces of parochial pride that came from its place in history. Bolivia lost its only access to the sea, a blow that is a source of bitterness to this day.

The Cause of All National Disasters?

It is difficult to tell these histories without rendering the *caudillo* age as a story of national disasters. The internal violence, economic catastrophes, and territorial losses seem to bear this view out. Were these not somehow terror states, where people lived in fear of the dictator and civil rights were non-existent? Did this era not also signal an exodus of foreign and domestic capital from the region, little economic growth or development, because investors avoided putting their money into zones characterized by civil war? The answer to all these questions is yes, but in the same instance, we ought to be cautioned that there is more to this than meets the eye. Rather than identifying the *caudillo* as barbarian and reinforcing long-standing prejudices about Latin American backwardness, it may be worth imagining other ways to tell their story.

The first takes us to questions about local life in Latin America. Even before independence, the region was characterized by dynamic civic associations and cultures, though in the years after independence these associations usually functioned more effectively at the local than the regional or national level. People living outside of the capital cities took the opportunity provided by independence to assert their autonomy, and did not easily give it up. This was especially true for peasant and indigenous societies throughout the region, which had struggled for centuries to maintain their customs, privileges, land, timber, and water rights against centralized forms of authority. Strong central states might have been better able to promote national economic growth and development, but given the fact that these two phenomena historically came at the expense of poor rural people, it is no wonder that many rural communities flourished during the *caudillo* age. Rafael Carrera, the nineteenth-century Guatemalan *caudillo* widely hated by Central American liberal elites, was extremely popular among indigenous peoples, and drew many of his soldiers from the rural poor.

Caudillos such as Carrera and the Ecuadoran José María Urvina (president from 1851 to 1859) speak to a critical feature of political leadership in Latin America, which dates from the colonial period. In the deeply unequal and hierarchical societies that characterize this part of the world, successful leaders maintain their position by serving as interlocutors between marginalized peoples and more powerful groups (often the state, foreign interests, or national elites). Their power comes both from their ability to oversee large-scale patronage systems, distributing political spoils to their supporters (this is often called clientelism), and from their ability to cultivate a sense of closeness, of fictive kinship (known here as *compadrazgo*) in their followers because of their brotherly or fatherly concern for them. The Spanish King made himself relevant over time by occupying this position, as the ultimate defender of the rights and interests of Indians. This pact was in part acted out through elaborate symbolic acts, but it was also acted out through concrete acts, land grants, intercessions between local elites and indigenous peoples, and acts of clemency for crimes committed against the state. One cannot appreciate the importance of these types of interlocutors without also considering the deep historical inequality of this region, and the profound antipathies that have always existed between local elites and those who they dominate. The king, and later the *caudillo*, were figures who mediated this antipathy.

In the nineteenth century, peasants relied on the king/*caudillo* to defend their interests in the face of liberal attacks on village autonomy and communal landholding. These institutions played a central role in community survival strategies, historical bulwarks against *hacendados*[3] and others who might acquire property at the expense of the poor. For liberals, peasant communal lands were the essence of backwardness, signs of nations that lacked a coherent form, and property that remained unproductive because its owners lacked the ability to profit from its use.

Caudillos occupied contradictory roles in this conflict. Urvina, for example, mobilized indigenous support by positioning himself against the traditional exploiters of the Indians, the Catholic Church and the landlords of the highlands (on whose estates Indians lived in semi-serfdom). He attacked several practices, eliminating the despised Indian Protectorate[4] and tribute, and as such gained a great deal of support among Indians. But as a liberal, Urvina supported the parcelization of indigenous lands. One could also argue that his attacks on highland landlords were both aimed at re-invigorating the colonial state—Indian covenant at the expense of landlords and ultimately served to free up Indian laborers for service on the cacao estates of the coastal region (which were subject to severe labor shortages).

Indeed, one of the notable features of the *caudillo* age was that while political instability hurt national elites, it was generally good for people in the provinces. In order to understand why this was so we need to return to the colonial period. Prior to independence the state enforced social inequality, reserving economic and political privilege for a relative few, and policing a social order where one's ancestry defined one's trajectory through life. Moreover, during the years of colonial rule those inequalities were reinforced by the ways in which Latin America was integrated into the outside world. The principal exporting sectors— mining and plantation agriculture, along with niche commodities like cochineal—tended to exacerbate inequalities as workers in these sectors toiled for meager wages or as forced labor. In a pattern that would be repeated even after independence, as Latin America became more extensively linked to the outside world, inequalities deepened.

Independence disrupted the political and social order, while civil strife devastated those export dependent economic sectors that had prospered under colonial rule. In much of the region the mines and the plantations went into prolonged declines, impoverishing some elites and making it more difficult for them to maintain the labor regimes of the past. In this context poor rural people often found that they were able to live and work under conditions that were more equitable than in the past. Peasants across the region did not face pressure from expanding commercial agriculture. Demands for forced labor declined because of the shuttering of mines and plantations. And states that were weaker than ever before were less able to tax and draft their citizens into service. As in the past, economic decline on the macro level left many poor people with more control over their own destinies, better able to use their own labor power for themselves, and more likely to be able to negotiate the terms of their participation in political and military movements. Unlike a strong central state, which might draw on the resources of the entire nation (or colony) to make demands of poor peasant villagers, a *caudillo* could only command loyalty from his soldiers if he delivered the goods.

Historically, these villagers were loyal first and foremost to their home community. There was precedent for this: the colonial system made the town council (*cabildo*) one of the few political bodies that could represent local people against the state and more powerful economic interests, and unity on the local level has always been a strong bulwark against what villagers view as sinister outside forces. Indigenous peoples in particular were given a great deal of autonomy under the colonial system, an autonomy that was mostly exercised through the privileges accorded to local indigenous authorities by the colonial state. It is not surprising that, when it came to defending their own interests, most people in the region turned first to local institutions.

The defense of village autonomy was sometimes framed in terms of *usos y costumbres* (customary law), a concept that suggests that indigenous villages represent cultures that are distinct from the societies around them. While this was no doubt true for many indigenous communities during this era, it was also true of peasant communities across Latin America, where the defense of local customs and life-ways had long been bound up with other strategies for personal and community survival. Former slaves in Surinam (the Saramakas), Spanish speaking, Catholic peasants in the Andes, cowboys in Argentina (*gauchos*) and *mestizo*[5] ranchers in Mexico (*rancheros*) all sought to defend their communities against outsiders during these decades. All defined themselves as not quite white, not quite European, and believed that the things that made them particular were also qualities that they had a right to defend, by force of arms if necessary.

Because *caudillos* tended to eschew ideological agendas in favor of personal power, they were generally less concerned with extending the power of the government into peasant communities, with creating a more systematic program of national integration and development, than they were about simply managing their fragile coalitions. The appeal of the *caudillo* to these communities was inextricably tied up with this fact, because in return for loyalty, the *caudillo* tended to respect village autonomy. And that respect was not simply evidenced through a tendency not to meddle, it was demonstrated in the respect that the most successful *caudillos* showed for the dignity of the poor, *casta*[6] followers who made up their armies.

Such was clearly the case for the Argentine *caudillo* Juan Manuel de Rosas. The model for the image of the barbaric *caudillo* in Domingo Faustino Sarmiento's classic *Facundo: Civilization and Babarism,*[7] Rosas was in many ways an archetypical *caudillo*. Born to a wealthy landowning family, he made his name as a military man in the wars of independence, before becoming Governor of the Province of Buenos Aires in 1829, a position he would hold with only brief absences until he was overthrown in 1852. Like other *caudillos*, when he assumed the governorship he confiscated the property of his enemies and used it to pay his soldiers and provide recompense to the poor peons who had suffered losses in earlier conflicts. Rosas paid particular attention to courting the support of Afro-Argentines, as they represented around 30 percent of the population of Buenos Aires and represented a critical source of his power. His wife and daughter also maintained ties to the black community, while his official publications praised and defended their patriotism. His paper *La Gaceta Mercantil* not only called them "valiant defenders of liberty," but noted that "General Rosas so appreciates the mulattos and *morenos* that he has no objection to seating them at his table and eating with them."[8] Rosas' enemies among the Unitarians (including Esteban Echeverría), recoiled at these images, as they represented a direct repudiation of the deeply racist values that predominated among elites of the day.

Rosas' reign was brutal. Enemies were shown no mercy and the opposition was repressed by his personal army, the *Mazorca*. He positioned himself as the defender of order, a warrior for traditional values, but nurtured a personality cult around his Holy Federation that placed him at the symbolic center of the nation in ways that were not unlike the role assigned to the Spanish King in earlier times. Followers assiduously placed his portrait in their homes, and wore the red of the Holy Federation as much to deny disloyalty as to prove loyalty. In return for giving up any pretense to civil rights, they received the economic spoils and personal security gained from order—order as the antidote to the violence and dislocation produced in the wars of independence.

Traditional assessments of Rosas held that the terror of these years somehow precluded the creation of a nation. These judgments were originally penned by Argentines themselves, most notably Sarmiento. Rosas represented a kind of rural backwardness, whether cultural or racial, a kind of degeneration that prevented the advance of civilization. However, in recent decades a more complex narrative has emerged. The story begins by acknowledging that in the aftermath of Argentine independence, the odds of ruling this vast region through a strong centralized state were virtually nil. In the 1820s Bernardino Rivadavia tried to expand federal control and create a balanced economy with a powerful centralized and efficient state, but his efforts were undermined by recurring civil war. Not only were distances great and hard to travel, the regional strongmen who emerged during the wars for independence possessed their own armies, and were unlikely to cede authority to Buenos Aires. At this moment the complete dissolution of Argentina was possible, as Bolivia's, Paraguay's, and Uruguay's secessions revealed. Facing these facts on the ground, Rosas wove together a loose coalition of *caudillos*, each of whom was recognized as essentially autonomous, but who were expected to swear loyalty to the Holy Federation. In return for autonomy, they recognized Buenos Aires' right to control foreign policy and *porteño*[9] merchants' prerogative to dominate foreign trade. His position also allowed him to use the National Customs Houses to raise revenue.

Starting from this position of relative weakness, Rosas used customs revenues to gradually expand the authority of Buenos Aires across the national territory, bringing the other *caudillos* increasingly under the central state's authority. He never produced the strong centralized state that Unitarians might have wanted, but the practical series of alliances and agreements he oversaw maintained the peace and allowed the early development of Argentina's agricultural export economy, especially beef and hides (with some wheat). Under Rosas the patterns of land tenure and oligarchical rule that would later characterize the country's export boom were established. The state and private interests built roads, transportation and communications networks, and the transformation of the pampas from free range into private property gradually proceeded. Domination of the export sector eventually allowed Buenos Aires merchants to control the salted beef trade, and vast fortunes were made exporting beef to feed slaves in Brazil and Cuba. Without Rosas' particular style of rule, much of this may have been impossible. Whether that is a good thing or a bad thing depends on one's perspective.

Over time Rosas' enemies grew in number, but until the very end Rosas had considerable support from *estancieros*[10] in Buenos Aires, the Catholic Church, and the poor. In part this support was strategic, but his cultural appeal should not be underestimated. He defended religious tradition and placed Catholicism at the center of his symbolic repertoire, which stood in stark contrast to his liberal enemies. And his capacity to speak in a language that resonated with the rural and urban poor, along with his care in divvying up the spoils of power with his followers, generated a great deal of support. Just as the Spanish king had once positioned himself as a father to the poor, so could Rosas, in his own way.

The Document: Literature as History

When Latin Americans looked for a language to describe the anxieties they felt about their societies during the nineteenth century (and often into the twentieth century), the images they turned to were often rooted in a very specific binary—the struggle between barbarism and civilization. One was rooted in the past, the other oriented to the future. One held the promise of modern nationhood, the other poverty and dependence. Race, class, gender, and culture were all described through these lenses, producing clear visions of who promised to be enlightened citizens, and who promised to be drags on progress. Yet it was never quite so simple. The intelligentsia never dismissed the traditions that gave the region's cultures their form and specificity out of hand. Through the nineteenth and twentieth centuries, Latin American writers and intellectuals remained deeply ambivalent as they described the interplay between the traditional and the modern. Even though the national communities they described were themselves recent fictions, they did not want civilization to flatten out those things that made one an Argentine, a Brazilian, a Mexican, a Chilean.

Over many decades literature became one of the critical forums in which the interplay of local and universal values was dissected. Below (Document 2.1) is a short story that represents one of the brilliant early examples of this tradition, *The Slaughterhouse* (*El Matadero*), written by the Argentine Esteban Echeverría in 1838. Rather than a simple screed against either the traditional or the modern, *The Slaughterhouse* weaves an ambivalent story of change. Like other notable writers of his day, Echeverría imagined himself as a nationalist, a political activist, and a writer. He was a prominent member of several political clubs founded to oppose Rosas in the 1830s, including the *Asociación de Mayo*, named for Argentina's independence heroes. He used fiction to articulate a vision of the nation as it was and should be, and in many ways lived the tragedies he described through the experience of forced exile (in this, he was similar to Sarmiento). It was in exile in Uruguay that he wrote this powerful indictment of Rosas, and where he died while Rosas was still in power. *The Slaughterhouse* would not be published until 1871.

Echeverría's anxieties about barbarism were also evident in his other work, especially *la insurrección del sur* and *la cautiva*, his epic poem about a European woman kidnapped by Mapuche Indians. In this, he was very much like other liberal intellectuals of his day. Strong opponents of dictatorship and *caudillismo*, these figures are in some ways deeply sympathetic, yet they situate their opposition to dictatorship in ways that remind us of the elitism of the era. Theirs was an urbane intellectual liberalism, with little sympathy for the sensibilities and capacities of the rural folk who formed the backbone of Rosas' power. And in the end, their admiration of civilization would have its genocidal variant, as the logics of modernity under-girded decisions to simply eliminate those who were unwilling or unable to embrace the sensibilities they adored.

Other important texts in this literary cannon include *Facundo*, *Martín Fierro*, *Rebellion in the Backlands*, *Don Diego Sombra*, and *Birds Without a Nest*. From these texts we gain an appreciation of how struggles over violence, *caudillismo*, citizenship, and race, gender, and class were played out through the twin tropes of civilization and barbarism.

Document 2.1 Esteban Echeverría, *The Slaughterhouse* (*El Matadero*)

Source: Trans. Elizabeth Medina, with assistance from Marina Soldati; http://www.biblioteca.clarin.com/pbda/cuentos/matadero/matadero.htm.

Even though what I am about to tell is essentially history, I will not begin with Noah's Ark and his ancestors' genealogy, as the early Spanish chroniclers of the New World were wont to do and whose example we should emulate. I have many reasons for not following their example, reasons I will not elaborate on in order to avoid long-windedness. I will merely say that the events in my narration took place in the 1830s of the Christian era. It was, moreover, during Lent, a time of year when meat is scarce in Buenos Aires because the Church, in deference to Epictetus's precept of *sustine et abstine*—to bear and forbear—ordains that vigil and abstinence be imposed on the stomachs of the faithful as the flesh is sinful, and thus, as the proverb says: *flesh seeks flesh*. And since the Church, *ab initio* and by direct authorization from God Himself, holds material power over the consciences and stomachs that do not, in any way whatsoever, belong to the individual, then nothing more is fair or rational than for it to forbid what is evil.

The purveyors of meat, on the other hand—good Federalists all, and therefore good Catholics—knowing full well that the people of Buenos Aires possess the precious quality of an extraordinary docility for bowing to any kind of command, bring only the number of steers strictly necessary during the Lenten season to feed the children and the sick—who are excused from the abstinence mandated by the Papal Bull—and without any intention of letting a few intractable heretics stuff their gullets. For there is never any lack of such people, ever prepared to transgress the Church's meat commandments and spread the contagion of their bad example to society.

Thus, it happened that in those days, there was a very heavy rainfall. Roads were flooded. Marshes became lakes, and the streets that led into and out of the city overflowed with slushy mud. A huge torrent suddenly cascaded down Barracas Creek and majestically spread its murky waters until they reached the gully beds of Alto. The Río de la Plata swelled fiercely, propelling the turgid waters that were searching for a channel, making them rush over fields, embankments, groves, and hamlets, until they spread out like a vast lake across all the lowlands. Ringed from north to west by a swath of water and mud, and south by a whitish ocean on whose surface a number of small boats bobbed precariously about, and chimneys and treetops marked with black smudges, the city gazed at the horizon in astonishment from its towers and its ravines, as though imploring for protection from the Most High. The rain seemed to portend another Great Flood. Pious men and women wailed as they prayed novenas and recited endless litanies. Preachers stormed the churches and made the pulpits creak under their hammering fists. "This is Judgment Day," they said. "The end of the world is near. God's wrath is overflowing and spilling forth as floodwaters. Woe unto you, sinners! Woe unto you, wicked Unitarians[11] who mock the Church and its wise men, and fail to listen reverentially to the word of the Lord's anointed! Woe unto you who do not beg for God's mercy before the altars! The terrible hour approaches of useless gnashing of teeth and feverish cursing. Your wickedness, heresies, blasphemies, your horrendous crimes have caused the plagues of the Lord to veer towards our land. The Lord of the Federation's just hand will damn you."

The wretched women streamed out of the churches, overwhelmed and gasping for air, blaming the calamity, as was to be expected, on the Unitarians.

Still the heavy rains continued falling relentlessly and the flooding worsened, as if to confirm the preachers' predictions. Church bells began tolling, invoking divine aid, on the orders of the very Catholic and universalist Restorer,[12] who it seemed was rather worried. The libertines, the unbelievers—that is to say, the Unitarians—grew fearful at the sight of so many remorseful faces and at the sound of such a bedlam of profanity. There was already talk, as though the matter had been decided, of a procession that all the people would be obliged to attend, unshod and bareheaded, accompanying the Sacred Host to be carried by the Bishop beneath a canopy, to Balcarce Gully. There, thousands of voices would have to implore for divine mercy, exorcising the cause of the flood—the Unitarian devil.

Happily—or better said, unfortunately, for it would have been a sight to behold—the ceremony was not performed because as the Río de la Plata's floodwaters abated, the immense flood bed gradually drained away without any need of exorcism or supplications.

Now the most relevant circumstance for my story is that as a result of the flood, the Convalescencia Slaughter Yard saw not a single head of cattle for fifteen days, and in one or two days all of the farmers' and water sellers' oxen had been consumed in order to supply the city with beef. The poor children and the sick were fed on eggs and chicken, and the gringos[13] and renegade heretics bellowed for beefsteak and roast. Abstinence from meat was widespread among the common folk, who were blessed as never before by the Church, and thus millions upon millions of plenary indulgencies showered down on them. The price of a hen rose to six pesos while eggs went for four *reales* each, and fish was exorbitantly expensive. In those Lenten days, people did not consume fish and red meat in the same meal, nor indulge in gluttonous excess; but, on the other hand, innumerable souls rose straight to heaven and events took place that seemed the stuff of dreams.

Not a single live mouse was left in the slaughter yard, out of the thousands that had found shelter there before. They all died, either from starvation or from drowning in their burrows because of the incessant rain.

Swarms of black women, scavenging in the manner of *caranchos*[14] for viscera to steal, spread throughout the city like mythical harpies, ready to devour anything edible they could find. Their inseparable rivals in the slaughter yard, the seagulls and the dogs, migrated elsewhere in search of animal feed. A number of ailing elderly people contracted consumption for lack of nutritious broth. But the most striking event of all was the near-sudden death of some gringo heretics, who committed the transgression of gorging on Extremadura sausages, ham, and cod, and departed for the afterlife to atone for such an abominable sin as to partake of meat and fish in the same meal.

Some physicians expressed their opinion that if the scarcity of meat continued, then half of the population would suffer from fainting spells because their stomachs were so habituated to the fortifying juices of meat. One could not help noticing the stark contrast between these dire scientific predictions and the condemnations hurled down by the reverend fathers from the pulpits, against all carniferous nutriments and the combined consumption of meat and fish during those days, set aside by the Church for fasting and penance. This set off a kind of internecine warring between stomachs and consciences, stoked on one hand by unrelenting appetite, and on the other by the priests' no-less-implacable vociferations, duty bound as they are to brook no vice that might lead to a relaxing of Catholic customs. On top of this, there was the inhabitants' condition of intestinal flatulence from eating fish and beans and other somewhat indigestible fare.

This war was manifested by the jarring sobs and cries that were heard as the priests delivered their sermons, and in the rumblings and sudden explosive noises coming from the city's houses and streets, or wherever people gathered together. The Restorer's government—as paternal as it was far-sighted—grew rather alarmed. Believing that these instances of unrest were instigated by revolutionaries, and attributing them to the savage Unitarians themselves (whose wickedness, said the Federalist preachers, had brought down the flood of God's wrath upon the nation), the government took active measures. It sent out its spies among the populace, and finally, well apprized, issued a decree that was soothing for consciences as well as for stomachs, with a most wise and pious declaration, so that—at all costs and charging across high water if need be—cattle should be brought to the corrals.

And indeed, on the sixteenth day of the scarcity, on the eve of the Day of Sorrows,[15] a troop of fifty fattened steers waded across Paso de Burgos and entered the Alto Slaughter Yard. This number, incidentally, was a mere trifle, given that the population was accustomed to consuming 250 to 300 steers a day and at least a third of the inhabitants were under a special dispensation from the Church allowing them to eat meat. How strange that there should be stomachs subject to inviolable laws and that the Church holds the key to all stomachs!

But there really isn't anything strange about it at all, since the Devil customarily enters the body through the flesh, and the Church has the power to cast him out. It is a matter of reducing man to a machine, whose driving force is not his own will but that of the Church and the government. A time may come when it will be forbidden to breathe fresh air, take a walk, or even to have a conversation with a friend, without first obtaining permission from the competent authorities. This was how it was, more or less, in the happy times of our pious grandparents, which the May Revolution unfortunately disrupted.

In any event, upon the announcement of the government decree, the corrals of Alto filled up—despite all the mud—with butchers, scavengers for viscera, and curious onlookers, all of whom welcomed the fifty steers headed for the slaughter yard with boisterous shouts and applause.

"Smallish, but fat!" they exclaimed. "Long Live the Federation! Long Live the Restorer!"

My readers surely must know that in those days, the Federation was everywhere—even amidst the filth of the slaughterhouse—and just as there could be no sermon without St. Augustine, there was no festival without the Restorer. It is said that when they heard the wild shouting, the last of the rats that were starving to death in their rat holes sprang back to life and began madly scurrying about, for they realized that the familiar merriment and uproar were announcing the return of abundance.

The first steer butchered was gifted whole to the Restorer, who was known for his penchant for grilled meat. A committee of butchers marched off to deliver it in the name of the Federalists of the Alto Slaughter Yard, and they personally expressed their gratitude for the government's wise providence, their unlimited support for the Restorer, and their deep hatred of the enemies of God and man—the Unitarian savages. The Restorer responded to their harangue in the same vein, and the ceremony ended with the appropriate cheers and vociferations from spectators and actors. One must assume that the Bishop had granted the Restorer a special dispensation to eat meat, since being such a strict observer of the laws, such a good Catholic, and such a staunch defender of the faith, he would have set a bad example by accepting such a gift on a holy day.

The slaughter proceeded, and in one hour, forty-nine steers had been laid out in the slaughter yard, some skinned and others about to be. It was a lively and picturesque scene, though one that brought together the most hideous, filthy, malodorous, and deformed elements of the small proletarian class typical of the Río de la Plata. However, to enable the reader to readily picture the scene, a sketch of the venue is required.

The Convalescencia or Alto Slaughter Yard is a parcel of land near the country estates south of Buenos Aires. The large rectangular lot lies at the end of two streets, one of which stops there, while the other continues eastward. This south-sloping lot is divided by a rain-carved channel lined with innumerable rat holes, with the channel bed in the rainy season collecting all of the blood, both dry and fresh, from the slaughter yard. At the right-angle junction, to the west, stands what is known as the *casilla* or judge's quarters, a low building consisting of three small, sloping-roofed rooms, with a porch along its front that faces the street and a hitching post for horses. To the rear of the building are several corrals of *ñandubay* wood, with heavy gates for securing the cattle.

In the winter these corrals are veritable quagmires. The animals crowd together, buried up to the tops of their legs in the mud, stuck together, as it were, and nearly motionless. Corral duties and fines for violations of the regulations are collected in the *casilla*, where the slaughter yard judge holds court—an important personage, the caudillo of the butchers, who wields supreme power over this small republic by delegation of the Restorer. It isn't hard to imagine the kind of man required to perform such an office. As for the *casilla*, it is such a small and shabby building that no one in the corrals would give it any importance but for the association of its name with that of the feared judge and the garish red signs painted on its white walls: "Long Live the Federation"; "Long Live the Restorer and the Heroic Doña Encarnación Ezcurra"; "Death to the Unitarian Savages." They are signs fraught with meaning, symbolic of the political and religious faith of the slaughter yard's people. But some readers will likely be unaware that the aforementioned "heroine" is the Restorer's late wife, the butchers' beloved patroness, venerated by them after her death for her Christian virtues and Federalist heroism during the revolution against Balcarce.[16] It so happened that during an anniversary of that memorable feat by the *Mazorca*,[17] the butchers celebrated with a splendid banquet in the heroine's *casilla*, which she attended with her daughter and other Federalist ladies. There, before a great crowd, she offered her Federalist patronage to the gentlemen butchers in a solemn toast, whereupon they enthusiastically proclaimed her patroness of the slaughter yard, inscribing her name on the walls of the *casilla*, where it will remain until it is erased by the hand of time.

From a distance, the slaughter yard was a grotesque, bustling sight. Forty-nine cattle were laid out on their skins, and nearly two hundred people trudged around in the sloughy ground that was drenched with the blood from the animals' arteries. A group of people of different races and complexions gathered around each steer. The most prominent figure in each group was a butcher with knife in hand, his arms and chest bare, hair long and tangled, his shirt, *chiripá*,[18] and face smeared with blood. Behind him, following his every move, was a band of swarming, capering boys and black and mulatto women, these last scavengers for chitterlings, as ugly as the viragos of legend. Intermingled among them were some huge hounds that sniffed, growled, or snapped at each other as they wrangled over a prize piece of offal. Forty-some carts covered with blackened, worn hides were ranged unevenly along the entire length of the lot. A few men on horseback, wearing ponchos and with lassoes lightly and expertly held in one hand, rode their mounts at a brisk stride amid the crowds, while others slouched over their horses' necks, training an indolent eye on one of the lively groups. Meanwhile, above them, a swarm of blue-and-white gulls, drawn back to the slaughterhouse by the smell of flesh, fluttered in the air, blanketing the slaughter yard's din and babble with dissonant squawks and casting a shadow over the field of gruesome carnage. Such was the scene at the start of the butchering.

However, as the slaughter continued, the scene began to change. The groups broke apart and new ones formed, which took on assorted attitudes, and then the people scattered at a run, as though a stray bullet had hit where they stood or the jaws of a rabid mastiff had burst into their midst. In one group, a butcher hacked at a slaughtered animal's flesh; in a second, another butcher hung up the quartered sections on wagon hooks. One skinned a carcass here, another trimmed off the fat there. And from time to time, from among the ranks of the mob that eyed and waited for a piece of offal, a grimy hand holding a knife would dart out to slice a piece of fat or meat from a steer's quarters. This would set off the butcher's shouts and explosions of anger, the renewed swarming of the groups, and the young boys' jeers and jarring shouts.

"Hey, over there! That woman is slipping fat into her bosoms!" one of them shouted.

"That man stuffed it in his pants flap," retorted the black woman.

"Hey you, black witch, get out of here before I cut you open!" exclaimed the butcher.

"What have I done to you, ño Juan? Don't be mean—all I want is the belly and the guts."

"They're for that there witch—goddamn it!"

"Get the witch! Get the witch!" the young boys chanted. "She's taking the kidney fat and the liver!" And two chunks of clotted blood and some enormous mud balls began raining on her head.

In another part of the yard, two African women half-carried, half-dragged an animal's entrails. Over in another area, a mulatto woman was walking off with a ball of viscera when she suddenly slipped in a puddle of blood and fell flat on her backside, shielding her precious booty with her body. Farther away, huddled together in rows, four hundred black woman unwound a tangle of intestines in their laps. One by one, they picked off the last bits of fat that the butcher's miserly knife had left on the entrails. Meanwhile, others emptied out stomachs and bladders and filled them with air from their own lungs so that they could deposit offal inside them once they were dry.

Youths, gamboling about on foot and on horseback, smacked each other with inflated bladders or lobbed rolled pieces of meat at one another, scattering with the exploding balls of meat and their boisterous antics a cloud of seagulls that balanced in the air, celebrating the slaughter with their raucous screeching. Despite the Restorer's prohibition against swearing and the holiness of the day, profanities and obscenities were often to be heard, vociferations laden with the bestial cynicism that is so typical of the riffraff in our slaughter yards, and which I am disinclined to share with my readers.

Without warning a bloody lung would fall over someone's head, which was then passed on to someone else's, until some deformed hound grabbed it firmly, only to be accosted by a pack of other dogs that tried to wrest a piece of it away in a horrific melee of snarls and savage bites. An old woman set off in angry pursuit behind a young man who had smeared her face with blood. His friends, responding to the troublemaker's yelling and cursing, surrounded and harassed her the way dogs will badger a bull. She was pelted with pieces of meat and balls of dung, as well as with guffaws and repetitive shouts, until the judge commanded that order be restored and the field cleared.

To one side, two boys practiced handling their knives by throwing horrendous slashes and blows at each other. In another spot, four already-adolescent boys flicked knives at each other for the right to a thick length of intestine and a piece of tripe filched from a butcher. And not far from them, some dogs, gaunt from forced abstinence, employed the same means to see which one would carry away a mud-slathered liver. It was all a simulacrum in miniature of the barbaric ways in which individual and social issues and rights are resolved in our country. All told, the scenes unfolding in the slaughter yard were for seeing—not for consigning to paper.

One animal, with a short, thick neck and a fierce look, had been left behind in the pens. Opinions were divided regarding its genitals, because they seemed to be similar to both a bull's and a steer's. The animal's hour arrived. Two lassoers on horseback entered the corral, now surrounded by crowds milling about, some on foot, others mounted, and still others straddling the corral's gnarled timbers. The most grotesque, conspicuous group of all was standing by the gate: several expert lassoers on foot, their arms bare, each one armed with an unerring noose, bright red kerchiefs tied around their heads, wearing vests and red *chiripás*. Behind them were several riders and expectant onlookers, intently observing the scene.

The animal, a slipknot already around its horns, bellowed wildly, spraying foam from its mouth. But the devil himself could not get it to emerge from the thick slime that like glue mired down the beast and made it impossible to lasso its legs. The boys perched on the corral fence shouted at and heckled the animal, waving their ponchos and kerchiefs to no avail. The cacophony of whistles, clapping, high-pitched and guttural voices blaring from that extraordinary orchestra was something to hear.

The boorish comments and shouts of raillery and obscenities rolled from mouth to mouth, each one there making a spontaneous show of their cleverness and wit, excited by the scene or prompted by someone else's sallies.

"Son of a bitch, that bull."

"To hell with those castrated bulls from Azul."[19]

"Damned cheating driver passed a bull off for a steer."

"I'm telling you it's a steer—that's no bull!"

"Can't you see it's an old bull?"

"The hell it is—show me its balls if you're so sure, damn it!"

"There they are—he's got them between his legs. Can't you see, my friend? They're bigger than your chestnut horse's head. Or did you go blind on the way here?"

"Your mother would be the blind one, if she gave birth to a son like you. Can't you see that lump's nothing but mud?"

"You're as stubborn and ornery as a Unitarian. . ."

At the sound of the magic word they all shouted, "Death to the Unitarian savages!"

"Send the sons of bitches to One-Eye."

"Yes, to One-Eye—he's got the balls for fighting Unitarians. Flank steak[20] for Matasiete, executioner of Unitarians! Long Live Matasiete!"

"The flank steak to Matasiete!"

"There he goes!" shouted a man with a guttural voice, cutting short the bluster of cowardly bullies. "There goes the bull!"

"Watch out! Look sharp you, by the gate! He's headed there, mad as a devil!"

Indeed the animal—harassed by the shouting and, most of all, by two sharp cattle prods spurring his hindquarters—sensing that the noose had loosened, rushed the gate with a powerful snort, hurling fiery looks from side to side with its reddened eyes. The lassoer yanked the lariat and dislodged the noose on the bull's horn, making his horse fall back on its haunches. A sharp hiss flayed the air and, from atop a fence fork, a boy's head was seen to roll down, as though severed from the base of the neck by a hatchet blow, his motionless trunk still sitting astride its wooden horse and shooting out from every artery a long torrent of blood.

"The rope was cut!" some shouted. "There goes the bull!"

But others, bewildered and stunned, were silent, because everything had happened as quickly as though a lightning bolt had struck.

The group that was by the gate began to break up. Some crowded around the head and still-quivering body of the boy decapitated by the lasso, expressing horror at the final look of shock on its face. The others, horsemen who had not witnessed the tragedy, fanned out in different directions in pursuit of the bull, yelling and screaming, "There he goes!" "Intercept him!" "Watch out!" "Rope him, Sietepelos!" "Get away from him, Botija!" "He's furious, stay out of his way!" "Head him off, head him off, Morado!" "Spur that lazy horse!" "The bull's on Sola Street!" "The devil stop that bull!"

The riders' mad rush and the shouting were infernal. When they caught wind of the tumult, a handful of black women who had scavenged chitterlings and sat in a row along the water channel's edge curled up and crouched over the stomachs and entrails that they had been unraveling and rolling up with the patience of Penelope. This action surely saved them, because when the animal caught sight of them, it gave a terrifying snort, jumped sideways, then continued running straight ahead, the riders in hot pursuit. They say that one of the women soiled herself, another prayed ten Hail Marys in two minutes, and two promised San Benito[21] never to return to those accursed corrals and to abandon the occupation of collecting entrails. It is not known whether they made good on their promise.

Meanwhile, the bull entered the city through a long, narrow street that originates from the sharpest angle of the rectangle we had described before, a street enclosed by a water canal and a living fence of prickly pear. It was called "Sola" because it had no more than two adjacent houses on it. In its flooded center was a deep mud pool that covered the road's entire width, between one canal and the other. At that moment, an Englishman returning from his saltworks on a somewhat intractable horse was slowly wading across the bog and no doubt he was so absorbed in his mental calculations that he heard the bedlam of the onrushing riders with their infernal shouting only when the bull had already rushed into the pool of mud. Without warning, his horse spooked, bolted sideways, then broke into a gallop, leaving the poor man submerged in two feet of mud. The accident, however, neither stopped nor slowed down the headlong race of the bull's pursuers. On the contrary, they exclaimed, amid sarcastic guffaws, "The gringo screwed up!—back on your feet, gringo!" And as they crossed the morass, the mud churned up by their horses' hooves kneaded the man's miserable body. The gringo extricated himself as best he could, reaching the edge of the bog looking more like a devil browned by the fires of hell than a blond-haired white man. Farther ahead, four black women collectors of chitterlings who were heading home with their loot, upon hearing the shouts of "After the bull!" dove into the canal full of water, the only refuge left to them.

In the meantime, after having run some twenty blocks in various directions and frightening every living creature with its presence, the animal went through the palisade gate of a country home, where it met its doom. Though tired, it still showed vigor and a fierce mien. But it was surrounded by a deep canal and a thick fence of agaves, and there was no escape. Its persecutors had dispersed, but soon they banded together again and decided to use a team of oxen as a decoy and lead the bull back, to atone for its crime on the very spot where it had committed it.

One hour after its escape, the bull was back in the slaughter yard, where the few riffraff who had stayed around spoke of nothing but its misdeeds. The gringo's adventure in the mud hole aroused mainly derisive laughter and sarcasm. Of the boy decapitated by the lasso nothing remained, except for a puddle of blood—his body was in the cemetery.

Very quickly, they roped the animal's horns as it bucked, pawed its hooves, and bellowed with rage. They threw one, two, three lassoes at it to no avail, but the fourth snared a leg. The bull's vigor and fury redoubled—its tongue stretched out convulsively, froth spewed from its mouth, smoke from its nostrils. Its eyes blazed.

"Hamstring that animal!" a commanding voice exclaimed. Matasiete jumped off his horse, slashed the bull's hock in one swing, then, dancing around it, enormous dagger in hand, buried the blade up to the hilt in the animal's neck and showed the steaming red gash to the crowd. A torrent spurted from the wound, the bull exhaled one or two hoarse bellows. Then the proud animal collapsed, amid the mob's shouts, proclaiming Matasiete's prize of a flank steak. For the second time, Matasiete proudly stretched out his arm and the bloodstained knife, then bent down to skin the animal with his comrades.

The question of the dead animal's genitals still had to be settled, though it was provisionally classified as a bull because of its indomitable ferocity. However, everyone was so exhausted from the long exertion that the matter was momentarily forgotten. But just then, a rough voice exclaimed:

"Here are the balls!" Extricating two enormous testicles from the animal's belly, the man displayed them—the unmistakable marker of the animal's dignity as a bull—to the bystanders. His words were met with uproarious laughter and loud chatter—all of the lamentable incidents were now easily explained. It was an extreme rarity for a bull to turn up in the slaughter yard. It was even forbidden. The rules of proper social practice dictated that the animal be thrown to the dogs; but there was such a lack of meat, and so many inhabitants were going hungry, that His Honor the Judge was forced to turn a blind eye.

In a flash the wretched bull was skinned, quartered, and hung on the wagon. Matasiete slid the flank steak under his saddle blanket and prepared to set off. The butchering had ended at noon, and the few stragglers who had been there until the end were now leaving in groups, on foot and on horseback, or using their cinch straps to haul carts loaded with meat.

But, suddenly, a butcher shouted in a gravelly voice:

"Here comes a Unitarian!" And at the sound of the fraught word, the entire rabble stopped dead in its tracks, as though stunned.

"Can't you see his U-shaped side whiskers? He doesn't have a ribbon on his tail coat or a mourning band on his hat."

"Unitarian dog."

"He's a dandy."

"He rides English saddle, like the gringos."

"Give him the corncob."

"The shears!"

"He needs a whipping."

"He's got a pistol case on his saddle to look smart."

"All those Unitarian dandies are a bunch of show-offs."

"Bet you aren't up to it—eh, Matasiete?"

"Bet you he isn't."

"Bet you he is."

Matasiete was a man of few words and much action. When it came to violence, agility, skill with the hatchet, the knife, or the horse, he was closemouthed and acted swiftly. They had piqued him: he roweled his horse and galloped, loose reined, toward the Unitarian.

The man in question was young, aged 25, elegantly dressed and good-looking. He was heading for Barracas at a trot, unaware of any impending danger, at the same time that the mob was shouting out the exclamations just heard at the tops of their lungs. He then realized that the pack of slaughter-yard guard dogs was staring ominously at him, and his right hand automatically reached for the holsters on his English saddle. That was when the sideways blow from the chest of Matasiete's horse threw him backwards over his mount's haunches, landing him on his back some distance away, where he lay quite still.

"Cheers for Matasiete!" the rabble exclaimed in unison, madly rushing at the victim like rapacious *caranchos* alighting on the bones of a tiger-ravaged ox.

Still dazed, the young man got up, and hurling a fiery look at the ferocious men, began walking toward his horse, which stood motionless a short distance away, intent on getting vengeance and justice with his pistols. Matasiete leapt down from his horse, and blocking him, grabbed him by the cravat and threw him to the ground, at the same time drawing his dagger from his waist and pressing it against the young man's throat.

An explosion of laughter was followed by yet another resounding "Hurrah!" that rose in the air in praise of Matasiete.

What noble souls, what courage, that of the Federalists! Always in gangs and swooping down on their defenseless victims like vultures!

"Cut his throat, Matasiete; he was going for his pistols. Slit his throat like you did the bull's."

"Mischievous Unitarian. We need to cut off his sideburns."

"He's got a nice neck for the violin."

"Better to slit his throat."

"We'll give it a try," said Matasiete. He started smiling as he slid the dagger's blade across the fallen man's throat, as he pressed down on his chest with his left knee, and held his head rigid by grabbing his hair with his left hand.

"No, no—don't slit his throat," the slaughter-yard judge shouted in his imposing voice, as he approached from a distance on his horse.

"To the *casilla* with him. Prepare the corncob and the shears. Death to the Unitarian savages! Long Live the Restorer of Laws!"

"Long Live Matasiete!"

"Death!," "Long Live!" the spectators echoed in a chorus. And tying up his elbows, between blows and shoves, shouts and insults, like Christ's executioners they dragged the wretched youth to the torture bench.

In the middle of the receiving room in the *casilla*, there stood a large, massive table that was never cleared of glasses of drink and playing cards except when it was used for executions and torture by the slaughter yard's Federalist executioners. Also visible in one corner was another, smaller table with writing materials and a notebook, and a number of chairs, among which stood out the arm chair used by the judge. A man, apparently a soldier, was seated on one of the chairs, singing a *resbalosa* tune to the melody of a guitar. The song, about torturing Unitarians, was extremely popular among the Federalists. Just then, the gang reached the *casilla*'s front porch and shoved the young Unitarian toward the center of the room.

"It's your turn for the *resbalosa*," one of the men shouted at him.

"Commend your soul to the devil."

"He's as furious as a wild bull."

"The stick will tame you soon enough."

"He needs a whipping."

"For now, the pizzle[22] and shears."

"Otherwise, the candle."

"Better the corncob."

"Silence, and sit down!" exclaimed the judge, as he sank down on an armchair. Everyone obeyed, while the young man, who was standing, confronted the judge and exclaimed in a voice full of indignation.

"Miserable killers! What do you intend to do to me?"

"Calm down!" the judge said, smiling. "No reason to lose your temper. You'll find out in time."

The young man was, in fact, beside himself with rage. His entire body seemed to be in the throes of a seizure. His pallid, bruised face, his voice, his trembling lip showed the alteration of his heart, the agitation of his nerves. His burning eyes seemed about to burst out of their sockets, his lanky black hair bristled. The veins on his bare neck throbbed visibly and his chest heaved violently beneath his shirtfront.

"Are you trembling?" the judge said to him.

"With rage, because I can't strangle you with my bare hands."

"Would you have the strength and the courage for it?"

"More than enough will and courage for you, you snake."

"Let's see, bring the shears for trimming my horse's mane. Give him a trim, Federalist style."

Two men grabbed him, one by the rope binding his arms, the other by his head, and in a minute one of his side whiskers, that continued all the way down to his beard, had been sheared off. The audience exploded with laughter.

"Let's see," said the judge, "a glass of water to refresh him."

"I'd make you drink a glass of gall, you scum."

A diminutive black soon stood before him with a glass of water in his hand. The young man kicked his arm, sending the glass flying and crashing against the ceiling, spattering the spectators' astonished faces.

"This one's impossible."

"We'll break him soon enough."

"Silence," said the judge. "You've already gotten a Federalist shearing. All you need is a moustache. Don't forget to grow one. Now let's get down to business. Why aren't you wearing an insignia?"

"Because I don't want to."

"Don't you know that the Restorer orders it?"

"Livery is for you slaves, not for free men."

"The free men are made to wear one by force."

"Yes—force and bestial violence—those are your weapons, despicable wretches. Wolves, tigers, panthers are also strong like you; you ought to walk on all fours like them."

"Aren't you afraid that the tiger will tear you to pieces?"

"I prefer it to you tying me up and plucking out my entrails one by one, like a crow."

"Why don't you have a mourning sash on your hat in memory of the Heroine?"

"Because I wear one in my heart, in memory of the country you've murdered, you villains."

"Don't you know that the Restorer has decreed it?"

"You are the ones who've decreed it, you slaves, to flatter your master's pride and render him your disgraceful vassalage."

"Impudent fool! You've got your gorge up all right, but say another word and I'll have your tongue cut off. Pull the pants off this stupid dandy and give him the pizzle on his bare ass; tie him down tightly to the table."

Immediately the judge spoke, four blood-bespattered ruffians lifted the young man and stretched him out on top of the table, pressing down on his arms and legs.

"You'll have to cut my throat before I'll let you strip me, you bastard."

They gagged him and began to pull off his clothes. The young man curled up, kicked, clenched and grinded his teeth. Now his limbs became as pliant as a reed, now they were as hard as iron, and his spine was twisting, snake-like. Drops of sweat slid down his face, as large as pearls; his pupils flashed with anger, his mouth foamed and the veins beneath his pale skin were dark, as though turgid with blood.

"Tie him up first!" the judge shouted.

"He's roaring with rage," said one of the thugs.

Moments later they tied his legs at an angle to the table's four legs, turning his body face down. The same thing had to be done to do the same with his hands, and to do it they loosened the rope that had tied his hands behind his back. The young man felt that his hands were free, and in a violently abrupt movement that seemed to drain him of all his strength and vitality, he raised himself, first on his arms, next on his knees, then he collapsed on the table and murmured,

"You'll slit my throat first before you'll strip me, filthy scum."

His strength was gone.

They immediately tied him down in a crucified position and began the work of pulling off his clothes. That was when the blood gushed out, bubbling out of the young man's mouth and nose, then trickling down both sides of the table. The thugs stood motionless; the onlookers were dumbfounded.

"The savage Unitarian burst with rage," said one.

"He had a river of blood in his veins," muttered another.

"Poor devil, all we wanted was to have a bit of fun with him, and he took things too seriously," the judge declared, his tiger's brow contracted in a frown. "A report must be filed. Untie him, and let's go."

The order was carried out, they locked the door, and the mob soon trailed behind the judge as he rode his horse, head bowed, and silent.

The Federalists had concluded one of their innumerable achievements.

In those days, the slaughter yard's butchers-cum-executioners were the apostles who were spreading the gospel of the Rosas Federation at whip- and knife-point, and it is not hard to imagine what sort of federation had to emerge from their heads and knives. In keeping with the jargon invented by the Restorer, the patron of their brotherhood, they labeled a "savage Unitarian" anyone who was not an executioner, a butcher, a barbarian, or a thief; any man who was decent and whose heart was in the right place; any patriot with an education who was a friend of enlightenment and freedom. The events described above may allow us to see, in all clarity, that the center of the Federation was the slaughter yard.

For Further Reading

Chasteen, John Charles. *Heroes on Horseback: A Life and Times of the Last Gaucho Caudillos*. Albuquerque: University of New Mexico Press, 1995.

De la Fuente, Ariel. *Children of Facundo: Caudillo and Gaucho Insurgency during the Argentine State-Formation Process (La Rioja, 1853–1870)*. Durham, NC: Duke University Press, 2000.

Gootenberg, Paul. *Between Silver and Guano: Commercial Policy and the State in Postindependence Peru*. Princeton: Princeton University Press, 1991.

Guardino, Peter. *Peasants, Politics, and the Formation of Mexico's National State: Guerrero, 1800–1857*. Palo Alto: Stanford University Press, 2000.

Johnson, Lyman (ed.). *Death, Dismemberment, and Memory: Body Politics in Latin America*. Albuquerque: University of New Mexico Press, 2004.

López-Alves, Fernando. *State Formation and Democracy in Latin America, 1810–1900*. Durham, NC: Duke University Press, 2000.

Lynch, John. *Argentine Caudillo: Juan Manuel de Rosas*. Wilmington: Scholarly Resources, 2001.

Mallon, Florencia. *Peasant and Nation: The Making of Postcolonial Mexico and Peru*. Berkeley: University of California Press, 1995.

Méndez, Cecilia. *The Plebeian Republic: The Huanta Rebellion and the Making of the Peruvian State, 1820–1850*. Durham, NC: Duke University Press, 2005.

Sanders, James. *Contentious Republicans: Popular Politics, Race, and Class in Nineteenth-Century Colombia*. Durham, NC: Duke University Press, 2004.

Sarmiento, Domingo Faustino. *Facundo: Civilization and Barbarism*. New York: Penguin, 1998.

Shumway, Nicholas. *The Invention of Argentina*. Berkeley: University of California Press, 1993.

Thurner, Mark. *From Two Republics to One Divided: Contradictions of Postcolonial Nationmaking in Andean Peru*. Durham, NC: Duke University Press, 1997.

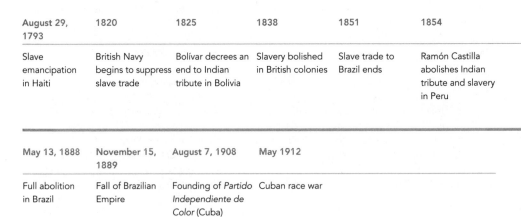

August 29, 1793	1820	1825	1838	1851	1854
Slave emancipation in Haiti	British Navy begins to suppress slave trade	Bolívar decrees an end to Indian tribute in Bolivia	Slavery bolished in British colonies	Slave trade to Brazil ends	Ramón Castilla abolishes Indian tribute and slavery in Peru

May 13, 1888	November 15, 1889	August 7, 1908	May 1912
Full abolition in Brazil	Fall of Brazilian Empire	Founding of *Partido Independiente de Color* (Cuba)	Cuban race war

Race and Citizenship in the New Republics   **3**

1861–1865	1862	September 22, 1862	1868–1878	1879–1880	October 7, 1886
Civil war in United States	Slave trade to Cuba ends	President Lincoln issues Emancipation Proclamation in United States	Ten Year War (Cuba)	Julio Roca's conquest of the desert in Argentina	Full abolition in Cuba

It is difficult to read the *Declaration of the Rights of Man and Citizen*, issued by the French National Constituent Assembly in August 1789, without imagining this as a critical moment in human history. Best summed up with the phrase all "men are born and remain free and equal in rights", the *Declaration* symbolized the convergence of revolutionary fervor and the ideals of perhaps the most important intellectual of the eighteenth century, Jean Jacques Rousseau. Repudiating a history in which rights had been apportioned according to lineage and special status (i.e. membership in a religious order), this made the citizen the only legitimate possessor of rights. To be sure, the *Declaration* did not include women, and its writer had no intention to free the slaves, but it was such a hopeful idea. And it would animate much of the nineteenth- and twentieth-century history of the world. Since that time one of the critical stories of humankind has been the struggle to become more free, to extend more rights to more people, and to establish universal standards and practices of justice. This was as true in Latin America as it was in any other place.

In most places and at most times freedom and equality before the law have been articulated as universal values (ideals that remain valid no matter what the context), but in practice they have always been the product of local circumstances. They are rights granted to citizens, those individuals designated as members of a national community, and during the nineteenth century citizenship itself was not always framed as a right. It was instead often seen as something for which one must qualify. In much of Europe, one needed to belong to the folk—through language, religion, or customs, to belong to the national community, and thus be a potential citizen. In the United States, already an ethnically diverse society, male whiteness was the essential precondition of citizenship. In most places property and age were also critical requirements. Even more, the very question of what set of practices constituted citizenship rights would be debated again and again during the course of the century. Political rights—the right to vote, to stand for office, to choose ones' rulers were but one among many types of contested rights, including the right to free speech, to freedom of religion, to freedom of assembly, to equality before the law, and so on. Added to this were other claims to rights, not always framed according to universal liberal values. Emancipated slaves sometimes saw recompense for their suffering (perhaps a plot of land, maybe more) as a right. Peasants might demand for a right to village autonomy. This expectation, once held by indigenous vassals of the king, would be recast as a citizenship claim made by villages that called themselves *comunidades ex-indios* (ex-Indian communities).

Latin Americans faced innumerable obstacles in defining suitable qualities of citizenship in their newly independent republics. Independence represented a kind of freedom—freedom from colonial rule—but in societies with so little tradition of liberal rights and such a long history of legally enshrined hierarchies—religious, social, and racial—the question how freedom from colonial rule translated into citizenship rights was a daunting one.

Caste Systems

While Latin Americans would for the most part defer struggles over gender rights until well into the twentieth century, race and caste were critical categories in the citizenship debates of the early republican period. Colonial society was predicated on caste hierarchies—in late colonial Mexico there were at least 18 caste categories—which determined where one lived, which occupations were available, and opportunities for marriage, political, and social advancement. Whites were at the top of those hierarchies, but the *criollos* (Europeans born in the Americas) who took power in the new republics were not always supporters of these forms of distinction, as they were often both liberals and felt the sting of standing second to peninsular Spaniards. Utopian liberals often wanted to strike down all barriers (again, except those that excluded women), pushing through emancipation declarations, prohibitions of the caste system, and constitutions that granted nearly universal citizenship rights to adult males in the early years of independence.

These were, however, idealistic moments. The law in Latin America has a long history of acting as a projection of how society might function, and not so much as a prescription for how it will function, and these laws were no exception. The urban, educated, middle-class and elite, white liberals who wrote these constitutions could not, for the most part, imagine people of the lower castes as their equals, and with independence formal discrimination would gradually be replaced by unofficial practices that accomplished the same ends. In some cases (in Peru in 1826, for example) old systems of tribute and forced labor would be reintroduced by states in need of resources, and in others informal exclusionary practices would simply supersede formal ones.

During the nineteenth century the old systems of hierarchy were gradually remade into new systems of direct exclusion based on the categories created by scientific racism, as ideas emanating from Europe and North America about the biological differences among the races found many adherents in the region. Race was a charged concept in this era. European theorists argued variously that the different races descended from different origins (i.e. Samuel Von Sommering), that different groups had innately different abilities (Johann Blumenbach), that the mixing of races led to the degeneration of the species (Arthur de Gobineau) and that society was responsible for maintaining and improving the gene pool (Francis Galton). Of course, these ideas had uneven impacts in Latin America, but the influences of new sciences like eugenics, phrenology, and craniometry were unmistakable. A colonial system favoring cleanliness of the blood (*limpieza de sangre*—a hierarchical system based on your ability to claim blood untainted by the infidels) was supplanted by another that gave whiteness a scientific virtue. Whites were smarter, more rational, more fit to govern, and more fit to be citizens of any society. Blacks, Indians, Asians, and those of mixed racial origins were seen to be a burden at best and a threat to civilization at worst.

Troubled by the prospects for their nations to become civilized because of the racial make-up of their societies, Latin American elites undertook any number of projects to improve the race. Where possible, they gradually erased the stain of blackness or Indianness through intermarriage or reclassification. As late as 1838 Afro-Argentines are 25 percent of Buenos Aires, but by 1887 only 2 percent. Many were reclassified as *trigueño*, or "wheat colored." Others hoped for redemption through education, modernization, hygiene, nutrition, healthy motherhood, and any number of other improvements, believing that if they could elevate the poor, racially compromised masses out of their civilizational slumber, their societies might prosper. Their vision was not so much egalitarian as it was rooted in a history of Catholic paternalism, of helping defenseless pathetic vassals.

Others took a darker view of the racial divide. Nationalists in Peru drew on the Inca past for their symbols, but actively despised living Indians. In the minds of *Limeños* (and for that matter highlanders), the regional geography of the country was also indelibly racial—a white/mestizo city and coast confronted an Indian highlands and countryside. This deep fragmentation would ultimately harden into the system Peruvians called *gamonalismo*, in which landlords and merchants who controlled the highlands like feudal kingdoms were tolerated both because they delivered loyalty to the national government, and because *Limeños* had little faith in the capacity of Andean peoples for citizenship.

The racial geographies of places like Mexico and Argentina were less well defined, as most of rural Mexico and the *pampas* had indeterminate racial origins. Where, however, race could be clearly linked to a region's identity, it was sometimes turned to genocidal ends. In Chiapas, the Indian highlanders who were forced into *enganche* (forced contract) labor on the coastal coffee plantations earned little sympathy from outsiders. In Mexico's North, the government of Porfirio Díaz forcibly moved approximately 15,000 Yaquis from their homes in Sonora and condemned them to labor on henequen plantations in the Yucatán following their military defeat at the hands of the army in the early 1900s. Julio Roca's Conquest of the Desert in Argentina (1879–1880) was informed by similar attitudes towards race, and left over 1,300 indigenous dead. In both cases, the clearing of indigenous lands left new territory open for white speculators and settlers to turn to "productive" ends.

Indigenous peoples were left in a series of binds by these conflicts. Though some tried to appropriate the language of liberalism, demanding their rights as citizens, fighting in national wars (thousands of indigenous Mexicans fought in Benito Juárez' liberal armies against the

French invasion of Mexico, 1861–7), they were hamstrung in a variety of ways. Liberal elites were not inclined to recognize the participation of racial others in their great national struggles. Even though they relied on armies made up of the great unwashed masses, they quickly erased them from their historical memory once they consolidated power. Neither were popular groups served well by their own versions of liberal rights. When peasant or indigenous villagers came to the liberal cause, they generally interpreted the right to freedom to mean village autonomy. Individual rights were transformed into the right of local communities to set their own laws, to live free of interference from the outside world. Just as importantly, indigenous peoples were as likely to be tied up in fratricidal struggles with neighboring communities as they were national or international elites. The net result was that indigenous peoples generally did not generate visionaries who thought in national terms, and the terrain for national leadership was left to those who saw the Indian, the *mestizo*, the peasant, as little more than fodder for their own dreams.

The break-up of communal peasant villages, accomplished mainly by liberal states which had relied on these same peasants to consolidate their hold on power, would be both one of the great tragedies of the nineteenth century and a source of enduring grievances into the twentieth. Across the region land surveyors, speculators, and investors took advantage of liberal legislation to gobble up a great deal of land that was deemed vacant, largely because it was occupied by indigenous peoples. Former peasants were increasingly thrust onto the labor market, forced to work in export agriculture as debt peons[1] or day laborers. This in turn is part of the reason why village autonomy would remain a critical peasant demand across the region for generations to come (including in violent conflicts in Mexico in 1910, Bolivia in 1952, Peru in 1968, and arguably Mexico in 1994).

The Stain

Slaves created the first republic in the Caribbean, and yet just fifty miles away, simple emancipation would take nearly a century longer. This contrast reminds us that the story of freedom and citizenship is a varied one across the region, invariably rooted in local histories, cultures, and circumstances. Those places where slavery was not a centrally important institution generally produced different kinds of histories than those where it was.

Slaves existed in most parts of the region at the beginning of the nineteenth century. On the eve of independence there were 30,000 slaves in La Plata, 78,000 in New Granada, 64,500 in Venezuela, and 89,000 in Peru. They worked on Peruvian sugar plantations and wineries, on cacao and sugar estates in Venezuela, in Colombian gold mines, and ranches in Argentina. They were also common in urban areas, toiling as servants, and skilled and unskilled workers. In most of these regions they were important, but not critical sources of labor, often working alongside free laborers. By contrast, plantation agriculture in the Caribbean and Brazil relied on slavery for its very existence. In Brazil, slaves were also central to gold and diamond mining in Minas Gerais, and to an emerging coffee economy in and around São Paulo.

It is not really sufficient to describe societies in the region as characterized by the presence or absence of slaves. Across the region there were too many distinctions even within slavery to do this. Take the United States, for instance. In the nineteenth century the United States had a slave population that was unlike any other in the region. Whereas in most regions a considerable percentage of slaves were of African origin, in the United States the vast majority of slaves were native born. Perhaps because of the historical cost of importing slaves and the relative poverty of U.S. plantation societies, North Americans had only a marginal presence in the history of the slave trade, importing something like 500,000 slaves over several centuries (4.4 percent of the total, as compared to 4 million or 35 percent for Brazil).

The slave population of the United States was among the largest in the Americas in the early nineteenth century, but that population was the product of natural increase and extremely low levels of manumission. Because so few were ever freed, to be black in the United States (and particularly the South) in the nineteenth century was almost certainly to be a slave. Miscegenation produced more blacks, more slaves, and the European ancestry of many slaves was erased. Furthermore, those who were free enjoyed little better treatment than slaves (except, to some extent, in Louisiana). Among other prohibitions, many Southern states forbade free persons of color from becoming preachers, selling certain goods, tending bar, staying out past a certain time of night, or owning dogs.

Just a few hundred miles away, Haiti's history of slavery was quite different. A marginal colony until the end of the seventeenth century, during the eighteenth century St. Domingue emerged as one of the richest colonies in the world, due to a booming sugar plantation complex and the importation of 790,000 slaves. The story of Haitian independence was told in Chapter 1, but it is worth recalling that unlike in the United States, in Haiti slavery and race were not entirely contiguous. In fact, much of the wealth in the colony was in the hands of free people of color. Their role in independence was ambiguous. Free blacks first struggled for rights for themselves, but as slave-owners, were not universally in favor of emancipation. Over time, some free blacks advocated slave emancipation, but their reasons were not always clear. Some seem to have genuinely desired emancipation. Others used it simply to win slaves onto their side in the civil war that engulfed Haiti during the 1790s.

Across a narrow straight, slavery remained essential to a colonial Cuban economy well into the nineteenth century. With the demise of the sugar industry in Haiti, Cuban planters grew more cane, imported more slaves. Still, while slavery played a critical role in maintaining Cuba's colonial status early in the century, the logics that underpinned this option gradually grew less compelling in the decades after the 1820s. North American investment began to supplant the power of Spanish capital, and Cuba grew more diverse (in part due to European immigration, which was promoted to dilute the African blood of the island's population) and more distant from its Spanish overlords. As the British government intensified its pressure on the slave trade, Cuban planters looked elsewhere for labor. With the end of slavery in sight, by mid-century the planters in Santa Clara and Matanzas (the most prosperous sugar zones) began to recruit indentured Chinese laborers in significant numbers. Even so, Cuban planters actually imported 400,000 slaves between 1835 and 1864.[2]

Cuba's booming economy enriched a growing number of free blacks during this era. Black professionals and petty merchants with middle-class aspirations marked the face of a changing Havana, and like elsewhere, offered a model of upward mobility for other free but poor blacks. This caused alarm in some quarters, and colonial officials ultimately tightened the caste restrictions, making it harder for blacks to move up the social ladder and also restricting the movement of people of color into and out of the country. Fearing that Cuban and foreign blacks were fomenting rebellion among the slaves, royal officials launched a major campaign against free blacks in 1844 (the *Escalera*) arresting two thousand and exiling several hundred. This profoundly shaped the experience of emancipation in Cuba, where free people of color were increasingly made into objects of fear and official discrimination as slavery drew to its close.

In Brazil, government officials did the opposite, loosening colonial era restrictions that limited the upward mobility of free people of color in response to an increasingly upwardly mobile Afro-Brazilian population. By the mid-nineteenth century *libertos* (former slaves) even enjoyed the right to vote as long as they met property qualifications. Non-whites could be found across the professions, in government, and among the nation's most important writers and intellectuals by the 1870s, and faced no formal social prohibitions. To be sure, mulattos[3] generally fared better in society than blacks, but by this time most of the discrimination in Brazil was informal, outside of the law.

As international pressure brought the slave trade to an end, the patterns of slavery across the hemisphere changed. Slavery became more rural, more closely tied to the most profitable export commodities (cotton in the United States, coffee in Brazil, sugar in Cuba), more absent from the quotidian life of the cities and from less prosperous regions. Cuba was an increasingly divided place, as some regions depended even more on slavery than they had in the past, and others increasingly did not rely on slavery at all. Complicating this situation further, a growing number of Cubans openly argued for both freedom from Spain and freedom from slavery, identifying both as a kind of bonded servitude that crippled the nation. The racist elements of this sentiment were sometimes explicit, as many believed that the continued presence of large numbers of black slaves represented a barrier to true Cuban nationhood.

Slaves and former slaves were active participants in this struggle. Runaway slaves and slave revolts in Cuba and elsewhere in the Caribbean reminded Cuban whites of the injustices of the institution. *Cofradias* (fraternal societies organized by slaves and former slaves) kept pressure on the system by raising funds to purchase freedom and agitating for rights. Whenever laws were passed to ameliorate the harshest conditions of slavery in Cuba, slaves used their extensive oral networks to pass the news. Once armed with this knowledge slaves actively challenged their overseers and claimed whatever rights they believed they had. The refusal of overseers to respect those rights (which in some cases may be as simple as the right to talk back) could at times ignite a volatile situation. Moreover, planters could be put at a severe disadvantage by these information networks. Rumor and speculation could transform relatively minor reforms into something much more significant. Whispers of imminent emancipation (and the belief that planters were defying orders from above) helped launch the Haitian revolution, revolts in Barbados (1816), Demerara (1823), and Jamaica (1831).[4]

The issue of slavery came to a head during Cuba's independence wars, beginning with the Ten Years War (1868–78). The war took place largely in Oriente, a relatively poor and remote region of the island at the time. Perhaps because Oriente had relatively few sugar *ingenios* (mills), and thus relatively few slaves, both the rebels and Spanish promised freedom to Afro-Cubans who fought on their side. Neither side imagined extensive emancipation, but slaves actively joined both in significant numbers. Simultaneously, the fear of emancipation emanating from the east helped keep the rich sugar planting areas in Santa Clara and Matanzas resolutely in the royalist camp.

Even though limited to eastern Cuba, the war initiated the process of emancipation, and once begun it was hard to reverse. The international slave trade had ended. Along with Brazil,

Cuba was one of only two places in the Americas where slavery remained legal. Furthermore, low reproduction rates on the island meant that the competition for slaves would only become fiercer. Those with sufficient resources turned to other (principally Chinese) forms of labor servitude. For their part, former slaves pressed the system with increasing confidence, pooling their resources to purchase the freedom of friends and relatives, and pressuring the judicial authorities whenever they could to limit abuses and punish masters who broke the law. In some senses, slavery was becoming unworkable.

During the war (in 1870) the Spanish *Cortes* passed the Moret Law, which declared that all individuals born on the island henceforth would be born free (thus the name, a Free Womb Law), but the law required a 22-year apprenticeship for children born to slave mothers. Under increasing pressure from abolitionists, including former slaves, ten years later the Spanish *Cortes* passed a law calling for gradual abolition, which included an 8-year period of indentured servitude for the former slaves (this was called the *patronato*). Increasingly unwilling to allow any limits to their freedom, slaves challenged the *patronato* with such effectiveness that it was abolished 2 years early on October 7, 1886. Slavery in Cuba had come to its end (Table 3.1).

The active role that slaves played in their own emancipation in Cuba is striking, in part because Cuba seems to stand out from societies like the United States and Brazil. This is, however, a trick of the light. In all cases in the Americas emancipation was a complex story of pressures from the outside world, internal elite conflicts, and pressure from slaves themselves. In Cuba, as in Haiti, slaves took hold of their freedom in the context of civil wars. In the United States, cross-class unity among whites limited the possible ways blacks might

Table 3.1 Emancipation in the Americas

Country	Dates
Haiti	1793
Argentina	1813 (free womb), 1851 (full)
Chile	1823
Mexico	1829
Venezuela	1830 (children), 1854 (full)
Bolivia	1831
British colonies	1833
Uruguay	1842
Danish colonies	1847
French colonies	1848
Colombia	1851
Peru	1854
Ecuador	1854
Dutch colonies	1863
United States	1865
Cuba	1870 (free womb), 1886 (full)
Brazil	1871 (free womb), 1888 (full)
Puerto Rico	1873

participate in the civil war, but pressure from former slaves helped to mobilize northern whites against the abomination of slavery. In Brazil, the story of emancipation is similarly complex.

The first real pressures on Brazilian slavery came from abroad. As early as 1815 Brazilians submitted to British pressure to limit the Atlantic slave trade, and the government formally committed to gradually end the trade in the 1830s. Still, until the British finally pressured Brazil into abolishing the legal slave trade in 1851, Brazilian slave imports remained robust. During the nineteenth century Brazil imported 1.3 million slaves, including 371,000 in the 10 years prior to the end of the trade (The United States, by contrast, imported just 51,000 slaves during the nineteenth century.) Brazil suffered some spectacular slave rebellions during these years (especially in 1835, in Bahia), and during this era public sentiment gradually turned against slavery (Brazilian liberals believed the country's failings in their war with Paraguay during the 1860s were a result of slavery), but until the 1850s slavery remained important enough to the economies of the northeast, south, and southwest of the country that abolition gained relatively little purchase in the country as a whole.

With the end of the slave trade, however, the demographics of slavery in Brazil began to change. After 1851 slaves as a percentage of labor force and capital gradually declined. As access to slaves became more limited, they tended to become concentrated around a few commodities. Slaves were transferred from declining regions (like the northeast) to the more robust coffee and mining regions (particularly Rio de Janeiro and Minas Gerais). Also, although São Paulo had one of the most robust coffee economies in the country, planters there increasingly recruited European and Asian migrants, relying less on slaves (coffee exports would surpass sugar by the 1850s). While planters in some regions still relied on slaves, after the 1850s more and more regions of the country either did not use large-scale slavery or depended increasingly on other forms of labor. By 1884 slaves accounted for more than 10 percent of the population in less than half of Brazil's provinces, and in the northeast slave populations were comparable to the United States North around the time of abolition (5 percent of the total). In this context the moral arguments against slavery gradually gained more adherents.

After a series of failed efforts, the Brazilian Parliament eventually passed a free womb law (the Rio Branco Law) in 1871. The law established a fund to purchase the freedom of slaves, but it also required the "free" children of slaves to work for their masters to the age of 21, and compensated slave-owners for their losses. Inadequate though it was, it did signal the eventual end of slavery. Wealthy planters redoubled their efforts to find alternative labor sources, and opponents simply resolved to put more pressure on the system. Over the course of the next 15 years slaves and former slaves protested, marched, and pressured the Imperial government to end slavery, forming the backbone of a popular abolitionist movement. Black and mulatto intellectuals wrote extensive tracts decrying the evils of slavery. Free black dockworkers and others struck or otherwise mobilized against slavery. In response, local governments in several regions passed acts of emancipation, declaring slavery-free zones. Ceará declared itself a free state in 1884, followed by Amazonas in 1885. In the South, a November 1886 strike by free workers forced the city of Santos to declare itself free. By the end of the year the city housed 10,000 runaway slaves.

White liberals also participated, writing letters to the newspapers, traveling to slave plantations to monitor the conditions of slaves and report abuses, and as a result of these combined pressures, slavery became increasingly untenable—a system that was driving the country towards chaos. Attempting to stave off this threat, the Brazilian Parliament passed a law freeing all slaves over 65 in 1885, and then its Golden Law—emancipation without recompense to the owners for Brazil's 723,000 remaining slaves—in 1888. By this time three-quarters of Brazil's slaves toiled the three major coffee provinces of São Paulo, Minas Gerias, and Rio de Janeiro.

Different Paths

Critics of slavery in the nineteenth century described this institution as not simply a stain on humankind, but as hopelessly antiquated and ultimately unproductive. The historical record from Cuba and elsewhere, however, suggests something to the contrary. Here, as in Brazil, slaves worked alongside free laborers, in skilled and unskilled positions, and often in industries that produced immense profits. Slave-owners may have wanted to preserve this institution in part because of their own cultural sensibilities, but it also seems that the wealth they had tied up in slaves was, in fact, extremely productive. The problems they faced came from an increasingly fragile supply chain and an increasingly powerful opposition. The rate of natural increase in the slave population might have allowed slavery to continue for some time, but the importance of the trade in these regions suggested that once it was ended, slavery's days were numbered.

Why did Cuban and Brazilian planters rely so heavily on the slave trade to replenish their supply of slaves? In part it was simply because the trade had always been more developed in these areas, bringing in more slaves. In part it was because the life span of slaves on plantations in these regions was shorter than in the United States. More than half of Brazilian slaves died within the first three years of arriving. Life expectancies for slaves were two-thirds that of whites (in the United States it was 90 percent of whites). This would seem to suggest a more benign slavery in North America, but such comparisons can be deceiving.

Because slaves were more costly in the north, planters in the United States had more incentive to see that their slaves lived long lives. Likewise, slaves in the United States tended to work on smaller plantations and in smaller numbers than elsewhere, meaning that each slave's value to their owner as a portion of their capital tended to be greater. This also meant that a North American planter had more economic incentive to see a son born of a slave as a unit of production than a Brazilian planter. A Brazilian slave-owner may have been less concerned about the health of an easily replaced slave than his North American counterpart, but they were also more willing to consider manumission. Legally enforceable contracts in which slaves and their masters agreed to a price for their freedom were relatively common in Brazil. They had no history in the United States. Furthermore, in both contexts slaves who worked as household servants, or on small estates where they enjoyed face-to-face relationships with their owners, would have experienced slavery far differently than those who worked on large commercial estates.

One of the rather significant differences among these societies—and one that would have important implications for the rights blacks acquired after slavery, lay in the ways race and slavery were linked in these societies. Unlike in the United States, in Brazil and Cuba slavery and race were never coterminous.

In Cuba, the population of free blacks during the nineteenth century amounted to 39 percent of the people of African origin on the island. In Brazil it was more than 75 percent. The urban working class of cities like Rio de Janeiro included significant numbers of free blacks, while free people of color also worked in agriculture, owned land, even owned slaves. In Bahia, Afro-Brazilians owned both sugar plantations and slaves in significant numbers.

And so, while during the years preceding abolition in both the United States and Brazil slave-holding was increasingly confined to large-scale landowners, in Brazil the black population as a whole was never isolated within a single social system (Table 3.2). In the United States the opposite happened. North American planters used this situation to build a regional coalition with poor whites in defense of slavery—playing on themes of a southern culture unified in its whiteness. In Brazil (Rio and São Paulo, particularly, where most slave holding was concentrated) the owners did not manage to produce these regional cross-class coalitions opposing abolition. Brazilian elites feared the racially heterogeneous masses that characterized their countryside and cities, and would not imagine mobilizing them into a coalition either opposed to or in favor of abolition. We see this in certain curious distinctions between Brazil and the United States. For example, representatives from Pernambuco and Bahia supported the Rio Branco law, even though between 12 percent and 20 percent of the population in these states were slaves. Delaware refused to support compensated emancipation in 1861 even though there were only 2,000 slaves in the state.

Rights and the Color Line

The history of rights for people of color in the United States is well known. After a moment in which blacks in the defeated South embraced the franchise and a Radical Republican Congress tried to punish a recalcitrant South by letting former slaves, carpetbaggers, and scalawags take the reins of government, northern reformers gradually retreated and southern whites created local political systems characterized by the Black Codes, Jim Crow Laws, the Ku Klux Klan, and a landscape where the threat of lynching was ever present. The cross-class alliance that defined the secessionist movement evolved into a political alliance rooted in anti-black hysteria. American historians generally agree that all but the most enlightened of thinkers never really believed African Americans deserved equal citizenship rights, and that in the North as well as the South blacks had few opportunities to press for their legal rights during the ensuing century. Equally important, the United States' "one drop rule," enforced

Table 3.2 The eve of emancipation: United States, Cuba, Haiti, Brazil

Country	Total population	Free people of color	Slaves
Haiti (1789)	523,000	28,000	465,000
USA (1860)	31,443,321	488,070	3,953,760
Cuba (1862)	1,396,530	232,433	370,533
Brazil (1872)	9,930,000	4,250,000	1,510,00

rigorously across the country, erased the possibility that miscegenation would entail a proliferation of categories. If you had a black ancestor, you were black. And you had better not forget that.

Latin American societies did not generally see a legal codification of discrimination based on race, a fact that many Latin American nationalists have used to argue that the region is more enlightened when it comes to matters of race. Some have even taken this as evidence that Latin Americans are not really racists (the Brazilian Gilberto Freyre and Mexican Manuel Gamio are famous examples). Early in the century, North American blacks who visited Brazil described their experiences here as a welcome relief from what they experienced at home. Still, the absence of violent codified discrimination did not exactly translate into the presence of rights, in Brazil, Cuba, or anywhere else. Former slaves in the region confronted a great deal of prejudice, lived in an era of virulent scientific racism, and at the very least faced the prospects of being very poor in poor countries; nations without the means to ameliorate their poverty even if they had possessed the will.

Because the states that governed post-emancipation societies were weak, local power brokers would determine the terms and nature of labor arrangements throughout the region. Coercive but somewhat flexible labor systems like debt peonage, share cropping, and contract labor would prevail in many areas, and the political connections between landowners and political elites would undermine most efforts to enforce existing labor laws or the civil rights of newly emancipated citizens. Planters in Cuba, Mexico, Jamaica, Brazil, and elsewhere also turned to migrant labor to meet their needs. As a result, some former slaves were left without any form of work.

Former slaves in Brazil had differing experiences. In São Paulo, slaves tended to move away from their former masters. At first they had trouble integrating into the growing urban and agricultural economy, for several reasons. Planters and the state worked together to flood the São Paulo labor market with subsidized immigration as abolition got underway. For their part, the *libertos* often demanded respect, an end to corporal punishment, respect for their family units, and wages that planters would not offer. However, once subsidized immigration ended, and the new immigrants found their footing, former slaves were increasingly incorporated into São Paulo's emerging industrial workforce. By contrast, in Bahia former slaves often remained tied to their former owners, working on their estates as agricultural laborers, and only migrating away from estates that suffered economic catastrophes in the aftermath of emancipation.

These distinct experiences helped produce a series of new images of Brazil that would supplant older ones. The northeast—poor, black, remote from the capital, tropical—came to be understood as a backwards region, filled with people not exactly ready now (if ever) for citizenship. Rio de Janeiro—the capital, the intellectual and cultural center—and São Paulo—the engine of economic growth and industry—came to be imagined as both less black and more modern than the rest of the country. It did not make sense for Brazilians to create formal systems of racial discrimination, as the northeast–southwest distinction did not align perfectly with racial classifications, and the centuries-old free-black community in Brazil had both intermarried with Europeans and produced its own share of wealthy, prestigious families. Instead, what Brazilians saw was the emergence of a series of softer designations that could maintain the hierarchies that existed under slavery. These soft gradations also allowed Brazilians to embrace the image of Brazil as a racially mixed society.

Somewhere between the rich white *paulista*[5] and poor black *nordestina*[6] was a mulatto, sometimes rich, sometimes poor, and sometimes a little of both.

On the national level, many former slaves supported the monarchy as a potential ally in the fight against discrimination and for voting and other rights, largely because the monarchy had been behind many anti-slavery measures over the years. This alliance was short-lived, however, because elites in Rio de Janeiro, along with *paulista* planters, conspired to overthrow the crown and create a republic in 1889. Power in the new republic was highly decentralized, and while the only restrictions on male suffrage were literacy, politics increasingly became an entirely elite affair, with very little popular participation. Brazilians of color first tried to defend their old allies through a series of black guards, and later tried to organize independently in defense of their rights in newly formed clubs and militias, but the new elites were prepared, and aggressively put down all forms of popular mobilization. The new planter state, in effect, eliminated the one element of the government to whom Brazilian blacks had looked for support. Moreover, because people of African ancestry could hope to move up the social hierarchy by acquiring wealth, prestige, and power, a confrontational struggle for civil rights quickly gave way to more individual strategies of advancement after 1889. If you followed the rules of the system, you might get ahead. If you protested, you were certain to be left behind.

Such was not the case in Cuba. Former slaves in Cuba did what slaves did elsewhere, often putting family and community interests ahead of the struggle for individual rights. Many moved eastward to Oriente, away from the sugar zones of Santa Clara and Matanzas in search of a better life. Still, when Cuba's final war for independence broke out in 1895, thousands of free blacks joined in the independence wars even though they were already free. Their participation reminds us that the meaning of freedom to slaves was neither universal nor simply tied to bondage. White Cubans and North American liberators would later try to erase their critical role in the struggle, but for those Afro-Cubans who fought for independence (in some cases twice), their sacrifices would represent an indelible claim on citizenship. Indeed, Cuba's 1902 Constitution granted all adult males the right to vote, regardless of color. This right, and the related claim that a voter had a right to be a full and equal participant in the political life of the nation, framed many of the political battles that would shape early republican Cuba.

In the aftermath of independence a significant number of Afro-Cubans demanded rights and privileges (pensions and positions in the government, for example) based on the 1902 Constitution, and based on their sacrifices in the struggle for independence. White Cubans responded both by trying to erase those contributions, and by increasingly defining blackness as a threat to the nation. The Cubans of color who demanded their rights as citizens, who demanded a share of positions in the bureaucracy, representation among elected officials, and the elimination of discrimination against blacks, were increasingly cast as dangerous primitives, threats to the nation's capacity for progress.

Cuba was thus like Brazil in that Cuban whites did not formally exclude all blacks from positions of privilege based on the qualities of their blood. They instead focused on a series of practices, and specifically Afro-Cuban religious traditions, arguing that significant numbers of former slaves were simply unfit for civilization. As in Brazil, where *capoeira*[7] was criminalized during the nineteenth century, Afro-Cuban religious traditions became a particular target. Images of the black Cuban as non-Christian, as a practitioner of witchcraft, of animal

La Política Cómica

La justicia del pueblo

CASTIGANDO EL CRIMEN

Figure 3.1 "Justice by the people: punishing the crime" political cartoon

Source: Courtesy of Alejandra Bronfman

and human sacrifices, and particularly of the kidnapping of white children for the purposes of ritual sacrifice, filled Cuban newspapers in the early years of independence (Figure 3.1). Police, scientists, criminologists, and elected officials railed against a perceived epidemic of savagery, and in the process laid the groundwork for recasting thousands of patriotic veterans (and citizens) as threats to the nation. The two processes were intertwined—the more Afro-Cubans demanded rights, the more stories of strange rituals and the kidnapping of white children circulated.

Facing these obstacles, or perhaps because of them, in the decade after independence Afro-Cubans increasingly began to organize for civil rights, rights built around a complex mix of universal values and rights won through the struggle. In 1908 Evaristo Estenoz, Pedro Ivonet, Gregorio Surín and several others founded the Independent Party of Color (*Partido Independiente de Color*, PIC), which was mainly made up of veterans of the wars for independence. The PIC was the first race based political party in the Americas, and was banned by the Cuban Congress shortly after it was founded (incidentally, the Morúa Amendment, the law that made the PIC illegal by banning parties based on race or class, was proposed by an Afro-Cuban). PIC supporters did not back down, and in spite of attempts to paint them as seditious, continued to protest for rights after the Morúa Law was passed. Their opponents were similarly resolute, and after 1910 stirred up fears of race war and black sexual violence, generally tying blackness to sedition and barbarism. The conflict came to a head after a series of protests in May 1912, which the press reported as the beginnings of a race war that would imperil the nation. In the following weeks some party supporters and poor peasants did engage in violent protests, but the response by the Cuban army was swift and decisive. Perhaps as many as 6,000 PIC supporters were massacred. In the aftermath, Afro-Cubans would need to find new means to struggle for their rights.

The Documents: Limiting Citizenship

As one would expect, it is relatively easy to find texts representing the views of both abolitionists and advocates of slavery from across the Americas during the nineteenth century. Abolition was one of the great issues of the day, debated in venues as diverse as the British Houses of Parliament and street corners in Rio de Janeiro. The written record of these struggles however, tends to reflect the limited access that individuals in the nineteenth century had to the written word. It was mostly middle- and upper-class white males who were even literate, let alone who had the means of publishing their views. In that record we therefore gain a rather narrow appreciation of the process and meanings of abolition. Slavery was attacked, defended, and modified largely through a Christian, prosperous, moralizing, and nationalistic lens. Even when the horrors of slavery were described, we rarely find the victims themselves describing their experiences.[8] We get very little sense from these documents of the roles that the slaves themselves played in first ending slavery and then in acquiring civil rights.

The record in Brazil is relatively thin, as most of the ex-slaves who became literate and prosperous seem to have preferred ascending the already existing social hierarchies to actively arguing for rights as Afro-Brazilians. Brazil's significant number of free people of color at emancipation, the fact that some limited access to power and prestige already existed for Afro-Brazilians, and the largely conservative political climate in Brazil may help to explain this.

In fact, the writer of Document 3.1 may have been an example of this. Raimundo Nina Rodrigues (1862–1906) began his career as a provincial intellectual and ultimately emerged as one of Brazil's most important social scientists, psychiatrists, and interpreters of race. Scholars have long believed that Nina Rodrigues' position in Brazil's debates about race were made even more complex because he was in fact mulatto. This is open to speculation though, because it is possible that his critics painted him as a mulatto when he was not, in effect using the taint of race to argue that what he had to say about race was somehow tainted. The logic of this claim is made more complex by the fact that his views about blacks were exceptionally negative.

Rodrigues did view mulattos more favorably than blacks (and this in stark contrast to the United States, where mulattos were often represented as the most degenerate, criminal, and lazy of blacks), arguing for the possibility that they could be civilized, but his views on race are perhaps most notable for the ways that he links a series of cultural and religious practices to blackness and backwardness, and ultimately suggests that the state ought to intervene in the private lives of Afro-Brazilians, prohibiting certain practices, because they represented a kind of civilizational peril. Strongly influenced by the Italian criminologist Césare Lombroso, his efforts to link race, culture, and crime are unmistakable. Nonetheless, Rodrigues also offers a sort of guide to how Afro-Brazilians might become civilized. Their backwardness, in his view, is not an essential quality, but something susceptible to modification.

Rodrigues' work was widely read in Latin America, and he had an important influence on the Cuban criminologist Fernando Ortiz. Working within a milieu in which North American ideas of racial separation and Afro-Cuban demands for rights based on their participation in the struggle for independence came into constant conflict, Ortiz' scholarly writings and work as a public official helped to shift the terrain on which Cubans struggled for their rights. Rather than denying rights based upon race, Ortiz, with the collaboration of a series of newspapers and other public officials, highlighted the dangers that Afro-Cuban religions represented to civilization. In part the images used were grotesque, but the larger impression he created was that Afro-Cubans were not Christian, were cannibalistic and dangerous, and needed to be controlled. Even as some Afro-Cubans organized for civil rights based on the fact that they faced discrimination for being black (see Document 3.2), in the very act of highlighting their blackness, they fed white hysteria over the black threat.

It is within this milieu that Document 3.3 must be read. It was written in the aftermath of the massacre of 1912, when it became impossible to organize a party around blackness. Some Afro-Cubans responded to these events by asserting that they were, indeed, civilized. Some eschewed separatist politics (Nicolás Guillén, senator and father of the poet, for example), insisting that there was no real racism in Cuba and that they were happy to work within the system. Others denied the claim that all Afro-Cubans practiced *brujería* (witchcraft), using Rodrigues' own logic to argue that they had erased their racial origins, and deserved to be treated as honorable and civilized. Fernando Guerra, however, was one of many who took on their enemies by openly defending Afro-Cuban religious forms. Guerra represents a particularly interesting case, because the author was in fact in close contact with Fernando Ortiz. He eventually even invited Ortiz to Lucumí ceremonies and initiated him into the religion. Having seen these eloquent defenses and participated in the rituals, Ortiz later muted his criticisms of Lucumí.

Document 3.1 Raimundo (Raymundo) Nina Rodrigues, *The Fetishist Animism of the Bahian Blacks (O Animismo Fetischistados Negros Bahianos)* (Excerpt)

Source: Excerpt from Raimundo (Raymundo) Nina Rodrigues, *O Animismo Fetischistados Negros Bahianos* (*The Fetishist Animism of the Bahian Blacks*, published 1896–1900). Translated by Diane Grosklaus Whitty.

The Fetishist Animism of Bahian Negroes

Only official science, because of the superficial, dogmatic nature of teaching, could insist in asserting even today that the population of Bahia is by and large a monotheistic

Christian one. This assertion must reflect either a systematic disregard for calculating the two-thirds African negroes and mixed-race mestizos that make up the great majority of the population, or a naïveté born of brute ignorance that blindly yields to outward appearances that will prove illusory and misleading upon the most superficial examination.

The prediction that this is not how it should be follows both from an understanding of the mental conditions prerequisite to the adoption of any religious belief and from these inferior races' psychic unfitness for the elevated abstractions of monotheism. But in the case at hand, citing this deduction as proof would of course be to commit a gross *petitio principii*, for here the opposite assertion is intended to do no less than stand as a tacit, formal disapprobation of the inductive conclusion reached by ethnographic researches. And only documented observation as thorough and rigorous as that exacted by the delicate nature of this subject matter should, in the final analysis, speak for or against the soundness and applicability of this principle, or for or against its repudiation.

More than once during my exercise of the teaching profession, the demands of psychological analysis in the field of forensic psychiatry have brought me practical experience with the problems raised by this controversy, where the facts always reveal themselves to be in formal contradiction with the ungrounded assertions of official science. Thus engaged in accurately ascertaining the nature and form of the religious feeling of Bahian negroes, I have endeavored to study the facts with the utmost neutrality and impartiality and have devoted nearly five years of time and effort to attentive observations. Considering the strictly scientific spirit in which these painstaking investigations were conceived in my quest to solve a serious issue in practical ethology, any preliminary declaration that they neither had nor have anything in common with controversies that debate "the metaphysics of matter and of the spirit" is hardly warranted.

Within the realm of that which is knowable, religious feeling is a positive psychological condition, which in no way presumes the animosities manifested between deists and atheists.

The persistence of African fetishism as an expression of the religious feeling of Bahian negroes and mixed-race mestizos is a fact that has not been disguised by the outward appearances of their apparently adopted Catholic worship, belied in the form of widespread hybrid associations between this worship and fetishism and also in the genuine practice of African sorcery, which thrives exuberantly and heartily alongside Christian worship there. In Bahia there exist deep-rooted fetishist beliefs and practices, established as ordinarily as those in Africa, neither hidden nor disguised but present in the full light of day; there exists a life that evinces its licitness in the police licenses granted for large annual festivals or *candomblés* and that enjoys the tolerance of public opinion, as reflected in how matter-of-factly the daily press reports on these gatherings, as if they were just another facet of our normal life; there exist practices whose activities reach into far broader realms than those in which they originated, and beliefs that are adopted and followed by the *soi-disant* civilized classes, in virtue of alliances formed with Catholic worship and the union forged with spiritual practices—that these manifold experiences exist lies within the spirit of the public and is fully known to all.

But observations that aspire to be scientific in nature and in value demand a rigor and precision that precludes simply using as references information which can be greatly adulterated or enlarged upon, even if only unconsciously. This subject does not require only authenticity and precision; it also calls for objective references to specific facts that are at any moment liable to verification and examination by those desiring to challenge them. Without a doubt, there arise all sorts of obstacles and stumbling blocks to a fair and just interpretation of facts of this nature, here more than anywhere. "Even dedicating much time and care to it," says Tylor (E. B. Tylor, *La civilisation primitive*, trans. Mme. Pauline Brunet, Paris, 1876, vol. 1, p. 489).

"it is not always easy to elicit from savages information on their theology. They customarily try to hide from the prying and contemptuous foreigner the details of their worship and all knowledge of their gods, who seem to tremble, like their worshippers, before the white man and his mightier Deity." As to not knowing their language, slavery must exacerbate in the African negro the savage's natural tendency to hide his beliefs.

The conviction that religious conversion is a simple matter of willingness and that nothing could be easier than annulling the negro's beliefs through punishment, to then replace these with the white man's, was shaped so as to satisfy the master's interests and thereby justify, as a veritable meritorious deed, all the violence employed to convert them to the Christian faith. However, the deeper reasons that incited the violence of masters and their agents against the fetishist practices of the negro slave were quite other than catechistic zeal.

In the first place, we have a fear that sorcery would be used in retaliation for the mistreatment and punishment inflicted on the slaves and a superstitious dread of cabbalistic practices of a mysterious, unknown nature; secondly, the indeed well-founded apprehension that religious practices and festivals would come to hinder the regular course of work and justify idleness; thirdly, the despotic deterrent power wielded by the master, who could not admit that the negro might have any will other than his own—these were the true reasons why candomblés were continually disbanded through violence, sanctuaries violated, and fetishes destroyed, even when licenses were granted to negroes so that they might amuse themselves to the monotonous sound of the drumbeat. Even freed, the negro could find no protection or aid from the law so that he might freely express his beliefs during the regime of slavery, because then the mission of the law was to preserve this regime. Under the pretext that candomblés were a steady source of conflict and affrays and the site of unbridled debauchery and licentiousness, the police would harshly suppress them and at times would hunt them out in the cities, where, considering their nature and location, they should be more protected from the direct action of slave masters than on sugar plantations.

As an overall consequence, since these negroes have been forced their whole lives to disguise and hide their faith and religious practices, the remembrance of persecutions suffered for their beliefs still persists today and will long persist in their memory, closely tied within their spirits to a fear of confessing and explaining these beliefs. As the elimination of slavery is still quite recent, the greatest part of fetishist priests are old Africans who were all slaves. In addition to these motives, a no less powerful reason for the negro's reserve and mystery is the sorcerer's interest in the enhanced prestige he derives from this secrecy. The faith of believers and the credulity of the superstitious are crudely and gainfully exploited by these sorcerers: divulging their practices would divest them of the prestige of the unknown and would seriously damage the influence they exercise.

Along with these multiple causes contributing to our problem of understanding, we find others involving the problem of interpreting the meaning and form of fetishist practices that have been greatly modified by their environment. Transported to American soil and supplanted by an officially taught Catholicism imposed through the violence of slavery, the African element has been diluted in a large heterogeneous social environment, and the purity of African practices and rituals has necessarily and inevitably vanished, replaced by mongrel practices and beliefs. The only whole, pure thing we should expect to find is the feeling that animates their beliefs, as fetishist when the objects of this belief are rocks, trees, or shells from the seashore as when they are the many Catholic saints.

In examining and analyzing this feeling as it presents itself and lives on in the negroes who have become part of the Brazilian population and as it broadly manifests itself in all aspects of our private and public lives, we have set ourselves the task of this study, which intends to deduce therefrom sociological laws and principles that generally go unnoticed or ignored. The Portuguese language that everyone speaks today and the medical profession that I practice have been of equal assistance to me in the accomplishment of this task. The latter has served me twofold, inspiring and strengthening my innermost confidence as a general practitioner, affording a multitude of observations, and creating opportunities to examine these freely.

This is my objective, less than uncovering the African phylogenesis of our negro fetishism and asking how purely these imported religious practices and beliefs have been preserved.

In the descriptions that follow—which are the premises grounding my final conclusions—an obligation to show that African fetishism prevails in Bahia, that it is the authentic manifestation of the religious feeling of the negroes and vast majority of mestizos here, and that it is not just some chance occurrence coming from this or that sporadic society of superstitious negroes or impostors obliges me to delve into minute details and particulars that under other circumstances could very well be omitted for the sake of clarity and succinctness.

Document 3.2 Political Program of the *Partido Independiente de Color*, 1908

Source: Used with permission from Aviva Chomsky, trans. First appeared in *The Cuba Reader: History, Culture, Politics*, ed. Aviva Chomsky, Barry Carr, and Pamela Smorkaloff, Durham, NC: Duke University Press, 2003.

The "Independent Association of Color" hereby constitutes itself as a national organization in the entire territory of the Republic. We seek to maintain a balance among all Cuban interests, spread love for the Fatherland, develop cordial relations and interest everybody in the conservation of Cuban nationality, allowing everybody born in this land to participate equally in public administration.

Our motto is an egalitarian, sovereign, and independent republic, without racial divisions or social antagonisms. All Cubans who are worthy should be able to be named to the diplomatic corps, and, as a matter of important and urgent necessity, citizens of the race of color should be named, so that the republic can be represented in all its hues.

We believe that all court trials that take place in the Republic should be trials by jury, and that the duty of serving on the jury should be mandatory and free.

We call for

The abolition of the death penalty, and for the creation of penitentiaries that fulfill the needs of modern civilization.

The creation of correctional School-ships (Barcos-escuelas) for youthful offenders who, according to the law, cannot suffer greater penalties.

Free and compulsory education for children from ages six to fourteen.

The creation of polytechnic (vocational) schools in each of the six provinces, free and compulsory for adults, to be considered as the second stage of compulsory education, and consisting Arts and Trades.

Official, national, and free university education available to all.

The regulation of private and official education, under the auspices of the state, so that the education of all Cubans will be uniform.

The creation of a Naval and Military Academy.

Free and faithful (leal) admission into military, administrative, government, and judicial services of citizens of color, so that all of the races can be represented in the service of the state.

Immigration should be free for all races, without giving preference to any. The free entrance of all individuals who, within sanitary prescriptions, come in good faith to contribute to the development of the public good.

The repatriation, at public expense, of all Cubans from foreign shores who want to return to their native land but lack the necessary resources.

The creation of a Law to guarantee that in employment in all public enterprises, in Cuba and abroad, Cubans will be given preference to foreigners, until the latter are naturalized, and preventing new enterprises from being established in other countries.

We will work to make the eight-hour day the norm in all of the territory of the republic.

The creation of a Labor Tribunal to regulate any differences that arise between capital and labor.

The promulgation of a law prohibiting the immigration of minors, and of women, except when they are accompanied by their families.

The distribution of plots of land from State reserves, or from lands acquired by the state for this purpose, among veterans of the War of Independence who lack resources and who wish to devote themselves to agriculture, giving preference to those who are not suited for public office.

Document 3.3 *Manifiesto, "Santa Rita de Casia," y "San Lázaro," Sociedad de Protección Mutua, Canto y Baile*

Source: Instituto de Literatura y Linguística, Havana, Cuba. Translated by Patricia Rosas.

We Are Religious People, Not Atheists

This manifesto is directed to the people who upon the death of our Director, señor Silvestre Erise, knew how to fulfill like true Christians the high mission of respect and consideration for the dead, as the lifeless material must not be profaned by anyone, much less by people educated and intellectual in matters of human understanding.

To all those who felt in their hearts the nostalgia of others' grief in the sad moments experienced by the family, friends, and members of the Society, the Board of Directors wishes to thank them. Together we felt the death of our Director of the "Santa Rita de Casia" and "San Lázaro" Society, the man who founded it in 1902 in the Barrio del Cerro.

We Christians who belong to the aforementioned society pray to the Supreme Being for the happiness and consolation of those people who, in the columns of certain newspapers, like *La Marina*, profaned the name of the person who in life was called SILVESTRE ERISE and who, we have heard, on various occasions donated 300 pesos to help build the Reina Mercedes Hospital and 500 more for a Cuban who is living in Spain.

As mourners and aggrieved friends, who loved the person who is gone, we would like to say something to those people who, despite their culture and social contacts, lack respect for those who mourn the death of a beloved person. If we say nothing, it is to show that the sentiments of our unwarranted enemies are not equal to those of the mourners and friends of the deceased.

We say this because, as true Christians, we beseech in our prayers to Providence for all kinds of happiness and comforts for those whose bodies, like that of Señor Erice [sic], will always have to cover the earth with its mantle of rocks and multi-colored roots. Like the social laws of nature, this makes us all equals.

We all know that to be born means to die and that we must comply with the immutable laws of Nature. For this reason, despite the human species feeling the great weight of death, the end and the beginning of social life in Nature teaches us to know what we are and for what purpose we serve here on earth: to be born, to die, and to die to be born.

All human beings, given that they are born, must necessarily take care of themselves, and for that, it is clear, one must assimilate whatever is appropriate for life and for the development of a person's being, whatever is befitting for the self-same transmission of life. This is necessary so that the species can reproduce with all of the conditions of a healthy and strong constitution, so that development may be what it ought to be, within biological laws.

Death is Nature's justice. Before it, we are all equals: scholar, philosopher, oppressor, tyrant, the proud, the haughty, the humble, rich and poor, the ignorant, ruler and the ruled, oppressor and the oppressed, the fulfilled person and the beggar, the civilized and the uncivilized, all on the earth who hate each other because of our human pre-occupations. As death is Nature's justice, thus all we are is dust, smoke, and ashes here on this earth.

After all that has come before, we move on to the duty that our Director left us before his passing, as well as encountering impassioned love for our fellow men, the bond felt by those who loved him. Thus, through the unity of those who profess the Lucumí religious doctrine, and with the justice of the Republic's laws, we shall be able to maintain the prestige and equilibrium of the Society, the object of his desires, sacrifices, and sorrows until the last moments of his Christian life, as a man faithful to God and fulfilling his duties as head of the family.

Nothing is so Christian, noble, and sacred in the conscience of social beings as fulfilling the request of a person on his deathbed. For this reason, we are inviting those people who are known in the province of Havana and who wish to formally join this Society for Mutual Protection, Song, and Dance.

We let it be known that the fee for joining is one peso; 20 centavos, weekly and 80 centavos, monthly. The allowance for ill members who are bedridden is one official peso coin. In the case of death, to defray the costs of the burial, 25 pesos in the same coin will be delivered to the family member closest to the deceased who had helped that person until the final moments of life.

The "Santa Rita de Casia" and "San Lázaro" Society does not require a member to have a medical certificate, since the person covered by the treasury must present himself in good health before the President, Secretary, Treasurer, and Director.

We also wish to announce that the Reformed Regulation of the aforementioned Society does not recognize chronic illnesses because it is a society of a distinct nature from the Socorros Mutuos (Mutual Aid Societies), which requires a medical certificate because members declared as suffering from a chronic disease are separated from other members. For that reason, we call attention to those of us who profess the African religion Lucumí, and to whom we are able to say that with the succor they give us during Sunday services, it is possible to pay the rental of a house and other expenses of the Society.

We also let it be known that the weekly and monthly membership fee is destined for cases of members' illnesses or death. For that reason, the Treasurer cannot hold an amount greater than 20 pesos, and the remainder of the money with the President's help will be deposited in the his bank in the capital.

Now, since those of us who profess the African religious doctrine of Lucumí have clearly taken into account what is mutual protection for the cases of illness and death, we are certain that we have complied with these words of Jesus: "love one another"— and to that we add—for our Father who art in Heaven, that he protect the collective unit of the oppressed and the abused, for those who as human beings are like us, of flesh and blood.

After all that has been explained in this manifesto, as religious people and not atheists, it remains for us to say to the members and protectors of the Society that on Sunday, October 17, we will begin our Sunday services with the recognition of the municipal mayor and the chief of police, señor Placido Hernandez, who respectful of the laws of the Republic faithfully fulfills what his superiors order him to do. And as the chief of police is the guarantor of public order in the Barrio del Cerro, the board of directors of the aforementioned Society respectfully salute him, señor Placido Hernandez, the officials, and other subordinates from the 11th police station.

For the Board of Directors,

Fernando Guerra, President

Havana, September 30, 1915

For Further Reading

Andrews, George Reid. *Blacks and Whites in Sao Paulo, Brazil, 1888–1988.* Madison: University of Wisconsin Press, 1993.

Andrews, George Reid. *Afro-Latin America, 1800–2000.* Oxford: Oxford University Press, 2004.

Borges, Dain. "'Puffy, Ugly, Slothful, and Inert': Degeneration in Brazilian Social Thought, 1880–1930," *Journal of Latin American Studies* 25:2 (1993), 235–56.

Bronfman, Alejandra. *Measures of Equality: Social Science, Citizenship, and Race in Cuba, 1902–1940.* Chapel Hill: University of North Carolina Press, 2004.

Butler, Kim D. *Freedoms Given, Freedoms Won: Afro-Brazilians in Post-Abolition Sao Paulo and Salvador.* New Brunswick: Rutgers University Press, 1998.

Ferrer, Ada. *Insurgent Cuba: Race, Nation, and Revolution, 1868–1898.* Chapel Hill, University of North Carolina Press, 1999.

Gotkowitz, Laura. *A Revolution for Our Rights: Indigenous Struggles for Land and Justice in Bolivia, 1880–1952.* Durham, NC: Duke University Press, 2007.

Graham, Sandra Lauderdale. *Caetana Says No: Women's Stories from a Brazilian Slave Society.* Cambridge: Cambridge University Press, 2002.

Grandin, Greg. *The Blood of Guatemala: A History of Race and Nation.* Durham, NC: Duke University Press, 2000.

Helg, Aline. *Our Rightful Share: The Afro-Cuban Struggle for Equality, 1886–1912.* Chapel Hill: University of North Carolina Press, 1995.

Helg, Aline. "Race and Black Mobilization in Colonial and Early Independent Cuba: A Comparative Perspective," *Ethnohistory* 44:1 (1997), 53–74.

Larson, Brooke. *Trials of Nation Making: Liberalism, Race, and Ethnicity in the Andes, 1810–1910.* Cambridge: Cambridge University Press, 2004.

Lasso, Marixa. *Myths of Harmony: Race and Republicanism during the Age of Revolution, Colombia, 1795–1831.* Pittsburgh: University of Pittsburgh Press, 2007.

Reis, João José. *Slave Rebellion in Brazil: The Muslim Uprising of 1835 in Bahia.* Baltimore: Johns Hopkins University Press, 1995.

Scott, Rebecca. *Slave Emancipation in Cuba: The Transition to Free Labor, 1860–1899.* Pittsburgh: University of Pittsburgh Press, 2000.

Scott, Rebecca, *Degrees of Freedom: Louisiana and Cuba after Slavery.* Cambridge, MA: Belknap Press, 2008.

Stepans, Nancy. *The Hour of Eugenics: Race, Gender, and Nation in Latin America.* Ithaca: Cornell University Press, 1993.

Viotti Da Costa, Emilia. *The Brazilian Empire: Myths and Histories.* Chapel Hill: University of North Carolina Press, 2000.

Williams, Derek. "Popular Liberalism and Indian Servitude: The Making and Unmaking of Ecuador's Antilandlord State, 1845–1868," *Hispanic American Historical Review* 83:4, 697–734.

1838	May 24, 1844	1859	1861	1864	1868–1874
First railroads built in Latin America in Cuba	Samuel Morse transmits first message by telegraph	Street cars introduced in Rio de Janeiro	Benito Juárez creates the *Rurales* (Mexican rural police)	Railway construction begins in Mexico	Domingo Faustino Sarmiento President of Argentina

The Export Boom as Modernity

4

With Mexico's tumultuous first century of independence coming to its conclusion, in September 1910 President Porfirio Díaz decided to throw a party. There was a great deal to celebrate. He had ruled Mexico for 34 years, and just been re-elected to another 6-year term. Mexico's government was more stable, the treasury healthier, and its infrastructure more developed than at any time since independence. New public works were evident everywhere. A new opera house was under construction in Mexico City, government office buildings were going up throughout the downtown core, and electric streetlights and automobiles were everywhere on the city's streets. Mexicans could also celebrate the success of massive engineering projects, including a drainage tunnel that emptied the waters of the Valley of Mexico, ending the threat of malaria in the capital city. Though it had slowed in recent years, Mexico's economy had been growing spectacularly since the 1880s, bringing along with it new agricultural wealth, new mines, and even an emerging industrial complex.

Díaz's party showcased these developments. He covered the city in lights, announced new public works projects, and held parades celebrating the long and now glorious history of the nation. Not everything was great in Mexico. The political opposition was in exile, plotting revolution, peasant unrest was evident in several regions, unemployment was high, and certain leading intellectuals believed the country was veering towards crisis. Nonetheless, the omnipresent signs of progress were breathtaking.

Throughout Latin America the late nineteenth century witnessed a very particular form of modernity. With the independence wars and fratricidal struggles of the nineteenth century in the past, and with slavery and other caste systems firmly abolished, some parts of the region were well situated to become important participants in that era's boom in global trade. The industrial economies of the north needed a variety of inputs—copper, nitrates, silver, oil, iron, rubber, coffee, sugar, tobacco and others—that could be found in abundance in Latin America, and in return promised a range of highly desired manufactures—steam engines, barbed wire, shoes, machine guns, cameras, medicines, and later, refrigerators, radios, telephones, and automobiles. All these goods circulated on global transportation networks at reduced costs, with a speed and in volumes never seen before. Ideas, fashions, and various cultural forms also entered global networks in new ways in the late nineteenth century, as steamships, railways, photographs, telegraphs, and recorded sound made once great distances seem small.

Sometimes called the golden age of the export oligarchy (an oligarchy, because both the political and economic realms were controlled by a small elite), this period can seem like Milton Friedman's idea of the Latin American Dream.[1] As efficient exporters of raw materials, most Latin American nations prospered because they could cheaply produce certain valuable commodities then in demand in the industrial north. Developed economies were sufficiently prosperous to invest the capital that Latin Americans needed in order to exploit those commodities, a phenomenon most powerfully symbolized through railroad development. Latin Americans lacked the resources needed to build railroads, but needed them more than most. Railroads could open otherwise isolated regions to export agricultural and mineral commodities. They could move people into and around their nations—a bonus where there were few navigable rivers, like Mexico, Colombia, Peru, and Chile. Railroads could also ensure central government control, and along with barbed wire (patented in the United States by Joseph Glidden in 1874) and machine guns (the Gatling Gun was patented in 1861) they facilitated central government control in ways that earlier technologies never could. Foreign investors could thus provide the tools to allow Latin Americans to become consumers in the global industrial chain, to make their countries more stable and modern, and to restore something of the wealth and elegance that was lost during decades of internecine conflict.

But wait: this is not the only way to begin this story. Milton Friedman is not terribly popular these days, and his critics might prefer to invoke a tragic tone, introducing the export boom as a sad tale of economic dependency, as a period when powerful foreign interests and a small elite came to monopolize Latin America's wealth, while the vast majority of people in the region remained poor. They would remind us that this was an era in which rich nations gained the economic upper hand because of the asymmetry involved in exporting raw materials while importing manufactured goods. As a result the gulf between the rich and poor nations only grew larger, reinforced as always through the use of violence.

The differences between these views are in part ideological (left versus right) and in part professional (economic versus social historians), but they also say a great deal about the types of stories we like to tell when we narrate the past. The export boom can be told as a tragedy where inequalities deepened and were further entrenched, where certain forms of violence were intensified and the victimization of the region at the hands of the outside world was re-inscribed through an unequal global system. It can also be told as a kind of epic, where

Latin Americans of a variety of classes struggled to make themselves and their societies more prosperous, more *modern*. Some tell it as a comedy, an era when foolish prognosticators imagined that Latin America had solved all its problems. Even more, this era can be told as a romance, a time when Latin Americans embraced a series of innovative phenomena—new ideas, commodities, and practices—because of what they promised for themselves personally and for their societies in general. The appeal of the telephone, of the horseless carriage, of the streetlight and the modern sewer is difficult to explain to those for whom these are now century-old relics. And even if these things transformed people's lives in uneven ways, they are nonetheless among the most significant measures of Latin America's first modern age.

Order, Then Progress

Order and Progress—the phrase is so critical to the story of the late nineteenth century in Latin America that it is emblazoned on the Brazilian flag. Unlike the liberal democracies of that era, most Latin American elites believed that their societies would never prosper, would never become modern, if order was not first established. They believed that democracy, a messy process everywhere, brought only chaos to regions like Latin America, because the people were not civilized enough to exercise their democratic rights responsibly. Indeed, neither conservatives nor liberals seemed to have much faith in the capacity of their societies to be orderly absent the threat of punitive violence. Rosas' *Mazorca*, like Juárez' *Rurales* (Mexico's rural police, founded 1861) of a later generation were charged with preserving the order by force of arms, appealing to the sense among many that Latin America had to be made safe by an iron hand before it could enter the modern world.

Still, order is a funny thing. While its advocates generally imagine order and stability as an intrinsic good, political stability is almost always stability *in someone's interest*. Instability at the national level during the nineteenth century was accompanied by a great deal of stability at the local level in some regions, because small communities had the power to live as they saw fit, controlling their lands, water, timber, and politics. Stability at the national level, especially if it was accompanied by the resources to build railroads, telegraphs, roads, and national armies, gave the state the power to reach into local affairs, to change the rules of land-ownership, to influence local political arrangements, and to force their citizens to sell their goods and perhaps their labor in an expanding national and international economy. Stability, in this sense, meant stability in the interest of those who would direct the project of modernization. Water once used to feed local interests would become a commodity, valuable to the export economy. Lands once given over to subsistence farming would become potential sources of cash crops for export. Marginalized peoples who had often lived far from the purview of the state would now represent either necessary workers or potential threats to the rule of law. Thus were the complex inter-weavings of the mantra of the export boom, *order and progress*.

This is a complex story, told time and again as Latin Americans wondered about the seeming persistence of certain forms of state sanctioned violence in their societies (and especially after the Dirty Wars of the 1970s). When modern states were created in Latin America, those modern states lacked the democratic processes or civil rights that characterized the states that were then emerging, if haltingly, in Western Europe and North

America. Over the decades historians have offered many explanations for this divergence. Some attribute it to the authoritarianism of the colonial past, or blame outsiders, who favored repressive regimes that defended their interests over unpredictable democratic processes.

Others blame the cultures of the region for the way order and progress became intertwined, suggesting that there was something intrinsic to the ways people in the region saw the world that favored dictatorships. It also makes sense to note that the anti-democratic practices of these states had a racial cast, that people of African and indigenous origins were most often the victims of Latin American modernization. We might similarly note that the history of the U.S. South was hardly more democratic during this era than Latin America. One could also argue that the particularly violent experience of the post-independence wars left a significant number of people in the region favoring order at almost any price. Capital, which needed to be attracted to the region because of what was lost in a half century of conflict, would not come without stability. Goods would not get to market without safe effective means of transport. Nothing would be built if the builders could not expect their constructions to stand.

In the end, it would seem that each of these explanations has elements of truth, especially given that the anxieties that accompanied the post-independence era were played out in very local ways through specific conflicts. If there was something generalizable in these fears, it was a sense that this region, once home of the richest colonies on the planet, was falling behind, and increasingly backwards not just in the eyes of Europeans, but of their North American cousins. Elites in the region did not just want an order that would save them from chaos (like that theorized by Thomas Hobbes in *Leviathan*), they wanted an order that produced modernization, progress.

During this era most Latin American elites, like many in the West, found some of the darker values to emerge from the Enlightenment particularly appealing. Often known by the label positivists (drawn from the writings of Herbert Spencer and Auguste Comte), they tended to reject liberal democratic values (the idea that the best society maximizes personal freedom) in favor of a kind of political and social system that would allow them to organize society along scientific lines, an order that would allow them to find rational/scientific solutions to the region's problems. Government should be managed according to scientific principles, economies made to run as efficiently as possible, and the fuzzy-headed, mystical, and backwards practices of the national folk should be eradicated. They should be taught to be patriotic, dress in modern (read European) style clothes, to embrace modern medicine (which at that point was about as likely to kill its patients as cure them), and eat more meat.[2]. Globally these were the early days of sciences like anthropology, criminology, phrenology, and any number of organizing practices designed to make modern nations out of the detritus of independence. It would be an order imposed from above, as the masses could not expect to understand their own interests, but where it succeeded, it promised a better life for all.

And so, with the help of modern technology and the incentives provided by a booming global economy, Latin American nations increasingly came to be characterized by order after the 1850s. In part that order was illusory, the result of careful public relations, but the region as a whole did exhibit enough signs of a gradual return to stability after the 1850s that foreign investors began to return. Investments became railroads, barbed wire, telegraphs, and modern weaponry for Latin American armies, which in turn became more order, and then progress. We see a powerful example of how this process took place in the ranching sector, which flourished across Latin America after 1850. Lands where thousands of cattle once roamed, the common property of herdsmen, became ranches. The cattle became the property of the landowner, and the herdsmen employees. Old cattle breeds were then eliminated (a process made possible by enclosure) and new scientific breeds were introduced, generating more wealth for ranchers, their employees, and the national treasury. Order had made progress, easily measured in exports, employment, income, and customs revenues.

Measuring a Golden Age

Statistics can be deceiving, especially when we choose a few select measures to represent the experience of dozens of countries over several decades. The export boom did not begin in all parts of the region at once, dating in some countries to the 1830s (mining in Chile, and a decade later guano in Peru), and not beginning elsewhere until the 1890s. That said, there seem to be some significant trends across the region during the latter decades of the nineteenth century, which generally continued until the beginning of the Great Depression in 1930. Most regions became more clearly integrated into the global economy by pursuing a strategy of using the export of commodities to promote economic growth (Table 4.1). Latin America as a whole saw significant increases in foreign investment. And consistent, sometimes spectacular economic growth became the norm. These observations, however, leave some critical questions unanswered. Did this growth benefit Latin America as a whole,

Table 4.1 Principal exports in Latin America, 1870–1930

Argentina	Corn, wheat, livestock
Bolivia	Tin, silver
Brazil	Coffee, rubber
Chile	Nitrates, copper
Colombia	Coffee, gold
Costa Rica	Coffee, bananas
Cuba	Sugar, tobacco
Dominican Republic	Cacao, sugar
Ecuador	Cacao, coffee
El Salvador	Coffee, precious metals
Guatemala	Coffee, bananas
Haiti	Coffee, cacao
Honduras	Bananas, precious metals
Mexico	Silver, copper, zinc, lead, oil, henequen, sugar
Nicaragua	Coffee, precious metals
Puerto Rico	Sugar, coffee
Paraguay	Yerba mate, tobacco
Peru	Copper, sugar, nitrates, cotton
Venezuela	Coffee, cacao
Uruguay	Beef, wool

Source: Courtesy of Victor Bulmer Thomas, *The Economic History of Latin America since Independence*, Cambridge: Cambridge University Press, 1994, p. 59

or did it re-inscribe a relationship between Latin America and the outside world that enriched the North at the South's expense?

Looking at lists not unlike Table 4.1, the Argentine economist Raúl Prebisch once famously lamented that Latin America was on the wrong side of the international division of labor. Prebisch influenced generations of scholars who became dependency theorists, writers who argued that Latin America simply replaced one colonial master with others (principally England and the United States) at independence, creating economies characterized by declining terms of trade, export enclaves that did not benefit larger national economies, monocrop dependence (in almost all countries one or two commodities made up more than 50 percent of exports, which meant that falling prices for a single commodity could have devastating repercussions throughout the economy), and extreme vulnerability to international economic cycles, especially given the fact that in some countries as much as 50 percent of capital was in foreign hands. Particularly popular on the political left during the 1960s and 1970s, this school of thought sometimes came to explain the tragedies that characterized Latin American society almost exclusively through reference to the global economic system.

Today, economic historians are not so sure about these explanations. They point out that some export-based economies have managed over the generations to be quite prosperous, that these countries used that prosperity to promote economic diversification (Asia's newly industrialized countries, or NICs, are the most prominent example). Contemporary economic historians also point out that many of the specific claims of dependency theorists about terms of trade, enclaves, and monocrops do not withstand the close scrutiny of actual case studies. What they offer instead is a complex rendering of a region that, lacking capital and domestic markets, relied on the export sector during the latter half of the nineteenth century to generate wealth that could not be created through any other means. Foreign capital paid for railroads, dock facilities, and communications infrastructures. Revenues collected at customs houses provided critical income for states in need of revenue to govern, police, and invest in their countries. In Chile, for example, the export tax on nitrates provided 50 percent of government revenue during the years 1890 to 1914. Across the region Finance ministries used these monies to pay off foreign debts, balance their budgets, and build a great deal of infrastructure; remarkable feats given the decades of chaos that followed independence.

Recent studies of the nineteenth century suggest that while the impacts of foreign investments were uneven, the ancillary benefits and linkages created by foreign investment in countries like Mexico, Argentina, Venezuela, Brazil, and elsewhere, were considerable. After having had almost no railroads 50 years earlier (Cubans built the first railway in Latin America in 1838), by the eve of the First World War Argentina had 31,859 km of railroads, Mexico 25,600 km, Brazil 24,737 km, Chile 8,069 km, and Colombia 1,061 km. Even if the results were ambiguous, without these railroads economic growth would have been impossible. Furthermore, along with these railroads these countries saw a considerable expansion of the middle class, along with the emergence of a waged working class, which worked in industries processing goods for export. In several countries local governments used revenues from export and import duties, along with the manipulation of tariff rates, to promote local industrial development, even in the late nineteenth century. Medellín, Buenos Aires, São Paulo, Mexico City, Monterrey, Santiago, and other cities across the region industrialized during this era by relying on profits from the export sector.

Industrial workers—a new social category—often found themselves able to take advantage of their new settings (concentrated in cities), to successfully agitate for better wages and living conditions, and they clearly had a higher standard of living than did their rural counterparts. Members of the urban working and middle classes became part of a small but growing community of consumers, purchasing goods made locally and imported from abroad, and contributing in dynamic ways to the growth of industries devoted to food processing, beverages, cigarettes, clothing and textiles, construction materials, and other goods. Though small relative to Europe and North America, in at least five countries (Mexico, Argentina, Peru, Brazil, and Chile) domestic manufacturing provided most of the local market's needs for manufactured consumer goods by the eve of the First World War.

Across the region exports and industrial production grew steadily from the mid-nineteenth century to the beginning of the First World War. Still, the question is not simply did these sectors grow, but did they create enough wealth to reduce poverty in significant ways? It seems the answer is that they did not. The manufacture of consumer goods was focused exclusively on limited domestic markets, highly dependent on the state and unable to lift wages across the economy (and non-existent in some parts of the region), and was thus not suitable for any strategy for generating significant increases in gross domestic product[3] (GDP). Exports really lay at the center of Latin American efforts to spur significant economic growth.

Given the lack of domestic capital, technology, and expertise, export growth was likely the only viable strategy to foment substantial economic growth, but the challenges to such a project were significant. In order to produce per capita GDP growth that was comparable to that in the United States and Europe, Latin American economies needed annual per capita GDP growth of 1.5 percent during this period (this would double per capita GDP in fifty years). Region-wide, export growth would have had to be 4.5 percent in order to produce that level of per capita growth in the GDP. Yet this level of growth was extremely difficult to achieve (Table 4.2). Only two countries (Chile and Argentina) saw this rate of growth during this period.[4]

Some scholars dispute these measures, arguing that changing local conditions in several countries did produce significant growth.[5] Still, even if we agree that this is too conservative an approach, what does it mean to say that per capita income doubled in societies with histories of extreme inequality? In every country in the region except Argentina and Uruguay agricultural wages actually fell even as per capita GDP rose during these years, and inequality increased. The privatization of landholdings in Mexico may have increased exports and GDP, but by 1910 more than half the land in the country was in the hands of 1 percent of the population, and 97 percent of Mexicans were landless. Small-scale peasants could rarely produce documents that proved they owned the land they worked, and even if they did, they confronted recalcitrant government officials and corrupt brokers who preferred to place land in the hands of investors who promised to grow cash crops. And since land ownership was so critical to prosperity, the concentration of landholdings was closely linked to increasing inequality. Workers on large estates oriented towards commodity crops (sugar, cacao, tobacco, coffee, henequen, etc.) sometimes wound up working under conditions that were little different from slavery.

Table 4.2 Annual percentage rates of export growth, 1850–1912

Argentina	6.1
Brazil	3.7
Bolivia	2.5
Chile	4.3
Colombia	3.5
Costa Rica	3.5
Cuba	2.9
Ecuador	3.5
Guatemala	3.6
El Salvador	3.5
Mexico	3.0
Nicaragua	2.9
Paraguay	3.9
Peru	2.9
Uruguay	3.4
Venezuela	2.7

Source: Courtesy of Victor Bulmer Thomas, *The Economic History of Latin* America *since Independence*, Cambridge: Cambridge University Press, 1994, p. 63

Signs of Civilization

In the early twentieth century Argentines could proudly claim that theirs was one of the ten richest countries in the world. Buenos Aires, like a number of Latin American cities, was a shiny, modern showpiece with a population of 1.5 million people, complete with new mansions, electric lights, department stores, and trolleys. *Porteños* could also point to the immense population growth of their nation in recent decades, which because it relied principally on European immigrants, had the effect of increasingly erasing any sense of the muddy racial origins of the country. In Argentina half of the population growth during 1884–1913 was due to immigration, and with almost 5 million European immigrants in their midst, Argentines could claim that theirs was a white country. Brazilians likewise successfully turned to European migration (attracting 1.6 million) to whiten their nation, though the regional impacts of migration were quite distinct. The waves of Asian migration were viewed less favorably, but Asians were nonetheless preferable to the degraded racial stock of the region.

Latin Americans recorded their progress in a number of ways. Statistics were critical, telling the story of railroads, canals, and roads constructed, public works completed, economies that were growing, budgets that were balanced. Populations were increasingly measured, though many of the measures that would characterize the twentieth century— literacy and education, crime statistics, health, wages, working conditions, voter turnouts, and hygiene would not appear until some time later. Beyond statistical representations, modernity was also a visceral experience, felt in particular ways. As latecomers to modernity, Latin Americans modeled their idea of progress on trends and technologies acquired from abroad, on their capacity to both emulate and equal the societies everyone knew were the most modern of places. *Tropicalista* doctors in Salvador dedicated themselves to operating at the cutting edge of tropical medicine, and Brazilians claimed that one of their own, Alberto Santos-Dumont, was the first to fly an airplane unassisted in 1906. Many Mexicans marveled when their president installed an elevator in Chapultepec Castle.

In a way, there was no more powerful symbol of this transformation than the photograph. Photography and modernity are powerfully linked. The photographic medium was invented in the nineteenth century, one of the first representational practices that was itself produced through technological innovation. Photographs offered a powerful means with which to capture reality, distinct from other forms that seemed more deeply mediated by the hand of the artist. They could document Latin America for outsiders, render Indians, slaves, and the geographies of the region as curiosities, phenomena in some cases on the verge of disappearing. The subjects of the photos often had little choice, as their photographers used them to show racial types, criminal types, and a variety of forms of rural and urban poverty.

Indeed, one of the early critical forms of photography in the region were *type* photographs, which became common in the 1860s. These photographs introduced viewers to the Indian, the peasant, the agricultural laborer, the *cargador*, and others (see Figure 4.1).

Figure 4.1
Black and white photograph of two young indigenous men

Source: Courtesy of: www.catedras.fsoc.uba.ar/ cicerchia/expfr.htm

Collected and used by the state to document its population, they were also turned into postcards, mementos of sojourns that circulated among wealthy aficionados in the urban centers of Latin America and elsewhere. As Deborah Poole argues, these photos could fix the racial identity of their subject in ways that were often more powerful than any other means. The types that emerged from them were defined not just by phenotype and shape, but through dress, background, and accessories, all of which gave the subject in the photo a racial identity.

Over time, many of the photographers who initially made their living with these photos established portrait studios and took clients who were not curiosities, but instead individuals who *wanted* to have their pictures taken. These portraits revealed a great deal about the complex ways in which modernity was experienced during this period, the ways in which individuals of both European and non-European ancestry aspired to define themselves as both modern and traditional through dress, grooming, and the poses they assumed in these photographs. In sitting for a family portrait, the subjects could choose Western attire (i.e. suits) or traditional dress, could look squarely into the camera or avert its gaze, each gesture indicating something about the subject's engagement with modernity. These portraits also spoke to gender norms, as one could regularly find the males and females wearing different kinds of dress—typically the males a more modern style and the females a more traditional— representing a notion of who worked towards the future and who rooted the family in the past.[6] Upwardly mobile individuals with indigenous and African ancestries regularly used these portraits to reveal their modernity in sharp contrast to the racial types that populated photographs of peasants and slaves. Consider the following image of Benito Juárez, the Mexican President, in 1861. Though of Zapotec origin, Juárez erased his indigenous past through dress, manner, and profession, all aptly summed up in Figure 4.2.

Figure 4.2 Benito Juárez
Source: Courtesy of Getty Images

Figure 4.3
A Peruvian soldier
and his wife

Source: Courtesy of
Library of Congress

More complicated still are those photographs where the meanings are more oblique. In Figure 4.3 (which dates to 1868) it is not clear that the subjects, a Peruvian soldier and his wife, asked to be photographed or simply consented. A complex mix of the modern and traditional can be seen in this photo, as the wife retains Andean dress, a long braid, and a somewhat frayed version of European bowler that marked Andean female identity in this era. Still, it is unclear whether the husband chose a military uniform to mark his participation in the modern project of Peruvian nationhood, or was marked as disciplined into the modern nation by the photographer's choice to place him in uniform. During this and later eras white elites across the Americas sought to impose order on unruly indigenous masses through military discipline, even as some Andean peoples sought upward mobility through service in the armed forces. While we can see a story of modernity told through this photograph, we cannot be certain which story it is.

Photographs were also critical in documenting the material signs of progress. Construction projects, new buildings, national festivals, electrical lights, paved roads—all were avidly photographed during the export boom. In part these photos simply documented new things (Figure 4.4), a trolley, a train, a tram, a road excavated in order to build a modern sewage system, but many mixed new aesthetic sensibilities with a desire to represent modernity as more than just something that derived from Europe. Latin Americans wanted to prove that their countries were as capable as any other of being sources of the endless cycles of innovation—artistic and scientific—that characterized modernity. Images like the one in Figure 4.5, of Buenos Aires' Retiro train station in 1915, remind us of this desire. Modernity, represented in this building and the photo that captures it, is a deeply aesthetic experience. Modern nations were prosperous, they were rational, they were scientific, and they were sites of innovation and creativity, where the future was made. Inasmuch as this was scientific innovation, new manufactured goods, and new aesthetics, Latin Americans could most easily embrace the latter as their preserve.

Figure 4.4   Image of an early tram system, Belem, early twentieth century

Source: Courtesy of tram website photo: http://www.tramz.com/br/be/be.html

Figure 4.5 *Estación Retiro del Ferrocarril*, Central Argentino

Source: Margarita Gutman (*editora*) Buenos Aires 1910: *Memoria del Porvenir, Buenos Aires: Gobierno de la Ciudad de Buenos Aires, Facultad de Arquitectura Diseño y Ubranismo de la Universidad de Buenos Aires, Instituto Internacional de Medio Ambiente y Desarrollo IIED-America Latina*, 1999

One final photograph completes this section. Figure 4.6 in many ways embodies all the qualities of the previous four. It is a photo of indigenous subjects in modern dress, where the participation of the subjects in the photo can neither be understood as coerced or voluntary. They are students in Mexico City's *Casa del Estudiante Indígena* (House of the Indian Student) part of a group of indigenous students who were often forcibly recruited to this school, but who then remained there voluntarily and refused to leave Mexico City once their studies were complete.[7] This photo then, reveals a very interesting play on the type photograph, which was still common in Mexico in the 1920s. These were Indians, who just two years earlier might have been photographed to establish their racial alterity, now participating in a photograph that showed their capacity to be modern subjects. Modernity here is a series of qualities—the substitution of modern dress for peasant clothes, the presence of the automobile workshop and the auto in the photo, and the fact that these students were being trained as mechanics. That this photo was in fact taken after Mexico underwent a massive social revolution reminds us that the logics that underpinned the export boom would remain powerful even after its conclusion.

Figure 4.6 *La Casa del Estudiante Indígena*: male students working around a table
Source: Courtesy of SEP, *La Casa del Estudiante Indígena*

The Document: On the Eve of Revolution

During the first decade of the twentieth century Mexico was awash with writings about its past, present, and future. Many described conditions in the country in optimistic terms, while some described social conditions in Mexico largely negatively. Given that we know what happened next, it is tempting to pit the two trends against one another in what could be an elaborate game of historical *gotcha*. Critics like the Flores Magón brothers and Andrés Molina Enríquez become prescient about their country's problems, while those who marveled at the achievements of the Díaz regime are revealed to be naïve at best, and capitalist lackeys at worst.

This practice is both unsatisfying and misleading. Some Mexicans suggested that their country had serious problems in the years before the collapse of Porfirio Díaz' dictatorship, but their descriptions of the nation's ills were not always particularly accurate or influential. The Flores Magón brothers' newspaper *Regeneración* (see the website) while now an important historical artifact, was not widely read in Mexico. Their anarchism never found much purchase among Mexican workers, and for the most part appealed to a small group of dissident intellectuals. Andrés Molina Enríquez' 1909 indictment of the regime *los grandes problemas nacionales* (the great national problems—sections of this too can be found on the website) offered its own particular view of the national problems, but as a prescription for what ailed Mexico in 1910 it is highly problematic (nonetheless, it was extremely influential on later generations of social reformers). Molina Enríquez found fault not in the process of development per se, but in the ways that development had undermined the Indian *pueblo* as a social and juridical institution, thus undermining the natural evolution of Indian communities (in this, he was deeply positivist). While sympathetic to Indians, he saw them as fundamentally backwards. Even the oppositional tome published by Francisco Madero, Díaz' opponent in the 1910 elections (*la succesión presidencial en 1910*), offered little that would help explain much of what would follow.

This then, is one of the problems in reading documents that precede momentous events. We have the benefit of hindsight, and tend to impose meaning and importance on these texts, reading them to look for a writer's capacity to predict the future rather than gleaning from the text what was interesting about the present. Ultimately this is not the most compelling or useful reading of these texts. Rather, the document provided below (Document 4.1), an interview between the American journalist James Creelman and Porfirio Díaz from 1908, is included to offer readers an opportunity to contemplate the values and ideas that informed its composition. In particular, readers can explore the *ways of seeing* that animated the text, the things that were made visible, and the things that were invisible.

The meeting of these two figures is indeed a telling story of the early twentieth century. Díaz, the 78-year-old dictator, 32 years in power, uses the interview to reflect on what he has made of his country and what it might become. Creelman, the 49-year-old *yellow* journalist, famous for taking up arms against the Spanish even as he reported on the Spanish-American War for the *New York World*, reveals his own sensibilities when he describes what is modern in Mexico. In part it is from his distinctly North American view of the world that Díaz emerges as the "Hero of the Americas," though his views seem to have resonated south of the border. While it gained very little attention in the United States, Creelman's interview was reproduced in several important Mexican newspapers, including *El Imparcial* and *El Tiempo*.

Document 4.1 James Creelman, "Porfirio Díaz, Hero of the Americas" (Excerpts)

Source: *Pearson's Magazine*, March, 1908.

From the heights of Chapultepec Castle President Díaz looked down upon the venerable capital of his country, spread out on a vast plain, with a ring of mountains flung up grandly about it, and I, who had come nearly four thousand miles from New York to see the master and hero of modern Mexico—the inscrutable leader in whose veins is blended the blood of the primitive Mixtecs with that of the invading Spaniards—watched the slender, erect form, the strong, soldierly head and commanding, but sensitive, countenance with an interest beyond words to express.

A high, wide forehead that slopes up to crisp white hair and over hangs deep-set, dark brown eyes that search your soul, soften into inexpressible kindliness and then dart quick side looks—terrible eyes, threatening eyes, loving, confiding, humorous eyes—a straight, powerful, broad and somewhat fleshy nose, whose curved nostrils lift and dilate with every emotion; huge, virile jaws that sweep from large, flat, fine ears, set close to the head, to the tremendous, square, fighting chin; a wide, firm mouth shaded by a white mustache; a full, short, muscular neck; wide shoulders, deep chest; a curiously tense and rigid carriage that gives great distinction to a personality suggestive of singular power and dignity—that is Porfirio Díaz in his seventy-eighth year, as I saw him a few weeks ago on the spot where, forty years before, he stood-with his besieging army surrounding the City of Mexico, and the young Emperor Maximilian being shot to death in Queretaro, beyond those blue mountains to the north—waiting grimly for the thrilling end of the last interference of European monarchy with the republics of America.

It is the intense, magnetic something in the wide-open, fearless, dark eyes and the sense of nervous challenge in the sensitive, spread nostrils, that seem to connect the man with the immensity of the landscape, as some elemental force.

There is not a more romantic or heroic figure in all the world, nor one more intensely watched by both the friends and foes of democracy, than the soldier-statesman, whose adventurous youth pales the pages of Dumas, and whose iron rule has converted the warring, ignorant, superstitious and impoverished masses of Mexico, oppressed by centuries of Spanish cruelty and greed, into a strong, steady, peaceful, debt-paying and progressive nation.

For twenty-seven years he has governed the Mexican Republic with such power that national elections have become mere formalities. He might easily have set a crown upon his head.

Yet to-day, in the supremacy of his career, this astonishing man—foremost figure of the American hemisphere and unreadable mystery to students of human government—announces that he will insist on retiring from the Presidency at the end of his present term, so that he may see his successor peacefully established and that, with his assistance, the people of the Mexican Republic may show the world that they have entered serenely and preparedly upon the last complete phase of their liberties, that the nation is emerging from ignorance and revolutionary passion, and that it can choose and change presidents without weakness or war.

It is something to come from the money-mad gambling congeries of Wall Street and in the same week to stand on the rock of Chapultepec, in surroundings of almost unreal grandeur and loveliness, beside one who is said to have transformed a republic into an autocracy by the absolute compulsion of courage and character, and to hear him speak of democracy as the hope of mankind.

This, too, at a time when the American soul shudders at the mere thought of a third term for any President.

The President surveyed the majestic, sunlit scene below the ancient castle and turned away with a smile, brushing a curtain of scarlet trumpet-flowers and vine-like pink geraniums as he moved along the terrace toward the inner garden, where a fountain set among palms and flowers sparkled with water from the spring at which Montezuma used to drink, under the mighty cypresses that still rear their branches about the rock on which we stood.

"It is a mistake to suppose that the future of democracy in Mexico has been endangered by the long continuance in office of one President," he said quietly. "I can say sincerely that office has not corrupted my political ideals and that I believe democracy to be the one true, just principle of government, although in practice it is possible only to highly developed peoples."

For a moment the straight figure paused and the brown eyes looked over the great valley to where snow-covered Popocatapetl lifted its volcanic peak nearly eighteen thousand feet among the clouds beside the snowy craters of Ixtaccihuatl—a land of dead volcanoes, human and otherwise.

"I can lay down the Presidency of Mexico without a pang of regret, but I cannot cease to serve this country while I live," he added.

The sun shone full in the President's face but his eyes did not shrink from the ordeal. The green landscape, the smoking city, the blue tumult of mountains, the thin, exhilarating, scented air, seemed to stir him, and the color came to his cheeks as he clasped his hands behind him and threw his head backward. His nostrils opened wide.

"You know that in the United States we are troubled about the question of electing a President for three terms?"

He smiled and then looked grave, nodding his head gently and pursing his lips. It is hard to describe the look of concentrated interest that suddenly came into his strong, intelligent countenance.

"Yes, yes, I know," he replied. "It is a natural sentiment of democratic peoples that their officials should be often changed. I agree with that sentiment."

It seemed hard to realize that I was listening to a soldier who had ruled a republic continuously for more than a quarter of a century with a personal authority unknown to most kings. Yet he spoke with a simple and convincing manner, as one whose place was great and secure beyond the need of hypocrisy.

"It is quite true that when a man has occupied a powerful office for a very long time he is likely to begin to look upon it as his personal property, and it is well that a free people should guard themselves against the tendencies of individual ambition.

"Yet the abstract theories of democracy and the practical, effective application of them are often necessarily different—that is when you are seeking for the substance rather than the mere form.

"I can see no good reason why President Roosevelt should not be elected again if a majority of the American people desire to have him continue in office. I believe that he has thought more of his country than of himself. He has done and is doing a great work for the United States, a work that will cause him, whether he serves again or not, to be remembered in history as one of the great Presidents. I look upon the trusts as a great and real power in the United States, and President Roosevelt has had the patriotism and courage to defy them. Mankind understands the meaning of his attitude and its bearing upon the future. He stands before the world as a states-man whose victories have been moral victories.

"In my judgement the fight to restrain the power of the trusts and keep them from oppressing the people of the United States marks one of the most important and significant periods in your history. Mr. Roosevelt has faced the crisis like a great man.

"There can be no doubt that Mr. Roosevelt is a strong, pure man, a patriot who understands his country and loves it well. The American fear of a third term seems to me to be without any just reason. There can be no question of principle in the matter if a majority of people in the United States approve his policies and want him to continue his work. That is the real, the vital thing—whether a majority of people need him and desire him to go on.

"Here in Mexico we have had different conditions. I received this Government from the hands of a victorious army at a time when the people were divided and unprepared for the exercise of the extreme principles of democratic government. To have thrown upon the masses the whole responsibility of government at once would have produced conditions that might have discredited the cause of free government.

"Yet, although I got power at first from the army, an election was held as soon as possible and then my authority came from the people. I have tried to leave the Presidency several times, but it has been pressed upon me and I remained in office for the sake of the nation which trusted me. The fact that the price of Mexican securities dropped eleven points when I was ill at Cuernavaca indicates the kind of evidence that persuaded me to overcome my personal inclination to retire to private life.

"We preserved the republican and democratic form of government. We defended the theory and kept it intact. Yet we adopted a patriarchal policy in the actual administration of the nation's affairs, guiding and restraining popular tendencies, with full faith that an enforced peace would allow education, industry and commerce to develop elements of stability and unity in a naturally intelligent, gentle and affectionate people.

"I have waited patiently for the day when the people of the Mexican Republic would be prepared to choose and change their government at every election without danger of armed revolutions and without injury to the national credit or interference with national progress. I believe that day has come."

Again, the soldierly figure turned toward the glorious scene lying between the mountains. It was plain to see that the President was deeply moved. The strong face was as sensitive as a child's. The dark eyes were moist.

And what an unforgettable vision of color, movement and romance it was!

Beneath the giant trees still surrounding the rock of Chapultepec—the only rise in the flat valley—Montezuma, the Aztec monarch, used to walk in his hours of ease before Cortés and Alvarado came with the cross of Christ and the pitiless sword of Spain, to be followed by three hundred terrible years in which the country writhed and wept under sixty-two Spanish viceroys and five governors, to be succeeded by a ridiculous native emperor and a succession of dictators and presidents, with the Emperor Maximilian's invasion between, until Díaz, the hero of fifty battles, decided that Mexico should cease to fight, and learn to work and pay her debts . . .

As we paced the castle terrace we could see long processions of Mexican Indians, accompanied by their wives and children, with monstrous hats, bright colored blankets and bare or sandaled feet, moving continuously from all parts of the valley and from the mountain passes toward Guadalupe; and two days later I was to see a hundred thousand aboriginal Americans gather about that holiest of American shrines, where, under a crown of emeralds, rubies, diamonds, and sapphires that cost thirty thousand dollars merely to fashion, and before a multitude of blanketed Indians, kneeling with their wives and babies, holding lighted candles and flowers, and worshiping with a devotion that smote the most cynical spectator into reverence, the resplendent Archbishop of Mexico celebrated mass before the alter-enclosed blanket of the pious Indian, Juan Diego, upon whose woven surface the image of the Virgin Guadalupe appeared in 1531 . . .

"It is commonly held that true democratic institutions are impossible in a country which has no middle class," I suggested.

President Díaz turned, with a keen look, and nodded his head.

"It is true," he said. "Mexico has a middle class now; but she had none before. The middle class is the active element of society, here as elsewhere.

"The rich are too much preoccupied in their riches and in their dignities to be of much use in advancing the general welfare. Their children do not try very hard to improve their education and their character.

"On the other hand, the poor are usually too ignorant to have power.

"It is upon the middle class, drawn largely from the poor, but somewhat from the rich, the active, hard-working, self-improving middle class, that a democracy must depend for its development. It is the middle class that concerns itself with politics and the general progress.

"In the old days we had no middle class in Mexico because the minds of the people and their energies were wholly absorbed in politics and war. Spanish tyranny and misgovernment had disorganized society. The productive activities of the nation were abandoned in successive struggles. There was general confusion. Neither life nor property was safe. A middle class could not appear under such conditions."

"General Díaz," I interrupted, "you have had an unprecedented experience in the history of republics. For thirty years the destinies of this nation have been in your hands, to mold them as you will; but men die, while nations must continue to live. Do you believe that Mexico can continue to exist in peace as a republic? Are you satisfied that its future is assured under free institutions?"

It was worth while to have come from New York to Chapultepec Castle to see the hero's face at that moment. Strength, patriotism, warriorship, prophethood seemed suddenly to shine in his brown eyes.

"The future of Mexico is assured," he said in a clear voice. "The principles of democracy have not been planted very deep in our people, I fear. But the nation has grown and it loves liberty. Our difficulty has been that the people do not concern themselves enough about public matters for a democracy. The individual Mexican as a rule thinks much about his own rights and is always ready to assert them. But he does not think so much about the rights of others. He thinks of his privileges, but not of his duties. Capacity for self-restraint is the basis of democratic government, and self-restraint is possible only to those who recognize the rights of their neighbors.

"The Indians, who are more than half of our population, care little for politics. They are accustomed to look to those in authority for leadership instead of thinking for themselves. That is a tendency they inherited from the Spaniards, who taught them to refrain from meddling in public affairs and rely on the Government for guidance.

"Yet I firmly believe that the principles of democracy have grown and will grow in Mexico."

"But you have no opposition party in the Republic, Mr. President. How can free institutions flourish when there is no opposition to keep the majority, or governing party, in check?"

"It is true there is no opposition party. I have so many friends in the republic that my enemies seem unwilling to identify themselves with so small a minority. I appreciate the kindness of my friends and the confidence of my country; but such absolute confidence imposes responsibilities and duties that tire me more and more.

"No matter what my friends and supporters say, I retire when my present term of office ends, and I shall not serve again. I shall be eighty years old then.

"My country has relied on me and it has been kind to me. My friends have praised my merits and overlooked my faults. But they may not be willing to deal so generously with my successor and he may need my advice and support; therefore I desire to be alive when he assumes office so that I may help him."

He folded his arms over his deep chest and spoke with great emphasis.

"I welcome an opposition party in the Mexican Republic," he said. "If it appears, I will regard it as a blessing, not as an evil. And if it can develop power, not to exploit but to govern, I will stand by it, support it, advise it and forget myself in the successful inauguration of complete democratic government in the country.

"It is enough for me that I have seen Mexico rise among the peaceful and useful nations. I have no desire to continue in the Presidency. This nation is ready for her ultimate life of freedom. At the age of seventy-seven years I am satisfied with robust health. That is one thing which neither law nor force can create. I would not exchange it for all the millions of your American oil king."

His ruddy skin, sparkling eyes and light, elastic step went well with his words. For one who has endured the privations of war and imprisonment, and who to-day rises at six o'clock in the morning, working until late at night at the full of his powers, the physical condition of President Díaz, who is even now a notable hunter and who usually ascends the palace stairway two steps at a time is almost unbelievable.

"The railway has played a great part in the peace of Mexico," he continued. "When I became President at first there were only two small lines, one connecting the capital with Vera Cruz, the other connecting it with Queretaro. Now we have more than nineteen thousand miles of railways. Then we had a slow and costly mail service, carried on by stage coaches, and the mail coach between the capital and Puebla would be stopped by highwaymen two or three times in a trip, the last robbers to attack it generally finding nothing left to steal. Now we have a cheap, safe and fairly rapid mail service throughout the country with more than twenty-two hundred post-offices. Telegraphing was a difficult thing in those times. To-day we have more than forty-five thousand miles of telegraph wires in operation.

"We began by making robbery punishable by death and compelling the execution of offenders within a few hours after they were caught and condemned. We ordered that wherever telegraph wires were cut and the chief officer of the district did not catch the criminal, he should himself suffer; and in case the cutting occurred on a plantation the proprietor who failed to prevent it should be hanged to the nearest telegraph pole. These were military orders, remember.

"We were harsh. Sometimes we were harsh to the point of cruelty. But it was all necessary then to the life and progress of the nation. If there was cruelty, results have justified it."

The nostrils dilated and quivered. The mouth was a straight line.

"It was better that a little blood should be shed that much blood should be saved. The blood that was shed was bad blood; the blood that was saved was good blood.

"Peace was necessary, even an enforced peace, that the nation might have time to think and work. Education and industry have carried on the task begun by the army."
. . .

"And which do you regard as the greatest force for peace, the army or the school-house?" I asked.

The soldier's face flushed slightly and the splendid white head was held a little higher.

"You speak of the present time?"

"Yes."

"The schoolhouse. There can be no doubt of that. I want to see education throughout the Republic carried on by the national Government. I hope to see it before I die. It is important that all citizens of a republic should receive the same training, so that their ideals and methods may be harmonized and the national unity intensified. When men read alike and think alike they are more likely to act alike."

"And you believe that the vast Indian population of Mexico is capable of high development?"

"I do. The Indians are gentle and they are grateful, all except the Yacquis and some of the Mayas. They have the traditions of an ancient civilization of their own. They are to be found among the lawyers, engineers, physicians, army officers and other professional men."

Over the city drifted the smoke of many factories.

"It is better than cannon smoke," I said.

"Yes," he replied, "and yet there are times when cannon smoke is not such a bad thing. The toiling poor of my country have risen up to support me, but I cannot forget what my comrades in arms and their children have been to me in my severest ordeals."

There were actually tears in the veteran's eyes …

Throughout the valley moves a wondrous system of electric cars, for even the crumbling house of Cortés is lit by electricity, and an electric elevator runs through the shaft of Chapultepec hill by which the Montezumas used the escape from their enemies.

It is hard to remember that this wonderful plain was once a lake and that the Aztecs built their great city on piles, with causeways to the mainland. President Díaz bored a tunnel through the eastern mountains and the Valley of Mexico is now drained to the sea by a system of canals and sewers that cost more than twelve million dollars . . .

"In my youth I had a stern experience that taught me many things (said Díaz). When I commanded two companies of soldiers there was a time when for six months I had neither advice, instructions nor support from my government. I had to think for myself. I had to be the government myself. I found men to be the same then as I have found them since. I believed in democratic principles then and I believe in them yet, although conditions have compelled stern measures to secure peace and the development which must precede absolutely free government. Mere political theories will not create a free nation . . ."

(Díaz) was the son of an inn-keeper. An institution of learning now stands memorially on the site of his birth. Three years after he was born his father died of cholera and his Spanish–Mixtec mother was left alone to support her six children.

When the grown boy wanted shoes, he watched a shoemaker, borrowed tools, and made them himself. When he wanted a gun he took a rusty musket-barrel and the lock of a pistol, and constructed a reliable weapon with his own hands. So, too, he learned to make furniture for his mother's house.

He made things then, as he afterward made the Mexican nation, by the sheer force of moral initiative, self-reliance and practical industry. He asked no-one for anything that he could get for himself.

Go from one end to the other of Mexico's 767,005 square miles, on which no more than 15,000,000 persons live to-day, and you will see everywhere evidence of this masterful genius. You turn from battlefields to schools to railways, factories, mines and banks, and the wonder is that one man can mean so much to any nation, and that nation an American republic next in importance to the United States and its nearest neighbor.

He found Mexico bankrupt, divided, infested with bandits, a prey to a thousand forms of bribery. To-day life and property are safe from frontier to frontier of the republic.

After spending scores of millions of dollars on harbor improvements, drainage works and other vast engineering projects, and paying off portions of the public debt—to say nothing of putting the national finances on a gold basis—the nation has a surplus of $72,000,000 in its treasury—this, in spite of the immense government subsidies which have directly produced 19,000 miles of railways.

When he became President, Mexico's yearly foreign trade amounted to $36,111,600 in all. To-day her commerce with other nations reaches the enormous sum of $481, 363,388, with a balance of trade in her favor of $14,636,612.

There were only three banks in the country when President Díaz first assumed power, and they had a small capital, loaning at enormous and constantly changing rates.

To-day, there are thirty-four chartered banks alone, whose total assets amount to nearly $700,000,000, with a combined capital stock of $158,100,000.

He has changed the irregular and ineffective pretense of public instruction, which had 4,850 schools and about 163,000 pupils, into a splendid system of compulsory education, which already has more than 12,000 schools, with an attendance of perhaps a million pupils; schools that not only train the children of the Republic, but reach into the prisons, military barracks and charitable institutions …

There are nineteen thousand miles of railways operated in Mexico, nearly all with American managers, engineers and conductors, and one has only to ride on the Mexican Central system or to enjoy the trains de luxe of the National Line to realize the high transportation standards of the country.

So determined is President Díaz to prevent his country from falling into the hands of the trusts that the Government is taking over and merging in one corporation, with the majority stock in the Nation's hands, the Mexican Central, National and Inter-oceanic lines-so that, with this mighty trunk system of transportation beyond the reach of private control, industry, agriculture, commerce and passenger traffic will be safe from oppression.

This merger of ten thousand miles of railways into a single company, with $113, 000,000 of the stock, a clear majority, in the Government's hands, is the answer of President Díaz and his brilliant Secretary of Finances to the prediction that Mexico may some day find herself helplessly in the grip of a railway trust.

Curiously enough, the leading American railway officials representing the lines which are to be merged and controlled by the Government spoke to me with great enthusiasm of the plan as a distinct forward step, desirable alike for shippers and passengers and for private investors in the roads.

Two-thirds of the railways of Mexico are owned by Americans, who have invested about $300,000,000 in them profitably.

As it is, freight and passenger rates are fixed by the Government, and not a time table can be made or changed without official approval.

It may surprise a few Americans to know that the first-class passenger rate in Mexico is only two and two-fifths cents a mile, while the second-class rate, which covers at least one-half of the whole passenger traffic of the country, is only one cent and one-fifth a mile—these figures being in terms of gold, to afford a comparison with American rates.

I have been privately assured by the principal American officers and investors of the larger lines that railway enterprises in Mexico are encouraged, dealt with on their merits and are wholly free from blackmail, direct or indirect. . .

More than $1,200,000,000 of foreign capital has been invested in Mexico since President Díaz put system and stability into the nation. Capital for railways, mines, factories and plantations has been pouring in at the rate of $200,000,000 a year. In six months the Government sold more than a million acres of land.

In spite of what has already been done, there is still room for the investment of billions of dollars in the mines and industries of the Republic.

Americans and other foreigners interested in mines, real estate, factories, railways and other enterprises have privately assured me, not once, but many times, that, under Díaz, conditions for investment in Mexico are fairer and quite as reliable as in the most highly developed European countries. The President declares that these conditions will continue after his death or retirement.

Since Díaz assumed power, the revenues of the Government have increased from about $15,000,000 to more than $115,000,000, and yet taxes have been steadily reduced.

When the price of silver was cut in two, President Díaz was advised that his country could never pay its national debt, which was doubled by the change in values. He was urged to repudiate a part of the debt. The President denounced the advice as foolishness as well as dishonesty, and it is a fact that some of the greatest officers of the government went for years without their salaries that Mexico might be able to meet her financial obligations dollar for dollar.

The cities shine with electric lights and are noisy with electric trolley cars; English is taught in the public schools of the great Federal District; the public treasury is full and overflowing and the national debt decreasing; there are nearly seventy thousand foreigners living contentedly and prosperously in the Republic—more Americans than Spaniards; Mexico has three times as large a population to the square mile as Canada; public affairs have developed strong men like Jose Yves Limantour, the great Secretary of Finances, one of the most distinguished of living financiers; Vice-president Corral, who is also Secretary of the Interior; Ignacio Mariscal, the Minister of Foreign Affairs, and Enrique Creel, the brilliant Ambassador at Washington.

And it is a land of beauty beyond compare. Its mountains and valleys, its great plateaus, its indescribably rich and varied foliage, its ever blooming and abundant flowers, its fruits, its skies, its marvelous climate, its old villages, cathedrals, churches, convents—there is nothing quite like Mexico in the world for variety and loveliness. But it is the gentle, trustful, grateful Indian, with his unbelievable hat and many-colored blanket, the eldest child of America, that wins the heart out of you. After traveling all over the world, the American who visits Mexico for the first time wonders how it happened that he never understood what a fascinating country of romance he left at his own door.

It is the hour of growth, strength and peace which convinces Porfirio Díaz that he has almost finished his task on the American continent.

Yet you see no man in a priest's attire in this Catholic country. You see no religious processions. The Church is silent save within her own walls. This is a land where I have seen the most profound religious emotion, the most solemn religious spectacles—from the blanketed peons kneeling for hours in cathedrals, the men carrying their household goods, the women suckling their babies, to that indescribable host of Indians on their knees at the shrine of the Virgin of Guadalupe.

I asked President Díaz about it while we paced the terrace of Chapultepec Castle.

He bowed his white head for a moment and then lifted it high, his dark eyes looking straight into mine.

"We allow no priest to vote, we allow no priest to hold public office, we allow no priest to wear a distinctive dress in public, we allow no religious processions in the streets," he said. "When we made those laws we were not fighting against religion, but against idolatry. We intend that the humblest Mexican shall be so far freed from the past that he can stand upright and unafraid in the presence of any human being. I have no hostility to religion; on the contrary, in spite of all past experience, I firmly believe that there can be no true national progress in any country or any time without real religion."

Such is Porfirio Díaz, the foremost man of the American hemisphere. What he has done, almost alone and in such a few years, for a people disorganized and degraded by war, lawlessness and comic opera polities, is the great inspiration of Pan-Americanism, the hope of the Latin-American republics.

Whether you see him at Chapultepec Castle, or in his office in the National Palace, or in the exquisite drawing-room of his modest home in the city, with his young, beautiful wife and his children and grandchildren by his first wife about him, or surrounded by troops, his breast covered with decorations conferred by great nations, he is always the same—simple, direct and full of the dignity of conscious power.

In spite of the iron government he has given to Mexico, in spite of a continuance in office that has caused men to say that he has converted a republic into an autocracy, it is impossible to look into his face when he speaks of the principle of popular sovereignty without believing that even now he would take up arms and shed his blood in defense of it.

Only a few weeks ago Secretary of State Root summed up President Díaz when he said:

"It has seemed to me that of all the men now living, General Porfirio Díaz, of Mexico, was best worth seeing. Whether one considers the adventurous, daring, chivalric incidents of his early career; whether one considers the vast work of government which his wisdom and courage and commanding character accomplished; whether one considers his singularly attractive personality, no one lives to-day that I would rather see than President Díaz. If I were a poet I would write poetic eulogies. If I were a musician I would compose triumphal marches. If I were a Mexican I should feel that the steadfast loyalty of a lifetime could not be too much in return for the blessings that he had brought to my country. As I am neither poet, musician nor Mexican, but only an American who loves justice and liberty and hopes to see their reign among mankind progress and strengthen and become perpetual, I look to Porfirio Díaz, the President of Mexico, as one of the great men to be held up for the hero-worship of mankind."

For Further Reading

Bulmer Thomas, Victor. *The Economic History of Latin America Since Independence*. Cambridge: Cambridge University Press, 1994.

Coatsworth, John. *Growth against Development*. Dekalb: Northern Illinois University Press, 1981.

Haber, Stephen. *Industry and Underdevelopment: The Industrialization of Mexico, 1890–1940*. Palo Alto: Stanford University Press, 1995.

Haber, Stephen. *How Latin America Fell Behind: Essays on the Economic Histories of Brazil and Mexico*. Palo Alto: Stanford University Press, 1997.

Hispanic American Historical Review, Special Issue: Can the Subaltern See? Photographs As History 84:1 (2004).

Kouri, Emilio. "Interpreting the Expropriation of Indian Pueblo Lands in Porfirian Mexico: The Unexamined Legacies of Andrés Molina Enríquez," *Hispanic American Historical Review* 82:1 (2002), 69–118.

Peard, Julyan. *Race, Place, and Medicine: The Idea of the Tropics in Nineteenth-Century Brazil*. Durham, NC: Duke University Press, 2000.

Poole, Deborah. *Vision, Race, and Modernity: A Visual Economy of the Andean World*. Princeton: Princeton University Press, 1997.

Tenorio-Trillo, Mauricio. *Mexico at the World's Fairs: Crafting a Modern Nation*. Berkeley: University of California Press, 1996.

1895	1895–1898	1907	1910	November 25, 1911	November 1914
José Martí returns to Cuba, is quickly killed in action	Cuban War of Independence	Global Depression results in repatriation of thousands of Mexican migrant workers in the United States	Francisco I Madero issues the *Plan de San Luis Potosí*, calling for an uprising in Mexico against Porfirio Díaz, to begin November 20, 1910	Peasants in Morelos, led by Emiliano Zapata, issue the *Plan de Ayala*, beginning a rebellion against the government of Francisco Madero	Zapatistas and Villistas converge on Mexico City

Signs of Crisis in a Gilded Age

5

April 10, 1919	January 1919	1919	July 20, 1923	1924
Emiliano Zapata ambushed by government forces during negotiations for a truce	Tragic week in Buenos Aires during general strike	Argentine Patriotic League founded	Pancho Villa killed	APRA (*Alianza Popular Revolucionaria Americana*) Founded by Peruvian Víctor Raúl Haya de la Torre

The challenges we encounter in attempting to render the histories of a region as diverse as Latin America become immediately apparent with one simple question: When did the golden age of the export oligarchy end? Was it 1907 (with the onset of a global recession), 1910 (with the beginning of the Mexican Revolution), 1914 (with the beginning of the First World War), 1919 (with the economic crisis at the end of the war), 1929 (with the onset of the Great Depression), or perhaps some other date? The question becomes even more complex when we attempt to characterize the export boom. With all the talk about economic growth and modernity it is possible to lose sight of the fact that there were significant numbers of people in each country in Latin America who never enjoyed the benefits of economic growth, and for whom this period represented a loss of rights, lands, and autonomy. Moreover, the threat of imperialism, instability, and violence were never far from people's minds throughout this golden age. In short, Latin Americans lived in a fragmented world; someone's boom was always another's crisis. This should remind us that general assessments of civic life, the economy, and society are not always useful in regions where poverty, inequality, and conflict are common.

It would, however, be misleading to represent this as a period of looming crisis. At any given moment in Latin America's history it is possible to find any number of seemingly contradictory signs about the future. James Creelman may have been wrong to think that Porfirio Díaz would be remembered as the "hero of the Americas," but many today remember him for introducing lasting and arguably positive transformations in Mexico. Neither are his critics remembered as somehow misguided, but as individuals who saw the same fractured reality differently. This is how we must attempt to read the voices raised in protest as the golden age drew on and towards its end. Progress came at a great cost—with deeper inequality, greater dependence on the global economy (and the United States in particular), economic and political instability. It entailed the forced elimination of certain ways of life, sometimes with great attendant violence. And on some level, the process was never entirely complete. Latin Americans today continue to live in multiple worlds, at the same time ultramodern and deeply traditional. Néstor García Canclini calls the cultures of this region *hybrid*, a concept he uses to suggest the simultaneity of two different worldviews, often in the same person.[1]

It may be telling that even as some writers celebrated Latin America's great leaps forward, others lamented imperialist and other threats. José Martí's 1891 essay *Our America* (Document 5.1) immediately alerts its readers to a series of crises, of the need for Latin Americans to find their common voice in order to strengthen the region in the face of North American expansion. Writing from his exile in New York, Martí wrote of a crisis in nationhood that in some ways links him more closely to José Hernández (whose gaucho Martín Fierro was a national hero quite opposed to the modern world Domingo Faustino Sarmiento wanted to create) than to many of the liberal social critics of his day. Like these critics he was raised to believe in the possibilities of progress, but unlike them he sees the price of that process as a new era of outside domination (which in the case of Cuba, was coming even before the previous imperial era ended), and an obliteration of what was virtuous and original in his America. Months after publishing the poem he would found the *Partido Revolucionario de Cuba* (the Cuban Revolutionary Party), which was designed to bring Cuban exiles in the United States together to press the struggle for independence and against U.S. annexation (the alternative favored by many in Washington at that time). He would return to Cuba to lead the struggle in 1895, only to be killed in battle with the Spanish a short time later.

Our America circulated widely across the region precisely because he eloquently gave voice to the fear that the boom and its attendant version of modernity were coming at too high a price. Others followed. José Enrique Rodó's *Ariel* (1900), and Rubén Dario's "A Roosevelt" (1905)[2] were complex meditations on the threat that the United States represented to Latin American sovereignty, and defenses of local Hispanic cultures. There was relatively little in their work to suggest an embrace of the indigenous or African cultures of the region, but later generations would do just that as they sought to come to terms with U.S. hegemony. For still other writers (e.g. José Mariátegui), it would be a combination of factors, including the persistence of grinding inequality, economic crises brought on by the volatility of the export economy, and the growing appeal of leftist ideologies after 1917 (and the Russian revolution) that offered signs of a new era of crisis.

Crises in the Countryside

José Martí did not need to tell the rural poor that the export boom had come at a great price. In Mexico, almost every mile of railway construction was accompanied by some minor conflict. Rural groups were neither as compliant nor as easily controlled as Porfirio Díaz would have had foreign investors believe. Araucanians in Argentina and Mapuches in Chile could only be displaced through military campaigns. Brazil had its own rebellions, the most famous being the millennial movement led by Antônio Conselhiero at Canudos in the 1890s.[3] Indeed, as certain forms of violence faded at the national level during the boom, violence intensified in the countryside. Local and national elites used the police and the military to ensure *order*. Political thugs "recruited" labor, "bought" land from unwilling peasants, and ensured that they had a monopoly on legitimate violence. Political parties did exist for some, but it was a fixed game, controlled by a small oligarchy, who perpetually deferred the promise that once order and progress were assured, democracy would follow.

Those rural peoples excluded from the game had few options. They could migrate to more marginal regions, other countries, or the cities. They could remain behind and become workers on estates growing commodities for export. Or they could fight. Historically this last option was risky, though not necessarily fatal. Limited rebellion long formed an important part of the peasant's political repertoire, used quite effectively in negotiations with more powerful groups. However, by the late nineteenth century this option was increasingly closed off. In part this was due to the fact that modern technologies of violence (railroads, telegraphs, machine guns) made it easier to simply repress rural protest. During this era central authorities also made sense of rural protest differently than they had in the past. Rendering rebellion as the sobs of primitive, inferior people, they concluded that rural protest was best dealt with through a type of repressive violence that would clear the way for more civilized people. Unrest in the countryside thus became an excuse for the nineteenth- century equivalent of "shock and awe," used to clear the land for more productive purposes.

The growing intensity of the violence mobilized against peasants did not mute their grievances. It simply made the stakes of the struggle much higher. At times they steeled themselves for *wars to the end of the world* (e.g. Canudos 1897, Tomochic, Mexico, 1892). At others they compensated for the losses they suffered through surreptitious means, stealing cattle and food, sabotaging the property of their overlords. At still others they waited quietly for an opportunity to strike back against their oppressors. Elite conflicts, larger social or economic crises, wars and disasters of all kinds could fracture the ruling classes. If the collapse was sufficient, the rural poor might have a chance to step in and reshape the order of things, to negotiate a new ruling pact at a time when their superiors were at their most weak and divided. In Mexico, 1910 provided such an opportunity.

Porfirio Díaz made one substantial blunder in his interview with James Creelman (Document 4.1). He implied that he was not going to run for re-election in 1910, declaring that the country was ready for democracy. His (off hand) promise set off a wave of political activity. Millions of middle-class Mexicans seized the opportunity to take part in the first political opening in the country in more than three decades. For the most part they supported the opposition candidate Francisco Madero, a prosperous northern *hacendado* who promised to modernize the political system. Díaz however, changed his mind about not running, and won an obviously fixed election (notable for the fact that Madero was jailed before election and then exiled). Madero in turn called for Mexicans to overthrow the regime by the force of arms in a rebellion that began in November 1910 (see his *Plan de San Luis Potosí* on the website). When his rebellion forced Díaz to flee the country in May 1911, Madero proposed new elections, which he won the following November. To his mind, this ended the Mexican revolution.

He was wrong. Díaz was sitting on a powder keg in 1910, and the collapse of the regime unleashed waves of violence that would not be easily contained. Madero fell quickly, as did his successors, so that within a couple of years the country was wracked by civil war. As much as anything, the chaos reminded Latin Americans that certain problems that many believed had been left in the past—the unruly peasant, the backwards Indian—were not entirely buried. At no point was that more obvious than in December 1914, when the peasant armies of Francisco (Pancho) Villa and Emiliano Zapata converged on Mexico City, turning Mexico's most modern city into the site of a stunning social inversion. Among the most famous records produced in this was a photo of two Zapatista soldiers, faces creased by age and hands calloused by years of agricultural labor, sitting at the lunch counter in Sanborns, one of the most exclusive restaurants in Mexico City, drinking chocolate and eating rolls (Figure 5.1). The photo taken of this moment is today one of the most easily recognized images of the revolution.

Costing over a million lives and lasting a decade, Mexico's revolution was an immensely complex series of conflicts. Some revolutionaries demanded land and liberty, others had specific grievances against local landlords and government officials. Some were committed to democracy, the rule of law, or social reforms that would ameliorate inequality. Others

Figure 5.1   Two Zapatistas eating at Sanborns

Source: © (inventory number 33532 / Zapatistas en Sanborns). CONACULTA. INAH-SINAFO-FN-Mexico

Figure 5.2 Villa and Zapata in Mexico City

Source: Courtesy of Underwood Photo Archives/SuperStock

may simply have been carried with the wind. Yet the images produced by the Zapatista and Villista convergence in Mexico City have come to symbolize the crisis brought on by the revolution more than any others (Figure 5.2).

To contemporary eyes the moments captured in Figures 5.1 and 5.2 evoke the carnivalesque. Mexico City was a profoundly segregated space, where class, culture, and ethnicity produced impermeable boundaries, boundaries that everyone understood and no one transgressed. Indigenous peasants knew better than to even look a white, middle-class Mexican in the eye or to speak to them without due reverence. To occupy the physical spaces monopolized by members of polite society was beyond the pale. And here they were, a northern cattle rustler (Villa) and a Nahautl-speaking peasant (Zapata), sitting on the thrones of Maximilian and Carlotta, while their armies ruled the streets and ate in fancy restaurants. Still, if one looks closely, is there not just a hint of discomfort in Zapata's eyes as he sits on the throne, or in the eyes of the Zapatistas drinking chocolate? In the end they were not driven out of the city, they left of their own accord.

The Zapatistas left the city for obvious reasons. They were not city folk. Their revolution was about regaining lands and liberties taken from them by Porfirio Díaz. And by December 1914 they had established that the only way they could claim these victories and defend them was through the force of arms. An extended stay in Mexico City did nothing to further these ends, and in fact extended absences from their home communities might imperil hard won victories.[4]

Villistas had an even more complicated agenda. Inasmuch as the Zapatistas had a declaration that identified their goals (the *Plan de Ayala*, included below), Villistas came from a cross-class alliance of people defined mostly by their northern frontier traditions. Alan Knight describes them as *serrano* revolutionaries, products of independent traditions who chafed, on some deep level, at the ways that a generation of economic development and political centralization had undermined their autonomy. In this, the *serrano* revolutionary harkened back to a romantic past, a time when their physical movement was not impeded by barbed wire and railroads, when land was plentiful and cheap, when people had the ability to work for themselves rather than as employees in some larger enterprise, and when the corrupt government officials who now imposed their will so capriciously lacked the ability to enforce rules drafted in Mexico City.

In this the Villistas, not unlike the Zapatistas, spoke of a society that had disappeared during the export boom. Both wanted freedoms and rights, along with material possessions, that they no longer had. Their visual appearance, the Indian peasant and the gun-toting frontiersman, both spoke of a past that urbane Mexicans wanted to leave behind. As such, when they occupied Mexico City, the clash was all the more stunning. They reminded all Mexicans that traces of a certain past remained, but that reminder was not guaranteed to produce a return to that past. Urban Mexicans responded to the thought of their country in the hands of the Zapatistas and Villistas with horror, and the meanings they made of the occupation of their city would in many ways serve to seal the fate of these revolutionaries. Zapatistas became backwards Indians. Villistas became bandits. And the Constitutionalists, a diverse collection of liberals, intellectuals, modernizers, and even elements of the old regime, became the men who would save the nation from chaos.

Perhaps the aftermath is just as important. Zapata and his followers retreated to Morelos. Villa returned to the north. Neither seemed capable of producing a ruling coalition with the other. In the end it was their enemies, the Constitutionalists, who emerged from this convergence re-energized. Using the new military technologies that were then being tested on the battlefields of Europe, Constitutionalist armies routed Villa at Celaya in April 1915, and then set out to establish a new state. In 1917 they passed a constitution, which while promising to return land to the peasants who had lost it during Porfirio Díaz's dictatorship, to educate the masses, and protect workers, was for the most part not terribly different from the constitution that an earlier generation of liberals had written in 1857. Political stability would again become paramount, and the new state would put off most reforms, instead preferring to exercise its power by silencing their enemies. Zapata was assassinated as he attempted to negotiate a truce with the government in April 1919. Villa, who represented a permanent threat even after he retired from the field, was murdered in July 1923.

To the Barricades

Peasants, by their nature, face limits to their ability to affect national politics. Their politics begin and end with local grievances, and this generally undermines sustained participation in national movements. States have historically responded to their grievances by mixing local concessions with local repression, cleaving off one peasant group from another by dealing directly with each. Rural rebellion may be difficult to defeat, but as long as rebels remain isolated in small groups, they rarely have the ability to threaten the survival of the state.

Urban populations present an entirely different kind of challenge to any state. City dwellers can disrupt national-level politics in ways that rural people generally cannot because their proximity to power and their capacity to act in a concerted manner threaten the state in ways that rural people cannot. Because their subsistence depends on national and international networks, city dwellers of all classes have interests that extend beyond their neighborhoods. Rebellion in the cities has thus always been a distinct kind of problem. It grew even more serious towards the end of the nineteenth century, when urban proletariats emerged across Latin America.

Industrial growth in Latin America was accompanied by the development of an industrial working class. Most lived in a series of growing cities in the region—places like Monterrey, Mexico City, Havana, Medellín, São Paulo, Buenos Aires, and Santiago, where the processing of goods for export and domestic manufacturing were concentrated.[5] Some were the descendants of long-term city dwellers. Others were recent migrant from the countryside, some of them former slaves. Still others came from the waves of European and Asian migration that arrived in Latin America in the late nineteenth century. Walking into their factories, workers entered an incredibly fluid setting; a place where limited grievances over wages and working conditions were at times resolved simply, and at others turned into violent confrontations with lasting repercussions. Factories produced novel social relationships, based on negotiations over wages and working conditions, but they were also sites where workers' and employers' attitudes towards one another were shaped by more opaque concepts like respect and propriety, the proper (and sometimes beloved) boss, and the honorable worker.

Recent studies of industrial workers in cities like Medellín, Havana, Monterrey, São Paulo, and Buenos Aires reveal workers who were willing to strike for their interests, who supported unionization and labor actions, and who contested the authority of their bosses both on and off the shop floor, but who, unlike their rural counterparts, were deeply invested in their role as participants in the industrial economy; proud to be industrial workers. They also reveal employers who were often concerned about the well being of their workers—who while authoritarian nonetheless wanted their factories to be *modern* places, with healthy, fairly treated workers, good morale, and loyal workforces. Factory owners in Medellín cultivated the idea that they were devoutly Catholic patrons, building social clubs, providing housing subsidies, and attempting to educate their workers. The Braden Copper Company in Chile promoted "family values" among their workers, and tried to eliminate sex workers and promote nuclear families at their mines. Workers took advantage of these programs when it suited them, though they struck relatively often.

The Catholic factory owners in Medellín did not respond well when their workers were not loyal. Strikes, protests, and other forms of "immoral" behavior undermined their sense of order, and threatened their positions as beneficent patrons overseeing the industrialization of their city. They revealed the fragile nature of the pact of domination that framed the development of an industrial proletariat, one in which factory owners positioned themselves as feudal lords, or *caudillos*, and workers were expected to accept their beneficence compliantly. But simple compliance was rarely seen. Freed of the constraints of rural life, brought together in factories, housing, and the street in ways that they had never been before, workers embraced any number of strategies to press their economic, social, and political interests. This did not preclude swearing loyalty to the factory, when it suited them, but in many cases it also included turning to the union, and the strike, to exercise their newfound power.

Buenos Aires in 1919 was a stunning example of this practice. Once a relatively sleepy capital, positioned mainly to collect taxes on wheat and hide exports and European imports, the export boom transformed Buenos Aires into one of the largest cities in the Americas, and an important industrial center. The city attracted 800,000 immigrants during the boom, growing to over 1.6 million. International migrants formed a considerable part of the working classes in a number of Latin American cities, including Havana, São Paulo, Rio, and Caracas, but Buenos Aires was almost singular in the size of its foreign born population, which came to make up half of the city by 1910. By 1914 the foreign born represented two-thirds of the skilled and white-collar workers in the capital, and 80 percent of unskilled labor in the city.[6]

These immigrants could not vote, and lacked political rights. Politics in Argentina were a tightly controlled affair, and at the end of the nineteenth century the political system remained entirely in the control of the oligarchy. It was not until 1891 that the opposition *Unión Civica Radical* (UCR) was founded, and it was not until the 1912 Sáenz-Peña electoral law that all native born and naturalized males were granted the vote. This gave middle-class Argentines a political voice in the form of the Radical Party (the Radical Hipólito Yrigoyen was elected president in 1916), but left millions of immigrants, most of whom had never become citizens, with no voice at all. Drawn mostly from the middle class, Radical Party members sympathized with the economic interests of the oligarchs, as their own prosperity was derived from the same export economy that made the rich, rich, and left the poor, poor.

Middle-class Radicals, like members of the oligarchy, did not trust immigrants. For all their racial virtue, they spoke foreign tongues, ate alien foods, did not celebrate the national traditions or owe any loyalty to the nation. Worse still, some brought with them objectionable ideas about workers rights, anarchism, and democracy. Moreover, because of immigration Buenos Aires was a city beset by a series of social crises. Sex ratios were skewed, single-motherhood widespread (20 percent of children were born to single mothers), and the sex trades were more prominent here than in all but a few other cities in the Americas. The oligarchs shared with most middle-class radicals a deep anxiety about slums, anarchism, strikes, loose morals, family decay, and crime in the immigrant neighborhoods. They also feared that "true" Argentines were in danger of being swamped by the foreign (often represented as Jewish[7]) element. When workers protested or struck, their actions were construed as the work of foreign agitators, not the product of legitimate grievances.

It is unsurprising that these conflicts came to a head in 1919. The war, known in various parts of Latin America as the *dance of the millions*, brought high commodity prices and immense wealth for some, but rising prices and stagnating wages for workers. During the war the cost of living in Buenos Aires climbed 60 percent, while wages fell by 16 percent. Workers responded by striking in increasing numbers. Elsewhere in Latin America (Cuba, the Amazon, Chile) the end of the war saw also widespread labor unrest and economic crisis, but few contexts were as volatile as Buenos Aires at the time. Living in their crowded tenements with a growing array of grievances, and cognizant of the recent successes of the Bolshevik revolution in Russia, Argentine workers were ready for a confrontation. Many simply wanted to win better wages and working conditions, but some workers—supporters of anarchist and socialist unions, or the Socialist Party—saw this as a revolutionary moment, a chance to participate in a movement that was coalescing around the western world. Their weapon: the general strike.

Such was the case in Buenos Aires in January 1919. Workers struck the Vasena Metallurgical workshop on January 7, demanding a reduction in the workday from 11 to 8 hours, better working conditions, Sundays off, better wages, and the reinstatement of fired union delegates. The company responded by hiring strike-breakers and non-union workers, and in the ensuing conflict the police were brought in and fired on workers. Four workers were killed, and more than thirty wounded in the melee. The story to this point was relatively unremarkable, as it was common to labor conflicts across the region during this period, but as workers gathered to care for the dead and take them to the Chacarita Cemetery, police again opened fire on the assembled. The following day *La Prensa* reported eight deaths, while others claimed more than fifty. In the ensuing hours, as stories circulated about the conflict, a growing number of *porteño* workers agitated for some sort of significant response from working people. Some were no doubt caught up in the anger and excitement of the moment, but the *Federación Obrera Regional Argentina* (Argentine Regional Worker's Federation—FORA), the coalition that organized the strike, was not. Leaders of the FORA (which had 20,000 members in 1919), believed this was Argentina's revolutionary moment. They launched a general strike on January 9, and it quickly spread to the provinces.

It would be a gross understatement to say that the FORA overestimated their strength. General strikes are dangerous things, perhaps successful when a regime is so discredited and weak that a widespread civic disturbance can topple the government, but perilous when unarmed workers face a militarized regime with substantial popular support. However real their grievances, and however thrilling the first turn at the barricades was, it was not only the Radical government of Yrigoyen the strikers had to confront, but a large population of Argentines who for years had been nursing a hysterical fear of immigrant workers, and who would support extreme measures to rein them in.

Almost immediately a militia made up of middle-class and wealthy young men joined the military and police in responding to the strike. They targeted striking workers, immigrants, and members of the political left with breathtaking violence. The *semana trágica* (tragic week) of the general strike left 1,000 dead, 4,000 injured, and around 50,000 imprisoned. Foreshadowing the extreme (and extremely xenophobic) measures that conservatives would use against their foes at various points during the twentieth century, they also used the pretext of the general strike to target Jewish neighborhoods in an effort to dismantle a supposed "Argentine Soviet" that in fact never existed. Yrigoyen repudiated the violence, but did little to punish those who were responsible. Having courted popular sympathies in running for election in 1916, he then sacrificed any chance that he might build an alliance with workers to challenge the oligarchy's political power. For their part, workers were reminded that they had no rightful place in the system.

Indeed, the most significant political movement to emerge out of the semana trágica was the *Liga Patriótica Argentina* (Argentine Patriotic League). The league was an extreme right-wing organization that was formed from the militias that terrorized workers and immigrants during the general strike. Given aid and training by the Argentine Army, the Church, and the wealthy, it was xenophobic, anti-communist, anti-Semitic. By the early 1920s it had about 300,000 members in over 600 brigades, who participated in any number of violent campaigns in defense of "Fatherland and Order." Catholic workers who were committed to capitalism and self-improvement were welcomed in the League, as long as they eschewed any interest in principles like equality. League members believed egalitarian values were utopian and dangerous, that society was naturally hierarchical and should remain so.

The Documents: Questioning a Golden Age

In some senses Document 4.1 and those included here have a great deal in common. All were penned during the export boom. All try and make sense of that boom in ways that draw moral conclusions about the kinds of economic and political transformations the region had seen in the recent past. Each however, offers a very different account of what has happened, and what is happening. In Creelman we see an optimistic sense that the future is bright, and in the three that follow we see angst, anger, and a demand for change. Reading any one of them for a true sense of the past seems a fool's errand. Readers will favor some and feel antipathy for others, largely based on their own sympathies. What seems more interesting here are the variety of ways the same experience can be rendered, and the underlying assumptions and values that each text reveals.

Presented below are three iconic examples of the voices raised in protest during this era. The first (Document 5.1) is one of the most famous essays ever penned by a Latin American intellectual, José Martí's *Our America*. In part a contemplative piece of philosophy, and in part a direct call to political action, Martí used this essay to argue both for Cuban independence and for a larger project of Latin American unity—a call that in many ways harkens back to Simón Bolívar. In this sense, his essay is not only about the crisis of a nation as yet chained to its colonial overlords, but about the problem of forging a strong, united, and independent Latin America.

Martí's essay is followed by the *Plan de Ayala*, penned by Emiliano Zapata and the Nahuatl speaking villagers of the highlands of Morelos in 1911 (Document 5.2). Their declaration was a direct repudiation of Francisco Madero, whom they supported in the overthrow of Porfirio Díaz. As such, their grievances were in some senses quite specific, a quasi-legal explanation and justification for their own perilous act of rebellion. Still, there was much more to the *Plan de Ayala*. Embedded within the document are a series of assumptions and claims about the rights of villagers, and how the violation of those rights justifies rebellion. Though much more practical than Martí, their larger insights were no less profound.

The final document (5.3) is excerpted from the book *Seven Interpretive Essays on Peruvian Reality*, written by the Peruvian intellectual José Carlos Mariátegui in 1928. Similar themes emerge here as in the previous essays, but again, Mariátegui wrote from a particular viewpoint. An avowed Marxist, he combined the political ideology of those who advocated the 1919 general strike in Buenos Aires with a focus on the rural problems that shaped the Peruvian left (Mariátegui was an advocate of workers rights, and supported Peru's 1919 strikes). Mariátegui was an early supporter of Raúl Haya de la Torre's *Alianza Popular Revolucionaria Americana* (American Popular Revolutionary Alliance -APRA), though he left the party just prior to the publication of *Seven Essays* to establish his own Socialist Party.

What makes this essay particularly important is that it represents a form of Marxism that sought organic national origins in the plight of Andean peoples, rather than from an emergent (often immigrant) working class. It draws on the specific histories of the Andes, where Indian–white relations were far more clearly contentious than elsewhere, where the possibility of pan-Indian movements seemed more likely, and where the Inca past remained a subject of romantic memories even into the twentieth century. Moreover, unlike *Our America* and the *Plan de Ayala*, *Seven Essays* was penned at a time when a growing community on the left, buoyed by Russia's 1917 revolution, truly believed in the likelihood of a global socialist revolution. Mariátegui was therefore a writer with a foot in two different worlds—he drew from the nationalist, anti-imperialist traditions of writers like Martí, but looked towards a future in which the battle between left and right would be fought on a global stage.

Document 5.1 José Martí, "Our America," from *La Revista Ilustrada*, New York, January 1, 1891

Source: "Our America" from *The America of José Martí* translated by Juan de Onís. Translation copyright © 1954, renewed 1982 by Farrar, Straus, & Giroux, Inc. Reprinted by permission of Farrar, Straus and Giroux, LLC.

The prideful villager thinks his hometown contains the whole world, and as long as he can stay on as mayor or humiliate the rival who stole his sweetheart or watch his nest egg accumulating in its strongbox he believes the universe to be in good order, unaware of the giants in seven-league boots who can crush him underfoot or the battling comets in the heavens that go through the air devouring the sleeping worlds. Whatever is left of that sleepy hometown in America must awaken. These are not times for going to bed in a sleeping cap, but rather, like Juan de Castellanos' men, with our weapons for a pillow, weapons of the mind, which vanquish all others. Trenches of ideas are worth more than trenches of stone.

A cloud of ideas is a thing no armored prow can smash though. A vital idea set ablaze before the world at the right moment can, like the mystic banner of the last judgment, stop a fleet of battleships. Hometowns that are still strangers to one another must hurry to become acquainted, like men who are about to do battle together. Those who shake their fists at each other like jealous brothers quarreling over a piece of land or the owner of a small house who envies the man with a better one must join hands and interlace them until their two hands are as one. Those who, shielded by a criminal tradition, mutilate, with swords smeared in the same blood that flows though their own veins, the land of a conquered brother whose punishment far exceeds his crimes, must return that land to their brother if they do not wish to be known as a nation of plunderers. The honorable man does not collect his debts of honor in money, at so much per slap. We can no longer be a nation of fluttering leaves, spending our lives in the air, our treetop crowned in flowers, humming or creaking, caressed by the caprices of sunlight or thrashed and felled by tempests. The trees must form ranks to block the seven-league giant! It is the hour of reckoning and of marching in unison, and we must move in lines as compact as the veins of silver that lie at the roots of the Andes.

Only runts whose growth was stunted will lack the necessary valor, for those who have no faith in their land are like men born prematurely. Having no valor themselves, they deny that other men do. Their puny arms, with bracelets and painted nails, the arms of Madrid or of Paris, cannot manage the lofty tree and so they say the tree cannot be climbed. We must load up the ships with these termites who gnaw away at the core of the patria that has nurtured them; if they are Parisians or Madrileños then let them stroll to the Prado by lamplight or go to Tortoni's for an ice. These sons of carpenters who are ashamed that their father was a carpenter! These men born in America who are ashamed of the mother that raised them because she wears an Indian apron, these delinquents who disown their sick mother and leave her alone in her sickbed! Which one is truly a man, he who stays with his mother to nurse her though her illness, or he who forces her to work somewhere out of sight, and lives off her sustenance in corrupted lands, with a worm for his insignia, cursing the bosom that bore him, sporting a sign that says "traitor" on the back of his paper dress-coat? These sons of our America, which must save herself through her Indians, and which is going from less to more, who desert her and take up arms in the armies of North America, which drowns its own Indians in blood and going from more to less! These delicate creatures who are men but do not want to do men's work! Did Washington, who made that land for them, go and live with the English during the years when he saw the English marching against his own land? These *incroyables* who drag their honor across foreign soil, like the *incroyables* of the French Revolution, dancing, smacking their lips, and deliberately slurring their words!

And in what patria can a man take greater pride than in our long-suffering republics of America, erected among mute masses of Indians upon the bloodied arms of no more than a hundred apostles, to the sound of the book doing battle against the monk's tall candle? Never before have such advanced and consolidated nations been created from such disparate factors in less historical time. The haughty man thinks that because he wields a quick pen or a vivid phrase the earth was made to be his pedestal, and accuses his nature republic or irredeemable incompetence because its virgin jungles do not continually provide him with the means of going about the world a famous plutocrat, driving Persian ponies and spilling champagne. The incapacity lies not in the emerging country, which demands forms that are appropriate to it and a grandeur that is useful, but in the leaders who try to rule unique nations of a singular and violent composition, with laws inherited from four centuries of free practice in the United States and nineteen centuries of monarchy in France. A gaucho's pony cannot be stopped in mid-bolt by one of Alexander Hamilton's laws. The sluggish blood of the Indian race cannot be quickened by a phrase from Sieyes. To govern well, one must attend closely to the reality of the place that is governed. In America, the good ruler does not need to know how the German or Frenchman is governed, but what elements his own country is composed of and how he can marshal them so as to reach, by means and institutions born from the country itself, the desirable state in which every man knows himself and is active, and all men enjoy the abundance that Nature, for the good of all, has bestowed on the country they make fruitful by their labor and defend with their lives. The government must be born from the country. The spirit of the government must be the spirit of the country. The form of the government must be in harmony with the country's natural constitution. The government is no more than an equilibrium among the country's natural elements.

In America the natural man has triumphed over the imported book. Natural men have triumphed over an artificial intelligentsia. The native mestizo has triumphed over the alien, pure-blooded criollo. The battle is not between civilization and barbarity, but between false erudition and nature. The natural man is good, and esteems and rewards a superior intelligence as long as that intelligence does not use his submission against him or offend him by ignoring him—for that the natural man deems unforgivable, and he is prepared to use force to regain the respect of anyone who wounds his sensibilities or harms his interests. The tyrants of America have come to power by acquiescing to these scorned natural elements and have fallen as soon as they betrayed them. The republics have purged the former tyrannies of their inability to know the true elements of the country, derive the form of government from them, and govern along with them. Governor, in a new country, means Creator.

In countries composed of educated and uneducated sectors, the uneducated will govern by their habit of attacking and resolving their doubts with their fists, unless the educated learn the art of governing. The uneducated masses are lazy and timid about matters of the intellect and want to be well-governed, but if the government injures them they shake it off and govern themselves. How can our governors emerge from the universities when there is not a university in America that teaches the most basic element of the art of governing, which is the analysis of all that is unique to the peoples of America? Our youth go out into the world wearing Yankee- or French-colored glasses and aspire to rule by guesswork a country they do not know. Those unacquainted with the rudiments of politics should not be allowed to embark on a career in politics. The literary prizes must not go to the best ode, but to the best study of the political factors in the student's country. In the newspapers, lecture halls, and academies, the study of the country's real factors must be carried forward. Simply knowing those factors without blindfolds or circumlocutions is enough—for anyone who deliberately or unknowingly sets aside a part of the truth will ultimately fail because of the truth he was lacking, which expands when neglected and brings down whatever is built without it. Solving the problem after knowing its elements is easier than solving it without knowing them. The natural man, strong and indignant, comes and overthrows the authority that is accumulated from books because it is not administered in keeping with the manifest needs of the country. To know is to solve. To know the country and govern it in accordance with that knowledge is the only way of freeing it from tyranny. The European university must yield to the American university. The history of America from the Incas to the present must be taught in its smallest detail, even if the Greek Archons go untaught. Our own Greece is preferable to the Greece that is not ours; we need it more. Statesmen who arise from the nation must replace statesmen who are alien to it. Let the world be grafted onto our republics, but we must be the trunk. And let the vanquished pedant hold his tongue, for their is no patria in which a man can take greater pride than in our long-suffering American republics.

Our feet upon a rosary, our heads white, and our bodies a motley of Indian and criollo we boldly entered the community of nations. Bearing the standard of the Virgin, we went out to conquer our liberty. A priest, a few lieutenants, and a woman built a republic in Mexico upon the shoulders of the Indians. A Spanish cleric, under cover of his priestly cape, taught French liberty to a handful of magnificent students who chose a Spanish general to lead central America against Spain. Still accustomed to monarchy, and with the sun on their chests, the Venezuelans in the north and the Argentines in the south set out to construct nations. When the two heroes clashed and their continent was about to be rocked, one of them, and not the lesser one, turned back. But heroism is less glorious in peacetime than in war, and thus rarer, and it is easier for a man to die with honor than to think in an orderly way. Exalted and unanimous sentiments are more readily governed than the diverging, arrogant, alien, and ambitious ideas that emerge when the battle is over. The powers that were swept up in the epic struggle, along with the feline wariness of the species and the sheer weight of reality, undermined the edifice that had raised the flags of nations sustained by wise governance in the continual practice of reason and freedom over the crude and singular regions of our mestizo America with its towns of bare legs and Parisian dress-coats. The colonial hierarchy resisted the republic's democracy, and the capital city, wearing its elegant cravat, left the countryside, in its horsehide boots, waiting at the door; the redeemers born from books did not understand that a revolution that had triumphed when the soul of the earth was unleashed by a savior's voice had to govern with the soul of the earth and not against or without it. And for all these reasons, America began enduring and still endures the weary task of reconciling the discordant and hostile elements it inherited from its perverse, despotic colonizer with the imported forms and ideas that have, in their lack of local reality, delayed the advent of a logical form of government. The continent, deformed by three centuries of a rule that denied man the right to exercise his reason, embarked—overlooking or refusing to listen to the ignorant masses that had helped it redeem itself—upon a government based on reason, the reason of all directed toward the things that are of concern to all, and not the university-taught reason of the few imposed upon the rustic reason of others. The problem of independence was not the change in form, but the change in spirit.

Common cause had to be made with the oppressed in order to consolidate a system that was opposed to the interests and governmental habits of the oppressors. The tiger, frightened away by the flash of gunfire, creeps back in the night to find his prey. He will die with flames shooting form his eyes, his claws unsheathed, but now his step is inaudible for he comes on velvet paws. When the prey awakens, the tiger is upon him. The colony lives on in the republic, but our America is saving itself from its grave blunders—the arrogance of the capital cities, the blind triumph of the scorned campesinos, the excessive importation of foreign ideas and formulas, the wicked and impolitic disdain for the native race—through the superior virtue, confirmed by necessary bloodshed, of the republic that struggles against the colony. The tiger waits behind every tree, crouches in every corner. He will die, his claws unsheathed, flames shooting form his eyes.

But "these countries will be saved," in the words of the Argentine Rivadavia, who erred on the side of urbanity during crude times; the machete is sill-suited to a silken scabbard, nor can the spear be abandoned in a country won by the spear, for it becomes enraged and stands in the doorway of Iturbide's Congress demanding that "the fair-skinned man be made emperor." These countries will be saved because, with the genius of moderation that now seems, by nature's serene harmony, to prevail in the continent of light, and the influence of the critical reading that has, in Europe, replaced the fumbling ideas about phalansteries in which the previous generation was steeped, the real man is being born to America, in these real times.

What a vision we were: the chest of an athlete, the hands of a dandy, and the forehead of a child. We were a whole fancy dress ball, in English trousers, a Parisian waistcoat, a North American overcoat, and a Spanish bullfighter's hat. The Indian circled about us, mute, and went to the mountaintop to christen his children. The black, pursued from afar, alone and unknown, sang his heart's music in the night, between waves and wild beasts. The campesinos, the men of the land, the creators, rose up in blind indignation against the disdainful city, their own creation. We wore epaulets and judge's robes, in countries that came into the world wearing rope sandals and Indian headbands. The wise thing would have been to pair, with charitable hearts and the audacity of our founders, the Indian headband and the judicial robe, to undam the Indian, make a place for the able black, and tailor liberty to the bodies of those who rose up and triumphed in its name. What we had was the judge, the general, the man of letters, and the cleric. Our angelic youth, as if struggling from the arms of an octopus, cast their heads into the heavens and fell back with sterile glory, crowned with clouds. The natural people, driven by instinct, blind with triumph, overwhelmed their gilded rulers. No Yankee or European book could furnish the key to the Hispanoamerican enigma. So the people tried hatred instead, and our countries amounted to less and less each year. Weary of useless hatred, of the struggle of book against sword, reason against the monk's taper, city against countryside, the impossible empire of the quarreling urban castes against the tempestuous or inert natural nation, we are beginning, almost unknowingly, to try love. The nations arise and salute one another. "What are we like?" they ask, and begin telling each other what they are like. When a problem arises in Cojimar they no longer seek the solution in Danzig. The frock-coats are still French, but the thinking begins to be American. The young men of America are rolling up their sleeves and plunging their hands into the dough, and making it rise with the leavening of their sweat. They understand that there is too much imitation, and that salvation lies in creating. Create is this generation's password. Make wine from plantains; it may be sour, but it is our wine! It is now understood that a country's form of government must adapt to its natural elements, that absolute ideas, in order not to collapse over an error of form, must be expressed in relative forms; that liberty, in order to be viable, must be sincere and full, that if the republic does not open its arms to all and include all in its progress, it dies. The tiger inside came in through the gap, and so will the tiger outside. The general holds the cavalry's speed to the pace of the infantry, for if he leaves the infantry far behind, the enemy will surround the cavalry. Politics is strategy. Nations must continually criticize themselves, for criticism is health, but with a single heart and a single mind. Lower yourselves to the unfortunate and raise them up in your arms! Let the heart's fires unfreeze all that is motionless in America, and let the country's natural blood surge and throb through its veins! Standing tall, the workmen's eyes full of joy, the new men of America are saluting each other from one country to another. Natural statesmen are emerging from the direct study of nature; they read in order to apply what they read, not copy it. Economists are studying problems at their origins. Orators are becoming more temperate. Dramatists are putting native characters onstage. Academies are discussing practical subjects. Poetry is snipping off its wild, Zorilla-esque mane and hanging up its gaudy waistcoat on the glorious tree. Prose, polished and gleaming, is replete with ideas. The rulers of Indian republics are learning Indian languages.

America is saving herself from all her dangers. Over some republics the octopus sleeps still, but by the law of equilibrium, other republics are running into the sea to recover the lost centuries with mad and sublime swiftness. Others, forgetting that Juárez traveled in a coach drawn by mules, hitch their coach to the wind and take a soap bubble for coachman—and poisonous luxury, enemy of liberty, corrupts the frivolous and opens the door to foreigners. The virile character of others is being perfected by the epic spirit of a threatened independence. And others, in rapacious wars against their neighbors, are nurturing an unruly soldier caste that may devour them. But our America may also face another danger, which comes not from within but from the differing origins, methods, and interests of the containment's two factions. The hour is near when she will be approached by an enterprising and forceful nation that will demand intimate relations with her, though it does not know her and disdains her. And virile nations self-made by the rifle and the law love other virile nations, and love only them. The hour of unbridled passion and ambition from which North America may escape by the ascendancy of the purest element in its blood—or into which its vengeful and sordid masses, its tradition of conquest, and the self-interest of a cunning leader could plunge it—is not yet so close, even to the most apprehensive eye, that there is no time for it to be confronted and averted by the manifestation of a discreet and unswerving pride, for its dignity as a republic, in the eyes of the watchful nations of the Universe, places upon North America a brake that our America must not remove by puerile provocation, ostentatious arrogance, or patricidal discord. Therefore the urgent duty of our America is to show herself as she is, one in soul and intent, rapidly overcoming the crushing weight of her past and stained only by the fertile blood shed by hands that do battle against ruins and by veins that were punctured by our former masters. The disdain of the formidable neighbor who does not know her is our America's greatest danger, and it is urgent—for the day of the visit is near—that her neighbor come to know her, and quickly, so that he will not disdain her. Out of ignorance, he may perhaps begin to covet her. But when he knows her, he will remove his hands from her in respect. One must have faith in the best in man and distrust the worst. One must give the best every opportunity, so that the worst will be laid bare and overcome. If not, the worst will prevail. Nations should have one special pillory for those who incite them to futile hatreds, and another for those who do not tell them the truth until it is too late.

There is no racial hatred, because there are no races. Sickly, lamp-lit minds string together and rewarm the library-shelf races that the honest traveler and the cordial observer seek in vain in the justice of nature, where the universal identity of man leaps forth in victorious love and turbulent appetite. The soul, equal and eternal, emanates from bodies that are diverse in form and color. Anyone who promotes and disseminates opposition or hatred among races is committing a sin against humanity. But within that jumble of peoples which lives in close proximity to our peoples, certain peculiar and dynamic characteristics are condensed—ideas and habits of expansion, acquisition, vanity, and greed—that could, in a period of internal disorder or precipitation of a people's cumulative character, cease to be latent national preoccupations and become a serious threat to the neighboring, isolated and weak lands that the strong country declares to be perishable and inferior. To think is to serve. We must not, out of a villager's antipathy, impute some lethal congenital wickedness to the continent's light-skinned nation simply because it does not speak our language or share our view of what home life should be or resemble us in its political failings, which are different from ours, or because it does not think highly of quick-tempered, swarthy men or look with charity, from its still uncertain eminence, upon those less favored by history who, in heroic stages, are climbing the road that republics travel. But neither should we seek to conceal the obvious facts of the problem, which can, for the peace of the centuries, be resolved by timely study and the urgent, wordless union of the continental soul. For the unanimous hymn is already ringing forth, and the present generation is bearing industrious America along the road sanctioned by our sublime forefathers. From the Rio Bravo to the Straits of Magellan, the Great Cemi, seated on a condor's back, has scattered the seeds of the new America across the romantic nations of the continent and the suffering islands of the sea!

Document 5.2 Emiliano Zapata, The *Plan de Ayala*, 1911

Source: From *Zapata and the Mexican Revolution* by John Womack, Jr., copyright © 1968 by John Womack, Jr. Used by permission of Alfred A. Knopf, a division of Random House, Inc.; Thames & Hudson Ltd., London.

Liberating Plan of the sons of the State of Morelos, affiliated with the Insurgent Army which defends the fulfillment of the Plan of San Luis, with the reforms which it has believed proper to add in benefit of the Mexican Fatherland.

We who undersign, constituted in a revolutionary junta to sustain and carry out the promises which the revolution of November 20, 1910 just past, made to the country, declare solemnly before the face of the civilized world which judges us and before the nation to which we belong and which we call [*sic, llamamos*, misprint for *amamos*, love], propositions which we have formulated to end the tyranny which oppresses us and redeem the fatherland from the dictatorships which are imposed on us, which [propositions] are determined in the following plan:

1. Taking into consideration that the Mexican people led by Don Francisco I. Madero went to shed their blood to reconquer liberties and recover their rights which had been trampled on, and not for a man to take possession of power, violating the sacred principles which he took an oath to defend under the slogan "Effective Suffrage and No Reelection," outraging thus the faith, the cause, the justice, and the liberties of the people: taking into consideration that that man to whom we refer is Don Francisco I. Madero, the same who initiated the above-cited revolution, who imposed his will and influence as a governing norm on the Provisional Government of the ex-President of the Republic Attorney Francisco L. de Barra [*sic*], causing with this deed repeated sheddings of blood and multiplicate

misfortunes for the fatherland in a manner deceitful and ridiculous, having no intentions other than satisfying his personal ambitions, his boundless instincts as a tyrant, and his profound disrespect for the fulfillment of the preexisting laws emanating from the immortal code of '57, written with the revolutionary blood of Ayutla;

Taking into account that the so-called Chief of the Liberating Revolution of Mexico, Don Francisco I. Madero, through lack of integrity and the highest weakness, did not carry to a happy end the revolution which gloriously he initiated with the help of God and the people, since he left standing most of the governing powers and corrupted elements of oppression of the dictatorial government of Porfirio Díaz, which are not nor can in any way be the representation of National Sovereignty, and which, for being most bitter adversaries of ours and of the principles which even now we defend, are provoking the discomfort of the country and opening new wounds in the bosom of the fatherland, to give it its own blood to drink; taking also into account that the aforementioned Sr. Francisco I. Madero, present President of the Republic, tries to avoid the fulfillment of the promises which he made to the Nation in the Plan of San Luis Potosí, being [sic, siendo, misprint for ciñendo, restricting] the above-cited promises to the agreements of Ciudad Juárez, by means of false promises and numerous intrigues against the Nation nullifying, pursuing, jailing, or killing revolutionary elements who helped him to occupy the high post of President of the Republic;

Taking into consideration that the so-often-repeated Francisco I. Madero has tried with the brute force of bayonets to shut up and to drown in blood the pueblos who ask, solicit, or demand from him the fulfillment of the promises of the revolution, calling them bandits and rebels, condemning them to a war of extermination without conceding or granting a single one of the guarantees which reason, justice, and the law prescribe; taking equally into consideration that the President of the Republic Francisco I. Madero has made of Effective Suffrage a bloody trick on the people, already against the will of the same people imposing Attorney José M. Pino Suárez in the Vice-Presidency of the Republic, or [imposing as] Governors of the States [men] designated by him, like the so-called General Ambrosio Figueroa, scourge and tyrant of the people of Morelos, or entering into scandalous cooperation with the científico party, feudal landlords, and oppressive bosses, enemies of the revolution proclaimed by him, so as to forge new chains and follow the pattern of a new dictatorship more shameful and more terrible than that of Porfirio Díaz, for it has been clear and patent that he has outraged the sovereignty of the States, trampling on the laws without any respect for lives or interests, as has happened in the State of Morelos, and others, leading them to the most horrendous anarchy which contemporary history registers.

For these considerations we declare the aforementioned Francisco I. Madero inept at realizing the promises of the revolution of which he was the author, because he has betrayed the principles with which he tricked the will of the people and was able to get into power: incapable of governing, because he has no respect for the law and justice of the pueblos, and a traitor to the fatherland, because he is humiliating in blood and fire Mexicans who want liberties, so as to please the científicos, landlords, and bosses who enslave us, and from today on we begin to continue the revolution begun by him, until we achieve the overthrow of the dictatorial powers which exist.

2. Recognition is withdrawn from Sr. Francisco I. Madero as Chief of the Revolution and as President of the Republic, for the reasons which before were expressed, it being attempted to overthrow this official.

3. Recognized as Chief of the Liberating Revolution is the illustrious General Pascual Orozco, the second of the Leader Don Francisco I. Madero, and in case he does not accept this delicate post, recognition as Chief of the Revolution will go to General Don Emiliano Zapata.

4. The Revolutionary Junta of the State of Morelos manifests to the Nation under formal oath: that it makes its own the plan of San Luis Potosí, with the additions which are expressed below in benefit of the oppressed pueblos, and it will make itself the defender of the principles it defends until victory or death.

5. The Revolutionary Junta of the State of Morelos will admit no transactions or compromises until it achieves the overthrow of the dictatorial elements of Porfirio Díaz and Francisco I. Madero, for the nation is tired of false men and traitors who make promises like liberators and who on arriving in power forget them and constitute themselves as tyrants.

6. As an additional part of the plan we invoke, we give notice: that [regarding] the fields, timber, and water which the landlords, científicos, or bosses have usurped, the pueblos or citizens who have the titles corresponding to those properties will immediately enter into possession of that real estate of which they have been despoiled by the bad faith of our oppressors, maintaining at any cost with arms in hand the mentioned possession; and the usurpers who consider themselves with a right to them [those properties] will deduce it before the special tribunals which will be established on the triumph of the revolution.

7. In virtue of the fact that the immense majority of Mexican pueblos and citizens are owners of no more than the land they walk on, suffering the horrors of poverty without being able to improve their social condition in any way or to dedicate themselves to Industry or Agriculture, because lands, timber, and water are monopolized in a few hands, for this cause there will be expropriated the third part of those monopolies from the powerful proprietors of them, with prior indemnization, in order that the pueblos and citizens of Mexico may obtain ejidos, colonies, and foundations for pueblos, or fields for sowing or laboring, and the Mexicans' lack of prosperity and wellbeing may improve in all and for all.

8. [Regarding] The landlords, científicos, or bosses who oppose the present plan directly or indirectly, their goods will be nationalized and the two third parts which [otherwise would] belong to them will go for indemnizations of war, pensions for widows and orphans of the victims who succumb in the struggle for the present plan.

9. In order to execute the procedures regarding the properties aforementioned, the laws of disamortization and nationalization will be applied as they fit, for serving us as norm and example can be those laws put in force by the immortal Juárez on ecclesiastical properties, which punished the despots and conservatives who

in every time have tried to impose on us the ignominious yoke of oppression and backwardness.

10. The insurgent military chiefs of the Republic who rose up with arms in hand at the voice of Don Francisco I. Madero to defend the plan of San Luis Potosí, and who oppose with armed force the present plan, will be judged traitors to the cause which they defended and to the fatherland, since at present many of them, to humor the tyrants, for a fistful of coins, or for bribes or connivance, are shedding the blood of their brothers who claim the fulfillment of the promises which Don Francisco I. Madero made to the nation.

11. The expenses of war will be taken in conformity with Article II of the Plan of San Luis Potosí, and all procedures employed in the revolution we undertake will be in conformity with the same instructions which the said plan determines.

12. Once triumphant the revolution which we carry into the path of reality, a Junta of the principal revolutionary chiefs from the different States will name or designate an interim President of the Republic, who will convoke elections for the organization of the federal powers.

13. The principal revolutionary chiefs of each State will designate in Junta the Governor of the State to which they belong, and this appointed official will convoke elections for the due organization of the public powers, the object being to avoid compulsory appointments which work the misfortune of the pueblos, like the so-well-known appointment of Ambrosio Figueroa in the State of Morelos and others who drive us to the precipice of bloody conflicts, sustained by the caprice of the dictator Madero and the circle of científicos and landlords who have influenced him.

14. If President Madero and other dictatorial elements of the present and former regime want to avoid the immense misfortunes which afflict the fatherland, and [if they] possess true sentiments of love for it, let them make immediate renunciation of the posts they occupy and with that they will with something staunch the grave wounds which they have opened in the bosom of the fatherland, since, if they do not do so, on their heads will fall the blood and the anathema of our brothers.

15. Mexicans: consider that the cunning and bad faith of one man is shedding blood in a scandalous manner, because he is incapable of governing; consider that his system of government is choking the fatherland and trampling with the brute force of bayonets on our institutions; and thus, as we raised up our weapons to elevate him to power, we again raise them up against him for defaulting on his promises to the Mexican people and for having betrayed the revolution initiated by him, we are not personalists, we are partisans of principles and not of men!

Mexican People, support this plan with arms in hand and you will make the prosperity and well-being of the fatherland.

Ayala, November 25, 1911
Liberty, Justice, and Law

Document 5.3   José Carlos Mariátegui, "The Problem of the Indian," from *Seven Interpretive Essays on Peruvian Reality*, 1928

Source: From *Seven Interpretive Essays on Peruvian Reality* by José Carlos Mariátegui, translated by Marjory Urquidi, copyright © 1971. Used by Permission of the University of Texas Press.

A New Approach

Any treatment of the problem of the Indian—written or verbal—that fails or refuses to recognize it as a socioeconomic problem is but a sterile, theoretical exercise destined to be completely discredited. Good faith is no justification. Almost all such treatments have served merely to mask or distort the reality of the problem. The socialist critic exposes and defines the problem because he looks for its causes in the country's economy and not in its administrative, legal, or ecclesiastic machinery, its racial dualism or pluralism, or its cultural or moral conditions. The problem of the Indian is rooted in the land tenure system of our economy. Any attempt to solve it with administrative or police measures, through education or by a road building program, is superficial and secondary as long as the feudalism of the gamonales continues to exist.

Gamonalismo necessarily invalidates any law or regulation for the protection of the Indian. The hacienda owner, the latifundista, is a feudal lord. The written law is powerless against his authority, which is supported by custom and habit. Unpaid labor is illegal, yet unpaid and even forced labor survive in the latifundium. The judge, the subprefect, the commissary, the teacher, the tax collector, all are in bondage to the landed estate. The law cannot prevail against the gamonales. Any official who insisted on applying it would be abandoned and sacrificed by the central government; here, the influences of Gamonalismo are all-powerful, acting directly or through parliament with equal effectiveness.

A fresh approach to the problem of the Indian, therefore, ought to be much more concerned with the consequences of the land tenure system than with drawing up protective legislation. The new trend was started in 1918 by Dr. José A. Encinas in his *Contribución a una legislación tutelar indígena*, and it has steadily gained strength. But by the very nature of his study, Dr. Encinas could not frame a socio-economic program. Since his proposals were designed to protect Indian property, they had to be limited to legal objectives. Outlining an indigenous homestead act, Dr. Encinas recommended the distribution of state and church lands. Although he did not mention expropriating the land of the latifundium gamonales, he repeatedly and conclusively denounced the effects of the latifundium system and, thereby to some extent ushered in the present socio-economic approach to the Indian question.

This approach rejects and disqualifies any thesis that confines the question to one or another of the following unilateral criteria: administrative, legal, ethnic, moral, educational, ecclesiastic.

The oldest and most obvious mistake is, unquestionably, that of reducing the protection of the Indian to an ordinary administrative matter. From the days of Spanish colonial legislation, wise and detailed ordinances, worked out after conscientious study, have been quite useless. The republic, since independence, has been prodigious in its decrees, laws, and provisions intended to protect the Indian against exaction and abuse. The gamonal of today, like the encomendero of yesterday, however, has little to fear from administrative theory; he knows that its practice is altogether different.

The individualistic character of the republic's legislation has favored the absorption of Indian property by the latifundium system. The situation of the Indian, in this respect, was viewed more realistically by Spanish legislation. But legal reform has no more practical value than administrative reform when confronted by feudalism intact within the economic structure. The appropriation of most communal and individual Indian property is an accomplished fact. The experience of all countries that have evolved from their feudal stage shows us, on the other hand, that liberal rights have not been able to operate without the dissolution of feudalism

The assumption that the Indian problem is ethnic is sustained by the most outmoded repertory of imperialist ideas. The concept of inferior races was useful to the white man's West for purposes of expansion and conquest. To expect that the Indian will be eman-cipated through a steady crossing of the aboriginal race with white immigrants is an anti-sociological naiveté that could only occur to the primitive mentality of an importer of merino sheep. The people of Asia, who are in no way superior to the Indians, have not needed any transfusion of European blood in order to assimilate the most dynamic and creative aspects of Western culture. The degeneration of the Peruvian Indian is a cheap invention of sophists who serve feudal interests.

The tendency to consider the Indian problem as a moral one embodies a liberal, humanitarian, enlightened nineteenth-century attitude that in the political sphere of the Western world inspires and motivates the "leagues of human rights." The antislavery conferences and societies in Europe that have denounced more or less futilely the crimes of the colonizing nations are born of this tendency, which always has trusted too much in its appeals to the conscience of civilization. González Prada was not immune to this hope when he wrote that "the condition of the Indian can improve in two ways: either the heart of the oppressor will be moved to take pity and recognize the rights of the oppressed or the spirit of the oppressed will find the valor needed to turn on the oppressors." The Pro-Indian Association (1900–1917) represented the same hope, although it owed its real effectiveness to the concrete and immediate measures taken by its directors in defense of the Indian. This policy was due in large measure to the practical, typically Saxon idealism of Dora Mayer, and the work of the Association became well known in Peru and the rest of the world. Humanitarian teachings have not halted or hampered European imperialism, nor have they reformed its methods. The struggle against imperialism now relies only on the solidarity and strength of the liberation movement of the colonial masses. This concept governs anti-imperialist action in contemporary Europe, action that is supported by liberals like Albert Einstein and Romain Rolland and, therefore, cannot be considered exclusively Socialist.

On a moral and intellectual plane, the church took a more energetic or at least a more authoritative stand centuries ago. This crusade, however, achieved only very wise laws and provisions. The lot of the Indian remained substantially the same. González Prada, whose point of view, as we know, was not strictly Socialist, looked for the explanation of its failure in the economic essentials: "It could not have happened otherwise; exploitation was the official order; it was pretended that evils were humanely perpetrated and injustices committed equitably. To wipe out abuses, it would have been necessary to abolish land appropriation and forced labor, in brief, to change the entire colonial regime. Without the toil of the American Indian, the coffers of the Spanish treasury would have been emptied." In any event, religious tenets were more likely to succeed than liberal tenets. The former appealed to a noble and active Spanish Catholicism, whereas the latter tried to make itself heard by a weak and formalist criollo liberalism.

But today a religious solution is unquestionably the most outdated and antihistoric of all. Its representatives—unlike their distant, how very distant, teachers—are not concerned with obtaining a new declaration of the rights of Indians, with adequate authority and ordinances; the missionary is merely assigned the role of mediator between the Indian and the gamonal. If the church could not accomplish its task in a medieval era, when its spiritual and intellectual capacity could be measured by friars like Las Casas, how can it succeed with the elements it commands today? The Seventh-Day Adventists, in that respect, have taken the lead from the Catholic clergy, whose cloisters attract fewer and fewer evangelists.

The belief that the Indian problem is one of education does not seem to be supported by even a strictly and independently pedagogical criterion. Education is now more than ever aware of social and economic factors. The modern pedagogue knows perfectly well that education is not just a question of school and teaching methods. Economic and social circumstances necessarily condition the work of the teacher. Gamonalismo is fundamentally opposed to the education of the Indian; it has the same interest in keeping the Indian ignorant as it has in encouraging him to depend on alcohol. The modern school—assuming that in the present situation it could be multiplied at the same rate as the rural school-age population—is incompatible with the feudal latifundium. The mechanics of the Indian's servitude would altogether cancel the action of the school if the latter, by a miracle that is inconceivable within social reality, should manage to preserve its pedagogical mission under a feudal regime. The most efficient and grandiose teaching system could not perform these prodigies. School and teacher are doomed to be debased under the pressure of the feudal regime, which cannot be reconciled with the most elementary concept of progress and evolution. When this truth becomes partially understood, the saving formula is thought to be discovered in boarding schools for Indians. But the glaring inadequacy of this formula is self-evident in view of the tiny percentage of the indigenous school population that can be boarded in these schools.

The pedagogical solution, advocated by many in good faith, has been discarded officially. Educators, I repeat, can least afford to ignore economic and social reality. At present, it only exists as a vague and formless suggestion which no body or doctrine wants to adopt.

The new approach locates the problem of the Indian in the land tenure system . . .

Those of us who approach and define the Indian problem from a Socialist point of view must start out be declaring the complete obsolescence of the humanitarian and philanthropic points of view which, like a prolongation of the apostolic battle of Las

Casas, continued to motivate the old pro-Indian campaign. We shall try to establish the basically economic character of the problem. First, we protest against the instinctive attempt of the criollo or mestizo to reduce it to an exclusively administrative, peda-gogical, ethnic, or moral problem in order to avoid at all cost recognizing its economic aspect. Therefore, it would be absurd to accuse us of being romantic or literary. By identifying it as primarily a socio-economic problem, we are taking the least romantic and literary position possible. We are not satisfied to assert the Indian's right to edu-cation, culture, progress, love, and heaven. We begin by categorically asserting his right to land. This thoroughly materialistic claim should suffice to distinguish us from the heirs or imitators of the evangelical fervor of the great Spanish Friar, whom, on the other hand, our materialism does not prevent us from admiring and esteeming.

The problem of land is obviously too bound up with the Indian problem as to be conveniently mitigated or diminished. Quite the contrary. As for myself, I shall try to present it in unmistakable and clearcut terms.

The agrarian problem is first and foremost the problem of eliminating feudalism in Peru, which should have been done by the democratic-bourgeois regime that followed the War of Independence. But in its one hundred years as a republic, Peru has not had a genuine bourgeois class, a true capitalist class. The old feudal class—camouflaged or disguised as a republican bourgeois—has kept its position. The policy of disentailment, initiated by the War of Independence as the logical consequence of its ideology, did not lead to the development of small property. The old landholding class lost its supremacy. The survival of *latifundistas*, in practice, preserved the latifundium. Disentailment struck at the Indian community. During a century of Republican rule, great agricultural property actually has grown stronger and expanded, despite the theoretical liberalism of our constitution and the practical necessities of the development of our capitalist economy.

There are two expressions of feudalism that survive: the latifundium and servitude. Inseperable and of the same substance, their analysis leads us to the conclusion that the servitude oppressing the indigenous race cannot be abolished unless the latifundium is abolished.

When the agrarian problem is presented in these terms, it cannot be easily distorted. It appears in all its magnitude as a socio-economic, and therefore a political, problem, to be dealt with by men who move in this sphere of acts and ideas. And it is useless to convert it, for example, into a technical-agricultural problem for agronomists.

Everyone must know that according to individualist ideology, the liberal solution to this problem would be the breaking up of the latifundium to create small property. But there is so much ignorance of the elementary principles of socialism that it is worthwhile repeating that this formula—the breaking up of the latifundium in the favor of small property—is neither utopian, nor heretical, nor revolutionary, nor Bolshevik, nor avant-garde, but orthodox, constitutional, democratic, capitalist, and bourgeois. It is based on the same liberal body of ideas that produced the constitutional laws of all democratic-bourgeois states. In the countries of Central and Eastern Europe— Czechoslovakia, Rumania, Poland, Bulgaria, et cetera—agrarian laws have been passed limiting land ownership, in principle, to a maximum of five hundred hectares. Here, the Great War razed the last ramparts of feudalism with the sanction of the capitalist West, which since then has used precisely this bloc of anti-Bolshevik countries as a bulwark against Russia.

In keeping with my ideological position, I believe that the moment for attempting the liberal, individualist method in Peru has already passed. Aside from reasons of doctrine, I consider that our agrarian problem has a special character due to an indisputable and concrete factor: the survival of the Indian "community" and of elements of practical socialism in indigenous agriculture and life.

If those who hold a democratic-liberal doctrine are truly seeking a solution to the problem of the Indian that, above all, will free him from servitude, they can turn to the Czechoslovakian or Rumanian experience rather than the Mexican example, which they may find dangerous given its inspiration and process. For them it is still time to advocate a liberal formula. They would at least ensure that discussion of the agrarian problem by the new generation would not altogether lack the liberal philosophy that, according to written history, has governed the life of Peru since the foundation of the republic.

Colonialism-Feudalism

The problem of land sheds light on the socialist or vanguardist attitude toward the remains of the vice-royalty. Literary *perricholismo* does not interest us except as an indication or reflection of economic colonialism. The colonial heritage that we want to do away with is not really the one of romantic damsels screened from sight behind shawls or shutters, but the one of a feudal system with its *gamonalismo*, latifundium, and servitude. Colonial literature—nostalgic evocation of the viceroyalty and its pomp—is for me only the mediocre product of a spirit engendered and nourished by that regime. The viceroyality does not survive in the *perricholismo* of troubabdors and storytellers. It survives in a feudalism that contains the germs of an undeclared capitalism. We decry not only our Spanish but our feudal legacy.

Spain brought us the middle ages: The Inquisition, feudalism, et cetera. Later it brought us the Counter Reformation: a reactionary spirit, a Jesuit method, a scholastic casuistry. We have painfully rid ourselves of most of these afflictions by assimilating Western culture, sometimes obtained through Spain itself. But we are still burdened with their economic foundations embedded in the interests of a class whose hegemony was not destroyed by the War of Independence. The roots of feudalism are intact and they are responsible for the lag in our capitalist development.

The land tenure system determines the political and administrative system of the nation. The agrarian problem, which the republic has yet to solve, dominates all other problems. Democratic and liberal institutions cannot flourish or operate in a semi-feudal economy.

The subordination of the Indian problem to the problem of land is even more absolute, for special reasons. The Indigenous race is a race of farmers. The Inca people were peasants, normally engaged in agriculture and shepherding. The industries and arts were typically domestic and rural. The principle that life springs from the soil was truer in the Peru of the Incas than in any other country. The most notable public works and collective enterprises of Tawantinsuyo were for military, religious, or agricultural purposes. The irrigation canals of the sierra and the coast and the agricultural terraces of the Andes remain the best evidence of the degree of economic organization reached by Inca Peru. Its civilization was agrarian in all its important aspects. Valcárcel, in his study of the economic life of Tawantinsuyo, writes that "the land, in native tradition, is the common mother, from her womb come not only food but man himself. Land provides all wealth. The cult of Mama Pacha is in a part with the worship of the sun and, like the sun, Mother Earth represents no one in particular. Joined in the aboriginal ideology, these two concepts gave birth to agrarianism, which combines communal ownership of land and the universal religion of the sun."

Inca communism, which cannot be negated or disparaged for having developed under the autocratic regime of the Incas, is therefore designated as agrarian communism. The essential traits of the Inca economy, according to the careful definition of our historical process by César Ugarte, were the following:

Collective ownership of farmland by the ayllu or groups of related families, although the property was divided into individual and non-transferable lots; collective worship of waters, pasture, and woodlands by the marca or tribe, or the federation of ayllus settled around a village; cooperative labor; individual allotment of harvests and produce.

Colonization unquestionably must bear the responsibility for the disappearance of this economy, together with the culture it nourished, not because it destroyed autochthonous forms but because it brought no superior substitutes. The colonial regime disrupted and demolished the Inca agrarian economy without replacing it with an economy of higher yields. Under the indigenous aristocracy, the natives made up a nation of ten million men, with an integrated government that efficiently ruled all its territory; under a foreign aristocracy, the natives became a scattered and anarchic mass of a million men reduced to servitude and peonage.

In this respect, demographic data are the most convincing and decisive. Although the Inca regime may be censured in the name of modern liberal concepts of liberty and justice, the positive and material historical fact is that it assured the subsistence and growth of a population that came to ten million when the conquistadors arrived in Peru, and that this population after three centuries of Spanish domination had fallen to one million. Colonization stands condemned not from any abstract, theoretical, or moral standpoint of justice, but from the practical, concrete, and material standpoint of utility.

Colonization, failing to organize even a feudal economy in Peru, introduced elements of a slave economy.

For Further Reading

Belknap, Jeffrey and Raúl Fernández (eds.). *José Martí's "Our America": From National to Hemispheric Cultural Studies*. Durham, NC: Duke University Press, 1998.

Deutsch, Sandra McGee. *Counterrevolution in Argentina, 1900–1932: The Argentine Patriotic League*. Lincoln: University of Nebraska Press, 1986.

Deutsch, Sandra McGee and Ronald H. Dolkart (eds.). *The Argentine Right: Its History and Intellectual Origins, 1910 to the Present*. Wilmington: Scholarly Resources, 1993.

Farnsworth-Alvear, Ann. *Dulcinea in the Factory: Myths, Morals, Men, and Women in Colombia's Industrial Experiment, 1905–1960*. Durham, NC: Duke University Press, 2000.

Frías, Heriberto. *The Battle of Tomochic: Memoirs of a Second Lieutenant*. Oxford: Oxford University Press, 2006.

García Canclini, Néstor. *Hybrid Cultures: Strategies for Entering and Leaving Modernity*. Minneapolis: University of Minnesota Press, 1995.

Guy, Donna. *Sex and Danger in Buenos Aires: Prostitution, Family, and Nation in Argentina*. Lincoln: University of Nebraska Press, 1991.

Katz, Friedrich. *The Life and Times of Pancho Villa*. Palo Alto: Stanford University Press, 1998.

Klubock, Thomas. *Contested Communities: Class, Gender, and Politics in Chile's El Teniente Copper Mine, 1904–1951*. Durham, NC: Duke University Press, 1998.

Knight, Alan. *The Mexican Revolution* (2 vols.). Cambridge: Cambridge University Press, 1986.

Levine, Robert M. *Vale of Tears: Revisiting the Canudos Massacre in Northeastern Brazil, 1893–1897*. Berkeley: University of California Press, 1995.

Martí, José. *Selected Writings*. New York: Penguin Classics, 2002.

Piccato, Pablo. *City of Suspects: Crime in Mexico City, 1900–1931*. Durham, NC: Duke University Press, 2001.

Rock, David. *Authoritarian Argentina: The Nationalist Movement, Its History and Its Impact*. Berkeley: University of California Press, 1995.

Rodó, José Enrique. *Ariel*. Teddington, England: Echo Library, 2008.

Sabato, Hilda. *The Many and the Few: Political Participation in Republican Buenos Aires*. Palo Alto: Stanford University Press, 2001.

Vargas Llosa, Mario. *The War to the End of the World*. New York: Picador, 2008.

Womack, John. *Zapata and the Mexican Revolution*. New York: Vintage, 1970.

1845	1847–48	1853	1867	1898	1899
Texas is annexed by the United States	In war with Mexico, United States acquires territories of Alta California and Santa Fé de Nuevo México	In Gadsden purchase, United States acquires parts of New Mexico and Arizona from Mexico	United States purchases Alaska	Spanish–American War	Founding of United Fruit Company

1927	1934	1950	1954
Augusto Sandino releases his political manifesto	Sandino is killed by elements of the Nicaraguan National Guard, led by Anastasio Somoza García	Jacobo Arbenz elected President of Guatemala	Guatemalan exiles overthrow Arbenz with CIA aid

Commerce, Coercion, and America's Empire

6

"It's down that way, by the white man, who make the chicken."

Getting directions on a Kingston street one May afternoon, I was reminded of what a complicated task it is to render the history of the United States in the wider world. The white man, it turned out, was Colonel Sanders, such a ever-present image in North America that today he registers simply as the cartoon icon of a fast food empire, and neither "white," nor a "man." Yet in this conversation he was both of those things, with a slight twist. Whereas in other settings he is a powerful symbol of American capitalism, here this was not so important. He was instead a curiosity, odd enough that amidst all the landmarks on a busy street, his face was the one that stood out. Who ever heard of a white man who cooked chicken?

To be sure, we cannot be certain why Colonel Sanders was rendered simply as the "white man, who make the chicken." Indeed, we cannot know whether the comment referred to his skin, his hair, his clothes, or all three, but this indeterminacy is exactly the point. The American[1] presence in Latin America is often represented in simple terms, as a violent oppressor or noble savior. These images serve immediate political interests but offer little access to what lies beneath. The United States has been a violent and often unwelcome presence in Latin America. The United States has also been an appreciated source of aid and investment, and the source of many of the mass cultural phenomena that shaped the region during the course of the twentieth century. Unlike the European empires of a bygone era, which were formal administrative systems founded on political, economic, and social control, the magic of the American Empire lay in the ways it was a relatively voluntary association, rooted in a burgeoning international mass market. The United States provided desirable objects (comestibles, modern conveniences, music, films, and television) and though they often came with asymmetrical power arrangements attached, the bargain inherent in U.S. global domination was not one sided. Recalling Colonel Sanders, we could say that just as the United States consumed the region, gobbling up its resources, land, and even its people, so too did Latin Americans consume the United States during the twentieth century. This was the driving logic of what historians came to called the American Century.

Here we will focus principally on American influence in Latin America in the decades prior to 1959, leaving later U.S. engagements in the region for other chapters. The temporal choice is an obvious one, marked by the fairly sudden change in U.S. attitudes towards Latin America that came with the Cuban Revolution, Fidel Castro's turn to the Soviet Bloc, and the sense after 1959 that political developments in Latin America truly could threaten U.S. security and prosperity. Before the Cuban revolution North Americans often saw threats coming from the South, but American hegemony (that is, the domination of one place by another) was a more nuanced phenomenon, driven more by commercial interests than hysteria. It was, if you will, the halcyon days of American imperialism, when one could imagine that in spite of Great White Fleets and American Expeditionary Forces, U.S. influence brought with it a great deal of good. In a nutshell, the United States promised to make Latin America modern.

Empire?

We encounter our first problem with the term itself. Formal empires were the stuff that made Europe modern. They were systems that linked ideological domination (often through Christian evangelism), physical domination (the mighty European military machines of the sixteenth to twentieth centuries), and economic control in formal imperial systems, governed from European capitals. Until the mid-twentieth century it was common for members of the European aristocracy to simply assume that they came to dominate the globe through their wit and ingenuity, but there has long been a counter-argument, articulated most beautifully by the Trinidadian historian Eric Williams, that Europe grew rich through the toil of slaves, that European domination of the planet was simply a system of brutal inequality that made Europe wealthy, and their colonies poor.[2]

Recent generations of scholars have modified Williams' thesis, demonstrating that colonial systems were complex terrains in which dominated peoples often had a certain amount of room to maneuver. Nonetheless, outside of Europe, where longings for empire can still be seen, the term is generally a dirty word. Nowhere is this more evident than in the United States, a nation forged through anti-imperial struggle, where the principles of freedom and self-determination are inextricably woven into what it is to be American. And yet while a strictly anti-imperial rhetoric has served certain ideological purposes within the United States, it has never easily translated into the practice of foreign policy. Since the very beginning the United States has been an expansionist nation, at times by acquiring territory, and at others by using American military and economic power to defend specific interests. Whether or not we call this imperialism is more a matter of political leanings than fact.

American expansion has taken a number of different forms, beginning even at the dawn of the nineteenth century. Following their own historical precedents, in the early years of the century settlers from the east gradually encroached on both indigenous lands and lands claimed by other European empires, moving into the Ohio Valley and Mississippi Basin, Florida, Louisiana, and other regions to the west. During the first half of the century the United States was a generally prosperous, stable society, with an expanding population. Farm-children from the east needed land to work, and it makes some sense that American expansion either came at the expense of increasingly weak European empires or nation states that were in the midst of fratricidal struggles and economic decline. North Americans fought two separate wars with Mexico, the first over Texas in 1836 (which was not technically a war with the United States) and the Mexican–American War in 1847–8. Several years later U.S. President Franklin Pierce bought a slice of territory from Mexican President Antonio López de Santa Anna (the Gadsden Purchase), bringing an end to the latter's iconic career. Alaska was purchased from the Russians in 1867.

From the South these wars were seen as acts of imperial aggression. From the North they were not. They were acts of *manifest destiny*, material reminders that God had given to the United States the responsibility of ruling North America. Moreover, these conquered territories did not become colonies. They were gradually incorporated into the United States, their residents newly minted as citizens of the United States (with all the explicit racial and gendered caveats of the day).

These acts stand in stark contrast to American expansion elsewhere. The easiest way to understand this is in racial terms. The American West, imagined as empty land, was incorporated into the political territory of the United States as a land that would, when peopled, be white. Americans viewed other regions—Mexico, Central America, and the Caribbean in particular—more skeptically, as poor racial candidates for incorporation into the United States. In a country whose self-image was anti-imperialist, there was not enough political will to colonize these places, yet they had the raw materials American factories needed, were ideal markets for American exports, and were the jumping off points for American aspirations to global military power.

Two major military conflicts at the turn of the twentieth century signaled the moment when U.S. military power and colonial aspirations coincided. The first was the Spanish–American war. The pretexts for the war (the protection of American lives, retaliation for the sinking of the *Maine*), were quickly overshadowed when, in the aftermath of a quick defeat of Spanish forces in Cuba, Puerto Rico, and the Philippines, the price the U.S. government demanded for peace was the transfer of the remaining fragments of the Spanish Empire to American control. In the Philippines this meant the United States would be the military overlord, reserve the right to dominate the islands politically and economically. In Puerto Rico it meant a quasi-colonial status under which islanders would receive U.S. citizenship in 1917. In Cuba, it meant the Platt Amendment, which gave the United States the right to meddle in the internal affairs of the island, to control its foreign policy, and the right to maintain a military base on the island (Guantánamo Bay). American forces did not depart the Island until the Platt Amendment was incorporated into the 1902 Cuban constitution, and it remained the law of the land until it was abrogated in 1934 (see the Platt Amendment on the website).

The second military conflict that signaled U.S. ascendance was the brief War for Panamanian independence in 1903. After the acquisition of California in 1848, American businessmen and filibusterers spent decades embroiled in the internal affairs of several Central American countries (particularly Nicaragua), trying to construct a canal across the isthmus that would allow the U.S. Navy and merchant ships to easily move from the Atlantic to Pacific coasts of the country, with no success. Panama, which probably had the best geography for a canal, was not a viable option because the French Panama Canal Company had already signed a contract with the Colombian government, and there was simply no way the Americans could have taken on both the French and the Colombians. Still, the construction of a canal across the isthmus was a gargantuan task, and after thousands of deaths, immense technical problems, scandals and bankruptcy, the Panama Canal Company abandoned the project in 1893. When the U.S. government offered to take over the project and Bogotá refused to agree to the terms offered, President Roosevelt threw his support to a group of conservative landowners who had long supported Panamanian independence from Colombia. After a short conflict Panamanian independence was won.

Roosevelt then undertook negotiations with the Panamanian Ambassador to the United States, the French engineer and canal booster, Phillipe-Jean Bunau Varilla. The resulting agreement (the Hay-Bunau Varilla Treaty) gave the United States rights to a Canal Zone that extended five miles on either side of the proposed canal in perpetuity, in return for an initial payment of $10 million and annual rent of $250,000. Work was resumed on the canal in 1904, and the 48-mile-long Canal was completed in 1914.

The cost of the project was enormous, measured both in dollars and human lives. The U.S. government spent a total of $375 million to build the canal, and at times employed nearly 50,000 workers in the construction process, most of whom came from a variety of islands in the Caribbean. More than 27,500 people died in the construction process, though only 5,609 of them died during the ten-year period during which the United States government oversaw construction.

That the United States saw many fewer deaths in spite of the fact that the majority of the work on the canal was undertaken after 1904 was a testament to the complex ways in which modernization and American power were linked. Most of those who died during the building of the canal were either victims of yellow fever or malaria. These diseases had long been endemic to the Caribbean, taking thousands of lives annually. These tropical maladies limited the capacity of European powers to rule outside of temperate zones, killing soldiers and administrators indiscriminately, and crippling colonial armies (the French faced enormous challenges in trying to control Mexico during the 1860s in part because of their high casualty rate due to yellow fever). Locals who survived their bouts with yellow fever emerged with some immunity, but even they suffered repeatedly at the hands of malaria. Most doctors believed that human contact spread these diseases, and tried to isolate patients in hospitals.

In 1881 the Cuban doctor and etymologist Carlos Finley discovered that the vector for yellow fever was the Stegomyia Fasciata mosquito, an insect that could be found abundantly in the cisterns, sewage canals, cesspools, and other sources of open water that surrounded urban areas. Perhaps because Finlay was a colonial subject, his discovery gained almost no attention, but when the U.S. army started suffering considerable casualties from yellow fever in Cuba, Major Walter Reed, a doctor in the U.S. army, was sent to investigate. He came across Finlay's findings, tested them, and concluded that mosquitoes were indeed the cause of the malady. Reed recommended a series of measures that were carried out immediately in Havana. The incidence of yellow fever in the city fell from 1,400 in 1900 to 37 in 1901.

The new measures to combat yellow fever, which included putting screens on dwellings, fumigating houses, providing running water, building sewer systems, and putting oil or kerosene in all sources of standing water, had a dramatic impact on the canal project. The last case of yellow fever in Panama was reported in 1905. Later efforts, which included reducing vegetation near work and housing, draining swamps and building ditches, and even introducing larvae-eating minnows to the water supply, also reduced malaria in the canal zone.

We could then claim that science, as applied by the U.S. government in this era, saved thousands of lives in the Caribbean. Those lives were in turn placed in the service of the American project. At first that project was mostly commercial. As a growing industrial power, the United States needed raw materials from Latin America in order to protect their growing industrial economy. Within a few decades American industrialists would also look to Latin Americans as potential consumers of their products. Later the same logic would be extended to include the concept of national security. The United States would not be safe as long as hostile states existed in the region. In all cases, while the rhetoric of freedom, democracy, and self-determination remained crucial to the American self-image, in practice these ideals were made secondary to more practical needs.

Table 6.1 provides a stark example of the implications of U.S. domination in the Americas. While the formal apparatuses of imperialism were for the most part never created (with the notable exceptions of Puerto Rico, Guantanamo Bay, and Panama), the region saw dozens of military interventions by U.S. forces in the years after the Spanish–American War. Always explained as necessary to defend U.S. lives and property, these interventions created a permanent U.S. military presence in the region, either through ongoing occupations or through the threat of future invasions. Unlike formal empires, American officials foresaw an end to each occupation, and were invariably committed to training U.S.-friendly security forces that would permit their withdrawal. Like formal empires, U.S. occupations sometimes lasted for decades, creating a sense of their own permanence.

The sheer number of these interventions suggests an American military with vast reach and aspirations. Close scrutiny reveals something else. For the most part United States interventions in Latin America during the early twentieth century were limited to the relatively small nations of the Caribbean. When the United States took on larger nations the results were not always favorable. General John Pershing's "Punitive Expedition" in Mexico (March 1916 to February 1917) was a case in point. Sent across the border to capture Pancho Villa, who had the temerity to attack Columbus, New Mexico, the expedition returned home demoralized, its objectives unmet. The U.S. government did not even seriously contemplate military intervention in most of Mexico's large South American neighbors during these decades.

It was instead in the small countries of the Caribbean and Central America where American officials could flex their military muscles in the support of U.S. foreign policy.

Table 6.1 U.S. Military interventions in Latin America, 1898–1959

Country	Date
Cuba	1898–1902
Puerto Rico	1898–
Nicaragua	1898
Nicaragua	1899
Honduras	1903
Dominican Republic	1903–4
Cuba	1906–9
Nicaragua	1907
Honduras	1907
Panama	1908
Nicaragua	1910
Honduras	1911
Cuba	1912
Panama	1912
Honduras	1912
Nicaragua	1912–33
Mexico	1913
Dominican Republic	1914
Mexico	1914–18
Haiti	1914–34
Dominican Republic	1916–24
Cuba	1917–33
Panama	1918–20
Honduras	1919
Guatemala	1920
Costa Rica	1921
Panama	1925
El Salvador	1932
Uruguay	1947
Puerto Rico	1950
Guatemala	1954
Panama	1958

Source: Marc Becker, www2.truman.edu/~marc/resources/interventions.html

Increasingly these nations depended on U.S. markets for their exports, and elites in these societies relied on U.S. aid and periodic military interventions to deal with their rivals. American investors in these countries often looked to the United States when their interests were threatened, but so too did many in the struggling middle classes or landed elites. American military power was a useful tool in their struggles against workers, peasants, and leftists, and it was not uncommon for these conservative interests to align with foreign investors in demanding U.S. intervention in the name of protecting lives, property, and order.

Bananas Are Our Business

There are very few commodities that explain American interests in Central America and the Caribbean as powerfully as the banana, a fruit that is infertile, highly vulnerable to disease, and delicious. North Americans were first introduced to bananas in 1870, and quickly took to them. By 1914 almost every American household could afford bananas, at least once in a while, and consumers in the United States purchased 45 million bunches per year. Bananas would not grow in the United States, but were easily cultivated in Central America, drawing more North American capital to a region already coveted for its sugar, coffee, and potential for a canal.

In 1899 a group of North American plantation and railroad entrepreneurs created the United Fruit Company (UFCO) in order to dominate this emerging business. At its founding it became the largest banana company in the world, with plantations in Colombia, Costa Rica, Cuba, Jamaica, Nicaragua, Panama, and the Dominican Republic. The company had a fleet of ships (41 by 1912) that conveyed a booming two-way trade. Bananas came north, and construction materials and merchandise traveled south. They also controlled hundreds of miles of railroad in the Caribbean, employed tens of thousands of workers, and operated stores, schools, hospitals, radio stations, breweries, banks, and hotels.

The UFCO was a model for the modern, vertically integrated corporation. Bananas were grown on UFCO plantations and transported on roadways and railroads it built and owned to its own ports (UFCO essentially owned Puerto Barrios in Guatemala). The UFCO's Great White Fleet would then transport the bananas to the United States, where they would ripen artificially in UFCO owned warehouses before distribution to wholesalers and supermarkets. This system gave the UFCO a degree of market domination that, over time, allowed the company to eliminate smaller producers in most places, and act as the principal employer in large parts of Central America, the Caribbean, and Colombia. While most scholars today reject the idea that the UFCO controlled enclaves (geographically, economically, and socially cut off from other parts of the country), its presence in some regions was overwhelming.

The unique characteristics of the banana facilitated this type of integration. Bananas are descended from a plant that many thousands of years ago grew wild in Oceania, but spread slowly across Asia and into Africa by the beginning of the Common Era (AD). Over many generations banana growers tinkered with the plant's characteristics, turning a rather bitter fruit that was difficult to eat into the fruit we know today. Genetic modifications ultimately produced a fruit with a tough exterior that protects the inner fruit, and which needs to be cultivated because it cannot regenerate naturally. Modern bananas do not ripen on the branch, which means that they require human intervention in order to be palatable.

The Gros Michel, the most important banana of the early twentieth century, could withstand schooner travel because it grew in very large bunches that did not protrude outwards, and ripened very slowly, meaning that significant quantities of product could be transported to North American markets without spoiling. The Gros Michel's principal drawback was that it was susceptible to Panama disease, which could easily wipe out entire plantations (a problem that became more acute after most production was turned over to this variety). Because of this the UFCO and its competitors claimed that they required millions of acres of potential plantation tracts, lands that could be colonized in the event of blight at existing plantations.[3]

Beyond tending to existing plants, banana workers had to constantly clear new land, exposing themselves to malaria and other tropical illnesses. Indeed, work in the banana business was arduous. Cultivation, processing, and harvesting required a constant influx of migrant labor, workers who moved along labor circuits in the Caribbean by the tens of thousands. Living in company housing, workers earned meager wages, were often away from their families for months or years at a time, and often found themselves in communities where they did not speak the local language. The standard markers of these types of communities—alcohol abuse, prostitution, and violence—were common to banana zones, in spite of occasional company efforts to produce stable and salubrious communities.

These conditions lent themselves to charges that the UFCO was an agent of imperialism, probably no more powerfully than in Guatemala. Thanks to a close relationship between oligarchical interests in Guatemala and the UFCO, the company became perhaps *the* dominant actor in the country virtually from its creation. In 1901 Guatemalan President Manuel Estrada Cabrera gave the UFCO a monopoly over the country's banana business. It could have seemed like a reasonable decision. The monopoly made Guatemala one of the most important components of the UFCO's empire, and promised to turn hitherto unproductive lands (at least in the eyes of the state, if not those of the peasants who occupied those lands) into sources of national wealth. Export agriculture produced fortunes and brought a certain kind of economic development, and in return the UFCO was allowed a veto power over any legislation or government initiatives that might prejudice the company's interests.

Guatemalans responded in a variety of ways to these circumstances. Workers for the UFCO sometimes chafed at their conditions and pay, but were often deeply aware that the opportunities afforded by the UFCO were better than those from any other employer. For some in the middle class and elites, the benefits bestowed on the country through its association with the UFCO seemed substantial enough to outweigh the costs. Material wealth, public services and infrastructure spawned by the UFCO seemed to promise a future that was better than the past. Others took a more cynical view, recognizing that the UFCO acted only in its own interest, but taking advantage of the only game in town. Still others however, viewed the total domination of Guatemalan society by a single foreign company and industry with distaste, chafing at the loss of national sovereignty and deep inequalities that characterized their country under the UFCO. The Guatemalan government, like other Caribbean *banana republics*, was beholden to the UFCO, repressive, and anti-democratic. Here as elsewhere, even in the 1920s a new generation of guerrillas, political activists, and intellectuals found their voice in calling for radical change.[4]

In the Guatemalan case, the first leader to truly challenge UFCO/U.S. hegemony was Jacobo Arbenz Guzmán. In 1944, as a relatively junior officer teaching at the Guatemalan Military Academy, he participated in the conspiracy that brought down the dictatorship of Jorge Ubico. He then became a minister in the government of Juan José Arévalo (president, 1944–1950) before running for president in 1950. Looking on their country, the revolutionaries of 1944 saw a profoundly unequal society. Two percent of the population owned 72 percent of agricultural land. Rural poverty was extreme, and getting worse as coffee and banana cultivation spread.

Arévalo and later Arbenz faced a difficult task in reversing these tendencies. As committed democrats, nationalists, and reformers, both were viewed with suspicion by the UFCO, which had cultivated close relationships with Ubico and earlier presidents in order to secure its interests. And by any measure, these interests were vast. The company was the largest landowner in the country (the UFCO owned 42 percent of the land). It owned the nation's railroad system, along with the utility that provided electricity to the Capital. Though the largest business in the country, the UFCO paid almost no taxes or duties to the government. The company not only had the power to paralyze the national economy, transportation, and power grids, it could also count on the support of the U.S. government in defending its interest.

Arévalo maintained cordial, if strained, relations with the United States, largely because he avoided direct confrontations with the UFCO. Arbenz however, took a different path. Elected in with 65 percent of the popular vote in 1950, he enacted important reforms almost immediately. Within months of coming to office he legalized the Communist Party, and threatened to expropriate the UFCO's railroads (International Railroads of Central America—IRCA). In response, the U.S. government threatened trade sanctions, and ramped up a propaganda war depicting Arbenz as threat to American national security. It seemed likely that U.S. pressure would quickly force Arbenz to backtrack, because at the time 85 percent of Guatemala's foreign trade was with the United States. Sanctions could rapidly cripple the country.

Arbenz did not back down. Instead, in 1952 he undertook his most radical steps, introducing an Agrarian Reform Law called Plan 900. The law allowed the government to expropriate unused land from large estates and redistribute it to peasants. Landowners would be compensated with 25 year bonds that paid 3 percent interest, and compensation would be based on the value of the land as assessed in 1952 tax declarations.[5] It was a bold maneuver, aimed at creating a new political base for leftist reforms, and shifting at least some production away from export commodities and towards staple crops.

The government made some new allies through the Plan 900, but it also made many powerful enemies. Not just the UFCO, which lost 234,000 acres, but Guatemalan elites, conservatives, and those whose livelihoods were tied to banana exports opposed what they viewed as a communist agenda. Moreover, the UFCO, which in 1952 cultivated only 139,000 acres of its 3 million acres in holdings in the country, vigorously rejected the $1 million in compensation offered for their lands. Knowing full well that the company vastly understated the value of its lands in its tax filings, Arbenz essentially used the UFCO's own books against it in making this offer.

The UFCO adopted multiple strategies to fight expropriation. First, they insisted that if they were to lose the land they should receive at least $16 million, as that was the fair value of the land. They also argued that the nature of banana cultivation should leave them exempt from seizure, because the ever- present threat of Panama disease meant that they might have to abandon their current plantations at any time. Without their reserves, they could be forced out of business, and this would be disastrous for everyone.

The company also launched a propaganda campaign against the government. Company spokesmen in the United States warned the American public of the threat emerging in Guatemala. Working in concert with their supporters in the Eisenhower administration, company officials publicly labeled Arbenz a communist, evoking images of the Soviet Union gaining a foothold in America's backyard. This label was a particularly powerful descriptor in the United States at the time, which was in the midst of a series of waves of anti-Communist hysteria, fed by fears of nuclear war (Stalin exploded an atom bomb in 1949), the Maoist revolution in China, and the ever present fear of a fifth element inside the United States that was committed to destroying the American way of life (Joseph McCarthy reached the height of his influence between 1950 and 1954). It was still early in the cold war, and millions of Americans genuinely believed that the dominoes were falling in their direction.[6] Naturally, it did not hurt that two key administration figures, Secretary of State John Foster Dulles and CIA director Allen Dulles, had close ties to the UFCO.[7]

The greatest risk, of course, was that Arbenz might succeed in both improving the standard of living in the countryside and building sufficient support to allow his regime to both withstand U.S. pressures and serve as a beacon to other reformers in the region. This was, in the end, what made the domino theory compelling logic. Americans were not so much motivated by the fear that communism was an expansive form of totalitarianism, as they were by a fear that successful reforms in Guatemala might offer a model for reform in other deeply unequal societies. If Guatemalans managed to turn the UFCO's lands into prosperous peasant farms, what about Nicaragua, Honduras, Cuba, and Mexico? If these countries followed suit, American interests in Latin America would truly be imperiled.

In order to stave off this disaster U.S. officials began plotting the overthrow of Arbenz as early as 1952. The CIA played a particularly important role in the plans, establishing training camps for a rebel invasion on UFCO owned lands in Honduras. When, in May 1954 U.S. officials learned that Arbenz had begun to import weapons from the Soviet bloc, the CIA sprang into action with Operation PBSUCCESS. On June 17 a small rebel force under the command of Colonel Carlos Castillo Armas invaded the country, relying on arms, intelligence, aircraft, and an information blitz (radio broadcasts, overstating the size and power of the rebels, phone calls threatening enemies with death, etc.) provided by the CIA. Without suffering a major defeat, on June 25 the army abandoned Arbenz. He resigned and fled to Mexico two days later.[8]

If ever there was a case for arguing that a specific result was over-determined, Arbenz' fall is clearly that. Close business ties between UFCO and the administration, genuine CIA fears of growing Soviet influence, anxiety about the potential a success of socialist reforms, and the U.S. government's inability to distinguish nationalism from communism all worked against Arbenz. He was popular, to be sure, but this alone could not guarantee his survival.

Arbenz may have mistaken popular support for strength. In Latin America political leaders with strong regional bases, support from the military, and connections to the outside have historically been better positioned than those who are simply popular in the broad sense. This is especially true for reformist regimes, and in particular those that position themselves as representatives of marginalized groups. Arbenz was a well-loved president, but he faced powerful enemies in the UFCO and its supporters (middle level managers, businessmen who profited from their connections to the company, anti-communists, and large portions of the military). Any democratic reformer would be hard pressed to prevail against such an array of adversaries.

Cultures of Consumption

American military power has a naked quality to it. The explicit use of violence to defend a specific vision of order—order that benefits American interests—does not sustain a great variety of interpretations. The UFCO, working with the CIA, orchestrated the overthrow of Jacobo Arbenz and the installment of a friendly government in June 1954. These are facts that describe a series of events that took place over several days. They do not, however, describe what we might call the everyday quality of the American presence in Latin America during the twentieth century. Every day millions of people in the region went to work for companies that were based in or did business with the United States. Millions more purchased products, heard sounds, saw images, or felt desires that linked them to their northern neighbor.

For the remainder of this chapter we turn away from the story of military and economic domination and towards the more ambiguous but no less important story of the cultural flows that shaped both Latin America and the United States during the early twentieth century. In the South the United States generated contradictory feelings and sensibilities. It was the home of the tourists who came to your cities, ruins, and beaches and acted in sometimes boorish and disrespectful ways, but left their money behind. It was the country of cold Anglo-Saxons, hard-hearted but rational people who had become rich because they lacked the passions and *joie de vivre* of their southern neighbors. It was a land of little culture, but much wealth, a land where diversity (indigenous peoples, Africans) was crushed instead of embraced. More than all this though, it was the land of the future, of new things, freshly unwrapped cellophane. It was a land of industrial invention, the best, largest, and fastest cars, trains, airplanes, and ships. It was the land of unimagined scientific innovation, of great cities, of new food and drink, possessed of properties never before imagined. And it was the land of glamorous movie stars, people so beautiful and wealthy that it was difficult to watch them without feeling desire to be them, to be like them, or be with them.

During the twentieth century American products, along with the aura of progress and wealth that they embodied, circulated across Latin America. Jazz, baseball, Coca-Cola, and movie stars were among the early American icons in the region,[9] to be later supplemented by radio, television, and fast-food. Though objects of mass production and intended for a mass market, they were anything but one-size-fits-all impositions on a foreign consumer. American products that found markets did so by marrying what was appealing with the foreign (its newness, its association with wealth and modernity) to what was appealing in the local (specific and often long-standing tastes and desires).

This goal was accomplished by making American products through local partnerships, and modifying them slightly to suit local tastes. Brands as varied as Budweiser, Coca-Cola, and Elvis Presley were recast to represent amalgams of North American modernity and specific Latin American sensibilities. In each instance foreign interests needed to find the right mixture, which they often did by manufacturing products locally and linking them to distinct regional symbols, while retaining the qualities in their products that made them more desirable, more modern. Take the advertisement reproduced as Figure 6.1, selling cigarettes made by the British American Tobacco Company, which was one of a series that appeared in the Mexico City newspaper *El Universal* in late December 1949.[10]

The advertisement links a number of powerful images—the cigarette with the foreign name, the ubiquitous *Hecho in Mexico* symbol, the chocolate of the ancient Aztecs, and industrialization—and is accompanied by the following text:

> As an authentically Mexican product, our original "chocotl-atl" has been a globally
> important source of nutrition for centuries. And when it comes to satisfying the

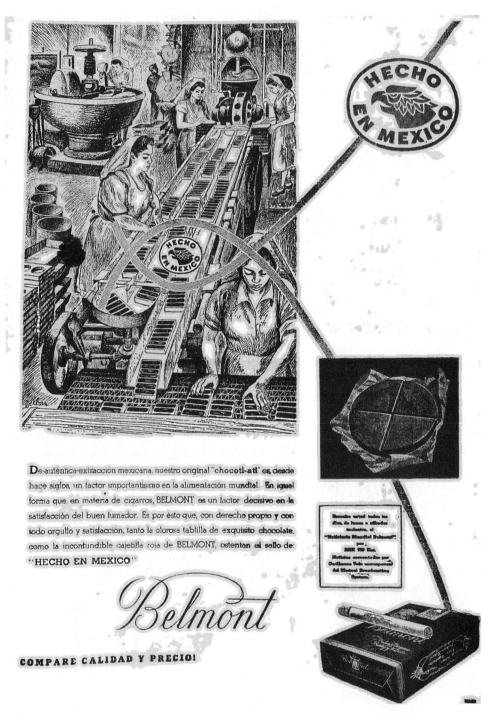

Figure 6.1 Belmont Cigarettes magazine ad

Source: *El Universal*, December 22, 1949

intelligent smoker, Belmont does the same for cigarettes. That is why, just as with the sweet smelling tablet of exquisite chocolate, we take great pride and satisfaction in our right to imprint the unmistakable red BELMONT package with the *"Made in Mexico"* seal.

We see here the complex alchemy of the foreign and the national that lay at the core of the new American empires. A British–American cigarette was appealing in part because it was a foreign cigarette. To smoke it was to show that you could afford something more expensive, classy. Like chocolate it was also part of both the particular national past and the universal industrial present. And like other advertisements in the series, which linked Belmont to the Mexican film industry, Mexican ceramics, and the revolutionary muralists, the advert ties Belmont to the deep past, the industrial workers who produced both chocolate and cigarettes, and a series of icons of Mexican revolutionary nationalism. If the muralists (perhaps even Diego Rivera?) smoked Belmonts, why shouldn't you?

Cartoon Figures

Such were the complexities of the cultural flows that characterized the early decades of the American century. Objects—a cigarette, a drink, a movie star—acquired complex meanings within a series of asymmetrical exchanges. And interestingly, no object was more ambiguously woven into these exchanges than the commodity with which we began this story, the banana. Bananas have for more than a century signaled the tropical essence of their place of origin. Even today, when we peel the label off our Chiquita banana (for the record, it is now a Cavendish and not a Gros Michel), we come face to face with the image of Carmen Miranda. In our memory she is a sultry Latin belle, sexually inviting, colorfully dressed, her head adorned with tropical fruit (Figure 6.2).

Stereotypes are funny things. They can silence and marginalize individuals and groups, but they can also be quite useful, even to those who are stereotyped. On an individual level, they create a language that can sometimes be used to the personal benefit of the stereotyped. On a group level, they provide symbols that people may rally around in order to feel a sense of belonging. Even more, they can be comical signs of that group identity, points of departure for laughter as the collective chortles, "oh, that is us." Bananas and banana culture formed a part of this for tropical Latin Americans. The banana was a symbol (however skewed) of a tropical culture that stood as an alternative to the alienated industrial lifestyles of the North. Banana cultures were typified by sensuous women, men who played romantic tunes on their guitars, people who drank strong drink on their verandas, overlooking verdant palm forests, white-sand beaches, and clear blue waters. This was the image that Miranda parleyed to fame first in Brazil, then elsewhere.

Miranda became a Brazilian icon as a samba star in that country's developing film industry, beginning with the documentary *A Voz Do Carnaval* in 1933, and the feature film *Alo, Alo, Brazil* in 1935. Truly an amalgam, this Portuguese-born woman gained fame by appropriating the dress and music of the Afro-Brazilian *favela* (slum). Tellingly, the more Miranda became an international star, the more she faced scorn in her own country as a sell-out. Featured in a number of hit films, including *Down Argentine Way* (1940), *That Night in Rio*

Figure 6.2   Photograph of Carmen Miranda
Source: © Hulton-Deutsch Collection/CORBIS

(1941), and *The Gang's All Here* (1943), after the late 1930s Miranda increasingly focused her career in Hollywood instead of Brazil, providing Brazilians both with a sense of pride (she did, after all make it), but also with a reminder that the United States had the capacity to lure away their most powerful stars, in effect to consume not just Brazilian music, but Brazilians themselves. Brazilians, like other Latin Americans, have a long tradition of feeling a mixture of pride and betrayal when they see their brightest stars leave for another stage. It is a reminder that individually they are as good as anyone, but that collectively they are second-class.

Bitterness over her international stardom was complicated by the fact that others in Brazil continued to benefit from her fame even after she left. Brazilian musicians and singers developed international audiences. The samba grew more popular as a national art form in Brazil. American tourists were drawn both to Rio de Janeiro and to other tropical paradises in search of the mystique she embodied. Drawn to the romance of the Carioca, American filmmakers started to feature Brazil as early as 1933, when Thornton Freelan made *Flying Down to Rio.*

Freelan's film starred the Mexican actress Dolores del Río as the Brazilian beauty Belinha de Rezende, reminding Latin American audiences that in the eyes of the North, the sultry women of one Latin American country could be easily substituted for those of another. Indeed, interchangeability even played a part in Carmen Miranda's story. When asked, many Americans of a certain age remember that Miranda starred in a Disney cartoon, *The Three Caballeros,* released during 1945.[11] In fact it was not her, but her sister Aurora, who starred in the film that introduced a generation of Americans to the South.

It may be somehow fitting that one of the most enduring symbols we have of the United States presence in Latin America during the first half of the twentieth century is a Disney cartoon. Perhaps more than any other company, Disney created products that were simultaneously globally popular, and indisputably associated with the United States (we leave aside the German origins of many Disney images). *The Three Caballeros,* along with 1943's *Saludos Amigos*[12], captured a great deal of what was at stake in the emergence of the United States as a global power during the twentieth century. The films were made by Walt Disney after he agreed to a request by the Coordinator of Inter-American Affairs at the U.S. State Department to conduct a goodwill tour of Latin America. These tours were attempts by the U.S. government and industry to build friendly and supportive relationships with their Latin American neighbors—relationships that would favor both commerce and security. In the films that came out of these experiences we see both Disney animators and Disney characters traveling to Latin America, only to become entranced by the cultures, geography, and mysteries of the region.

Reading these films is not as easy as it may seem. The cultural critic could easily jump on the gendered and racializing practices in the texts. Latin America becomes exotic, sexually inviting, as Donald Duck, the American tourist, is taken on a wild ride by the gun toting Mexican Panchito Pistoles, and the sophisticated but androgynous Carioca Joe. Donald falls head over heels for Aurora Miranda, induced into a hallucinogenic stupor by her beauty (or perhaps, somebody put something in his drink?). Elsewhere in these films the Argentine gaucho is represented by Goofy (arguably a racial stereotype, but at the very least one that inspires little awe in the gaucho's manliness), and the Andes become a frightening, mystical place, cut off from western civilization, and best avoided through the modern wonder of the airplane (in this case, little Pedro).

American audiences laughed, no doubt enjoyed the Disney movies for their humor, the music, the aesthetically pleasing quality of the cartoons, and probably the stereotypes (was goofy not like some version of the Appalachian hick?). But then, it appears that Latin American audiences loved the movies as well, as both movies were quite successfully released in Latin America. Indeed, both films debuted in Latin America before being released in the United States.

How do we explain this? We begin by remembering that even when two different audiences enjoy a film, the meanings they take away from that film can be quite different. Would Latin Americans have laughed at the bumbling fool Donald, easily tricked by his Latin American hosts, always lost, never quite at ease in a foreign land? Would they have been comforted by the fact that Joe and Panchito were much more in charge, much more in command of their faculties, than Donald? Would they have enjoyed the pleasing quality of the cartoons, and laughed at the stereotypes of themselves in the films because, after all, a cartoon by its very nature is a caricature, and these ones were funny? Given their own tendency to view the countryside as racially inferior, would urban modern Argentines have even recognized their own stereotypes of the *gaucho* in Goofy? Would they have been happy to see beautiful images of their modern cities in the films, images that contrasted with the ways Americans often represented their homes? Did they like the films simply because Donald was already a huge draw for Latin American audiences? We do not know.

What we do know is that these films, like Carmen Miranda, like the banana, formed parts of the terrain on which United States–Latin American relations were negotiated during the twentieth century. Even after U.S. attitudes hardened during the cold war (and especially after the 1959 Cuban revolution), the American presence in Latin America and the Latin American presence in the United States were framed as much by the market—each consuming the other—as they were by the simple imperatives of military and economic might. We ought not lose the significance of this fact in the face of otherwise overwhelming images of violent acts carried out in the name of U.S. domination, because the market gave the United States a far greater reach than its military ever could.

The Documents: Contesting Hegemony

No single text can convey the complexity of the American presence in Latin America. Because of that, below we have a selection of four different documents, each of which narrates a small part of that history. Our first is a fairly traditional text, the manifesto composed by guerrilla leader Augusto Sandino (1895–1934) in 1927 as he confronted the most visible sign of U.S. hegemony, the Marines. Political strife was commonplace in Nicaragua at the time. Groups denoted by the labels "Liberal" and "Conservative" continually clashed under the watchful eye of the U.S. government, which in turn used these conflicts to press its own advantage. Sandino was an unusual figure in these struggles, because his experience of exile between 1921 and 1926 reshaped the way he understood the conflict. Looking beyond parochial struggles, he came to see the United States as the real enemy.

When the Liberals and Conservatives agreed to a U.S.-brokered truce in 1927, Sandino rejected the accord, and released the manifesto included below (Document 6.1). This document represents a signature expression of a new, anti-imperialist guerrilla war, a vision that at times explicitly invoked Simón Bolívar's dream of a Latin America united against imperialism.[13] Indeed, while Sandino conflated his domestic enemies and foreign invaders in ways that make the notion that his war was simply anti-imperial unsustainable, he was one of the first Latin American guerrillas to specifically go to war against the United States. In light of this, Sandino's manifesto needs to be understood as much as a text that produces the enemy as describes it. The conflicts he participated in were as much about long-standing and often personal local grievances (class, ethnic, and kinship conflicts in the Segovias region) as they were about the presence of the United States in Nicaragua. That he was able to conflate all these into a struggle of us (Nicaraguans) versus them (the United States) was a testament to his skill as an ideologue.[14]

Document 6.2 represents an interesting example of a different version of United States—Latin American relations, the Good Neighbor Policy. During his presidency Franklin Roosevelt funneled U.S. aid and investment into friendly countries, positioning that aid as the most effective means of promoting economic progress and modernization. Supplemented at the end of the Second World War with the World Bank, the International Monetary Fund and later USAID, the Peace Corps, and Kennedy's Alliance for Progress, these initiatives sought to help Latin Americans by paying for doctors and vaccines, teachers, agronomists, and engineers, and investing millions of dollars to build schools, homes, hospitals, electrical grids, dams, and improve infrastructure more generally. The aid was also meant to thwart American enemies in Latin America by revealing the ways that capitalism could alleviate hunger and end poverty.

Our text, the documentary film *Silent War*, brings together a series of the tendencies of FDR's Good Neighbor Policy. Like others of its day, (notably *Good Neighbor Family* and *Roads South*) the film suggests that the United States can use its position on the cutting edge of all things modern to help Latin America. The progress described in the film (in this case, a yellow fever vaccine) serves U.S. strategic interests and saves the lives of the villagers in Popoyán; the kind of benefit that a contemporary management consultant might call *synergy*. In this, it is not unlike earlier efforts to reduce the impact of mosquito-borne illnesses, undertaken during construction of the Panama Canal. This was what made the logics of American influence in Latin America so compelling. American officials, and many Latin Americans, in fact believed that they were doing good deeds.

Idealism is not so easily evident in Document 6.3, the nakedly propagandistic film, *Journey to Banana Land*, which evidently premiered on board the S.S. *Talamanca* of United Fruit Company's "Great White Fleet" in 1950. The film is as close to a simple apologia for the UFCO as one could ever find. Under pressure in Guatemala because of its vast landholdings, the company used this film to show a North American audience its positive effect on Guatemala, the country's relative modernity, and the ways in which banana production was benefiting everyone, worker and consumer alike. The film also represents a powerful source for interrogating a series of other assumptions about class, gender, and ethnicity (in both Guatemala and the United States).

Document 6.4 returns us to where we began, with a slight shift. Ariel Dorfman's critique of U.S. imperialism during the 1960s begins by arguing that we must understand a set of assumptions about the modern and the primitive in order to understand American imperial practices. Written during the United States' war in Vietnam, in the aftermath of both the overthrow of Arbenz and the Cuban revolution, Dorfman's text is a product of new circumstances. Dorfman describes a nakedly imperialist United States. His evidence for this: *Donald Duck* cartoons, icons of popular culture read across the hemisphere.

Dorfman's critique is powerful and illuminating, and provides a clear reading of cartoons that today seem quite troubling (indeed, far more troubling than *The Three Caballeros*, given their content). Still, we are left wondering whether or not his critique of Pato Donald and Huey, Lewey, and Dewey tells us more about the assumptions of the cartoon's creators than it does about Donald's readers. *Journey to Banana Land, Donald Duck, Silent War*, and other texts may have been intended as instruments of imperialism, but it seems somehow unlikely that the audiences who experienced these texts were entirely naïve consumers. North American school children may have thought the family in *Journey* silly, boring, or unlike theirs. Did they throw spitballs at the screen, go to sleep at their desks, or cut class? Latin American audiences may have laughed at *The Three Caballeros* because Donald was such a buffoon, a reminder of how unsophisticated North American tourists were. And that man on the street may have thought it odd, inexplicable, that the white man made the chicken. We will never know. But then again, that is the magic of the mass consumption that accompanied the American Century. Just as long as you bought a ticket, you could make the meanings your own.

Document 6.1 Augusto Sandino, Political Manifesto, Nicaragua, July 1927

Source: Bruce, Marcus (Ed). *Nicaragua: Sandinista Peoples' Revolution Speeches by Sandinista Leaders*. United Kingdom, Pathfinder Press, 1985, First Trade.

A man who does not ask his homeland for even a handful of earth for his grave deserves to be heard, and not only heard, but believed.

I am Nicaraguan and I am proud that in my veins flows, more than any other, the blood of the American Indian, whose regeneration contains the secret of being a loyal and sincere patriot. The bonds of nationality give me the right to assume responsibility for my actions on matters of Nicaragua and, therefore, of Central America and the entire continent that speaks our language, without concerning myself over what the pessimistic and cowardly eunuchs may call me.

I am a city worker, an artisan as they say in my country, but my ideals are broadly internationalistic in nature and entail the right to be free and demand justice, although to achieve this state of perfection it may be necessary to shed my own blood and that of others.

The oligarchs, who act like geese in a quagmire, will say I am plebeian. It doesn't matter. My greatest honor is to have emerged from the bosom of the oppressed, who are the soul and nerves of the race, who have lived put off and at the mercy of the shameless assassins who helped incubate the crime of high treason: the Nicaraguan Conservatives who wounded the free heart of the homeland and who pursued us ferociously as though we were not children of the same nation.

Sixteen years ago Adolfo Díaz and Emiliano Chamorro ceased being Nicaraguans, because their greed destroyed their right to claim that nationality, as they tore from its staff the flag that flew over all Nicaraguans. Today that flag hangs idle and humiliated by the ingratitude and indifference of its sons who don't make the superhuman effort to free it from the claws of the monstrous eagle with the curved beak that feeds on the blood of this people while the flag that represents the assassination of defenseless peoples and the enmity of our race flies in Managua's Mars Field.

Who are those who tie my homeland to the post of ignominy? Díaz and Chamorro and their bootlickers who still want the right to govern this hapless land, supported by the invaders' bayonets and Springfield rifles. No! A thousand times no!

The Liberal revolution is on the march. There are those who haven't betrayed, who haven't halted, who haven't sold their rifles to satisfy Moncada's greed. It is on the march and today stronger than ever, because the only ones who remain are the brave and the selfless.

The traitor Moncada naturally failed in his duties as a soldier and a patriot. Those who followed him weren't illiterate and neither was he an emperor, to have imposed such greedy ambition upon us. I place before his contemporaries and before history this deserter Moncada, who went over to the foreign enemy with his cartridge pouch and all. An unpardonable crime that demands vindication!

The big men will say that I am very little to have undertaken such a task; but my insignificance is surmounted by the loftiness of my patriotic heart, and so I pledge before my country and history that my sword will defend the national honor and will be the redemption of the oppressed.

I accept the invitation to the struggle and I myself will provoke it, and to the challenge of the cowardly invader and the traitors to my country I answer with my battle cry. My chest and that of my soldiers will form walls that the legions of Nicaragua's enemies will crash upon. The last of my soldiers who are soldiers for Nicaragua's freedom, might die, but first, more than a battalion of you, blond invader, will have bitten the dust of my rustic mountains.

I will not be Magdalena, begging on bent knee for the pardon of my enemies—who are the enemies of Nicaragua—because I believe that nobody on earth has the right to be a demigod. I want to convince the cold-hearted Nicaraguans, the indifferent Central Americans, and the Indo-Hispanic race, that in the spur of the Andean mountains there is a group of patriots who know how to fight and die like men.

Come, you gang of morphine addicts; come murder us in our own land, I am awaiting you, standing upright before my patriotic soldiers, not caring how many you may be. But bear in mind that when this occurs, the destruction of your grandeur will shake the Capitol in Washington, reddening with your blood the white sphere that crowns your famous White House, the den where you concoct your crimes.

I want to advise the governments of Central America, especially that of Honduras, that you need not fear that, because I have more than enough troops, I will militarily invade your territory in an attempt to overthrow it. No. I am not a mercenary, but a patriot who will not permit an offense against our sovereignty.

I wish that, since nature has given our country enviable riches and has put us at the crossroads of the world, and since that natural privilege is what has led others to covet us to the point of wanting to enslave us, for that same reason I wish to break the bonds that the disgraceful policies of Chamorro have bound us with.

Our young country, that tropical brown-skinned woman, should be the one to wear on her head the Phrygian cap with the beautiful slogan that symbolizes our "red and black" emblem, and not that country raped by Yankee morphine addicts brought here by four serpents who claim to have been born here in my country.

The world will be imbalanced if the United States of North America is allowed to be the sole owner of our canal, because that would put us at the mercy of the decisions of the colossus of the North—to whom we would have to pay tribute—those practitioners of bad faith, who with no justification whatsoever seek to become its owners.

Civilization demands that a canal be opened in Nicaragua, but it should be one with capital from the whole world, and not just U.S. capital. At least half the costs of construction should be paid with capital from Latin America and the other half from the rest of the countries of the world that want to hold stock in such a company, and the United States of North America could have only the three million that they gave to the traitors Chamorro, Díaz, and Cuadra Pasos; and Nicaragua, my homeland, will receive the tariffs that by right and justice belong to it, with which we will have sufficient income to build railroads across our territory and educate our people in a real environment of effective democracy, and at the same time we will be respected and not looked upon with the bloody contempt that we suffer today.

Brothers and sisters of my people: having expressed my most ardent desires for the defense of our homeland, I welcome you in my ranks regardless of political affiliation, as long as you come with good intentions, remembering that you can fool all of the people some of the time, but you can't fool all of the people all the time.

Document 6.2 *Silent War* (Film)

To view this film, please visit the book's companion website at www.routledge.com/textbooks/dawson

---

Document 6.3 *Journey to Banana Land* (Film)

To view this film, please visit the book's companion website at www.routledge.com/textbooks/dawson

---

Document 6.4 Ariel Dorfman and Armand Mattelart, "From the Noble Savage to the Third World" 1970

Source: From *How to Read Donald Duck* by Ariel Dorfman. Copyright © 1984 by Ariel Dorfman, reprinted with permissions of The Wylie Agency LLC.

> Donald (talking to a witch doctor in Africa): "I see you're an up to date nation! Have you got telephones?"
> Witch doctor: "Have we gottee telephones! . . . All colors, all shapes . . . only trouble is only one has wires. It's a hot line to the world loan bank."
> (TR 106, US 9/64)

Where is Aztecland? Where is Inca-Blinca? Where is Unsteadystan?

There can be no doubt that Aztecland is Mexico, embracing as it does all the prototypes of the picture-postcard Mexico: mules, siestas, volcanoes, cactuses, huge sombreros, ponchos, serenades, machismo, and Indians from ancient civilizations. The country is defined primarily in terms of this grotesque folklorism. Petrified in an archetypical embryo, exploited for all the superficial and stereotyped prejudices which surround it, "Aztecland," under its pseudo-imaginary name becomes that much easier to Disnify. This is Mexico recognizable by its commonplace exotic identity labels, not the real Mexico with all its problems.

Walt took virgin territories of the United States and built upon them his Disneyland palaces, his magic kingdoms. His view of the world at large is framed by the same perspective; it is a world already colonized, with phantom inhabitants who have to conform to Disney's notions of it. Each foreign country is used as a kind of model within the process of invasion by Disney-nature. And even if some foreign country like Cuba or Vietnam should dare to enter into open conflict with the United States, the Disney Comics brand-mark is immediately stamped upon it, in order to make the revolutionary struggle appear banal. While the Marines make revolutionaries run the gauntlet of bullets, Disney makes them run a gauntlet of magazines. There are two forms of killing: by machine guns and saccharine.

Disney did not, of course, invent the inhabitants of these lands; he merely forced them into the proper mold. Casting them as stars in his hit-parade, he made them into decals and puppets for his fantasy palaces, good and inoffensive savages unto eternity.

According to Disney, underdeveloped peoples are like children, to be treated as such, and if they don't accept this definition of themselves, they should have their pants taken down and be given a good spanking. That'll teach them! When something is said about the child/noble savage, it is really the Third World one is thinking about. The hegemony which we have detected between the child-adults who arrive with their civilization and technology, and the child-noble savages who accept this alien authority and surrender their riches, stands revealed as an exact replica of the relations between metropolis and satellite, between empire and colony, between master and slave. Thus we find the metropolitans not only searching for treasures, but also selling the natives comics (like those of Disney), to teach them the role assigned to them by the dominant urban press. Under the suggestive title "Better Guile Than Force," Donald departs for a Pacific atoll in order to try to survive for a month, and returns loaded with dollars, like a modern business tycoon. The entrepreneur can do better than the missionary or the army. The world of the Disney comic is self-publicizing, ensuring a process of enthusiastic buying and selling even within its very pages.

Enough of generalities. Examples and proofs. Among all the child-noble savages, none is more exaggerated in his infantilism than Gu, the Abominable Snow Man (TR 113, US 6-8/56, "The Lost Crown of Genghis Khan"): a brainless, feeble-minded Mongolian type (living by a strange coincidence, in the Himalayan Hindu Kush mountains among yellow peoples). He is treated like a child. He is an "abominable housekeeper," living in a messy cave, "the worst of taste," littered with "cheap trinkets and waste." Hats etc., lying around which he has no use for. Vulgar, uncivilized, he speaks in a babble of inarticulate baby-noises: "Gu." But he is also witless, having stolen the golden jeweled crown of Genghis Khan (which belongs to Scrooge by virtue of certain secret operations of his agents), without having any idea of its value. He has tossed the crown in a corner like a coal bucket, and prefers Uncle Scrooge's watch: value, one dollar ("It is his favorite toy"). Never mind, for "his stupidity makes it easy for us to get away!" Uncle Scrooge does indeed manage, magically, to exchange the cheap artifact of civilization which goes tick-tock, for the crown. Obstacles are overcome once Gu (innocent child-monstrous animal—underdeveloped Third Worldling) realizes that they only want to take something that is of no use to him, and that in exchange he will be given a fantastic and mysterious piece of technology (a watch) which he can use as a plaything. What is extracted is gold, a raw material; he who surrenders it is mentally underdeveloped and physically overdeveloped. The gigantic physique of Gu, and of all the other marginal savages, is the model of a physical strength suited only for physical labor.

Such an episode reflects the barter relationship established with the natives by the first conquistadors and colonizers (in Africa, Asia, America and Oceania): some trinket, the product of technological superiority (European or North American) is exchanged for gold (spices, ivory, tea, etc.). The native is relieved of something he would never have thought of using for himself or as a means of exchange. This is an extreme and almost anecdotic example. The common stuff of other types of comic book (e.g. in the internationally famous Tintin in Tibet by the Belgian Hergé) leaves the abominable creature in his bestial condition, and thus unable to enter into any kind of economy.

But this particular victim of infantile regression stands at the borderline of Disney's noble savage cliché. Beyond it lies the foetus-savage, which for reasons of sexual prudery Disney cannot use.

Lest the reader feel that we are spinning too fine a thread in establishing a parallel between someone who carries off gold in exchange for a mechanical trinket, and imperialism extracting raw material from a mono-productive country, or between typical dominators and dominated, let us now adduce a more explicit example of Disney's strategy in respect to the countries he caricatures as "backward" (needless to say, he never hints at the causes of their backwardness).

The following dialogue (taken from the same comic which provided the quotation at the beginning of this chapter) is a typical example of Disney's colonial attitudes, in this case directed against the African independence movements. Donald has parachuted into a country in the African jungle. "Where am I," he cries. A witch doctor (with spectacles perched over his gigantic primitive mask) replies: "In the new nation of Kooko Coco, fly boy. This is our capital city." It consists of three straw huts and some moving haystacks. When Donald enquires after this strange phenomenon, the witch doctor explains: "Wigs! This be hairy idea our ambassador bring back from United Nations." When a pig pursuing Donald lands and has the wigs removed disclosing the whereabouts of the enemy ducks, the following dialogue ensues:

Pig: "Hear ye! hear ye! I'll pay you kooks some hairy prices for your wigs! Sell me all you have!"

Native: "Whee! Rich trader buyee our old head hangers!"

Another native: "He payee me six trading stamps for my beehive hairdo!"

Third native (overjoyed): "He payee me two Chicago streetcar tokens for my Beatle job."

To effect his escape, the pig decides to scatter a few coins as a decoy. The natives are happy to stop, crouch and cravenly gather up the money. Elsewhere, when the Beagle Boys dress up as Polynesian natives to deceive Donald, they mimic the same kind of behavior: "You save our lives. . . We be your servants for ever." And as they prostrate themselves, Donald observes: "They are natives too. But a little more civilized."

Another example (Special Number D 423): Donald leaves for "Outer Congolia," because Scrooge's business there has been doing badly. The reason is "the King ordered his subjects not to give Christmas presents this year. He wants everyone to hand over this money to him." Donald comments: "What selfishness!" And so to work. Donald makes himself king, being taken for a great magician who flies through the skies. The old monarch is dethroned because "he is not a wise man like you [Donald]. He does not permit us to buy presents." Donald accepts the crown, intending to decamp as soon as the stock is sold out: "My first command as king is . . . buy presents for your families and don't give your king a cent!" The old king had wanted the money to leave the country and eat what he fancied, instead of the fish heads which were traditionally his sole diet. Repentant, he promises that given another chance, he will govern better, "and I will find a way somehow to avoid eating that ghastly stew."

Donald (to the people): "And I assure you that I leave the throne in good hands. Your old king is a good king . . . and wiser than before."
The people: "Hurray! Long Live the King!"

The king has learned that he must ally himself with foreigners if he wishes to stay in power, and that he cannot even impose taxes on the people, because this wealth must pass wholly out of the country to Duckburg through the agent of McDuck. Furthermore, the strangers find a solution to the problem of the king's boredom. To alleviate his sense of alienation within his own country, and his consequent desire to travel to the metropolis, they arrange for the massive importation of consumer goods: "Don't worry about that food," says Donald, "I will send you some sauces which will make even fish heads palatable." The king stamps gleefully up and down.

The same formula is repeated over and over again. Scrooge exchanges with the Canadian Indians gates of rustless steel for gates of pure gold (TR 117). Moby Duck and Donald (D 453), captured by the Aridians (Arabs), start to blow soap bubbles, with which the natives are enchanted. "Ha, ha. They break when you catch them. Hee, hee." Ali-Ben-Goli, the chief, says, "it's real magic. My people are laughing like children. They cannot imagine how it works." "It's only a secret passed from generation to generation," says Moby, " I will reveal it if you give us our freedom." (Civilization is presented as something incomprehensible, to be administered by foreigners.) The chief, in amazement, exclaims "Freedom? That's not all I'll give you. Gold, jewels. My treasure is yours, if you reveal the secret." The Arabs consent to their own despoilation. "We have jewels, but they are of no use to us. They don't make you laugh like magic bubbles." While Donald sneers "poor simpleton," Moby hands over the Flip Flop detergent. "You are right, my friend. Whenever you want a little pleasure, just pour out some magic powder and recite the magic words." The story ends on the note that it is not necessary for

Donald to excavate the Pyramids (or earth) personally, because, as Donald says, "What do we need a pyramid for, having Ali-Ben-Goli?"

Each time this situation recurs, the natives' joy increases. As each object of their own manufacture is taken away from them, their satisfaction grows. As each artifact from civilization is given to them, and interpreted by them as a manifestation of magic rather than technology, they are filled with delight. Even our fiercest enemies could hardly justify the inequity of such an exchange; how can a fistful of jewels be regarded as equivalent to a box of soap, or a golden crown equal to a cheap watch? Some will object that this kind of barter is all imaginary, but it is unfortunate that these laws of the imagination are tilted unilaterally in favor of those who come from outside, and those who write and publish the magazines.

But how can this flagrant despoliation pass unperceived, or in other words, how can this inequity be disguised as equity? Why is it that imperialist plunder and colonial subjection, to call them by their proper names, do not appear as such?

"We have jewels, but they are of no use to us."

There they are in their desert tents, their caves, their once flourishing cities, their lonely islands, their forbidden fortresses, and they can never leave them. Congealed in their past-historic, their needs defined in function of this past, these underdeveloped peoples are denied the right to build their own future. Their crowns, their raw materials, their soil, their energy, their jade elephants, their fruit, but above all, their gold, can never be turned to any use. For them the progress which comes from abroad in the form of multiplicity of technological artifacts, is a mere toy. It will never penetrate the crystallized defense of the noble savage, who is forbidden to become civilized. He will never be able to join the Club of the Producers, because he does not even understand that these objects have been produced. He sees them as magic elements, arising from the foreigner's mind, from his word, his magic wand.

For Further Reading

Briggs, Laura. *Reproducing Empire: Race, Sex, Science, and U.S. Imperialism in Puerto Rico*. Berkeley: University of California Press, 2003.

Burton, Julianne. "Don (Juanito) Duck and the Imperial-Patriarchal Unconscious: Disney Studios, the Good Neighbor Policy and Packaging of Latin America," in Andrew Parker, Mary Russo, Doris Sommer, and Patricia Yaeger (eds.), *Nationalism and Sexualities*. New York: Routledge, 1992, pp. 21–41.

Cullather, Nick. *Secret History: The CIA's Classified Account of Its Operations in Guatemala, 1952–1954*. Stanford: Stanford University Press, 1999.

Dosal, Paul J. *Doing Business with the Dictators: A Political History of United Fruit in Guatemala 1899–1944*. Wilmington: Scholarly Resources, 1993.

Gilbert, Joseph M. Catherine LeGrand, and Ricardo Salvatore (eds.). *Close Encounters of Empire: Writing the Cultural History of U.S.–Latin American Relations*. Durham, NC: Duke University Press, 1998.

Gleijeses, Piero. *Shattered Hope*. Princeton: Princeton University Press, 1992.

Lafeber Walter. *Inevitable Revolutions: The United States in Central America*. New York: Norton, 1993.

McGuinness, Aims. *Path of Empire: Panama and the California Gold Rush*. Ithaca: Cornell University Press, 2007.

Mendible, Myra. *From Bananas to Buttocks: The Latina Body in Popular Film and Culture*. Austin: University of Texas Press, 2007.

Moreno, Julio. *Yankee Don't Go Home: Mexican Nationalism, American Business Culture, and the Shaping of Modern Mexico, 1920–1950*. Chapel Hill: University of North Carolina Press, 2003.

Pastor, Robert A. *Exiting the Whirlpool: U.S. foreign policy toward Latin America and the Caribbean*. Boulder: Westview, 2001.

Pérez, Louis Jr. *Cuba and the United States: Ties of Singular Intimacy*. Athens, GA: University of Georgia Press, 2003.

Pérez, Louis Jr. *On Becoming Cuban: Identity, Nationality, and Culture*. Chapel Hill, University of North Carolina Press, 2007.

Putnam, Lara. *The Company They Kept: Migrants and the Politics of Gender in Caribbean Costa Rica, 1870–1960*. Chapel Hill: University of North Carolina Press, 2001.

Schlesinger, Stephen and Stephen Kinzer. *Bitter Fruit: The Story of the American Coup in Guatemala*. Cambridge, MA: David Rockefeller Center for Latin American Studies; rev. exp. edn., 2005.

Smith, Peter H. *Talons of the Eagle: Dynamics of U.S.–Latin American Relations*. Oxford: Oxford University Press, 2007.

Soluri, John. "Accounting For Taste: Export Bananas, Mass Markets, and Panama Disease," *Environmental History* 7 (2002), 386–410.

Soluri, John. *Banana Cultures: Agriculture, Consumption, and Environmental Change in Honduras and the United States*. Austin: University of Texas Press, 2006.

Zolov, Eric. *Refried Elvis: The Rise of the Mexican Counterculture*. Berkeley: University of California Press, 1999.

1929	1930	1930	1943	October 1945	1946
Collapse of U.S. Stock Exchange signals beginning of global economic crisis	Vargas takes power in Brazil	Military coup begins the *Decada Infama* (infamous decade) in Argentina	Junior officers coup in Argentina	Juan Perón jailed by fellow officers	Juan Perón elected President of Argentina

1955 –	June 1973 –	July 1, 1974 –	March 24, 1976 –
Perón is overthrown, goes into exile	Perón returns from exile, is re-elected President in September	Perón dies, leaving Isabel, his third wife, president	Isabel Perón is overthrown, military begins the Process of National Re-organization (dirty war)

Power to the People   **7**

1937	1947	July 9, 1947	August 1951	December 1951	July 26, 1952
Vargas announces *Estado Novo* (New State)	Argentine women get the vote	Perón declares economic independence as foreign debt is paid off	Evita's *Renunciamiento*	Perón re-elected	Evita dies

Heard on the radio, or viewed on a newsreel, it could seem like a frightening spectacle. Here she was, the wildly popular wife of the Argentine president, addressing tens of thousands of crazed followers in the streets below. Her steady voice, simultaneously seductive, motherly, and commanding, was constantly interrupted by their chants; declarations that they were on her side and demands that she carry on as their leader. Evita had nothing of that apolitical, retiring sweetness that Latin Americans generally expected in prominent women. She attacked her enemies without mercy, and was loved and despised for it.

María Eva Duarte de Perón has long been categorized as a populist. Like many categories, it is not a very good one. Historians use it much like they use the term caudillo, to identify a vast array of politicians who cannot be easily classified according to the matrices of left versus right. Populists were charismatic, nationalist, and good at mobilizing industrial workers. Into this category we can place Víctor Raúl Haya de la Torre (Peru), Getúlio Vargas (Brazil), Carlos Ibañez (Chile), Jorge Eliéser Gaitán (Colombia), Juan and Eva Perón (Argentina), Lázaro Cárdenas (Mexico), and perhaps even Fulgencio Batista (Cuba), Anastasio Somoza (Nicaragua), and Rafael Trujillo (Dominican Republic). This list goes on in a deeply unsatisfying way, because almost every popular Latin American leader of the mid-twentieth century could be called a populist. The debate over who was and who was not a populist winds up becoming a little like arguing how many angels can fit on the head of a pin.

Our dilemma may lie in where we focus our attention. Populists were not just defined by a political style, they came of age in an era of significant social and technological change. We know Evita was a powerful speaker largely because she found her voice in the era of amplified, broadcast, and recorded sound (audio examples of her speech can be found on the website). Through these mediums she could expand the reach of her voice from a crowd of people within listening distance to tens of thousands, even an entire nation. Many of our most important traces of Evita include images of her speaking into a microphone, electronically enlarging her voice and mobilizing audiences far larger than politicians of an earlier era could have imagined. Her very skills at this were honed in years as a radio star, where she developed her melodramatic voice in *radionovelas* (radio soap operas), a tone that would serve her well when she addressed her beloved *descamisados* (shirtless ones) in later years. This was also the dawn of a visual age, for which she was well suited, but the dominant medium of her day remained broadcast sound, the loudspeaker, the microphone, and the radio. These technological innovations transformed what it was to be a politician, and what it was to be a member of the crowd.

Gathered in a public square, on a street, or in a private dwelling, individuals in the crowd were transformed through the experience of listening together. Even when they listened by themselves, they could understand that it was the voice of their leader they heard, and that millions of others were doing the same thing at the same time. Listening was a sentient experience that had connoted intimacy in the past; to hear the voice of a leader was to see them face to face, and to somehow be connected to power in that moment. In the radio age the act of listening to the leader still connected the listener to power, but instead of something that was individually empowering, it made the crowd into the people (Figure 7.1).

Figure 7.1 Evita at a microphone

Source: Courtesy of Wikimedia Commons

The Crowd

A century and a half before Evita addressed the crowd, individuals like Father Miguel Hidalgo used similarly vaunted rhetorical skills to stir his followers to action. Earlier leaders however, addressed a different kind of crowd. The groups were smaller, they were residents of a single town and its environs, and they were often intensely parochial in their worldviews. Hidalgo did not appeal to the crowd's Mexicanness, but to a much more local sense of self and idea of grievance. Their political ties were not horizontal, with other members of a national community, but to a distant king whose will was being subverted by venal officials. Indeed, the localistic sense of belonging that united those amassed in the town square in Dolores in 1810 was both a strength and a weakness of the popular movements that participated in nineteenth-century conflicts. Dispersed, and often divided by mutual feelings of hostility, Latin America's nineteenth-century crowds were threatening, but most often unable to sustain movements that went much further than the village boundary.

The twentieth century transformed the cognitive capacities of the crowd. Cities grew larger, producing urban working classes that often had a much greater sense of their shared interests and cultures, along with a capacity to disrupt the system that their rural brethren lacked. Moreover, the urban crowd was not just united through common work and living conditions, but through technologies that were as important to the twentieth century as the printing press was to the eighteenth. Face-to-face culture and politics were increasingly supplanted by interactions mediated through the radio, loudspeakers, and the photographic image. The notion of simultaneous time was no longer reserved for those literate enough to read a newspaper, but was shared by millions of people who had access to the new technologies. They could experience the feeling of fictive kinship by listening to the same speakers say the same thing at the same time. They could attend rallies that were larger, more disruptive, and more coherent than ever before. They could listen in the plazas, the schools, and their homes while national broadcasting companies (many government owned) broadcast the local and national news, and gave voice to a new generation of leaders. Politicians who were adept at using the new media found new, national audiences in these contexts, and their listeners constituted themselves as *the people*.

Music played a defining role in this process. Through recorded and amplified sound local songs increasingly became part of national repertoires. A song played again and again, heard in different places, reminded listeners that as they moved through space they remained rooted in a sentimental community comprised of millions of people whom they had never met. Popular music also contributed to the emergence of a novel kind of popular culture. Popular culture was no longer simply local practices that stood in opposition to elites, but it was also mass culture, the *radionovelas*, movies, *historietas* (comic books), and songs, and other mass phenomena. It was something that poor people shared, that gave them a sense of connectedness and of their own place in a modern world (as most of these cultural forms were fundamentally modern). Popular culture also sometimes blurred the boundaries between the classes. Middle class children might read the same comic books and go to the same movies as the poor. Elite nationalists could often belt out the same ballad as a poor shopkeeper, each with as much conviction as the other. Neither was false or fooled in their love of a national art form. Indeed, over time common tastes produced a new national culture.

The *Hora do Brazil*

Any close observer of Latin American society who utters the phrase "national culture" takes an enormous risk. Profoundly divided societies cannot generally be described as having national cultures. Yet if we discard the concept, we risk abandoning all efforts to understand how technology, style, and a sense of belonging came together in powerful ways to produce the phenomena that characterized Latin American politics in these years before the cold-war imposed a very different dynamic on the political life of the region. Few politicians better understood this convergence than Getúlio Vargas, who claimed the Brazilian presidency in a military coup in 1930. In some ways, Vargas was an unremarkable authoritarian ruler. Like many others, he promised a great deal and delivered relatively little. What instead marked this era as different from others were his (and his opponents') efforts to turn the radio into a means to create a national body politic.

Radio first arrived in Brazil in 1922, and was immediately popular, especially in urban areas. By the early 1930s there were 20 stations in the country, expanding to over 100 two decades later. By the mid-1930s, 85 percent of households in the country's two most populous cities, São Paulo and Rio de Janeiro, owned radios. Most early broadcasting was commercial, but the power of the new medium was not lost on Vargas and his appointees in the Department of Propaganda. Several government radio stations were founded in the early 1930s, charged with the twin responsibilities of publicizing the good works of the government (social and educational programs, labor laws, the passage of a minimum wage) and turning Brazilian listeners into a reliable political constituency.

Like bureaucrats everywhere, Vargas and his appointees did not always prove adept at using the medium. The managers of the three stations run by the government favored didactic programming, speeches by government officials and classical music. Listeners rarely tuned into these programs, favoring the musical selections of commercial radio instead. Indeed, the regime could only ensure an audience through decree. Under Vargas all stations in the country were required to broadcast the *Hora do Brazil* (*Brazil Hour*) every evening at 8 pm. Filled with speeches, public announcements, and cultural forms that spoke to elite sensibilities rather than popular tastes (marching music was more commonly played than samba), the *Hora* was widely ridiculed and ignored by radio listeners. Some stations simply refused to broadcast it, claiming they could not find the signal, or making some other excuse. It was popularly known as the *"hora fala sozinho"* or "hour that talks to itself."[1]

Vargas recognized that popular music was a powerful unifying force, and did attempt to link the samba to his regime. He supported samba schools and Carnival parades, and samba music was regularly broadcast on the government owned station *Rádio Nacional*[2], but his efforts to control the samba actually revealed how little control the regime had over its followers. In the mid-1930s federal officials tried to define acceptable limits to the subject matter of the samba. They promoted patriotic content, tried to censor anti-authoritarian, outlaw images (e.g. the *malandro*, a popular outlaw figure) in samba music. Fans of the music rejected the state's efforts, finding unsanctioned forums where they could listen to their preferred artists and songs. In fact much of the most popular samba music in the era was highly critical of the state.

As consumers of popular music poor Brazilians had more power than they did as workers or as citizens. Part of this was simply the freedom to consume what they desired, and reject what they did not, revealing the limits of any effort by the state or the music industry to indoctrinate through popular culture. Yet they also had the power to actually shape the art-form. Fans wrote samba lyrics and submitted them to artists and producers, and sometimes saw their songs recorded. They went to radio shows and applauded their favorite acts, helping to determine which songs became hits and which did not. In the process they distinguished good samba from bad, and Brazilian from foreign. In time, the popular embrace of the samba was so ubiquitous that samba became synonymous with the nation, something elites had to embrace if they wished to be perceived as Brazilian.

Mastering the Medium

It is easy to see why Vargas would have wanted to co-opt the samba and link it to himself and his *Estado Novo* (the vaguely fascist New State, which he inaugurated in 1937). Samba was enormously popular, and if he was identified with the art form he would attract a huge following. Yet it was the very popularity of the samba that undermined this project. There were too many samba artists, too many mediums through which it could be heard, and a fan base that was too vast and heterogeneous to ever allow the art form to be simply tamed, either by the state or the market. That was part of the magic of popular art forms in this era. They could be instruments of any number of cultural or political projects, because they resisted all efforts to strictly define or control them. Drawing on the samba was one thing, but Vargas was destined to fail if he tried to control it.

Just as importantly, Vargas proved ineffective at controlling and co-opting radio more generally, in part because commercial broadcasters understood the medium better than he did, and also perhaps because he lacked the kind of charisma that mattered most in the new electronic age. We see this dramatically when we turn to the Brazilian who did use the radio extremely effectively during this era, Vargas' bitter rival Carlos Lacerda. Lacerda's political constituency was middle class and conservative, but like most successful politicians in the age of mass communications he openly courted workers with his ardent nationalism and willingness to support a limited array of workers' rights. He was moralist, pro-traditional family, and vigorously attacked corruption, but most of all he was captivating.

In the early 1950s regime opponents put Lacerda on *Rádio Globo* and *TV Tupi*, the country's first television network. *Globo* had not been a successful station as a music and soap opera venture because of its small budgets, but found its niche in radio journalism. Lacerda joined *Globo* in 1953, and used his show to actively attack Vargas. He ran an improvisational and lengthy call-in program that used new tactics like media ambushes to produce electrifying radio. Though lambasted in the traditional media, the show was an immediate hit, turning *Globo* into the third most popular station in Rio by August 1954. As a radio and later television star, Lacerda continually demonstrated that elusive ability to turn listeners on, to draw them to his program, and keep them from changing the dial or turning off the set. This was a skill that became absolutely critical with the dawn of the radio and television age. Listeners suddenly had numerous options, and could not be compelled to pay attention.

Lacerda was in fact so successful at attacking Vargas that someone close to the president (if not the president himself) concluded that he needed to be eliminated. Armed assailants tried to kill Lacerda outside his Copacabana apartment on August 5, 1954, but he survived, while his bodyguard, an air-force officer, died. Lacerda and the dead bodyguard became heroes, and Vargas, who was seen as the intellectual author of a botched murder, suddenly faced a united opposition that openly talked about violent resistance to the regime. Vargas could still take to the airways to defend his positions and argue against his enemies, but at this point fewer and fewer Brazilians were listening.

That changed on August 24, 1954, when Brazilians listened to their radios with rapt attention as Vargas' suicide note was read on national radio just hours after his death (the note had actually been typed several days earlier). In part the note defended his specific policies, attempts to create national oil and electricity monopolies in order to promote industrialization, a national coffee department designed to maintain global coffee prices. It was also a dark attack on his enemies.

> Once more the forces and interests against the people are newly coordinated and raised against me. They do not accuse me, they insult me; they do not fight me, they slander me and refuse to give me the right of defense. They seek to drown my voice and halt my actions so that I no longer continue to defend, as I have always defended, the people and principally the humble . . . I have fought month after month, day after day, hour after hour, resisting constant, incessant pressures, unceasingly bearing it all in silence, forgetting everything and giving myself in order to defend the people that now fall abandoned. I cannot give you more than my blood. If the birds of prey wish the blood of anybody, they wish to continue to suck the blood of the Brazilian people. I offer my life in the holocaust. I choose this means to be with you always. When they humiliate you, you will feel my soul suffering at your side. When hunger knocks at your door, you will feel within you the energy to fight for yourselves and for your children. When you are scorned, my memory will give you the strength to react.[3]

Written as troops were preparing to overthrow the regime, the note exemplifies the novel ways in which radio contributed to that sense of belonging that is critical to popular nationalism. It did not matter whether or not Vargas actually wrote the note. Read nationally on the radio, it had the capacity to push hundreds of thousands of people into the streets, their anger and grief no doubt stoked by the simultaneity of their powerful emotions. Among other things, the crowds took out their anger on two radio stations that had been critical of the president in the weeks leading up to his death.

These outbursts did not indicate that poor Brazilians were ceaselessly loyal to Vargas. His regime never had the unquestioned support of working people, in part because working people in Brazil, as elsewhere, have always had a healthy skepticism for regimes that promise a great deal and deliver something less. Still, while their love was conditional, their grief at his loss was genuine and powerful. Poor Brazilians knew that they were better off with his unrealized promises than they had been in the past. Coming on the heels of the oligarchic republic, where the chasm between the *gente decente* (rich) and the *povo* (poor) was one of both wealth and dignity, Vargas spoke a language that resonated powerfully. He claimed to represent the poor, and actually passed laws in their favor.

Few Brazilians believed that these laws would be perfectly respected. When has that ever been the case in Brazil? Rather, these laws became tools that poor people used in their daily struggles to make ends meet. Some schools and hospitals were built, some roads completed, and wages for industrial workers in some sectors improved. And even if not always honored, the minimum wage (introduced in 1940) did impact the lives of millions of workers. Decades later, poor supporters would sum up their love of Vargas with the simple phrase "the president always remembered us,"[4] a powerful statement about how they were treated by the regimes that preceded and followed his.

Un Día Peronista[5]

Vargas proved capable of using new mediums to enhance his power, but unevenly so. Latching onto the radio, he tried to use it didactically, was sometimes wooden in his approach to courting the people, and was ultimately less successful than the opposition in turning broadcast media into public spectacle. This in turn has become a part of how Vargas is remembered. He is invoked much more for his politics and policies than for his style. The same cannot be said for Juan Domingo Péron and his wife Eva Duarte, whose particular political style, whose capacity to command the rapt attention of millions of Argentines, can stir up visceral feelings to this day.

The best place to begin the story of Peronism in Argentina is perhaps with the 1930s, a period that workers in that country called the *Decada Infama* (Infamous Decade). During the same years that Getúlio Vargas was courting support from Brazilian workers, their Argentine counterparts suffered a series of frustrating and humiliating experiences punctuated by right-wing military coups and deeply cynical politics. The military took power at the behest of the oligarchy in 1930, and immediately unleashed a wave of repression against organized labor. Two years later the military, conservatives, and Radicals formed a *concordancia* (accord) in which they agreed to share power, implement a series of oligarchy-friendly policies, and freeze workers out of the government entirely, all the while maintaining the appearance of democratic practice through electoral fraud and repression. Matters were made much worse by the fact that workers endured a disproportionate share of the economic pain suffered during these years.

There can be little doubt that the xenophobic nationalism of the *Liga Patriotica Argentina*[6] underpinned the *concordancia*, bringing middle-class and elite Argentines together in a shared anxiety about the threat of worker revolt. Across Latin America during this time leftward leaning regimes were courting support from workers, but in Argentina, where workers were more essential to the economy than elsewhere and dominated the social terrain of the country's capital, the antipathies between worker and oligarch were simply too deep, with too much history behind them, to be breached during these years.

To be a worker in Argentina during these years was to be in constant danger of arrest or assault from those who monopolized power, and to lack legitimate means of protesting your lot. This did not mean however, that workers remained quiet about their fate. They instead looked to other means, forums in which protest could be masked as something else. One could release frustration physically, through sport, manual labor, interpersonal violence, or heavy drinking. Just as importantly, one could turn on the radio, listen to a tango, and perhaps sing along. During these terrible years the tango became *the* quintessential medium through which workers could voice their grievances. Consider the lyrics to *Cambalache*, written by Enrique Santos Discépolo in 1935.

That the world was and it will be a pigsty
I know . . . In the year 510 and in 2000 too
There always have been thieves, hustlers, and fools
The happy and bitter, idealists and frauds
But, that the twentieth century is a display of insolent evil no-one can deny
We live wallowing in the mess.
And we are all covered by the same filth. . .

Today it doesn't matter
Whether you are decent or a traitor
Whether you are ignorant, a genius, a pickpocket
Generous or crooked
All is the same, none better than the other
The donkey is the same
As the great professor!
No one fails, no one has merit
The immoral have reached our level

If one man lives as an imposter
And the other steals for ambition's sake
It doesn't matter if it is a priest
A mattress-maker, the king of clubs
Huckster or tramp

There is no respect, no reason
Anyone is a gentleman, anyone a thief
Stavinsku, Don Bosco, and La Mignon
Don Chicho and Napoleon
Carnera and San Martin, all mixed together

Like in the jumbled window
of the bazaars
life is mixed up
and wounded by a sword without rivets
you can see a crying Bible
Beside a water heater

Twentieth century bazaar
Bizarre and fevered
If you don't cry, mama won't feed you
and if you don't steal you're a fool
Go ahead, Keep it up

We'll meet again
In Hell
No need to think
Just move out of the way.
No-one cares
if you were born honorable.
He who works
Day and night like a mule
Is no different than the one who lives off of others
No different than he who kills or heals
No different than an outlaw.[7]

Like the samba in Brazil, the tango was a popular art form, played on the radio, filled with *lunfardo* (profane slang) expressions, and beloved by the country's working classes. Stories of love betrayed, lives empty of meaning, of violence and social discord gave listeners the smallest of opportunities to describe the world they lived in after the *Semana Trágica* in January 1919. It was no surprise then, that the tango dismayed elites and was periodically censored by the Argentine state.

Among the powerful memories that Argentines have of Juan Perón is that he not only liberated the tango from censorship, but that he could speak the same language as the great tango singers. Their expressions, like their rage, were his as well. In this, he was unlike any other Argentine political leader in recent memory. Of relatively humble origins himself (he was after all, born to unwed parents), Perón was a sort of self-made man whose relationship to the oligarchy was always uneasy. He was a military man, but an admirer of the social compacts between workers, industrialists, and the state that he witnessed during postings in Europe during the 1930s. He imagined a new Argentina, no longer beholden to what was for all purposes a landed gentry, but was instead industrialized, broadly prosperous, and modern.

It was this desire to break the stranglehold that the oligarchy had on the system and forge a new society (one where social peace would be forged not by simply repressing workers) that motivated a group of relatively junior officers to overthrow the government in 1943. Among those officers, Perón stood out for his desire to change the face of Argentine politics. Put in charge of the Department of Labor (which he remade into the Department of Labor and Supply), he immediately began to construct a power base for himself through the department.

His timing was serendipitous. Workers may have been marginalized politically, but in the decade before the Junior Officers Coup the industrial workforce had been rapidly expanding. Global trade was severely disrupted during the 1930s, and Argentines suddenly found themselves unable to import many of the manufactured goods that had become commonplace in their country since the turn of the century. In response, local manufacturers increased domestic industrial production, often building branch-plants of larger European and American conglomerates, importing technology and machinery, but manufacturing locally (this was known as Import Substitution Industrialization, or ISI). Between 1935 and 1946 the number of industrial workers in Argentina grew from 435,816 to 1,056,673. Over the same period the number of industrial plants in Argentina doubled, from 38,456 to 86,400.

The challenge Perón faced lay in capturing the political loyalty of these new (and old) workers, and turning their energies towards even more rapid industrialization, as he had seen in countries like fascist Italy and Germany. In part, he pursued this goal by adopting a strategy from the Radical past, building clientelist networks[8] that could connect workers to Perón indirectly and offer material benefits to his supporters. This practice functioned through a series of formal and informal networks of poor and working people, run by local bosses who delivered jobs, fixed problems, provided public services, favors, money, food, and aid in emergencies. In return for these benefits, members had to come out in support of the leader, and deliver their votes on election day.

Perón did not stop here. He updated and enlarged the clientelist tradition by building a vast patronage network through government-affiliated unions that could, at least theoretically, ensure labor peace. He courted the large unions and promoted new unions among unskilled laborers. He attacked leftist unions and demanded that all workers, along with businessmen and industrialists, cooperate with the military to promote national development. Workers would be guaranteed wage increases (wages jumped 20 percent between 1943 and 1945), social security benefits, housing, education, and union representation (as long as they belonged to government unions), and industrialists would be granted government support through subsidies, preferential taxes, and a compliant workforce. Together with the state, these groups would work to make Argentina less dependent on foreign markets for its economic well-being. It would become a truly independent, industrialized nation.

It was a program that was destined to find adherents, and Perón's particular style represented an ideal vehicle for delivering this message. His use of *lunfardo* expressions, the way he mixed tango lyrics into his speeches, the fact that he actually delivered the goods, and his simple charisma—that nebulous capacity to draw those to whom you speak in, to make them feel connected to you—turned an otherwise technocratic project into a defining nationalist moment. He spoke to workers not as atomized individuals, but as powerful social actors, as Argentines, due the dignity and respect of anyone else. Peronism moreover recast citizenship to include a claim to social justice and pride in working people. Because of this, by 1945 Perón had become the most powerful political figure in the country, much to the chagrin of his fellow *junta*[9] members. That is why they jailed him on October 9, a move that Perón believed spelled the end of his political career.

Perhaps he felt this way because he was deeply aware of the fragile architecture upon which he had built his movement, but like the officers who arrested him, he was wrong to imagine that the workers would stand for this turn of events. While he sat in a military prison cell, resigned to his fate, the workers revolted. Unwilling to wait even for a protest planned by the *Confederación General del Trabajo* (General Confederation of Labor—CGT), on October 17 rank and file union members from all over the capital region converged on Buenos Aires, marched to the city's Plaza de Mayo, and demanded Perón's release. Workers remained throughout the day and night in the public spaces they had occupied, dancing and drinking, literally taking over the city from the wealthy. Faced with chaos, the regime released Perón that evening, and asked him to speak to the quarter of a million people gathered in the Plaza de Mayo in order to get them to disperse peacefully. Though they were accused of being drunken rioters in the mainstream press, as he spoke from the balcony Perón called them the true "Argentine People." Elections were called for 1946, and Perón won the presidency handily.

It was a fantastical moment, marked by the sudden power that working people seemed to possess, Perón's almost mythical stature, and made more significant because Argentina was about to embark on a post-war economic boom. Europe was devastated and hungry, and with the U.S. government poised to rebuild the continent, Argentina was entering a period in which demand for its exports and the price for those exports would be unusually high for the foreseeable future. The boom provided so much revenue to the state that the Argentine government paid off its foreign debt (1947), nationalized British-owned railroads, French-owned docks, and U.S.-owned telecommunications, and assumed control of the agency that marketed beef exports, all the while increasing worker's wages. Remarkably, revenues were so strong that all of this was undertaken at little cost to the export sector, leaving the oligarchy unscathed. Rising incomes alone led to a further jump in consumption, benefiting local industries. High tariffs would further help these industries, but it was the post-war export boom that made it seem that all of this was possible, with little sacrifice. It was the end of the boom and new waves of inflation after 1949 that revealed the real cost of these reforms, and the difficulty of building the prosperous industrial nation Peronists envisioned. Perón's plan for national economic liberation collapsed within a few short years.

Santa Evita

If the story of economic booms and political networks was all there was to Perón, his short regime (1946–55) would be remembered much like that of many other industrializing mass politicians. Whether thought of fondly or with disdain, figures like Getúlio Vargas and Lázaro Cárdenas (Mexico) for the most part lost their capacity to stir up extreme emotions long ago. Such is not the case with Perón, a man who could still produce riots in the streets as late as 2006, when his body was moved from his family crypt in Buenos Aires to a mausoleum at his country estate. In order to understand the continued capacity of Perón to evoke such passions, we shift our focus to the story of his second wife, Evita.

Perón was always a polarizing figure, a reformer who insisted on reconfiguring political power in Argentina. Nonetheless, he possessed certain forms of social capital that gave him access to elite Argentine society. He was a military man, strong, a son of the countryside. He was a product of good military schools, a loyal (to a point) soldier, and never one to over-turn social hierarchies entirely. Indeed, it seems that when he was jailed in October 1945 he resigned himself to the end of his political career because he never imagined that the crowd would both liberate him and put him in the presidency. We might imagine that this was because however great his skill at addressing the crowd, he remained a military man, his gaze fixed more on his place in the ranks than on the masses.

Evita's role in freeing him from jail remains shrouded in myth, but in popular memory she turned to the transformative capacity of the crowd in her efforts to free Perón. What is clear is that both her origins and her professional career gave her a perspective on the masses that was unique among members of the Argentine elite. Born in Junín in 1919 to parents who never married because her father already had a family, Eva Duarte grew up in a working-class household, and moved to Buenos Aires as a young woman to pursue a career in the theater. She won minor parts in radio dramas during the 1930s, and by the early 1940s she had become something of a star with a daily role in a drama on *Radio El Mundo*, the most popular station in the country. She met Perón at a charity event for the victims of the San Juan earthquake in 1944.[10] The two instantly became an item.

In the curious alchemy that is attraction, Eva and Perón seem to have been drawn to one another for a multitude of reasons, both personal and political. She was a beautiful starlet, but savvy, and popular among the poor and marginalized Argentines Perón aspired to represent. He was a powerful and handsome man, who promised to elevate Eva socially through their connection. His style and substance connected him to her listeners, and together each could further legitimize the standing of the other with that constituency. She was a willing participant in this endeavor, and actively transformed her status as a radio star into a vehicle for Peronism immediately after their affair began. Within months she was producing radio soap operas that dramatized Perón's accomplishments, and broadcasting recordings of his speeches over the air. She even told his life story in radio soap opera. She would use her radio program extensively to promote his 1946 presidential campaign, and make weekly radio addresses once he was elected.

The very same qualities that made Eva popular to some offended others. She had a powerful sexual presence, and like many accomplished women, was regularly accused of sleeping her way to the top. This rankled radio people, but since propriety was not the most important quality in the new media age, it did not impede her career trajectory. On the other hand, among the political classes, who tended to have extraordinarily narrow ideas about proper female behavior, her alleged sexual indiscretions and general comportment were viewed with horror. Her humble origins, her ways of speaking, and ultimately her place at Perón's side as an unmarried woman represented a complete affront to polite society. That she did these things while openly courting the admiration of working people further infuriated Argentine elites. In part because of this, rumor and innuendo would follow her incessantly. Dismissing Eva as little more than a prostitute, her enemies saw avarice and cruelty in her every act.

It is not clear that these attacks hurt her. The more the oligarchy (and middling sectors) hated her, the more she showed her contempt for them, the more everyday people found her utterly adorable. She stood in for them, was glamorous and defiant, and openly sought their approval—approval that re-inscribed their opposition to the oligarchy. Moreover, as she evolved from beautiful vamp to elegant benefactor of the poor (symbolized, literally, through an evolution in her wardrobe and hairstyle), she was able to cast herself in an increasingly defiant and self-sacrificing role—mother, sister, and lover of the people. Eva Duarte became simply Evita.

In Evita's rhetoric it was not the rich, but the *descamisados* who could claim to represent all that was worthy in the nation. She spoke to their sense of grievance, the feeling that they had been victimized for decades. Evita and Perón were simply their surrogates in a war against the nation's enemies, a revolution that required total loyalty to the cause. Whether railing against imperialist enemies, the Jockey Club, the oligarchy, the left, or liberal intellectuals, she was even more effective than Perón at moving the crowd.

Evita did deliver the goods, at least for a while (Figure 7.2). After being spurned by the proper society ladies of the *Sociedad de Beneficencia de la Capital* (Benevolent Society of the Capital), she managed to have their charitable foundation shuttered, and established her own, the *Fundación Eva Perón* (Eva Perón Foundation—FEP), in 1948. Begun with a donation from Evita herself of 12,000 pesos, the FEP accumulated assets of over $200 million

Figure 7.2
Evita at a table with people

Source: Courtesy of Getty Images

(U.S.), employed 14,000 workers, and purchased 400,000 pairs of shoes, 500,000 sewing machines, and 200,000 pots annually for distribution.[11] The FEP also established the Eva Perón School of Nursing (which by 1951 had graduated more than 5,000 nurses), built 12 hospitals, 1,000 schools, and supported the construction of affordable housing across the country. With resources donated from union dues, government grants, lotteries, and taxes, the FEP was the most important social agency in Argentina during Perón's presidency. These were remarkable developments in a country that until 1943 lacked a formal system of social service and aid.

Perón and Evita left ambiguous legacies. Dying young at age 33 in 1952 (before everything went sideways for the General), and leaving a beautiful corpse, she quickly became one of Argentina's enduring myths. Obviously frail in her last two years, she literally seemed to sacrifice her life for her husband and her *descamisados*. When she died, on July 26, 1952, the business of the nation came to a stop while millions grieved. In a tradition that reminds us of Santa Anna's leg, her body was embalmed, and kept in CGT headquarters until Perón was overthrown. She was then clandestinely moved around Buenos Aires for more than a year, and then spirited out of the country by the government. She was secretly buried under the name Maria Maggi de Magistris (an Italian born émigré to Argentina), in a small cemetery in Milan, in 1956.

This was still not the end for Evita, as she was dug up and returned to Perón in Madrid in 1971, where the body could occasionally be seen on the dining room table. Perón's third wife Isabel repatriated the remains in 1974, when they were given to her family. She was then placed in a high-security compartment in her family's crypt in the Recoleta Cemetery, a tomb that even today receives a steady stream of visitors.

Perón, overthrown in 1955 in the midst of an economic crisis, left behind a national system of Peronist unions that would remain focal point for political conflict in Argentine society for decades. Many of his efforts to centralize and coordinate education, healthcare, pensions, and welfare failed in the face of opposition from entrenched interests (sometimes undone by the very unions that served as his power-bases). The centralized state Perón imagined, where industrial capital and workers cooperated under the authority of the state, never materialized.

In exile however, Peronism seemed to thrive. Though Peronist images were banned after 1955, the symbolic power of Peronism as a form of opposition to oligarchical interests remained powerful in Argentina. Tough economic times and the fact that Argentines were not even allowed to say his name only increased Perón's mystique. Peronism ceased to be any sort of discrete ideology, and instead became a romantic longing for better times, expressed by a desire for the general's return.

That day came in 1973, when Perón was allowed to come home from Madrid. He was again elected president, but by this time he was an old man, and his movement was so fragmented that it offered Argentines little more than violent acts perpetrated against its perceived enemies. Perón died the following year, succeeded in office by his third wife, Isabel. Under her the country veered out of control, rocked both by economic crisis and waves of political violence. She was in turn overthrown in March 1976, succeeded by one of the bloodiest dictatorships in the history of the region. Peronists were again made into targets of repression under the ruling *junta*, which hoped to wipe them from the face of the nation once and for all.

They would not succeed. Memories of Juan, of Evita, and what they once promised persist to this day. In part this is due to the fuzzy ideological content of Peronism. In its current form it remains nationalist, impassioned, and rooted in simple concepts like the appeal to social justice. In a world where poor people continue to face repeated humiliations at the hands of the powerful, Peronsim remains a vivid symbol. Well into the 1980s elderly Argentine workers were said to refer to a sunny day as *un día peronista*.

The Documents: Evita Speaks

On the evening of August 22, 1951, a visibly frail, almost translucent Eva Perón gave one of the most memorable performances of her life. Facing over a million people on the Avenida Nueve de Julio at the *Cabildo Abierto* (Open Meeting) of the CGT, she discovered the power of the crowd. Attempting again and again to decline the honor of being named vice-president, she encountered an audience that would not accept her decision. They howled in protest, they refused to go home. At nightfall, they rolled newspapers into torches and lit them, and waited for the answer they demanded.

Evita Perón was not a retiring figure. In spite of her failing health, she was the head of the nation's largest social services organization, the head of the Peronist Women's Party (women, having received the vote in 1947, were critical in the November 11, 1951 elections), and she was adored by the people she addressed. Nonetheless, in this moment she was forced to come to terms with the fact that a million people, even when they come together in support of a speaker, have a kind of power all their own. Gathered from across the country largely due to Evita's largesse (the FEP paid train and bus fares, and fed the crowds), they were there to accomplish one thing: they were meant to pressure Perón into including Evita on the ticket for the 1951 elections. When things did not appear to be going as they hoped, neither the General, nor the union bosses, nor even Evita could calm the crowd. They interrupted her speech continually, refused to let others speak, and even seemed about to launch a spontaneous general strike. While the reasons they ultimately backed down are a little unclear, it seems likely that they only dispersed once she promised to do their bidding.

This was in many ways the apogee of Evita's political life, and the way it is remembered has long been a central narrative to her legend. It was a particularly important moment because the speech began as a stage-managed moment, but relatively quickly became an improvisation, a dialogue between Evita and the *descamisados*. We know this because the memories of the participants and newsreel footage show us a spectacle on the verge of turning into a revolt. Unfortunately though, when we endeavor to find out what really happened, we confront the fact that memories are faulty and the footage fragmentary.

The story of the *renunciamiento* (renouncement) has the power to make Eva Perón into an ambitious politician (she stoked the crowd to pressure Perón), a servant of the masses (she agreed to do as they wished), and a fool (she had no idea that events would get out of control). It also has the capacity to make the crowd into a powerful and disruptive political force (they do not leave until she agrees to their wishes), a mass that simply cannot sustain itself (they disperse because their energy dissipates, they may not even be able to hear what she says), or political dupes (they are fooled by Evita into dispersing). There are still other readings, which can render the moment variously as hopeful or sinister.

Presented below several different renderings of the *renunciamiento*, each with its own truth claims. Document 7.1 is the newspaper article from the *New York Times* reporting the event. The *New York Times* reported a great deal from Argentina that year, relishing in tales of Peronist corruption, repression, and fakery. Other reports around that time informed readers that the Peróns were repressing striking rail workers, refusing to let the opposition parties have access to government radio, fomenting virulent anti-Americanism, and spending lavishly on new luxury cars while the country suffered. Critics have long accused the *Times* of selectively reporting Latin American events, and describing American foes in the most negative terms. One wonders if these factors are at work in this story, and just how much the event is being reported, as opposed to imagined, in the *Times'* reportage.

Document 7.2 comes from the Peronist Party of Buenos Aires, and is their accounting of the *renunciamiento*. Proffered as her speech, with no other explanation, the text is notable both for the fact that the most important part of the event, the dialogue with the crowd, is missing, and for the fact that the words included in the text do not appear to be what she actually said. Were these the prepared remarks, written for Evita but never delivered? One wonders. If they were, they provide an excellent opportunity for us to understand how speakers deliver the texts prepared for them by speechwriters. It also reminds us of just how perilous it is to rely on written texts from archives in order to reconstruct a past that did not take place through the medium of the written word.

Document 7.3 offers readers our best approximation of what was actually said on August 22. It comes from a transcript prepared by the Argentine scholar Mónica Amaré, who assembles the dialogue from the bits and pieces of newsreel she has been able to acquire. Readers might also encounter heavily edited bits of those newsreels by searching for video of the *renunciamiento* on the web, or opt for a literary rendering of these clips in Tomás Eloy Martínez' *Santa Evita*. Nonetheless, while each of these texts offers a glimpse of the moment, they are partial; fragments that reveal as much about the method of representation and the person(s) representing the event as they do about the event itself.

For what it is worth, we know that Document 7.4 is an accurate rendering of what she said on the radio on August 31. We have the complete recording of the radio transmission, and it is word for word what we have here. Did she stick to her script in the absence of over a million screaming *descamisados*? It would seem so.

Document 7.1 Foster Hailey, "Peronists Will Head Argentine Ticket," *New York Times*, August 23, 1951

BUENOS AIRES, Aug. 22—Standing on a floodlit platform in Plaza Moreno before a crowd estimated all the way from 250,000 to 1,000,000 persons gathered from all over the nation, President Juan Perón and Señora Perón tonight accepted, in effect, a demand of the peronista party that they run for President and Vice President of Argentina.

The President's acceptance was unqualified. There was some doubt about his wife's decision, but it seemed to some listeners as unqualified as that of her husband.

"We subject ourselves to the decision of the people," said General Perón.

After first having asked for four days to make up her mind, then twenty-four hours, then two hours, Señora Perón's last words as she turned from the microphone were, "as General Perón says, we will do what the people want."

The Superior Council, meeting immediately after the rally disbanded, announced that its ticket for the November elections would be headed by the Peróns. It will officially convey this announcement to the President and his wife Friday.

Señora Perón did not make her promised appearance on the radio, apparently convinced that her silence would indicate consent.

The rally, which was not called by the official peronista party but by the General Confederation of Labor, was the culmination of months of organized supplications to President Perón to allow himself to be re-elected President for another six years. Nearly every day delegations have been presenting themselves at Casa Rosada pleading with the general to answer the demand of the people. Three weeks ago, the labor confederation entered Señora Perón in the list as its Vice Presidential choice.

An interesting feature of the speeches of both Peróns was that each recognized the opposition to her appearance on the ticket. Much of this opposition to her, Señora Perón said, might be that the opposition knew it could not attack General Perón directly because of the people's support of him, but felt it could attack him through her.

It has been no secret that there has been a serious split within the peronista party over her candidacy. Two members of the council were forced out a few days ago for having advocated the placing of Col. Domingo Mercante, Governor of Buenos Aires Province, in second place on the ticket. Colonel Mercante started an official trip through the province on Monday that would keep him out of the city through today. There was a report tonight that a delegation of 2,000 peronistas had come from La Plata with Mercante signs and been prevented from taking part in the rally.

Document 7.2 The Peronist Version of the Speech

Source: www.pjbonaerense.org.ar/peronismo/discursos_eva/discursos_eva.htm. Translated by Laura F. Temes and Patricia Rosas.

Your Excellency, Mr. President; my dear *descamisados* (shirtless ones) of our Nation:

It is a thrill for me to see the descamisados again, just as on October 17, and on all other dates when the people were present. Today, my General, at this Justicialist town hall meeting, the people who in 1810 gathered to ask what it all meant are gathered again to declare that they want General Perón to continue guiding the destiny of our Fatherland. It is the people, it is the women, the children, the elderly, and the workers who are here today because they have taken the future into their own hands, and they know that they will only find justice and freedom with General Perón at the helm of the Nation.

My General, your glorious vanguard of descamisados is present here today, as they were yesterday, and as they always will be, willing to give their lives for Perón. They fully understand that prior to the arrival of General Perón, they lived in slavery, and above all, they had lost all hope for a better future. They know it was General Perón who gave them social, moral, and spiritual dignity. They also know that the oligarchy, the mediocre, and the traitors of the Nation are not yet defeated, and that from their lairs, they undermine the people and the nation. But our oligarchy, who always sold itself for a pittance, does not expect the people to stand up this time nor does it realize that the Argentine nation is comprised of honorable men and women who are willing to die to finish off, once and for all, the traitors and the sellouts.

They will never forgive General Perón for improving conditions for the workers, creating *Justicialismo*, or establishing that dignity in our Fatherland is reserved only for those who work. They will never forgive General Perón for lifting up everyone they despise: the workers—whom they forgot—the children and the elderly and the women—whom they relegated to second place.

Those who made the country suffer an endless night will never forgive General Perón for raising the three flags that they should have raised over a century ago: social justice, economic independence, and the sovereignty of our Fatherland.

But today the people are sovereign, not only civically but also morally and spiritually. My General, we the people, your vanguard of descamisados, are willing to finish off, once and for all, the intrigue, the slander, the defamation, and the merchants who sell out their people and their country. The people want Perón not just because of the material gains—this Nation, my General, never thought of that. Instead, it thought of our country—the material, spiritual and moral greatness of our Fatherland. Because the Argentine people have a big heart, and they believe in values other than the material ones. For this reason, my General, they are here today, traveling the roads, and with thousands of sacrifices, taking shortcuts to come here to tell us that they want to be able to declare "Present!" at this Justicialist town hall meeting.

The Fatherland heeded the call of our compañeros from the General Labor Confederation to tell the Leader that a people stand behind him and that he should continue as he is doing now, fighting against those who are not patriots, against corrupt politicians, and against imperialism from the left and the right.

As for me, in General Perón, I always found a teacher and a friend, and he always stood as an example of unblemished loyalty to the workers. All these years of my life, I have devoted my nights and days to helping the humble people of our Fatherland, without consideration for the days or the nights or the sacrifices.

While by night the sellouts, the mediocre, and the cowardly plotted the next day's intrigues and infamy, I, a humble woman, only thought of the pain I had to alleviate and the people I had to comfort on your behalf, my General. For I know the deep affection you have for the descamisados and because I carry a debt of gratitude in my heart to them, the people who, on October 17, 1945, gave me back my life, my light, my soul, and my heart by bringing Perón back to me.

I am but a woman of the people, a *descamisada* of our Fatherland, a descamisada to the core. For I always wanted to rub shoulders with the workers, the elderly, the children, and those who suffer, working side by side and heart to heart with them to ensure that they love Perón even more, and to serve as a bridge of peace between Perón and the descamisados of our Fatherland.

My General, at this stunning sight, we witness once again the miracle that took place two thousand years ago. For it was not the wise, nor the wealthy, nor the powerful who believed, but rather the humble. The souls of the rich and the powerful are shut out from all the greed and the selfishness, but the humble, as they live and sleep out of doors, have the windows of their souls open to extraordinary things. My General, it is the descamisados who see you with the eyes of the soul, and that is why they understand you and follow you. That is why they only want one man and no other: Perón and no one else.

I take this opportunity to ask God to enlighten the mediocre, so they can see Perón and understand him. And also so that future generations will not point their fingers at us should they find out that there were Argentines who were such scoundrels that they made alliances with foreign interests to fight against a man like General Perón, who dedicated his entire life to trying to achieve greatness and happiness for our Fatherland.

I was never interested in deceit or slander when they unleashed their tongues against a frail Argentine woman. On the contrary, I felt happy inside, my General, because I wanted my bosom to shield any attacks directed at you, so they would hit me instead of you. But I was never fooled. Those who attack me do so not because of me, my General, but because of you. They are such traitors, such cowards that they do not want to say they do not love Perón. It is not Eva Perón they attack, it is Perón.

They are upset that Eva Perón has devoted herself to the Argentine people. They are upset that instead of devoting herself to the oligarchs' parties, she has devoted her hours, her nights and her days, to alleviating sorrows and healing wounds.

My General, before you stand the people, and I want to take the opportunity to thank all those who are humble, all the workers, all the women, children, and men of our Fatherland, who in their heart of hearts have praised a woman's name. I am a humble woman who loves them deeply and who doesn't mind devoting her life to them if it means bringing a little bit of happiness to one household in her Nation. I will always do what the people ask of me, but I say to my fellow workers, just as I told them five years ago, that I would rather be Evita than the President's wife if that Evita were uttered to soothe the pain in some household in our Fatherland. Today, I say to you that I prefer to be Evita, because in being Evita, I know that you will always carry me deep inside your heart. What glory! What honor! What more could a citizen aspire to than the love of the Argentine people!

I am so deeply moved. My humble person does not deserve the deep affection of all the workers of our Fatherland. You are placing a huge burden on the weak back of an Argentine woman. I do not know how to repay the affection and trust that the people have placed on me. I pay it back with love, by loving Perón and by loving all of you, which is like loving the Fatherland itself.

Compañeros, I want all of you, those in the provinces, those in metropolitan Buenos Aires, those in the capital, in short, people from all corners of the country, to tell the descamisados that all that I am, all that I have, all that I do, all that I will do, all that I think, and all that I possess, none of it is mine. It belongs to Perón because he gave me everything. By lowering himself to the level of a humble woman of the Fatherland, he raised her high up and placed her in the hearts of the Argentine people.

My General, if I could reserve any satisfaction for myself, it would be that of interpreting your dreams as a patriot, your concerns, and to have worked humbly, but steadfastly, to heal the wounds of the poor people of our Fatherland, to make hopes become reality and to alleviate sorrows, according to your wishes and your orders.

I have done nothing; everything is Perón. Perón is the Fatherland, Perón is everything, and we are all light-years distant from the Leader of the Nation. My General, before the people go to vote for you on November 11, with the full spiritual powers conferred upon me by the descamisados of our Fatherland, I proclaim you President of all Argentines. The Fatherland is saved because it is in the hands of General Perón.

To all of you, to my Fatherland's descamisados, and to all those who are listening, I hold you symbolically very, very, close to my heart.

Document 7.3 The *Renunciamiento* as Compiled from Newsreel and Archival Footage

Source: Compiled by Mónica Amaré. Translated by Laura F. Temes and Patricia Rosas.

[The event was scheduled to begin at 2:30 p.m. People, especially women, had camped out days in advance in the area surrounding the presidential balcony. Around 5:00 p.m., Perón arrived with his Ministers. The crowd gave him an ovation and immediately shouted out for Eva, who entered the balcony crying. José Espejo, Secretary General of the General Labor Confederation (CGT), spoke first. He ended his speech by proclaiming the Perón-Perón ticket for the following term. Next, Perón expressed his gratitude and promised to continue his government project. The crowd started chanting, "Perón with Evita!" Eva Perón began her speech.]

Your Excellency, Mr. President, dear descamisados of our Fatherland,
It is a thrill for me to see the descamisados again, just as on October 17, and on all other dates when the people were present. Today, my General, at this Justicialist town hall meeting, just as in 1810, the people ask, "what does it all mean?" Now, they know what it means, and they want General Perón to continue leading the destiny of our Nation.

With Evita! With Evita!

It is the people, it is the women, the children, the elderly, and the workers who are here today because they have taken the future into their own hands, and they know that they will only find justice and freedom with General Perón at the helm of the Nation.
My General, your glorious vanguard of descamisados is present here today, as they were yesterday, and as they always will be, willing to give their lives for Perón. They fully understand that prior to the arrival of General Perón, they lived in slavery, and above all, they had lost all hope for a better future.

Evita with Perón! Evita with Perón!

It was General Perón who gave them social, moral, and spiritual dignity. They also know that the oligarchy, the mediocre, and the traitors of the Nation are not yet defeated, and that from their filthy lairs, they undermine liberty and the people. But our oligarchy, who always sold itself for a pittance, does not expect the people to stand up this time nor does it realize that the Argentine nation is comprised of honorable men and women who are willing to die to finish off, once and for all, the traitors and the sellouts.

Fuel! Fuel! Fuel to the fire!

They will never forgive General Perón for lifting up everyone they despise: the workers—whom they forgot—the children and the elderly and the women—whom they relegated to second place. But today the people are sovereign, not only civically but also morally and spiritually. My General, we the people, your vanguard of descamisados, are willing to finish off, once and for all, the intrigue, the slander, the defamation, and the merchants who sell out their people and their country. The people want Perón not just because of the material gains—this Nation, my General, never thought of that. Instead, it thought of our country—the material, spiritual and moral greatness of our Fatherland. Because the Argentine people have a big heart, and they believe in values other than the material ones. For this reason, my General, they are here today, traveling the roads, and with thousands of sacrifices, taking shortcuts to come here to tell us that they want to be counted at this Justicialist town hall meeting.

The Fatherland heeded the call of our compañeros from the General Labor Confederation to tell the Leader that a People stand behind him and that he should continue as he is doing now, fighting against those who are not patriots.

As for me, in General Perón, I always found a teacher and a friend, and he always stood as an example of unblemished loyalty to the workers. All these years of my life, I have devoted my nights and days to helping the humble people of our Fatherland, without consideration for the days or the nights or the sacrifices.

While by night the sellouts, the mediocre, and the cowardly plotted the next day's intrigues and infamy, I, a humble woman, only thought of the pain I had to alleviate and the people I had to comfort on your behalf, my General. For I know the deep affection you have for the descamisados and because I carry a debt of gratitude in my heart to them, the people who, on October 17, 1945, gave me back my life, my light, my soul, and my heart by bringing the General back to me.

Evita with Perón! Evita with Perón!

I am but a woman of the people, one of the descamisadas of our Fatherland, a descamisada to the core. For I always wanted to rub shoulders with the workers, the elderly, the children, and those who suffer, working side by side and heart to heart with them to ensure that they love Perón even more, and to serve as a bridge of peace between Perón and the descamisados of our Fatherland.

[A paragraph is missing on which there is no agreement in the records.]

I was never interested in deceit or slander when they unleashed their tongues against a frail Argentine woman. On the contrary, it made me happy inside, because I served my people and my General. [Applause.]

But I was never fooled. Those who attack me do so not because of me, my General, but because of you. They are such traitors, such cowards that they do not want to say they do not love Perón. It is not Eva Perón they attack, it is Perón.

They are upset that Eva Perón has devoted herself to the Argentine people; they are upset that instead of devoting herself to the oligarchs' parties, she has devoted her hours, her nights and her days, to alleviating sorrows and healing wounds.

My General, before you stand the people, and I want to take the opportunity to thank all those who are humble, all the workers, all the women, children, and men of our Fatherland, who in their heart of hearts have praised a woman's name. I am a humble woman who loves them deeply and who doesn't mind devoting her life to them if it means bringing a little bit of happiness to one household in her Nation. I will always do what the people ask of me, [applause] . . . but I say to my fellow workers, just as I told them five years ago, that I would rather be Evita than the President's wife if that Evita were uttered to soothe the pain in some household in our Fatherland. Today, I say to you that I prefer to be Evita, because in being Evita, I know that you will always carry me deep inside your heart. What glory! What honor! What more could a citizen aspire to than the love of the Argentine people!

I am so deeply moved. My humble person does not deserve the deep affection of all the workers of our country. You are placing a huge burden on the weak back of an Argentine woman. I do not know how to repay the affection and trust that the people have placed on me. I pay it back with love, by loving Perón and by loving all of you, which is like loving the Fatherland itself.

Compañeros, I want all of you, those in the provinces, those in metropolitan Buenos Aires, those in the capital, in short, people from all corners of the country, to tell the descamisados that all that I am, all that I have, all that I do, all that I will do, all that I think, and all that I possess, none of it is mine. It belongs to Perón because he gave me everything. By lowering himself to the level of a humble woman of the Fatherland, he raised her high up and placed her in the hearts of the Argentine people.

My General, if I could reserve any satisfaction for myself, it would be that of interpreting your dreams as a patriot, your concerns, and to have worked humbly, but steadfastly, to heal the wounds of the poor people of our Fatherland, to make hopes become reality and to alleviate sorrows, according to your wishes and your orders.

I have done nothing; everything is Perón. Perón is the Fatherland, Perón is everything, and we are all light-years distant from the Leader of the Nation. My General, before the people go to vote for you on November 11, with the full spiritual powers conferred upon me by the descamisados of our Fatherland, I proclaim you President of all Argentines. The Fatherland is saved because General Perón governs it.

To all of you, to my Fatherland's descamisados, and to all those who are listening, I hold you symbolically very, very, close to my heart."

[Perón is the next to speak. The event would have ended after he finished speaking. However, the crowd clamors for Evita. Espejo approaches her and says, "Madam, the People are asking you to accept your post. . ."]

[Eva returns to the microphones]

I ask the General Labor Confederation and I ask you, given the affection that binds us, that for such a momentous decision in the life of this humble woman, you give me at least four days.

No! No! With Evita!

Compañeros . . . Compañeros, I don't want any workers from our Fatherland to wake up tomorrow and have no arguments to counter the resentful and the mediocre who did not or do not understand me, thinking that everything I do, I do on behalf of petty interests. . .

No! No! With Evita!

Companñeros, due to the affection that binds us, I ask you please, do not make me do what I do not want to do.

With Evita! With Evita!

[Eva asks for silence with her hands.]

When has Evita let you down? When has Evita not done what you want? Don't you realize that this moment is very important, for a woman just as for any other citizen, and that she needs at least a few hours, only that?

No! Strike! Strike! General strike!

[Crying] Companñeros, don't you think that if my taking on the responsibility of vice president was a solution that I would have answered "yes"? I do not relinquish my post in the struggle; I relinquish the honors.

No! No!

With General Perón in government, the post of vice president is nothing but an honor, and I aspire to nothing else but the honor of the affection of the humble people of my Fatherland.

Companñeros, companñeros. The General is asking me to tell you that if tomorrow I were to. . .

[The crowd again interrupts her.]

Companñeros, I ask you as a friend, as a comrade, to disperse, to. . .

No! Answer! Answer!

[José Espejo speaks: "Companñeros, companñera Evita has requested two hours. We will remain here. We will not budge until she gives us an affirmative response."]

I am surprised . . . Never in my heart as a humble Argentine woman did I think I could accept that post. . .

(Note: while Amaré does not include it in her compilation, several versions of the dialogue between Evita and the crowd include the further phrase, placed at various points in the dialogue.)

In the end, I will do as the people decide. . .

Thunderous Applause

Document 7.4 Eva Perón's Final Response Broadcast over the Airwaves at 8.30 p.m. on August 31, 1951

Source: http://www.lafogata.org/evita/evita2.htm.Translated by Laura F. Temes and Patricia Rosas.

"Compañeros,

I want to inform the Argentine people of my final and irrevocable decision to relinquish the honor that the workers and the people of this Fatherland wanted to bestow on me at the historic town hall meeting of August 22. That same marvelous afternoon that my eyes and heart will never forget, I realized that I should not trade my post in the Peronist movement's struggle for some other post. From that moment on, after conferring with my heart and with the people, I thought about this in the solitude of my own conscience, and I reflected on it with a cool head. I have reached my final and irrevocable decision and have presented it to the Supreme Council of the Peronist Party, before our supreme commander, General Perón. Now, I want the Argentine people to hear the reasons for my unwavering resignation directly from me. First, speaking as a proud Argentine woman and a Peronista, one who loves the cause of Perón, of my Fatherland, and of my people, I hereby state that this decision arises from the very core of my conscience, and thus, it is utterly free and carries the full force of my definitive will.

On October 17, I made a lasting vow in the presence of my own conscience to focus my efforts entirely on serving the descamisados, who are the humble people and the workers. I had an infinite debt to settle with them. I think I did everything in my power to keep my promise and pay my debt. Then as now, I have but one ambition, a single, great personal ambition: in the marvelous chapter that History will doubtlessly devote to Perón, may it say that next to Perón stood a woman who devoted her life to bringing the hopes of the people before the President, and that the people affectionately called this woman 'Evita.' That is who I want to be."

For Further Reading

Anderson, Benedict. *Reflections on the Origin and Spread of Nationalism.* London: Verso, 1983.

Auyero, Javier. *Poor People's Politics: Peronist Survival Networks and the Legacy of Evita.* Durham: Duke University Press, 2000.

Farnsworth-Alvear, Ann. *Dulcinea in the Factory: Myths, Morals, Men, and Women in Colombia's Industrial Experiment, 1905–1960.* Durham, NC: Duke University Press, 2000.

Fraser, Nicholas and Marysa Navarro. *Evita: The Real Life of Eva Peron.* New York: Norton, 1996.

Guillermoprieto, Alma. *Samba.* New York: Vintage, 1990.

Hayes, Joy Elizabeth. *Radio Nation: Communication, Popular Culture, and Nationalism in Mexico, 1920–1950.* Tucson: University of Arizona Press, 2000.

James, Daniel. *Resistance and Integration: Peronism and the Argentine Working Class, 1946–1976.* Cambridge: Cambridge University Press, 1988.

James, Daniel. *Doña María's Story: Life History, Memory, and Political Identity.* Durham, NC: Duke University Press, 2000.

Knight, Alan. "Populism and Neo-populism in Latin America, especially Mexico," *Journal of Latin American Studies* 30:2 (1998), 223–48.

Levine, Robert M. *Father of the Poor: Vargas and His Era*. Cambridge: Cambridge University Press, 1998.

Martínez, Tomás Eloy. *Santa Evita*. New York: Vintage, 1996.

McCann, Bryan. "Carlos Lacerda: The Rise and Fall of a Middle-Class Populist in 1950s Brazil," *Hispanic American Historical Review* 83:4 (2003), 661–96.

McCann, Bryan. *Hello, Hello Brazil: Popular Music in the Making of Modern Brazil*. Durham, NC: Duke University Press, 2004.

Taylor, Julie M. *Eva Peron: The Myths of a Woman*. Chicago: University of Chicago Press, 1979.

Vianna, Hermano. *The Mystery of Samba: Popular Music and National Identity in Brazil*. Chapel Hill: University of North Carolina Press, 1999.

Whitney, Robert. *State and Revolution in Cuba: Mass Mobilization and Political Change, 1920–1940*. Chapel Hill: University of North Carolina Press, 2000.

Williams, Daryle. *Culture Wars in Brazil: The First Vargas Regime, 1930–1945*. Durham, NC: Duke University Press, 2001.

July 26, 1953	October 16, 1953	May 1955	November 26, 1956	December 31, 1958	January 1, 1959
Castro leads assault on Moncada barracks	Castro, on trial, delivers "History will absolve me" speech	Castro released from prison in general amnesty, moves to Mexico, where he meets Che Guevara	Castro, Guevara, and 80 others leave Mexico for Cuba on the yacht *Granma*	Batista flees	The revolution is in power

September 28, 1960	October 1960 –	April 1961	May 1, 1961	1965	1965–1967
Committees for the Defense of the Revolution (CDRs) created	U.S. government declares partial embargo, increased to full embargo February 1962	U.S.-backed invasion takes place at Playa Girón (Bay of Pigs)	Castro declares Cuba a socialist nation	Che Guevara leaves Cuba to promote global revolution. He dies in Bolivia in 1967	Campaign against Bureaucracy

A Decade of Revolution in Cuba

8

April 1959	May 17, 1959	1960–1962	June 1960	July 6, 1960	August 23, 1960
Castro visits UN in New York	Agrarian reform law introduced	In Operation Pedro Pan, 14,000 Cuban children are sent without parents to United States	U.S. oil refineries refuse to refine Soviet crude, resulting in nationalization. More nationalizations follow	United States cuts Cuban sugar quota by 700,000 tons	Cuban Federation of Women (FMC) founded

1970 –
Ten million ton sugar harvest fails

Some fifty years on, the Cuban Revolution remains a powerfully polarizing symbol.[1] Ideologues on both the left and the right still invoke the Revolution as a story of good versus evil, as something that is vibrant or nearly dead, and seem largely incapable of imagining it in historical (as something that changes over time) or ambiguous terms. Fidel Castro and Che Guevara are Third World heroes, standing up to U.S. imperialism on behalf of the poor. They represent an evil authoritarianism, driving almost 10 percent of the island's population into exile. The Revolution taught the illiterate to read, provided healthcare to the poor, and reshaped the Cuban economy in spite of a crippling blockade. The revolutionaries were bumbling bureaucrats, relied on Soviet subsidies for decades, and ultimately made the island (once again) a haven for sex tourism in their effort to save themselves. Che was a model for the best kinds of youthful idealism and rebellion. Che was an incompetent ideologue who led a generation of naïve youths to their deaths.

Figure 8.1 Iconic Che cartoon

Source: *New Yorker* Magazine

Viewed together, these competing narratives provide a baffling portrait of revolutionary Cuba. Further, if we also consider our current tendency to fetishize and massify star power, stories of the Revolution veer into the absurd. As Figure 8.1 attests, the complex ways in which ideology, youthful rebellion, and mass marketing have become embedded in narratives of the Revolution can leave us shaking our heads. The Revolution becomes an empty signifier—it can represent just about anything you might desire.

Then again, Bart Simpson on a t-shirt worn by Che Guevara, in a cartoon in the *New Yorker*, actually makes some sense. We understand how all these images are linked together because the Cuban government has, for more than fifty years, taken a defiant attitude towards an imperial power through both its symbolic repertoire and its material acts. Bart may be no revolutionary, but we can easily understand his resistance to unjust systems of power (are Principal Seymour Skinner, Homer Simpson, and Nelson Muntz really legitimate authorities?). Bart also shares a certain charisma with the icons of the Revolution. Like Castro and Che, his character was quick witted, intelligent, and a born leader for the weak, willing to stand up to bullies at risk to his own life.

Of course, Bart is a cartoon, and Che and Fidel were idealistic revolutionaries, men willing to use violence in order to reshape Cuba in their image. Given this rather significant distinction, the fact that that we can relate to Che and Fidel through Bart Simpson ought to give us pause. It tells us something about how North Americans have made meaning of the events in Cuba since the 1950s, how they have made the Revolution into a legend that serves their narrative needs (a need, for example, for youthful rebel heroes or despotic villains), but it tells us very little about Cuba.

If we are to move beyond this problem we must attempt to understand the ways in which the Cuban Revolution, and Che and Fidel for that matter, are phenomena *in time*. Unlike cartoon figures, the Revolution and its leaders lived through specific historical moments, and changed along with global historical events. Even if part of Che's appeal was that he died young in a failed Bolivian Revolution (1967), he did leave a complex imprint on the historical record, and was fundamentally a man of the 1960s. Bart Simpson, on the other hand, will forever be ten years old, and seems to live out of time, which makes him a simple and enduring symbol of the youthful rebel spirit. Not so with real people, who either changed with the times or were left behind, dead or forgotten.

We might then begin by asking a simple question: *when was the Cuban Revolution?* A literal answer would focus on the violent conflict during 1957 and 1958, noting that a guerrilla movement led by Fidel Castro, his brother Raúl, Camilo Cienfuegos, Che Guevara, and others, fought Fulgencio Batista's regime to a standstill, helped discredit the government in the eyes of the United States (so that military support was cut off), and bided their time while a broad opposition coalition came together to force Batista out of power. The Revolution, in this sense, was won on January 1, 1959, when rebels marched gloriously through the streets of Cuban cities.

With Batista gone, it was unclear to many Cubans what would happen next. The rebels had not exactly been an army, but a collection of different opposition groups that came together in late 1958 mostly in the interest of ridding the country of Batista. It was then that the clarity and power of Fidel Castro's vision became evident. Castro marked this moment in dozens of speeches and public appearances, declaring over and over again both the end of tyranny and the beginning of some as yet unspecified process. He mostly avoided talking about agendas in these moments, and focused his energies on transforming himself into the undisputed savior of the nation.

This perhaps explains one of the most powerful images we have of these early days, a photo taken while Castro spoke at Camp Colombia, an old army barracks, on January 8, 1959. It was a speech not unlike many he gave during his victorious descent on Havana, full of exhortations to unity, promises of real change, and vague threats to his enemies. What made it powerful was that at some point during the speech doves were released in the crowd (rumors always had them descending from the sky, but this is myth), and flew through the air to alight on the podium, and Castro's shoulders (Figure 8.2). Critics claim the fix was in, that Castro had seed for the birds or that the spotlight trained on him attracted them. It did not matter. The doves, read popularly both as a sign of peace and of divine approval of

Figure 8.2 Fidel Castro and the doves
Source: © Granma/Handout/Reuters/Corbis

Castro's role as *El Comandante* (the Commander), sealed some unspoken deal. Castro, as the Revolution, would save the Cuban people.[2]

What happened next would be something different, more a process of regime consolidation than a revolution. The cross-class alliances that characterized the opposition to Batista rapidly disintegrated as Fidel asserted power within the new coalition and implemented a radical egalitarian transformation. Land reform, the nationalization of foreign property, and the decision to build closer ties to the Soviet Union were radical acts, but once implemented, and once the opposition was silenced or driven into exile, they were the acts of an authoritarian socialist regime, not a revolution.

The distinction is not simply academic. The very term revolution implies a transformation, and has been used across Latin America to denote moments in which the social and political order was overturned. The 1910 Mexican Revolution, the 1952 Bolivian Revolution, even the 1979 Nicaraguan Revolution saw old systems collapse and new political actors create more inclusive political orders. But at some point each of these new regimes seemed less like radical transformative governments and more like entrenched power blocs doing what power blocs do best, which is defend their own interests. The "Revolution" in each of these cases then became an argument. If you could claim to represent the Revolution, you were then the legitimate heirs of the last popular upheaval, and thus the representatives of the people. Mexico's *Partido Revolucionario Institucional* (Institutional Revolutionary Party—PRI) for example, ruled the country as the heirs of Pancho Villa and Emiliano Zapata for some seventy years. This claim suggested that the Mexican Revolution had never ended, and that the best way poor people could see their interests served was to work with, and not against the state.

A similar, but even more powerful sentiment has long been attached to the Cuban Revolution. Even in 1959 Fidel insisted that the Revolution was not an event, but a process. Over time, the long-standing antipathy of the United States and the sense of incompleteness that has plagued the island have reinforced this claim. If you take the regime's rhetoric at face value, the Revolution is still not over, the battle is still being fought, and Cubans must remain loyal, *forever, until victory.*[3]

For half a century, this merging of Revolution–nation–regime has affected life in Cuba in a number of ways. It has shaped politics, social life, and even private affairs, leaving what was once one of the most dynamic and open societies in Latin America closed to most forms of political expression. Near constant surveillance, or at least a fear of surveillance, has produced a society where distrust is ever-present, where acts of criticism are carefully framed to avoid detection, and where individuals are acutely aware of their powerlessness.

As masters of political management, the regime has spent decades perfecting the craft of responding to growing disaffection by making limited concessions, but rescinding those concessions just as quickly. Stressful moments may bring new busses or increased rations, restrictions on the entry into hotels might be lifted, or dollars (and even cell-phones) legalized, but these privileges may also be taken away in an instant. As long as the United States remains the enemy, Cubans must live in the Revolution, which links Cuban nationalism and Socialist revolution so seamlessly that to critique the Revolution is to be a traitor to the Cuban nation. And to do that is to opt for social and economic marginalization, the possibility of jail, and perhaps exile.

The threat may be constant, but the regime is not. There is little in the experience since the 1950s that suggests that the Revolution can be understood as a stable or singular phenomenon. Rather, the regime has taken a heterodox approach to changing Cuban society, keeping itself in power, coping with changing international circumstances, and dealing with their own successes and failures. Even Castro narrated different phases of the Revolution— the *Push towards Communism* during the 1960s (discussed below), the *Retreat to Socialism* of the 1970s (promoting soviet-style planning, material incentives, and limited private enterprise), the *Rectification* of the 1980s (when limited private enterprise was eliminated), and since 1989 the *Special Period in a Time of Peace* (the name seems fittingly empty of content). The only constant in Cuba's recent past has been the U.S. embargo, and the possibility of blaming all failures of the regime on the unflagging hostility of the U.S. government. One need not be too cynical to imagine that at critical moments of potential thawing in United

States–Cuban relations, Castro actively sought to renew this enmity, as without it he would have no one to blame for Cuba's problems. How many of us recall that the Clinton administration seemed to be on the verge of new diplomatic overtures to Castro when he shot down the Miami-based planes flown by *Brothers to the Rescue*, an anti-Castro group that was dropping pamphlets attacking the regime, in February 1996?

Making a Revolution

With an annual per capita income of $353 in 1959, Cuba was hardly a poor country by Latin American standards. Cuba was, however, a highly unequal society, one of the most unequal in the Americas. Rural workers earned only about $91 annually, leaving the country with a Gini coefficient of around 0.57.[4] The economic instability of the sugar industry (almost one-quarter of the workforce was employed in sugar, leaving them idle four months per year) and foreign domination of the economy (among other things, 75 percent of arable land was foreign owned), exacerbated these inequalities, and generated twin sets of grievances for ordinary Cubans. Though they relied on sugar and the United States for their prosperity, both were also a source of misery.

The appropriate means to liberate the country from these dependencies were far from clear. While the M-26-7 (named for the origins of their movement in the failed July 26, 1953 attack on the Moncada Barracks in Santiago de Cuba) under Fidel Castro grabbed most headlines and clearly led the opposition, the regime truly had fallen because of a concerted effort by rural guerrillas, an urban underground, and striking workers. The refusal of the police and military to support Batista in late 1958 sealed his fate. A small minority believed that all the opposition needed to do was topple the dictator, and that further reform was unnecessary. Many more believed that they needed to establish stable democratic institutions, like those imagined in earlier political struggles (as recently as 1940), but more resilient. Most Cubans agreed that Cuban political parties had rotted from the inside during the dictatorship, and needed to be remade with entirely new faces. There was likewise considerable popular support for limited economic and social reforms, especially those that would put foreign owned assets into the hands of Cubans.

The differing agendas proposed in 1959 were not easily reconciled, and any faction that managed to consolidate their hold on power would have to do so in a perilous setting. Too much change would alienate the United States and powerful economic interests, who in the past had been quite capable of scuttling even minor reforms (notably during the regime of Ramón Grau San Martín in 1933). Yet many of the groups that had been critical to the struggle to overthrow Batista were unwilling to settle for meager results, and could defend their interests with weapons. Eastern peasants demanded immediate land reform. Urban workers demanded immediate 20 percent wage increases, better working conditions, and more control of the shop floor. Others demanded rent freezes, housing, education reform, women's rights, the removal of pre-revolutionary officials, and any number of other changes.

That Fidel did not get steamrolled by the onslaught of demands attests both to his good fortune and acuity. Castro proved himself to be an extraordinarily savvy politician in this moment, finding ways through early 1959 to isolate (or execute) his rivals, to build a tight-knit and loyal following, to ensure his own survival, and concentrate power in his own hands.

That said, he also enacted concrete measures that responded to popular demands. The March 1959 Urban Reform Law mandated substantial rent reductions (50 percent for rent under $100). Telephone and utility rates were reduced, wages increased, and the property of high government officials seized. The Agrarian Law of May 1959 restricted landholdings to 1,000 acres, with limited exceptions. Together, these reforms dramatically reduced poverty in the early years of the Castro regime. By 1963 Cuba's Gini coefficient had fallen to 0.28.

Reform meant confrontation with the United States, and here Castro again proved incredibly adept at turning circumstances to his favor. As it became clearer during 1959–60 that radical reform meant a violent clash with the United States, Cuban society grew increasingly polarized. Though much of the opposition was Cuban in origin, Castro managed to cast acts of sabotage, attempted assassinations, and any number of protests as the work of the CIA (in part, because sometimes they were). Cubans, he argued, must unify to confront Cuba's internal and external enemies. He also increasingly argued that the only way to do this was through an embrace of communism. Over time, his efforts yielded fruit, as millions of Cubans came to link their idea of a liberated Cuban nation with his communist Revolution, and identify its opposite with treason.

With every successful confrontation with the United States, Cubans saw a leader who could defend their nation as no other ever had. He bravely went to New York and Washington, and took the rhetorical battle directly to the enemy. He survived their assassination attempts unscathed. And after the failed invasion at the Playa Girón (Bay of Pigs) on April 17, 1961, he could rightly claim to be one of a very few leaders anywhere to ever repel an American invasion. In the face of such a compelling heroic narrative, moderates who called for elections could be dismissed as bourgeois dupes, traitors to the Revolution who would allow an intractable enemy to weaken the nation by fomenting electoral discord. Dissent became criminal (100,000 suspected dissidents were in jail by the end of April 1961).

Radical economic policies had a similar effect on Castro's hold on power. By the end of 1961, Castro had nationalized 85 percent of Cuban industry. As more and more of the economy wound up in the hands of the state, the regime eliminated certain professions (like insurance, real estate, law), and many of Castro's enemies and rivals lost their livelihoods. Along with the repression they faced, this made exile an increasingly attractive option. The pull to leave was exacerbated by the Kennedy Administration's offer of asylum on exceptionally easy terms to Cubans, a policy designed to isolate the regime but which in fact made it easier for Castro to eliminate the opposition.[5] In their place revolutionary militants took over virtually all facets of the island's economic and political life.

Had the Castro regime been simply a run-of-the-mill authoritarian government, its success in consolidating its hold on the state and isolating or eliminating the opposition might have been viewed as an end in and of itself, or at the very least a propitious moment to begin stripping the country of its assets and opening off-shore bank accounts. But again, this was a moment when Castro demonstrated that his regime was unlike others. Castro wanted control, but he was also committed to creating a massive political apparatus that would simultaneously keep all Cubans engaged in the work of remaking, defending, and policing their nation. The principal means of accomplishing these goals were the mass organizations. In March 1960 the *Asocicación de Juventud Rebelde* (Association of Rebel Youth- AJR) was created, enlisting young people to the cause. In August 1960 the *Federación de Mujeres Cubanas* (Cuban Federation of Women—FMC) was founded. In September 1960, after a public rebuke from the OAS, the *Comités de Defensa de la Revolución* (Committees for the Defense of the Revolution—CDRs) were convened. The *Asociación Nacional de Agricultores Pequeños* (National Small Farmers Association—ANAP) and *Central de Trabajadores de Cuba* (Cuban Workers Confederation—CTC) were likewise turned into mass organizations.

In the heady days of the early 1960s these associations offered Cubans an opportunity to participate in a process that promised to liberate Cuba from its imperial past, and they attracted tens of thousands of members, who in turn provided critical support for the regime. By the end of 1961 there were 300,000 members in popular militias, and 800,000 in the CDRs. Explicitly charged with physically defending the country from invasion, these groups did much more. Together with other mass organizations they served as pressure groups, demanding any number of benefits from the state, and taking credit for revolutionary programs. They were also instruments for the dissemination of revolutionary fervor, charged with raising consciousness, administering healthcare, encouraging students to go to school and workers to go to work, and as always, seeking out enemies of the Cuban people.

When the labor ministry introduced new laws mandating secure and safe environments for women, The FMC used these laws to attract new members and new support for the regime. By 1962 the FMC had 376,000 members, many of whom could directly attribute significant life changes to the Revolution. In 1959 one quarter of the women in the workforce were domestic servants, a category that ceased to exist after the Revolution. During the early 1960s FMC efforts helped 19,000 former household servants attend special schools and find new jobs. Tens of thousands were provided scholarships, materials, and training to study for new professions, and over a thousand entered the revolutionary vanguard in public administration.

Utopias

Though often undertaken as practical efforts to shore up support for the regime, we should not underestimate the ways early revolutionary projects were linked to a utopian vision of what Cuba could become. Articulated most clearly by Che Guevara, the Revolution was, in many ways, a movement against history, an effort to remake the world. This made particular sense given the challenges the new regime faced. Utopian thinking seemed in some ways the only means to get out of the very real conundrums that Cuba faced as a monoculture society 90 miles away from a hostile super-power. At first, the utopian thinking came in a plan to shift the country away from its dependence on sugar exports, to diversify and industrialize Cuba in order to ensure its independence. As Minister of Industry and a principal architect of the land reform, Che directed this transformation.

Either out of pure naiveté or simple desperation, Guevara chose to forgo the socialist phase of revolutionary reform and push Cuba directly into communism. Che wanted to eliminate cash transactions for food, transportation, and rent, with an eye towards the end of money. Rejecting the suggestion that he keep market mechanisms in place in order to ensure productivity, Che insisted that Cubans could do away with the *law of value,* which after all allocated resources to where they were productive instead of to where they were most needed. His was a program of centralized planning, a program in which the state would directly intervene in all aspects of the economy to ensure "balanced" development. He would rely mostly on the willingness of people to sacrifice for the common good in order to make this happen.

Under Che's economic model, businesses would not be supported because of their viability or efficiency, or their capacity to generate enough revenues to cover their costs, but because they were deemed intrinsically good. Centralized budgeting would allow the government to allocate funds based on ideological rather than economistic (read bourgeois) reasons. Wage scales would be eliminated, as all workers deserved the same income, and bonuses and overtime would be eliminated. Even though material incentives were common in the Eastern Bloc, Che argued that they encouraged individualism and undermined the revolutionary project of creating "new men," with new forms of consciousness. Hard work would instead be recognized with moral rewards—banners, flags, pins, and plaques rewarding the contribution of workers to the Revolution. These would in turn help spur widespread revolutionary consciousness, which Che understood as an essential ingredient in the battle against Cuba's powerful enemies.

The gendered quality of this project was inescapable. Guevara's new man was just that. For all its pretenses to feminism and nods to Vilma Espín and the FMC, the leadership of the M-26-7 viewed males, females, and their sexuality in extraordinarily conservative ways. As images of Castro in the fields cutting sugar cane attested, the Revolution was the work of strong-backed men—men who enjoyed a cigar, a strong drink, and the pleasure of revolutionary women (Figure 8.3). This image was not just part of a charismatic myth, but critical

Figure 8.3 Castro cutting cane as a part of the 1970 Cuban sugar harvest
Source: Courtesy of Getty Images and *New York Times*, January 7, 2007

to the ways that Castro identified his own physical strength with the survival of the Revolution against its enemies.

We see this both in the ways that Castro's heterosexual masculinity was fetishized, and in the fact that homosexuals were actively persecuted by the regime into the 1990s. In the *machista* culture of the Revolution, their attraction to males was linked national weakness, decadence, and U.S. imperialism. Homosexuals were represented as obsessed with self-satisfying pleasure and debauchery; definitely counter-revolutionary traits.

Prostitutes likewise drew special ire from the regime, once the sex trades were banned in the early revolutionary period. Like homosexuality, prostitution was both linked to carnal pleasure, decadence, and U.S. imperialism (after all, North Americans were frequent sex-tourists in Cuba before 1959). The prohibition produced at least one memorable tale of a drug-dependent prostitute who turned her life around and received a university education as a result of the Revolution,[6] but one supposes that not all prostitutes viewed the regime's efforts to outlaw their profession favorably. The sex trades had always been one of the few ways that poor, uneducated women could earn a decent living, and quickly returned to prominence in Cuba once Castro embraced tourism as a means to earn foreign revenues in the 1990s.

In a larger sense, these phenomena remind us of just how complex it was to imagine the creation of a new man, or new society. The new Cuba was the vision of a revolutionary van-guard, and in creating the new society the regime invariably attempted to impose practices on Cubans that were not always welcome. The Revolution promised to liberate women, but drove millions (if you include domestic workers) out of work. Indeed, the end of domestic service, prostitution, and the flight of many middle-class women to the United States actually caused a reduction in the number of women in the workforce during the 1960s.

Later the Revolution would promise domestic equality under the Family Code (1975), which required Cuban males to do an equal share of the housework. Like the ban on prostitution and domestic service, it was a utopian idea, dreamed up in the vanguard, and its affect on actual Cuban women was quite uneven. Yet even if we mock these top-down reforms for their idealism we should not forget the substantive changes Cuban women saw in their lives during these years. In part because of the exodus after 1959, and in part because the Cuban state did open educational and professional opportunities for women, and in part due to the efforts of the FMC, by the end of the 1960s Cuban women found it easier to pursue a career, to get a divorce, and to make their own reproductive decisions than women anywhere else in Latin America. All could visit a doctor if they were sick, and virtually none faced the kind of desperate hunger that had affected millions before 1959, and still affected millions in other parts of the region.

Dystopias

There is no question that some aspects of Cuba's experience in the 1960s read best as comedies. In retrospect it seems quaint to think that anyone ever believed that moral incentives—asking workers to be more productive because it is good, rather than because they would personally benefit—would ever work. Few people today believe that the state has the capacity to transform consciousness in even small ways, let alone direct the massive transformation from individualistic thinking and towards the communist consciousness that Che advocated. Our own awareness of corruption, nepotism, and cronyism in Eastern Bloc countries (and Cuba) long ago put the lie to that promise.

We need only examine the rate of absenteeism in Cuba during these years to see the problems in Che's theories. By 1967 the daily absentee rate was about 20 percent across the country, and 50 percent in some regions, including Oriente (heartland of the Revolution). In part these rates were due to low morale, in part due to the fact that mismanagement elsewhere left workers standing in long lines for food, provisions, and buses instead of working, but even accounting for these factors, this tells us that Cubans effectively went on strike to protest moral rewards.

It was not simply moral incentives that failed. Economic diversification failed. Industrialization failed. Centralized budgeting failed spectacularly. By 1962, facing shortages, the government began rationing food, clothing and consumer items. By 1963 production volumes of any number of staple crops had plummeted and production across the economy had declined. The sugar harvest also fell, from 6.7 million tons in 1961 to 3.8 million in 1963. Facing pressure from the Soviets and an economy in chaos, Castro then turned his attention to increasing sugar exports in order to improve Cuba's balance of payments.

Even this was something of a disaster. As a part of a lurching series of policy shifts during the 1960s, Castro abandoned Che's management strategies in 1964 (and Che himself went off to promote worldwide revolution), and committed most of the country's productive capacity to producing a ten million ton sugar harvest by 1970. Nothing like that had ever been done before, and if successful, it would be a demonstration of the capacities of revolutionary Cuba. Road construction, manufacturing, port facilities, and agriculture were all refocused to serve sugar, while most other endeavors were neglected.

It may have made sense to prop up Cuban exports by reinvesting in the neglected sugar sector, but beyond emphasizing sugar, Castro also punished those sectors that might have dynamically supplemented sugar exports by selling to local markets. Renewed land reform in 1963 concentrated land in large state run export facilities (in sharp contrast to first land reform in 1959, which put land in to the hands of peasants). Peasants who since 1959 had provided a wide range of fruits and vegetables to the domestic market now increasingly had no access to land of their own under the logic that, if they possessed land, they would work on it to the detriment of the state farm.[7]

Fearing that small businessmen also represented a threat to the regime, Castro nationalized 57,000 small businesses in 1968, even though most had been established since 1959. Among the prohibited businesses were street vendors, sellers of fruit, bread, coffee, eggs, sandwiches, and other goods, who provided an essential service in daily life. Street vendors often sold black market foodstuffs, commodities grown on small farms and sent to market without the permission of the state, but they also filled a critical need for Cuban consumers. State cafeterias and stores already could not meet the needs of consumers, and since they could not hope to fill the void left by the absence of the informal economy, shortages became worse. Spare parts for cars, fresh fruit, and even coffee were increasingly available only through the underground economy. Minor protests flared here and there, and one could find graffiti attacking the regime on Havana's walls.

Even the mass organizations that earlier helped legitimize the revolutionary state were failing by the mid-1960s, their initial promise having faded into bureaucratic intransigence, nepotism, and a tendency to abuse their power and spy on ordinary Cubans. Castro responded with new efforts to win popular support, including a much ballyhooed program called *Local Power*, and the comical sounding *Campaign against the Bureaucracy* (hilariously parodied in Tómas Gutiérrez Alea's film, *The Death of a Bureaucrat*). Still, real popular power was not forthcoming; it never was. Local power was (as most Cubans knew) mostly an illusion, and by the mid-1960s most of the mechanisms that had once promised power to the people were chained to the state.

Workers, for instance, saw their unions wither away during these years. They lost the right to strike, to demand higher wages. Prior to 1964 grievance commissions arbitrated work-place conflicts, but because they sided with workers too often, they were abandoned in favor of work councils, which were indirectly charged with enforcing the will of the state and labor discipline. Workers were now invited into councils to work with management on productivity, but their right to make demands was curtailed. They were instead charged with increasing productivity, saving materials, reducing absenteeism, promoting voluntary labor, preventing accidents, and of course, promoting new consciousness. There would be no more bonuses, guaranteed sick days, or strikes.

In a tragically absurd combination of these initiatives, the very mechanisms created to improve the lives of Cubans sometimes did the opposite. During the late 1960s planning was impossible, as the principal planning agencies, JUCEPLAN[8] and the National Bank, lost 1,500 positions in the Campaign Against Bureaucracy, and could not function because receipts, taxes, cost accounting, interest were all abolished. Indeed, the budget itself ceased to exist between 1967 and 1970, jettisoned in favor of a series of *fidelista* mini-plans. Political control fell to an ever more vanguardist Cuban Communist Party (Fidel's version was founded in 1965), which spent most of its energies demanding revolutionary consciousness and self-sacrifice from Cubans. One supposes that they thought this an effective means of diverting the public's attention from the messes they had made.

By 1970 the GDP was barely higher than it had been in 1965, and in per capita terms it was lower. To be sure, more than mere incompetence hurt the Cubans. They faced the loss of professional technical expertise, and were not always up to the difficult task of reorienting Cuban trade away from the U.S. market and towards the East.

Larger freighters needed deeper harbors, more port facilities and warehouses. Inventory needed to be stored, and orders were not quickly filled. Cubans also had to deal with the challenges wrought by bad Soviet parts and general shortages of spare parts for their U.S.-made cars, trucks, appliances, and more. Still, in simple terms, Cubans were worse off in 1970 than they had been in 1959. So when it became clear that on top of all this the sugar harvest was going to fail to reach its goal (in the end it was 8.5 million tons), Castro appeared before an enormous crowd in the Plaza de la Revolucíon on July 26 to offer his resignation.

Cubans refused his offer, resoundingly. The question is, why? We might start with Castro's charisma. It is difficult to divorce the simple power of Castro's magnetism from his actual policies in the early years of his regime, because he was rare among politicians for his ability to stir the crowd. Cubans also responded to his common touch, his willingness to get down from his jeep and cut cane with the workers, his capacity to appear anywhere and every-where, his tirelessness, and his simple ability to stir up feelings of fraternal (and later paternal) love. These qualities could easily make certain failings worthy of forgiveness. Nonetheless, while Castro's appeal ought to inform our interpretation of these events, it does not fully explain why the crowd refused his resignation.

It may be that the crowd's response was some sort of common emotional catharsis, a sense that his failure was everyone's failure. While not exactly a democratic mandate for thirty-eight more years in office, we could interpret this as a sign of just how successful Castro had been in identifying himself and his revolutionary struggle as synonymous with the Cuban people. Still, even this is not enough to understand the enduring popularity of Fidel Castro in 1970 in spite of the repeated failures of the 1960s. To understand this we need to come to terms with the fact that millions of Cubans shared Castro's utopian dreams, his belief that Cubans had to remain ever vigilant in defending their nation against the United States, and his sense that many of these crises were the fault of sinister foreign elements.

We see this in more than just the crowd's response. Moral incentives, for example, produced high rates of absenteeism, but they also inspired millions of Cubans to sacrifice for *their* revolution. Volunteer work, begun in October 1959 to prepare the Havana waterfront for a convention of travel agents, drew many millions of participants during the 1960s. Two hundred thousand Cubans volunteered for a teacher's brigade committed to reducing illiteracy during the 1960s, which reduced the adult illiteracy rate from 21 percent to 13 percent by 1970. In 1970 alone 1.2 million Cubans left their jobs and worked in the sugar harvest.

Moral incentives may have been a planning disaster, but in many ways they were an ideological success. They highlighted the need for Cubans to make a commitment to the government, the need for sacrifice, and acted as a means of linking the people's sacrifice to a national revolutionary project that would not otherwise succeed. When Cubans suffered some form of deprivation, they were doing the work of the Revolution. One could be proud, and ought not complain. Moreover, Cubans did believe that they were a poor people living on a rich island. Who could challenge the argument that, absent the negative impact of neocolonialism and capitalism, Cubans would be prosperous, even as prosperous as the North Americans? And who could argue with the material benefits many poor people gained under Castro?

Their idealism spoke of a generational moment, framed both by the cold war and Cubans' long history of fighting imperial rule. Twenty years later their willingness to contribute to voluntary labor was not nearly as strong as it was early on, and Cubans would increasingly be noted more for their cynicism than their idealism, but this is the very point. These were heady times. Most Cubans were willing to suffer, and suffer a great deal, if they could believe it would lead to a better world.

The Documents: Narrating a Revolution

Knowing what would become of Cuba's revolution in the 1970s and beyond, it might be tempting to dismiss those cane-cutting revolutionaries as naïve. Like North American anti-war protestors, Mexican students who marched before the 1968 Olympics demanding greater democracy, and the jubilant Czechoslovakians who celebrated the Prague Spring before the Soviet tanks rolled in, today the Cubans who sacrificed themselves in pursuit of becoming *new men* seem so very young, and so very distant. It is good to have this perspective, because it reminds us that the 1960s were a specific historical era in Cuba and elsewhere. This perspective also reminds us that the era was short lived. Cuba's state was not alone in growing increasingly conservative and authoritarian after 1970. Their larger ideological agendas may have been different, but throughout the Americas the 1970s saw states that increasingly used violence and repression to ensure order.

It is because of this shift that narratives of the 1960s remain particularly important among Cubans. In remembering their idealism, Fidel's charisma, the utopianism of the moment, and even the ways in which the revolutionary state deployed violence against is enemies and critics, Cubans attempt to explain something about the longevity of the Castro regime. For obvious reasons, these memories tend to be extraordinarily polarized. There is what we might call the "official view," offered by the regime and a worldwide network of supporters. This tendency lionizes figures like Fidel, Che, and Camilo Cienfuegos, as brave revolutionary heroes who reshaped a nation (naturally with the help of lesser figures Vilma Espín, workers, women, peasants). Castro and Che in particular put a great deal of energy even at the time into shaping this memory. An example of this practice can be seen in Document 8.1, the speech given by Castro during the May Day celebrations in 1961, just weeks after his victory against the American backed invasion of Playa Girón (the entire text can be found on the website).

By 1961, a clear majority of those who remained on the island supported the regime, especially because of its success in defending the country from what Cubans understood as a foreign invasion. By this time intellectuals who spoke critically of the Revolution often found themselves in prison or forced out of the country, often the former leading to the latter. Once in exile in Miami, New York, or Madrid, their writing came to be characterized by bitter feelings of loss and a clear and unremitting hatred of Castro. Even if they had once been somewhat sympathetic to the reform agenda, in their stories the regime was violent, arbitrary, cynical, the worst kind of dictatorship.[9]

On the island these writers were often called *gusanos* (worms), an insult that suggested treason on their part. In the 1960s it was relatively easy to dismiss critics in this way, in part because on the island the Revolution had such an array of genuine boosters, including a new generation of artists, film-makers, poets and writers who were producing brilliant and innovative work in support of the regime. To be sure, much of that work was mildly critical of the government, mocking bureaucrats and demanding the best from the Revolution, but it was for the most part the work of intellectuals who were truly leftist idealists.

This happy state of affairs came to an abrupt end with the arrest of the poet Herberto Padilla in 1971. Imprisoned, tortured, and forced to make a humiliating confession and name supposed subversives in his circle of friends, his experience had a deeply chilling affect on Cuban intellectual life. In its aftermath the Cuban government began to exercise considerable control over the arts, and many of the intellectuals who had imagined themselves as revolutionaries during the 1960s increasingly found that there was no place for them in Cuban society. One of these figures was Reinaldo Arenas, who in Document 8.2 narrates his experience of the Playa Girón episode from the perspective of exile in the United States during the early 1990s. Arenas' autobiography *Before Night Falls* (the book from which this excerpt is drawn) is a deeply ambiguous story of his sympathies for and ultimate betrayal by the Revolution. Some might be inclined to view this book as a condemnation of the regime (especially given his personal experience as a homosexual persecuted by the state), but this is an overly simple reading of the text. In some ways Arenas longs for the promises made in Castro's May Day speech, but in his memory the sense of betrayal is just as strong.

Document 8.3 offers us yet another memorialization of the days surrounding the Playa Girón invasion. This time however, it comes from the novel *The Initials of the Earth*, written by the Cuban writer Jesús Díaz, who at the time of publication (1987) was one of the most important intellectuals in the country. Díaz won Cuba's *Casa de las Americas* prize for an earlier novel, *Los años duros* (*The Hard Years*, 1966), and spent nearly three decades at the heart of the Cuban cultural establishment as a writer and filmmaker. Like many of his generation he was both critical of the regime's failings and committed to the revolutionary project. Díaz remained in Cuba after the novel's publication, but ultimately chose exile in 1991. His departure from the revolutionary fold was prompted by official displeasure over his film, *Alice in Wonderland*, a scathing critique of the Cuban bureaucracy. While living in Berlin on a fellowship, he was warned that, should he return to Cuba, he would be in a great deal of trouble.

The Initials of the Earth is a fictional account of the life of Carlos Pérez Cifredo. He is the son of middle-class parents but also an active participant in many of the events that Cubans remember as central to this era, the anti-Batista protests, the revolutionary triumph, Playa Girón, the missile crisis, and the 10-million-ton sugar harvest. The text is hardly a whitewash of the 1960s, as Carlos is a deeply conflicted individual, at times a revolutionary idealist, and at others foolish, self-interested, bumbling, and disillusioned. He repeatedly joins the revolutionary struggle, only to withdraw, sometimes because he has been disgraced by his own "errors."

The novel is framed by Carlos' need to account for these errors, as he is confronting a panel of militants who will decide whether or not he is an "exemplary worker" based on their evaluation of his character. Of, course, his judges lack even the slightest sense of irony in judging a person who had given more to the cause than any of them. Their only concern is whether or not he is sufficiently possessed of the ideological qualities of a revolutionary.

The chapter we consider takes place during Playa Girón, and in it we see Carlos entangled in a series of trials, over the American invasion, his girlfriend's impending departure with the Literacy Brigades, the death of his father, and the arrest of his brother. Carlos is torn between remaining at the university (where he is doing the work of the Revolution as a student), trying to join with his unit fighting the invasion, and other more personal desires, such as making love to his girlfriend. Each dilemma offers a series of traps; should he be insufficiently committed to the cause, he will fail the Revolution.

Díaz' rendering of life within the revolution is compelling largely because he brilliantly captures the contradictions and ambiguities of life during these times. These tensions also play a prominent role in the life history interviews that the historian Elizabeth Dore and a team of Cuban researchers recently conducted on the island. Document 8.4 is Dore's write-up of one of those interviews. It is drawn from a conversation with a woman named Alma Rivera, conducted in the Vedado neighborhood of Havana in 2004. In the larger project Dore finds a remarkable diversity of experiences, from individuals who feel they have benefited greatly from the revolution or their place within the system, to individuals who credit the Revolution with little or nothing positive. Rivera fits in the latter category.[10]

Document 8.1   Fidel Castro, "Cuba is a Socialist Nation," Address to the May Day Celebrations, May 1, 1961 (Excerpt)

Source: lanic.utexas.edu/la/cb/cuba/castro.html.

Fight Against Imperialism

. . . Think of the men who died in recent battles and decide whether a single drop of blood was worth being lost to defend the past. Consider that these workers and youths, the children of workers, fell 10 or 12 days ago to defend what we have seen today. They fell to defend this enthusiasm, this hope, and this joy of today. That is why when today we saw a happy face or a smile full of hope, we though that each smile of today was a flower over the grave of the fallen hero.

It was like giving thanks to those who gave their lives in the battle against imperialism. Without them we would not have had the May Day parade. We would not have been able to see what passed in front of us today. What would have happened to our antiaircraft batteries, what would have happened to our cannons and our soldiers who marched here? What would have happened to our workers, wives, sisters, and factories? What would have happened if imperialism had established even a single beachhead on our territory? What would have happened if the imperialists succeeded in taking one part of our territory, and from there, with Yankee bombs, machineguns, and planes, would have launched an armed attack against us?

Let us not talk about what would have happened if the imperialist had won. There is no sadder picture than a defeated revolution. The uprising of slaves in Rome and their defeat should give us an idea of what a defeated revolution is. The commune of Paris should give us an idea of what a defeated revolution is. History tells us that a defeated revolution must pay the victors in blood. The victors not only collect the past debts but also try to collect future debts. But under certain circumstances, it is impossible to crush a revolution.

It has never happened in history that a revolutionary people who have really taken over power have been defeated. What would have happened this May Day if imperialism had won its game? That is why we were thinking of all we owed those who fell. That is why we were thinking that every smile today was like a tribute to those who made possible this hopeful day. The blood that was shed was the blood of workers and peasants, the blood of humble sons of the people, not blood of landowners, millionaires, thieves, criminals, or exploiters. The blood shed was the blood of the exploited of yesterday, the free men of today. The blood shed was humble, honest, working, creative blood—the blood of patriots not the blood of mercenaries. It was the blood of militiamen who voluntarily came to defend the revolution. It was spontaneously offered blood to defend an ideal.

This ideal was not the ideal with which the Yankees inculcated their mercenaries. It was not an ideal of parrots. It was not an ideal of the tongue, but of the heart. It was not an ideal of those who came to recover their lost wealth. It was not the ideal of those who always lived at the expense of others. It was not the ideal of those who sell their soul for the gold of a powerful empire.

It was the ideal of the peasant who does not want to lose his land, the Negro who does not want discrimination, the humble, those who never lived from the sweat of others, and of those who never robbed from others, an ideal that a poor man of the people can feel.

The revolution is all for him because he was mistreated and humillated. He defends the revolution because the revolution is his life. Before sacrificing this he prefers to lose his life. He knows that he may fall, but never in vain, and that the cause for which he falls will serve millions of his brothers.

Humble, honest blood was shed by the fatherland in the struggle against the mercenaries of imperialism. But what blood, what men did imperialism send here to establish that beachhead, to bleed our revolution dry, to destroy our achievements, to burn our cane? It was to be a war of destruction.

U.S. Planned Aggression

We can tell the people right here that at the same instant that three of our airports were being bombed, the Yankee agencies were telling the world that our airports had been attached by planes from our own airforce. They cold-bloodedly bombed our nation and told the world that the bombing was done by Cuban pilots with Cuban planes. This was done with planes on which they painted our insignia.

If nothing else, this deed should be enough to demonstrate how miserable are the actions of imperialism. It should be enough for us to realize what Yankee imperialism really is and what its press and its government is. It is possible that millions have heard only the report that Cuban planes piloted by defectors had attached our airports. This was planned, because the imperialists studied the plan to bomb and the way to deceive the entire world. This should serve to keep us alert and to understand that the imperialists are capable of the most monstrous lies to cover the most monstrous deeds.

U.S. leaders publicly confessed their participation—without any explanation which they owe the world for the statements made by Kennedy that they would never participate in aggression—and save us the effort of finding proof. Who were those who fought against those workers and peasants? We will explain.

Privileged Class Mercenaries

Of the first mercenaries captured, we can say that, without counting ships' crews, there were nearly 1,000 prisoners. Among that thousand we have the following: About 800 came from well-to-do families. They had a total of 27,556 caballerias of land, 9,666 houses, 70 industries, 10 sugar centrals, 2 banks, and 5 mines. So 800 out of 1,000 had all that. Moreover, many belonged to exclusive clubs and many were former soldiers for Batista.

Remember, during the prisoner interrogation that I asked who was a cane cutter and only one said that he had cut cane once. That is the social composition of the invaders.

We are sure that if we ask all those here how many owned sugar centrals, there would not be even one. If we asked the combatants who died, members of the militia or soldiers of the revolutionary army, if we compared the wealth of those who fell, surely there would be no land, no banks, no sugar centrals, or the like listed. And some of the shameless invaders said that they came to fight for ideals!

The invaders came to fight for free enterprise! Imagine, at this time for an idiot to come here to say that he fought for free enterprise! As if this people did not know what free enterprise is! It was slums, unemployment, begging. One hundred thousand families working the land to turn over 25 percent of their production to shareholders who never saw that land. How can they come to speak about free enterprise to a country where there was unemployment, illiteracy and where one had to beg to get into a hospital? The people knew that free enterprise was social clubs, and bathing in mud for the children because the beaches were fenced. The beaches were for the wealthy. One could never dream of going to Varadero, for that was for a few wealthy families. One could never dream of having a son study law. That was only for the privileged. A worker's son could never dream that his son might become a teacher or lawyer. Ninety percent of the sons of workers, or at least 75 percent of those who lived in places where there were no secondary schools had no chance to send their children to study. Not even in a dream could the daughters of the peasants dance here or parade here.

How can one of those who never knew labor say that he came to shed the people's blood to defend free enterprise? (Chanting, applause) And they did not stop at their fathers' mention of free enterprise; they included United Fruit and the electrical company. Those were not free enterprises; they were monopolies. So when they came here they were not fighting for free enterprise; they came for the monopolies, for monopolies do not want free enterprise. They were defending the monopolistic interests of the Yankees here and abroad. How can they tell the Cuban people that they were coming to defend free enterprise?

They also say that they came to defend the 1940 Constitution. How curious! That constitution was being torn into bits with the complicity of the U.S. Embassy, the reactionary church, and the politicians. So it is cynical for this group of privileged and Batista-type tyrants, criminals, and torturers to tell the people that they were coming to defend the Constitution of 1940, which has been advanced by the Revolutionary Government.

Who represented you in the congress? The corrupt politicians, the rich, the big landholders. There were only a handful of workers in congress. They were always in the minority. The means of disseminating ideas were all in the hands of the rich. It was hard to learn about the horrible conditions because of that. The deaths of thousands of children for lack of medicine and doctors did not bother the free enterprise men. There was never an agrarian reform law because congress was in the hands of the rich. Even though the Constitution said the land must be returned to the Cubans, and even though in 1959 the 1940 Constitution had been in effect 19 years, no law took land from the Yankee monopolies, which had huge expanses.

Up to 200,000 hectares were held by some foreign monopolies. The Constitution which said that land must be returned to the Cubans and the law setting a limit on landholdings were never enforced There were teachers without employment, while children lacked schooling.

The Batista group took over through a coup sponsored by imperialism and the exploiting class; they needed such a man as Batista, so that the rural guard would serve the landowners against the peasants. (Applause) It did not matter to them that the nation was being plundered. The landowners did not give anybody modern weapons to fight that regime; they gave arms to that bloody regime itself, not caring about how it violated the constitution. The Yankees did not give arms to anybody to fight Batista. None of the fine little gentlemen fought, because they still had their Cadillacs; they had a regime that guaranteed their frivolous life. They cared nothing about politics, for they had a very good life. Now that their privileges have ended, they found a Yankee government willing to give them arms to come here and shed the blood of workers and peasants. (Applause)

Those gentlemen spoke of elections. What elections did they want? The ones of the corrupt politicians who bought votes? Those elections in which a poor person had to turn over his ballot in return for work? Those fake elections that were just a means for the exploiting class to stay in power? Those elections which were not a military coup? There are many pseudo-democracies in Latin America; what laws have they passed for the peasants? Where is nationalization of industry? Where is their agrarian reform? (Applause)

A revolution expressing the will of the people is an election everyday, not every four years; it is a constant meeting with the people, like this meeting. The old politicians could never have gathered as many votes as there are people here tonight to support the revolution. Revolution means a thorough change.

What do they want? Elections with pictures on the posts. The revolution has changed the conception of pseudo-democracy for direct government by the people.

No Time for Elections

There had to be a period for abolition of the privileges. Do the people have time now for elections? No! What were the political parties? Just an expression of class interests. Here there is just one class, the humble; that class is in power, and so it is not interested in the ambition of an exploiting minority to get back in power. Those people would have no chance at all in an election. The revolution has no time to waste in such foolishness. There is no chance for the exploiting class to regain power. The revolution and the people know that the revolution expressed their will; the revolution does not come to power with Yankee arms. It comes to power through the will of the people fighting against arms of all kinds, Yankee arms.

The revolution stays in power through the people. What are the people interested in? In having the revolution go ahead without losing a minute. (Applause) Can any government in America claim to have more popular support than this one? Why should democracy be the pedantic, false democracy of the others, rather than this direct expression of the will of the people? The people go to die fighting instead of going to a poll to scratch names on paper. The revolution has given every citizen a weapon, a weapon to every man who wanted to enter the militia. So some fool comes along to ask if, since we have a majority why don't we hold elections? Because the people do not care to please fools and fine little gentlemen! The people are interested in moving forward.

They have no time to waste. The people must spend tremendous amounts of energy in preparing to meet aggression, when everybody knows we want to be building schools, houses, and factories. We are not warlike. The Yankees spend half of their budget on armaments; we are not warlike. We are obliged to spend that energy, because of the imperialists. We have no expansionist ambitions. We do not want to exploit any worker of another country. We are not interested in aggressive plans; we have been forced to have tanks, planes, machineguns, and a military force to defend ourselves.

The recent invasion shows how right we were to arm. At Playa Girón, they came to kill peasants and workers. Imperialism forced us to arm for defense. We have been forced to put energy and material and resources into that, although we would prefer to put them into more schools, so that in future parades there can be more athletes and school children. If our people were not armed, they could not crush mercenaries coming with modern equipment.

The imperialists would have hurled themselves on us long ago if we had not been armed. But we prefer to die rather than surrender the country we have now. They know that. They know they will meet resistance, and so the aggressive circles of imperialism have to stop and think.

So we are forced, by the threat of aggression to proclaim to the four corners of the world: All the peoples of America should rise in indignation at the statement that a country can intervene in another just because the first is strong. Such a policy would mean that the powerful neighbor takes the right to intervene to keep a people from governing themselves according to their own choice. It is inconceivable that there should be such miserable governments; after the aggression that killed peasants and workers, it is inconceivable that they have even begun a policy of breaking with Cuba, instead of breaking with Somoza, Guatemala, or the government in Washington that pays for planes, tanks, and arms to come here and kill peasants.

The Costa Rican government has said that, if mercenaries are executed, it will break with us. It has no reason at all for a break, so it seeks some pretext, and hits on the idea of "if there are executions." That government, in an insolent intervention, stated its disposal to break with us if any of the mercenaries are executed. It does not break with Kennedy who organized the expedition, or with Guatemala, or Nicaragua. We did not break with it; we merely answered the note.

Those who promote the policy of isolating Cuba at the orders of imperialism are miserable traitors to the interests and feelings of America. (Applause) These facts show us the rotten politics that prevail in many Latin American countries, and how the Cuban revolution has turned those corrupt forms upside down to establish new forms in this country.

New Socialist Constitution

To those who talk to us about the 1940 constitution, we say that the 1940 constitution is already too outdated and old for us. We have advanced too far for that short section of the 1940 constitution that was good for its time but which was never carried out. That constitution has been left behind by this revolution, which, as we have said, is a socialist revolution. We must talk of a new constitution, yes, a new constitution, but not a bourgeois constitution, not a constitution corresponding to the domination of certain classes by exploiting classes, but a constitution corresponding to a new social system without the exploitation of many by man. That new social system is called socialism, and this constitution will therefore be a socialist constitution.

Document 8.2 Reinaldo Arenas, "The Fire," from *Before Night Falls*

Source: "The Fire," from *Before Night Falls: A Memoir* by Reinaldo Arenas, translated by Dolores M. Koch, copyright © 1993 by the estate of Reinaldo Arenas and Dolores M. Koch. Used by permission of Viking Penguin, a division of Penguin Group (USA) Inc.

Undoubtedly all this had been planned since the beginning of the Revolution: the communist slogans, the communist texts, and the most convenient time to declare the communist nature of the Revolution. And in the midst of that wave of young men shouting slogans, I suddenly saw myself participating, carried away, marching and singing like all the others. At first I did not join in, but I did not protest either. I thought I could read in the faces of some of my friends from Holguín the same anguish or disenchantment that I felt, but naturally we did not talk about it. A few minutes later we were swept up by the parade, repeating slogans, which became more and more vulgar and offensive, against "Yankee imperialism" and against untold thousands of enemies suddenly discovered. Little by little the march turned into a sort of conga, into a grotesque carnival, where everybody, while moving their buttocks, began gesturing in an erotic and obscene manner. In a strange way that crowd, in less than a minute, had passed from socialism on to communism.

Heading the procession were the professors, the indoctrinators, the ideological guides, and Alfredo Sarabia. I understood that in reality we had been locked up for a year, as if in a monastery, where new religious ideas, and therefore new fanatic ideas, prevailed. We had been indoctrinated in a new religion and after graduation we were to spread that new religion all over the Island. We were the ideological guides of a new kind of repression, we were the missionaries who would spread the new official ideology among all the state farms in the Island. The new religion had in us its new monks and priests, and also its new secret police.

The atmosphere of the Revolution admitted no dissent whatsoever. Fanaticism and faith in a "brilliant" future, as our leaders incessantly hammered home, prevailed. This fanaticism reached its peak with the creation of the so-called ORI, that is, Integrated Revolutionary Organizations. Vulgarity and rabble behavior, encouraged by the Revolution, were logically a part of those organizations. One of the slogans was: "ORI Is Fire, Don't Say ORI, Say Fire." And everybody wiggled their butts, turned round and round, and sang to the conga beat of those songs and chants.

In fact, the Communist Party was, naturally, behind the ORI, and Fidel Castro became aware that those "Integrated Organizations" wanted to get rid of him and seize power; that is, the communists of the old guard wanted to remove Castro and take charge. But if Fidel Castro was ever loyal to anybody, it was to Fidel Castro. Later on, trials took place and some of those gentlemen received thirty-year sentences. And Castro affirmed that he was a Marxist and had always been a communist, that his political education had been Marxist-Leninist. So he became "the Fire," he became the ORI, the head of the "Integrated Organizations."

I finished my studies and became an agricultural accountant. I was assigned to the William Soler farm near Manzanillo, in the southernmost part of Oriente province. Before leaving for the farm, I spent some days in my grandfather's house.

Document 8.3 Jesús Díaz "Chapter 13," from *The Initials of the Earth*

Source: Jesús Díaz, "Excerpt," in *Initials of the Earth* by Jesús Díaz, translated by Kathleen Ross, pp. 195–203. Copyright © 1999, Piper Verlag GmbH, Munchen. Copyright 2006, Kathleen Ross, Translator. All rights reserved. Reprinted by permission of the publisher, Duke University Press.

Now the sky was clear, reddish, almost amber, and he couldn't stop looking at it from the flat roof of the Beca, the large residence hall. He was waiting for the war, he knew it was about to break out, had broken out, or was breaking out that very dawn of 16 April. He looked at the sky somewhat frightened, because now it was hiding a latent threat and during those days it was rare to see it so clean and pale, the stars becoming lost into the light like dissolving icicles. Only three weeks ago he had discovered the roof, a kind of ideal lookout from which, according to the Coachman, you could see all the nymphs of Vedado naked. Their successes were fleeting, limited, far-off, and undecipherable, but he stayed in the habit because he'd rediscovered the splendid magic of the cloud game. Suddenly he was the master of a ship, an elephant, or the rifle he'd lost when he abandoned the battalion, and his possessions were blue, gold, reddish, and ethereal, and always ended up dissolved into the wind, or silently swallowed by the unfathomable darkness of the night.

Then the stars came out, and Roal Amundsen Pimentel Pinillos, better known as Munse the Indian, would offhandedly share with them his knowledge, which he used to call galaxicology. Carlos—the Dude to his university classmates—quickly shared his enthusiasm and learned that not only Ursa Major and Minor existed, but also Giraffe, Hunting Dogs, Chameleon, Crow, Crane, Toucan, a whole bestiary of constellations. The firmament (Munse hated the word *sky*) was not even remotely filled by those animals. There were plant constellations as crucial as Hydra and Hydrus, mythological heroes like Hercules and Perseus, and also many instrument constellations: Microscope, Compass, Sextant. Although they couldn't make out more than a few with only their eyes, Munse always talked about the machine constellations, like the Furnace and the Air Pump; Carlos, for his part, felt a feverish inclination towards Berenice's Hair, the Painter's Easel, and Bird of Paradise.

In public, they always said their favorite constellation was *Cochero*, just to bother Osmundo Ballester who, owing to his legendary ugliness, was called Frankenstein's Coachman. Francisco Urquiola, known as Pancho the Ghost, liked to add "Tripleugly as his master," and Osmundo defended himself, "Tripleugly but white," and declaimed some verses learned from his father's lips: "To be white's a career, / mulatto, a profession, / black, a sack of charcoal / you can buy just anywhere." And that's how they were going along, ironic, enthusiastic friends, the day that God's Gift to Man surprised them with the news:

"The Russians put a man in the sky."

There wasn't time to explain to a guy like God's Gift that you didn't say Russians, but Soviets, or sky, but cosmos. They preferred running up to the lookout to see the blue that guarded the immemorial questions of its constellations, and they went up again in the evening, after classes. Munse, deeply moved, began to explain that man had crowned the legendary dream expressed in the winged myths of Icarus, Pegasus, and Chullima, in order to initiate a new phase in history, the Cosmic Era, while the Ghost beat out a rhythm on a case of sodas:

Yuri Gargar-in,
Yuri Gargar-on,
I'm headin' for the cosmos
In a rocket made of tin.

The Indian interrupted his explanation, how the hell did he dare to make fun of the Cosmic Era. "Because I'm inventing the Comic Era, asere," the Ghost replied, and they all started laughing about the cosmocomic and stopped on seeing the fire that suddenly broke out in the east, over El Encanto, and that grew with dizzying speed, devouring what was now no longer the most beautiful department store in Havana, sweeping it away and reddening the sky in the distance, as if it were burning the Bird of Paradise's song.

Twenty-four hours later the bombardment started. In the west, the sky blew up in explosions resembling the kinds of stars whose existence Munse had explained, wandering, binary, triple, multiple, shooting, fixed, with a deafening, sinister noise. The Coachman went down to get the news and returned, saying that airplanes of unknown origin were attacking the air force hangars in Ciudad Libertad. Carlos joined the cries of *Patria o Muerte* and felt sorry for the invaders, certain that this wasn't just a diversion like that of four months earlier: this time war had started.

He tried to rejoin his old battalion and was denied permission. He was a university student, the university would decide when and how to mobilize its units. He was thinking about breaking this absurd rule when they were informed that the compañeros killed during the bombardment would be laid out in the administration building, the Rectorado, and it would be their job to maintain order. On seeing the closed coffins, he thought about the La Coubre: now, too, the bodies would be charred or destroyed. He recalled Chava's warning. "The dead are watching," and cursed himself for leaving the combat battalion in order to accept a scholarship to the university. With the scholarship, he'd also gotten a place to live in the Beca, thus overcoming the fear in which he'd been living since leaving home and joining the militia. But now that war was going to break out, had broken out, was breaking out perhaps that night, now that the nine hundred comrades in his battalion were risking their hides for the motherland, he thought that the cost of his decision had been too high and realized he'd made it impulsively, out of anger because he'd been sanctioned for having left.

Life in the Beca meant a return to the lost paradise of normality. In the tall building, so like the one his father once owned, he shared a room with his buddies, had a bed, sheets, towel, a tiled bathroom with a blue toilet, and also received a stipend. On the first afternoon he went to the movies with Gisela, and on rediscovering the dream of life in the play of light and shadows, came to think that his life in the militia had all been a dream, and evoked the cold, the thirst, and the fatigue with the joy of someone who had awakened. From there, he went on to the hospital, giving his family's rigid customs as a reason not to take Gisela with him, and when he was alone, he felt like a heel. His father's old Buick was across from the pavilion; Jorge had stuck a decal on the windshield: I AM RELIGIOUS. IN CASE OF ACCIDENT CALL A PRIEST. He read it with a bitter smile, thinking how he could stick next to it the reply that decorated the car of the residence-hall director: I AM A REVOLUTIONARY. IN CASE OF ACCIDENT CALL A DOCTOR, or he could take Gisela along to visit, put her right in front of Jorge, and say to him, "Take a good look: a militant and a mulatta." Nevertheless, he'd kept her hidden, because he was a coward, as if her beautiful curly hair was a stigma. Rejoining his family, he calmed down. Jorge was still distant, but his mother thanked him with a kiss for his decision to stay and take care of his father, who smiled, happy that his two branches were there, next to their old trunk.

From then on, he lived intensely happy and sad days. Soon Gisela would leave with the Literacy Campaign, she'd spend a year far away, living with the peasants, and he was proud of her decision and encouraged her, telling her Toña's story, but at the same time wishing the day of her departure would never come. They'd go to the movies, dreaming that the show would last an eternity, while they discovered each other's bodies in the darkness. Going outside, they rediscovered their faces in the twilight, and Carlos would break off their happiness by making up unusual reasons for not taking her to visit. He would walk toward the hospital ruminating on his misery, telling himself that tomorrow he'd end his hypocrisy once and for all. But looking at his father's ever more-consumed face, he'd think he'd done the right thing, he had no right to assure his own happiness by showing up with a black woman and hurrying death: because for his father, there was no such thing as mulatto.

The nights he stayed to take care of him, Carlos felt a confusing happiness. Jorge wasn't there, and he wasn't obligated to make up friendly conversations about nothing under his mother's tender, inflexible gaze. His father had improved slightly, he spoke in a very low voice, said please when he asked for things and didn't make any wounding comments about politics, as if the nearness of death had sweetened his character. Carlos took advantage of the peacefulness in the room and the night to treat him tenderly, attentive to his urine, excrement, and sores, discovering the body that had engendered him as if he were discovering that of his own son. He would have liked to bathe and shave him, but didn't try because his mother would never give up that privilege. He contented himself with tickling him lightly on the chest, to see him smile, hear him murmur. "Cut it out, kid," feel him close, a buddy. But one night his father didn't respond to the tickling, took Carlos's hand to his chest and said, "I'm scared." "Of what?" he asked, ready to ask for help. His father held on to him with a tenacious anguish, repeating the phrase, and he too felt something empty, irreparable, dark, from which he could not escape, because it was *inside* his soul like the daño, and he knew that it was the final, inexplicable fear of children and the dying, and he told himself he had to be a man, and kissed his father's forehead murmuring, "Cut it out, kid, cut it out," before calling the nurse, who leaned over that emptiness against which neither doctors nor priests could do a thing.

He remained sunk in a strange stupor, in a fog resembling sleep or fatigue, surprised at not feeling a desire to weep. He telephoned his mother, told her simply, "You need to come," and she responded with a mutilated cry. But when she arrived she didn't weep, she asked permission to be alone with the body for five minutes, and Carlos consoled Jorge, who was sobbing like a little boy in the corridor. Hearing the bang of the door, they turned around. Their mother had emerged dressed in black, a dry suffering in her eyes, ready to take care of everything. During those hours, Carlos admired more than ever her practical sense of life, her natural capacity for work, and told himself that therein lay the source of her wrinkled beauty.

When they arrived at the funeral home it was dawn, a strange lilac light was floating in the room, they still hadn't brought the body. Little by little, distant friends of the family or of Jorge's arrived, greeting them by saying "My deepest sympathies" or "My thoughts are with you," to which Carlos invariably replied with a subdued "Thank you," while he watched them milling around his mother or his brother, and felt more and more alone. He asked himself if he had the right to call Gisela; if his father, so understanding after seeing the face of death, would have accepted her. He answered himself that he shouldn't do it without consulting his mother. Carlos was afraid that Jorge would snub her in a way he wasn't willing to put up with, he preferred to suffer through his solitude in silence, but then he'd never be able to convince Gisela of his love. He needed some advice, his buddies from the university still hadn't arrived, Pablo was in Cunagua, his battalion comrades in Escambray, his father dead.

A growing murmur startled him awake. Jorge was gesturing to their mother, and Gisela, Pancho, Osmundo, and Munse had paused at the threshold of the chapel. Carlos went towards his mother, almost running, and got to hear the last of Jorge's words, ". . . who are those people?"

"She's my girlfriend," he replied, with too loud a tone.

"Bring her here," his mother said, making Jorge stay beside her.

Carlos moved towards Gisela, who now had blended into the crowd, gave her a kiss on the cheek, and led her towards his mother, who gently caressed her face, kissed her forehead, and gave Jorge an order:

"Say hello to your *cuñada*."

Jorge held out his hand unable to control his resentful gaze, Gisela responded to his greeting with her head bowed, murmuring "My thoughts are with you," and a funeral home employee approached them.

"Señora Josefa Cifredo?"

His mother nodded her head yes.

"Please," said the employee, with a serious voice. "Who will dress the deceased?"

She looked at Jorge with a sad desperation, then at him, and replied: "His sons."

Carlos went down the stairs first, in silence, feeling a sudden shiver that turned into trembling on reaching the penumbra of the corridor, which got darker and darker. He entered the shadows remembering a night inhabited by souls in agony, the daño all along that unknown path that took him to the dark cave where for the first time he heard the echoes of death, which now sounded like his own footsteps as he headed towards the pale light at the end, under which his father lay naked, yellowish, poor, and able to put love in the place of hate and fear, to make him share with his brother the task that they carried out methodically, serenely, sobbing in silence.

And now, at the entrance gate to the Rectorado, he watched the relatives of the victims of the bombardment, thinking that they hadn't even been given the chance to dress their dead, to see them grow old, or to close their eyes. He felt like part of the wide human sea that spilled out over the wide staircase and the street, clamoring for vengeance. Across from the coffin where her boyfriend lay, there was a girl who refused to eat or to sit; she didn't weep, nor did she respond to the pleas of her family that she rest; she simply stood there, looking at the wood. Carlos searched for her eyes, to tell her silently that he was with her, but when their gazes met he felt it was useless: the girl couldn't see him. He asked himself where Gisela would be, in what remote place in Pinar del Río, maybe right there where the war would be starting, where other militiamen would protect her from death, like she had protected him from the loneliness into which he had plunged after the burial. Then, he had left the cemetery fearing that his mother would reinitiate the battle to shut him up at home with Jorge, knowing that precisely at that moment it would be impossible for him to say no. But on reaching the door of the house, she looked at him as if trying to memorize his face, before kissing his forehead and saying:

"Go live your life."

Hours later, waking up in his room, he felt as desolate as an orphan and ran to look for Gisela. They walked in silence along Avenida de los Presidentes, followed the seafront promenade, and sat on the wall, back turned on the sad March sea. Across from them, in the gardens of the Hotel Nacional, next to the rusting cannons of Spanish times, three antiaircraft batteries guarded the afternoon.

"I'm leaving tomorrow," she said.

Carlos didn't answer, her departure fit perfectly into his sadness; everyone was leaving, to teach, to Escambray, to Cunagua, or to die.

"I want to give you something."

He thought how a picture or a lock of hair wouldn't do any good.

"I know it's not the right time," she said, "but I'm leaving tomorrow."

Carlos turned around, ready to receive whatever it was, forcing a smile.

Gisela was tense, especially beautiful, set against the reddish sky like the blaze of a fire.

"If you don't want to, then, no," she said, and he took a second to understand that she was offering herself, just like that, for nothing, and he told her no, love, no, later on, when she came back, they'd get married.

"But I want to now." Gisela insisted, like a little girl. "I want you now."

The cheap hotel room was gray. Gisela didn't know what to do, and Carlos realized in horror that he didn't either, that Fanny and Gipsy had done everything, while he tried to find a dignified way to take off his pants and struggled to overcome the idea that he couldn't, that it wasn't the right place, or day, or hour, that his member wasn't going to respond because he was committing a sacrilege. Gisela had lost her self-assurance, her moment of madness, she took off her clothes in silence, head lowered like someone accepting punishment; she sat down next to him on the bed, turned her back to him, and asked him to help her. He thought he had no way to do that, and was going to say so when he realized she wanted him to undo her bra. But his clumsy fingers, damp with sweat, couldn't solve the mystery of a clasp that was neither a button nor a snap, but a sort of inexplicably complicated hook that she herself suddenly opened, turning around to take refuge in Carlos, who kissed her, feeling her small breasts fluttering against his chest, hearing her say, "Come" while she dragged him towards the bed and he felt his sex burning on contact with that warm skin, and his right hand and her left managed to pull off her panties leaving her open, waiting, and Carlos moved onto her and penetrated her and felt her cry and those serpent-like contractions devouring him, making him spill over in the very essence of pleasure.

"Finished?" she asked, and he burst out crying. He felt like an orphan, guilty and a failure, and he cried over the stupor of the hospital, the sadness of the funeral home, and the loneliness of the thud of his father's coffin in the ground. She let him cry on her breasts next to her warmth, breathe the scent of her hair, hear the beating rhythm of her heart, feel running on her groin that unique blend of blood and sap, harbor the marvelous, terrible thought that he, too, could have engendered a son. That was how he wanted to remember her the next day, when he said goodbye at the train amid the jubilation of thousands of literacy teachers and their relatives, and she murmured after kissing him:

"You are my husband."

But now, alone in his lookout, watching the almost completely blue sky, waiting for the war that was going to break out, had broken out, or was breaking out precisely then, he recalled her in the open train car, dressed in her uniform, with a backpack, a primer, and a huge cardboard pencil, radiant amid the racket of her compañeros, while he tried to cut a path through the crowd of relatives, the farewell committees, the music band, the vendors, and the locomotive's hoarse puffing, the departure whistle, and the vibrating crash of cymbals sounded, and he yelled a useless goodbye and saw her disappear behind the cloud of steam, singing in chorus with the crowd:

We're the Conrado Benítez brigades,

we're the vanguard of the Revolution . . .

And now, he mechanically repeated that goodbye on the roof, from the rear guard, feeling that something wasn't right, because in the movies, in books, in songs, it had always been the women who said goodbye to their heroes.

"Dude, your *pura*'s downstairs."

He didn't need to turn around to identify the Ghost, no one at the Beca managed to talk like that, although many tried. He went towards the elevator wondering what his mother might want. She'd never come to the Beca, it wasn't likely that she was sick. After his father's death, Carlos had taken her to the Archimandrite, who had found her hard and flexible, like a cedar branch. She had smiled, pleased with the diagnosis and even more with the prescription.

"Medicines will make you sick, my dear. Drink an infusion of jasmine, lily, or orange blossoms so your stomach won't be jumpy anymore."

Since then she had remained calm, resigned, telling him to bring her his dirty clothes and to come eat more often at the home that was as much his as his brother's, offering him half the money his father had left in the safe. Carlos gave her this pleasure only when Jorge wasn't there, because arguments with his brother had gone back to being about politics and it was almost impossible for them to talk without shouting. He knew that Jorge had kept the car for himself and was also trying to get the house and the money, saying that Carlos lost all his rights when he abandoned the family, but it didn't matter. He had a picture of his father in his wallet, he didn't need anything more.

When he found her sitting at the other end of the dining hall, he thought that the Ghost's obscure idiom was as clear as day: dressed in black, leaning slightly over the bagasse-board table, illuminated against the sunlight, his poor mother was the image of purity. He went forward without taking his eyes off her. She hadn't noticed his presence: through the glass wall, she in turn looked out at the street, where some militiamen began to move into formation to head for the burial. Carlos believed he knew the motive of her visit, she had come supposing that he'd be going to war, and he told himself that the fact that he wasn't going, that he was part of that stupid unit with black berets and cartridgeless rifles, would at least have the advantage of calming her.

"Hello," he murmured, kissing her on the cheek.

Startled, she turned around, anxiously taking his hands.

"Your brother's been arrested," she said.

"I warned him," murmured Carlos, shaking his head.

"He didn't do anything," she said, with conviction.

"I don't know that, Mamá, and neither do you."

She bit her lower lip, looking at him imploringly.

"Talk to your friends," she said.

He started to kick the floor with his boots, asking himself if his mother was able to understand that he didn't have any such friends, nor was he willing to intercede on Jorge's behalf, nor would he find anyone who would listen.

"I can't," he said. "There's a war on."

She wrung her small linen handkerchief over and over, as if saying a rosary.

The Coachman rapped on the glass with his knuckles, Carlos made signs to ask them to wait for him.

"Are you going?" she asked, with a defeated anguish.

"No," replied Carlos, looking into her eyes.

His mother stood up, pulled him to her, kissed him on both cheeks, and murmured thank goodness, while she opened up her inevitable black pocket-book with a gold clasp, from which she took out a grease-stained roll of paper.

"Here, take it," she said. "I brought you a steak."

Document 8.4 Elizabeth Dore, "Cubans' Memories of the 1960s"

Source: Reprinted from Elizabeth Dore, "Cuban Voices: Lives in the Revolution" (forthcoming). With permission from ReVista, The Harvard Review of Latin America.

September 2004, Vedado, Havana

It is the morning after Hurricane Ivan side-swiped the island, and the streets remain eerily empty. Roberto and I squeeze into Alma Rivera's miniscule apartment in a dilapidated building, a short walk from La Rampa, club-land for Havana's tourists. The three of us perch in the tiny combination kitchen-bedroom. A ladder in the corner leads to the barbacoa: the loft where Alma's three middle-aged sons sleep when they are not with girlfriends. Alma is 68 years old, black, petite and strong. Proudly pointing out the features of her room, she tells us, "I repaired the walls, installed the toilet, and built the barbacoa and the porch with my own hands. I had no proper tools." After her initial outburst, Alma becomes extremely solemn. "My life has been full of tears and suffering." Growing up in a poor peasant household in Pinar del Rio was "miserable, truly miserable. From the age of seven I worked in agriculture, mostly in the tobacco zone. I wanted to stay in school but my parents didn't let me. People before [the revolution] were foolish. [If I had studied] now I would be a great doctor." In 1961, Alma left her husband "because he was a womanizer," and moved to Havana with her two young sons.

"How did the triumph of the revolution affect you and your family," Roberto asks. Alma says nothing, and after an uncomfortable silence begins to tell us about the drudgery of her life in the 1960s.

"I worked in one cafeteria after another, cleaning floors and washing dishes." In a rare reference to the emancipatory effects of the revolution, she adds, "I didn't mind so much because I was in an atmosphere of freedom." A few years later Alma was fired from a good job at the Restaurant Cochinito because she refused to have sex with the manager. Echoing Fidel Castro's slogan about turning defeats into victories she says, with a certain smugness, "to quit at the right time is a victory." But adds in a voice that betrays her anger, "I got nailed. When I demanded my right to severance pay they refused. No one defended me. Not the management. Not the trade union. Not the Party. No one. They acted together. Not even the Woman's Federation. No. They were one."

Alma describes life in the 1960s as a string of battles with one bureaucrat after another. She tells a long, convoluted story about how she fought to keep her apartment, the one we are in. "I fought hard, finally they let me stay. They were going to send the police and all. But I am not afraid of anything. The head of the Committee for the Defense of the Revolution [the official "neighborhood watch"] was on my side, and she offered to talk to Fidel Castro about this. But I said no, so we went to the housing authority. The little whites [blanquitos] who worked there just looked at us. Then I said listen, we don't all have fancy foam mattresses to sleep on, now do we? Finally, they let us stay," she says, referring to her family, "but because of all that we didn't have a ration book [proof of residence needed to receive food] for three years."

After we leave, Roberto and I go to Rápido, a fast-food shop, to talk about Alma's life story. While we don't always agree, we both find her silence about the revolution striking. Alma seemed to take the opportunities provided by the state for granted. Her narrative thread is that she obtained what was rightfully hers thanks to her own persistence, struggle and intelligence. Not thanks to the revolution, the official slogan.

For Further Reading

Alvarez Borland, Isabel. *Cuban-American Literature of Exile: From Person to Persona*. Charlottesville: University Press of Virginia, 1998.

Anderson, Jon Lee. *Che: A Revolutionary Life*. New York: Grove, 1997.

Del Aguila, Juan M. *Cuba: Dilemmas of a Revolution*. Boulder: Westview, 1994.

Eckstein, Susan Eva. *Back from the Future: Cuba under Castro*. New York: Routledge, 2003.

Farber, Samuel. *The Origins of the Cuban Revolution Reconsidered*. Chapel Hill: University of North Carolina Press, 2006.

Higgins, Michael. "Cuba: Living the Revolution with Oscar Lewis," *Dialectical Anthropology* 3:4 (1978), 365–72.

Miller, Nicola. "The Absolution of History: Uses of the Past in Castro's Cuba," *Journal of Contemporary History* 38:1 (2003), 147–62.

Pérez, Louis A. Jr. *Cuba: Between Reform and Revolution*, 3rd edn. New York: Oxford University Press, 2005.

Pérez-Stable, Marifeli. *The Cuban Revolution: Origins, Course, and Legacy*. New York: Oxford University Press, 1993.

Quirk, Robert. *Fidel Castro*. New York: Norton, 1995.

Sweig, Julia E. *Inside the Cuban Revolution: Fidel Castro and the Urban Underground*. Cambridge, MA: Harvard University Press, 2002.

Valdes, Zoe. *Yocandra in the Paradise of Nada*. New York: Arcade, 1999.

October 3, 1968	November 4, 1970	September 11, 1973	March 24, 1976	1977	July 17, 1979
Juan Velasco overthrows government of Peru, institutes leftist reforms	Socialist Salvador Allende becomes President of Chile	Allende is overthrown in a military coup led by Augusto Pinochet	Argentine military overthrows Isabel Perón, begins Dirty War	Mothers of the Plaza de Mayo begin marching in protest of missing children	Somoza regime overthrown in Nicaragua, leftist *Sandinistas* come to power

June 19, 1990	April 5, 1992	September 12, 1992	October 16, 1998	November 2000	April 19, 2005
Alberto Fujimori elected President of Peru	In self-coup, Fujimori shuts down Congress and judiciary, and suspends the constitution	Sendero leader Abimael Guzmán captured	Augusto Pinochet arrested in London on charges brought by Spanish judge Baltaser Garón. He is eventually released because of poor health	Fujimori flees country after re-election because of corruption scandals	Adolfo Scilingo, only Argentine dirty warrior to ever confess, is sentenced to 640 years in prison for crimes against humanity by a Spanish court

Peru in an Age of Terror

9

On April 5, 1992, Peruvians awoke to discover that their president had overthrown his own government. Some were outraged, others cheered, but few Peruvians were particularly surprised. Elsewhere in Peru at least three armies of guerrillas were blowing up power stations and murdering their enemies (including feminists, human rights activists, and anyone insufficiently doctrinaire). In the countryside dogs hung from trees, the symbolic victims of Maoist[1] trials. And the only sector of the economy that seemed dynamic was the cocaine business, producing Peru's most profitable export. The guerrillas, army officers, and corrupt government officials were growing rich from the trade, but Peru was falling apart.

Alberto Fujumori's *autogolpe*,[2] the war against the guerrillas that followed, his brief tenure as the nation's savior, and his ultimate reckoning for both corruption and human rights violations, are stories that have corollaries across Latin America in the last quarter of the twentieth century. Between the 1960s and the 1990s the region as a whole went through one of the bloodiest periods since independence, as military and other authoritarian governments unleashed unprecedented levels of violence against what they invariably represented as a revolutionary communist threat. The statistics are staggering. Most governments in the region have never fully accounted for the dead, but truth commissions in Chile (the Rettig Commission) and Argentina (National Commission on the Disappearance of Persons, CONADEP) concluded that right-wing military dictatorships in those two countries murdered at least 2,279 and 9,000 persons respectively (though both commissions acknowledged that the actual numbers were far higher).[3] In Guatemala, a civil war during these years and accompanying state terror cost nearly 300,000 lives. Peru's Truth and Reconciliation Commission concluded that 69,280 people died or disappeared between 1980 and 2000 as a result of the armed conflict, about one-third of whom died at the hands of the government. These numbers do not include those who were arbitrarily imprisoned, tortured, and or forced into exile, numbers that reach into the millions for the region as a whole.

This period in Latin America's past is deceptively difficult to narrate. We often fall into a series of traps in telling the story of these conflicts, which are often referred to as the "dirty wars." Told as tragedy, we can become disturbingly caught up in the gruesome details of torture and murder, turned into voyeurs who symbolically re-enact these acts on their victims through our lurid fascination with the violence. Latin Americans become a shadowy people, unable to live by the rules of modern civility. Alternatively, we can make the victims (Salvador Allende's Popular Unity in Chile, Che Guevara's guerrillas in Bolivia, Mexican student protestors in 1968 and 1971, or even Peru's *Sendero Luminoso* [Shining Path]) into romantic heroes, victims who had no part in unleashing the waves of violence. While each of these may satisfy our mordant curiosity or desires to use the past to justify our own prejudices, neither is a particularly satisfying way to understand what happened.

Courts of law assign guilt and punishment for those convicted of crimes, and it is extraordinarily tempting to throw around terms like "crimes against humanity" when describing the dirty wars. It is also, in many cases, no doubt appropriate. Still, if we view these events simply as horrible crimes committed by evil men, we capture only a small part of this history. The twentieth century, and in Latin America's case, the late twentieth century, was an era of holocausts, acts of violence made all the more dramatic by the technologies of death that were developed in the twentieth century. Military men did not monopolize the blood-lust of the times. It could often be found on every side in a conflict. Inasmuch as the dirty wars are part of that larger experience, it is worth moving away from the individual pathologies of the warriors and placing the Latin American experience during these years into a larger context.

A Question of Origins

We are once again confronted with the problem of where we begin the story. Those who understand Latin America as an inherently violent place sometimes start with the sixteenth century conquest of the Americas, establishing an unbroken line of violence dating to the original sin.[4] Histories of torture, of extrajudicial killings take us deep into the Latin American past, and one could argue that the only thing new here is the fact that these acts are increasingly exposed.

This however, seems an exceptionally selective way of narrating the terror that engulfed the region between the 1960s and the 1980s. Latin America in 1960 was not the same as Latin America in 1600. Civilian governments ruled in most countries in the region. Those governments had imperfect records of respecting democratic processes and human rights, but most did rule with a democratic mandate. The phenomena we typically associate with democratic societies, a relatively free press, opposition political parties, an independent judiciary, could be seen in many countries in the region, though invariably these institutions were somewhat weak. At the very least, it did not seem at the time that the region as a whole was destined for a dark period of conflict and authoritarian rule. And then, in the years following the Cuban revolution civilian rule collapsed in country after country across the region. By 1980 almost no government in the region had come to power through the ballot box. The scale of violence that accompanied this collapse was unprecedented.

Certain macro-level explanations for Latin America's distinct path may be in order. While it is clear that during the 1960s and 1970s economic stagnation affected most western economies at some point, the economic problems that confronted Latin American nations during these years were much more severe than in the United States or Western Europe. Import substitution industrialization[5] (ISI), which provided steady growth in the region from the 1930s to the 1950s, had also produced some serious economic distortions, and by the late 1960s these were growing increasingly difficult to ignore. ISI depended on the state's ability to support industry and fund a broad array of educational, health, and welfare programs (including transportation, housing, and food subsidies), but as GDP growth slowed during the 1960s most governments in the region found themselves pressed by expanding debt, high rates of inflation, increased unemployment, and social unrest. They had to borrow from abroad simply to maintain their current levels of spending, much of which went to propping up inefficient industries that could not compete against foreign, higher quality and lower cost imports. This practice simply could not be sustained.

In part the unrest of the 1960s could be attributed to both local and global patterns—dimming economic prospects combined with youth culture, idealism unleashed by the Cuban revolution, and cold war politics. Most of the so-called civilized nations of the West saw periodic outbursts of violence between the 1960s and the 1980s. Student radicals disrupted campuses and challenged tradition from Paris to Berkeley. Radical movements kidnapped people from Quebec to Italy, robbed banks, set off bombs, and preached the demise of capitalism even in some of the most exclusive neighborhoods in the world. And in response, governments across the West armed themselves heavily and used their repressive capacities against their perceived enemies. Incidents like the massacre at Kent State University in May 1970, in which National Guardsmen opened fire on anti-war protesters, killing four and wounding nine, are merely emblematic of an era in which the United States government in particular spied on, harassed, and imprisoned its own citizens without the due process of law.

Latin Americans brought their own particular traditions to the conflicts that characterized these years. When young idealists attacked the government, they took on political systems with dubious reputations. Latin Americans typically believed their governments were exceptionally corrupt. Their politicians were known for using their offices for illicit gains, for doling out favors to well connected supporters, and for being relatively unresponsive to the popular will. They maintained the social peace by delivering the goods—education, healthcare, and other programs—but few people in Latin America really believed that their governments governed in the people's interest.[6]

Critics used terms like crony capitalism (a capitalist system where the state works mainly in the interest of big business) or clientelism (a state where the government functions principally by doling out favors and patronage to its supporters) to describe the logics that ruled Latin American politics. Given that most people in the region were poor and relatively marginalized, they played along, participating in a pact that guaranteed government stability as long as the system was able to deliver some goods. But the weakness of this system was easily revealed in moments of crisis. In these times violence acted as a kind of political currency, used by the state and its foes to press their interests.

Latin Americans were also burdened by another problem. Their nations were among the central sites for the proxy battles of the Cold War. Leaving aside the motives of both the United States and the Soviets, both superpowers intensified the volatility of already polarized nations through their struggles for hegemony in the region. American soldiers and arms flowed freely into Latin America during the cold war, matched (though hardly equaled) by an influx of Soviet AK-47s, munitions, and at least in one case, inter-continental ballistic missiles. Guerrilla armies could count on aid, training from Moscow, and safe haven in Cuba should their struggles fail. Their enemies could count on millions in military and economic aid from Washington.

Only rarely did the U.S. government opt for direct military intervention in Latin America during the Cold War. American officials found it much more cost effective to cultivate, arm and train their allies in the region. Conservative and elite groups who, like their American friends, increasingly identified all political opposition with communism, subversion, and an insidious Soviet threat, were often more than willing to undertake the battle themselves. While some no doubt believed that their enemies were communist revolutionaries (and some no doubt were), in identifying the political opposition as communist they were able to justify extreme measures, and ensure a steady supply of military aid and advice from the U.S. government.

The U.S. Army School of the Americas (established in Panama in 1945) trained several generations of junior military officers from across the region towards these ends. Trainees mostly came from institutions that had long focused more on ensuring internal order than fighting external enemies, and were encouraged to believe that a new revolutionary threat, concocted in Moscow but carried out by their own citizens, imperiled their nations. Students at the School of the Americas learned new tactics in counter-insurgency and the latest torture techniques. They forged relationships with American counterparts who could ensure the flow of weapons and aid. And they had any pre-existing anxieties about communism firmly reinforced.

After 1959 those anxieties intensified. Conservatives recoiled at the growing militance of communist led student movements and guerrilla insurgencies in Mexico, Venezuela, Colombia, Brazil, Argentina, and Peru. Curiously, both the extreme left and the extreme right responded to these developments in similar ways. Civil society, they agreed, was bankrupt. Civilian leadership and the political parties were either incompetent or completely in the hands of hidden enemies of the people. Violence, even spectacular violence, was the only answer (Figure 9.1).

"Your war is clean," reads the text in the poster in Figure 9.1, an advertisement in the Buenos Aires newspaper *La Nación,* in March 1976. It is in part an allusion to the fact that critics condemned the increasing use of torture and illegal detentions by the military as a "dirty" war, somehow beneath civilized people. The advertisement challenges this view, insisting that their actions were not just clean, but cleansing, that this was a just war. Both extreme left and right spoke in ritual ways about these acts, believing that they were

Figure 9.1 "You are not alone . . . your people are behind you."

Source: Courtesy of *La Nacion,* March 1976; also appears in Diana Taylor, *Disappearing Acts: Spectacles of Gender and Nationalism in Argentina's "Dirty War"* (Durham: Duke University Press, 1997)

somehow engaged in an exercise that would purify society, eliminate a cancer. Whether it was the cancer of bourgeois capitalism or communism, of patriarchy or feminism, of tradition or rebellion, or of terrorism (this accusation was traded throughout these years) did not matter. The enemy was corrupt, impure, foreign. For the nation to survive, the enemy had to be annihilated. Dehumanization was here turned to genocide, and the perpetrators of violence made into victims who sacrificed themselves to save the world.

To this day many Latin Americans refer to these experiences as wars. Conservatives, former military officers, and many others (in the case of Chile, as much as 30 percent of the population) believe that without the heroic acts of these military officers, their countries would have fallen into chaos. Others remain unconvinced. In most cases the dirty wars involved well-armed soldiers taking on a largely un-armed enemy, an enemy that represented little threat to take power. It was more of a massacre than a war. Students, union members, intellectuals on the left, and in many cases peasants with little interest in radical political change were systematically murdered by regimes that sometimes simply used the cover of a communist threat to go after their supposed enemies and enrich themselves.

Peru however, was different. While all the above mentioned phenomena could be witnessed here during the late Cold War, in this country an extreme leftist insurgency truly did come very close to toppling a democratically elected regime. More than this, in Peru we see an experience in which simple stories of evil soldiers and their innocent victims are exceptionally difficult to tell. The insurgents here were just as enamored of violence as their enemies, and were perhaps even more doctrinaire than the right. Fueled by rents from the cocaine trade, Peru's insurgents were also better able to arm themselves and sustain a war against a well-armed Peruvian state than their counterparts elsewhere in Latin America. Whereas Che's guerrilla army in Bolivia, and others in Mexico, Venezuela, and elsewhere failed in part because the insurgents could not count on the support of their erstwhile peasant allies, Peru's revolutionaries could draw enough from the drug trade to fund their war without much rural support. Peru's dirty war was thus both another cold-war conflict and something entirely new: an apocalyptic orgy of violence fueled by the insurgency's capacity to sustain itself through autonomous revenue streams. In this sense, Peru's terror links the Cold War to the contemporary wars on terror.

Sendero's War

Peruvians were introduced to *Sendero Luminoso* (Shining Path) when members of the movement burned the ballot boxes in the southern highland town of Chuschi, Ayacucho, on May 17, 1980, as the country held its first democratic elections in more than a decade.[7] *Sendero*'s decision to condemn the return of democratic rule seemed odd to many foreign observers, and even to many *Limeños*, but it made complete sense to many in the highlands. Democracy did not promise much to the poor and rural peoples of Ayacucho, who held a generally dim view of all power emanating from Lima. Neither did it appeal to Peru's extreme left, which viewed democracy as simply another bourgeois tool to oppress the masses and protect capitalism.

The particular constellation of events that explain *Sendero*'s rise from a quirky movement led by a provincial philosopher into a guerrilla army that almost toppled the Peruvian state may be best explained by beginning with another moment, twelve years earlier, when the military overthrew the civilian government of Fernando Belaúnde Terry. Belaúnde's fall was not the common story of conservative U.S.-backed soldiers toppling a left-leaning president. In fact, it was the reverse. The officers who took power in 1968 did so precisely to ensure that the state deliver on widespread promises of social reform, reforms aimed at ameliorating rural poverty and curtailing the revolutionary threat. Elected in 1963 on the promise that he would implement widespread reform, Belaúnde had done the opposite, resorting to the violent repression of both peasants and his critics on the left to stay in power. In the end, it was the men who were charged with carrying out his repressive policies who removed him. General Juan Velasco's regime nationalized many of the large firms that dominated the economy, and launched a major land reform, creating agricultural cooperatives out of the old estates in much of the highlands.

Some peasants benefited, but these reforms were limited in scale, and left millions of peasants (and particularly Ayacucho's poor) bitter for having been excluded.[8] Velasco's nationalization program was also burdened by bureaucratic incompetence and mismanagement, and in the early 1970s the economy sputtered. Velasco was overthrown in a coup within the coup in 1976, and his successors did their best to undo his left-leaning policies, with few positive results. Having seen failure heaped upon failure, the military had little prestige left when it gave up power in 1980. Still, very few people outside of Lima were pleased that Belaúnde, whose heavy-handed policies in the highlands produced lasting memories, won the 1980 election.

Belaúnde imposed severe austerity measures in an effort to promote exports and stem capital flight. His opponents on the left responded with a general strike in January 1981 that further crippled the already weak economy. By the end of 1982 inflation was running at 70 percent, and the foreign debt had ballooned to $11 billion. The national currency (the *sol*) lost 80 percent of its value during the year. It is unsurprising that in these circumstances radical solutions to Peru's problems would have found a constituency. Believing that free-market capitalism was the only solution to Peru's problems, the far right felt the need to dismantle any remaining remnants of ISI, through force if necessary. The far left, dominated by *Sendero*, was preaching the end of bourgeois capitalism.

In Ayacucho the economic crisis simply added one more set of problems to a region already at the breaking point by the late 1970s. Peasants here benefited relatively little from Velasco's land reforms, and had no cushion to fall back on as the national economy deteriorated. Students at the *Universidad Nacional San Cristóbal de Huamanga* in the city of Ayacucho were similarly discontented, as the path that has once signaled upward mobility—a university education—seemed less and less likely to provide them with what they desired in contemporary Peru. Always trending towards the left, university students here and elsewhere in Peru grew more and more radical during these years.

Taking a chapter from Chairman Mao, during the 1970s radical students in Ayacucho fell in love with the image of the disciplined, communal, and revolutionary peasant. They imagined that they would lead that peasant in a revolution that would over-run the cities, over-run hated Lima (hated both for its wealth and for their exclusion from that wealth), and destroy the capitalist state. Many were drawn to Abimael Guzmán, a professor of Philosophy and Mathematics at the University, and at his bidding left the city of Ayacucho after graduating from the university for the surrounding countryside, where they worked for years as teachers, preparing the peasants to accept the revolution that Sendero promised to launch. Guzmán would lead the revolution under the *nom de guerre* Presidente Gonzalo.

After coming out on election day in 1980, *Sendero* won some striking victories. Their teachers-cum-revolutionaries parleyed their moral authority into swift and summary justice, gaining enormous sympathy in the countryside. Peasant women saw female *senderistas* punishing drunken husbands and wife beaters and lent their support. What better image could there be of moral rejuvenation at a time of crisis than the image of a man punished by a woman's hand? The same could be said of *Sendero* justice against other targets who were widely hated by the region's poor. Corrupt government officials, landlords, and cattle thieves met ugly ends at the hands of *Sendero*'s *cadres* in the early 1980s. So too did the agrarian cooperatives, Velasco's panacea for rural poverty that in practice became hated symbols of the ways that reform had helped some peasants but excluded others. Landless *Sendero* supporters were encouraged to invade and occupy the cooperatives, effecting a bottom-up termination of state-directed agrarian reform.

In the early years the revolution expanded rapidly through the countryside. Belaúnde indirectly contributed to its growth by first failing to take Sendero seriously, and then by sending in the Marines, a branch of the military mostly recruited from the coast, which had little knowledge of the culture or politics of the highlands. Baffled by the complexities of the highlands and fearing terrorists around every corner, the Marines adopted a scorched earth policy in Ayacucho.

It was a disaster. The Marines were simply not up to the task of quelling the rebellion, both because they lacked the needed resources and because they were almost entirely out of their element. Indiscriminate killings simply made their position more vulnerable, turning more and more communities against the government and pushing many of these directly into *Sendero*'s camp. The presence of so many violent outsiders also produced a kind of hysteria in the highlands, a sense that the world really was coming to an end. In the midst of the crisis some highlanders turned to religion (evangelical Protestantism expanded significantly during these years), seeking spiritual rescue from the carnage. Others spread rumors that linked the Marines to apocalyptic fears. They were Argentine mercenaries sent to kill all rural folk. They were *pishtacos*, ravenous whites who murdered Indians for their fat, which was then used to make church bells.

It is not surprising that under these circumstance *Sendero* was able to expand its influence in rural areas beyond Ayacucho. It was particularly successful in the coca-rich upper Huallaga valley, where by the mid-1980s *Sendero* created a protection racket for the growers that could in turn fuel expansion elsewhere and the purchase of a growing military arsenal. As the highlands slipped from government control, bombings, blackouts, murders and kidnappings grew more frequent across the country, and especially in Lima. By the late 1980s *Sendero* controlled the poor barrios that ringed Lima, and the government seemed incapable of stemming its power.

Sendero never could have expanded in this fashion without a significant level of rural support, but that support was far from complete. Peasant sympathizers often saw in *Sendero* an opportunity to form a strategic alliance, but would just as easily turn on the revolutionaries when circumstances dictated. Indeed, the ties between peasant and *senderista* were always tenuous. The revolution was always much more an affair of urban educated intellectual guerrillas than it was a peasant war. *Senderistas* considered themselves Gang of Four

Maoists, painting the slogan "Death to the Traitor Deng Xiaopeng" on the walls of Andean communities, seemingly fighting simultaneous battles against the current Chinese government, the Peruvian state, and civil society.

As the war drew on, *senderistas* increasingly treated peasants as if they were ignorant tools of the revolution, to be called to arms or destroyed if recalcitrant. In contrast to the early years of the struggle, when their successes had in part been linked to their capacity to understand the desires and values of their erstwhile supporters, over time *senderistas* demonstrated less and less tolerance for local customs, local values, local age-based hierarchies, and increasingly treated indigenous cultures with contempt. In their blindness to local life-ways, they also failed to understand just how much a long history of violent conflicts with outsiders had fortified highland communities with a capacity for self-defense.

Communities that might have thrown their support behind *Sendero* for killing a corrupt government official often turned just as quickly against the movement when doctrinaire *senderistas* made demands they viewed as unfair. Others never had any sympathy for the guerrillas, and fought them without prompting. Just such an incident happened when seven *senderistas* were killed by *comuneros* (rebellious peasants) in the village of Huaychao, Ayacucho in January 1983. *Limeños*, who considered this a sign of peasant loyalty to the government, generally celebrated the incident. Their jubilance faded though, when a group of eight journalists on their way to Huaychao to write about the incident were murdered while passing through the village of Uchuraccay. This incident is the subject of Document 9.1 in this chapter.

Few of the movement's actual militants were ever peasants. In fact, most *senderistas* were current or former university students, drawn to the bloody path plotted by Guzmán. During the 1980s it was not just students from Ayacucho, but from Lima and other cities who organized *senderista* and other revolutionary cells on their campuses, preparing for the final battle against capitalism. Government forces in turn targeted the universities, imprisoning thousands of students for their suspected affiliations. Most of the *senderistas* who ever made it to a jail cell were urban, often middle-class students. Their rural comrades and sympathizers met different ends.

Sendero's appeal among students was in part the product of youthful enthusiasm, that belief among young people that if they are sufficiently committed, they can remake the world. To be sure, many of the students who were ultimately rounded up by security forces may have been simply experimenting with radical ideas, only to have those ideas harden into revolutionary anger and rage as a result of torture and long imprisonments (Figure 9.2). One easily loses faith in the system under torture.

Still, the fact that these students initially decided to attend a rally or meeting of revolutionaries, spoke of a cascading effect, the result of one crisis after another discrediting all forms of constituted authority. Aside from the human toll, one of most significant losses in all this was Peruvians' faith that moderate solutions might solve their problems. Both the extreme left and the extreme right obliterated all middle ground. Arbitrary arrests, detentions, and torture by the military no doubt had this effect, but so too did *Sendero's* acts. Anyone who was within *Sendero's* reach could be singled out for spectacular executions for the smallest reasons.

Part of what was so troubling in these acts was the fact violence often served as an end in and of itself for the *senderistas*. They came to be called monsters (*ñakaq*, or destroyers of

Figure 9.2   December 16, 1986: Peruvian police arrest a student from the state university of San Marcos during the protest organized by students and teachers of the state universities in Lima. Thousands of teachers and students marched through the streets of the capital and submitted a set of economic demands to the Economics Ministry

Source: Courtesy of Associated Press Photo

life) in many highland communities, where their enthusiasm for blood-letting disturbed many peasants. Still, these same peasants had little enthusiasm for the state. The military often treated Andean communities in similarly frightening ways. Caught in the middle of two armies, these peasants were forced to live a double life, always hiding their true affiliations and beliefs as an act of self-preservation in the face of murderous outsiders. Some even mobilized self-defense forces, known as *rondas-campesinas*. Though officially at war with *Sendero*, *ronda* members generally took a dim view of all outsiders (Figure 9.3).

The Peruvian state lagged in its responses to all these crises. Alan García was elected president in 1985 on the promise of restoring respect for human rights and fixing the economy, but did neither. In June 1986 he sent troops into three prisons in Lima and Callao against rioting *Sendero* inmates, killing 267. Under his administration Peru's foreign debt grew to nearly $20 billion (U.S.), and by 1989 the inflation rate was nearing 10,000 percent. Between 1988 and 1990 per capita GDP declined by 20 percent.

These were the issues that framed the 1990 presidential elections, in which the relatively unknown Alberto Fujimori was elevated to the nation's highest office. Systemic crises often favor candidates who can claim to be political outsiders, and Fujimori seized this role by trading on the fact that he was an ethnic outsider to Peru's elite community. He cast himself as a representative of Peru's poor and disenfranchised indigenous masses. He adorned himself in local costumes as he traversed the highlands in search of votes, and promised aid to those most affected by the economic and political chaos.

Figure 9.3 An unidentified young woman holds a home-made shotgun as she forms up with other members of a government-sponsored civil defense group near Ayacucho.

Source: Courtesy of Associated Press Photo

It must have seemed a little like a betrayal then, when Fujimori did an almost immediate about-face once assuming the presidency. In a practice that was distressingly common during these years, he immediately adopted the market-oriented economic priorities that he had lambasted his opponents for supporting. Within months he imposed a series of austerity measures (*fujishocks*), drastically reducing government spending, food subsidies, and price controls. Peruvians were further put at the mercy of international markets when he significantly reduced tariff barriers, opening the economy to cheap foreign imports and further weakening domestic manufacturers.

Fujimori also took on *Sendero* (and those he defined as terrorists more generally) in dramatic fashion. He legalized the *rondas campesinas*, providing them with arms and training. He stepped up the military presence in Ayacucho and relentlessly persecuted communities suspected of supporting *Sendero*. He expanded the role of the *Servicio Nacional de Inteligencia* (SIN—National Intelligence Service) in the war, creating a secret force called the *Grupo Colina* (Colina Group) to go after the terrorists. This category itself was expanded to include not just *Sendero*, but protesters, political opponents, journalists, and the occasional bystander.

The new president was fortunate that by 1990 much of the groundwork for success against *Sendero* was already complete. Alienated by the brutality and dogmatism of the *senderistas*, peasant support for the rebels had been on the wane since at least 1982. Moreover, after 1984 the government shifted the focus of its counter-insurgency program from the Marines to Army, bringing an end to many of the most problematic aspects of the government's efforts to combat *Sendero*. Army officers often came from the highlands, spoke Quechua, and were more sensitive to community needs and interests than their Marine counteraparts. They built roads, provided telephone service, and offered much needed supplies. They replaced indiscriminate killings with a more strategic approach to rooting out *Sendero* and winning popular support. Civic Action became a watchword for military officials aiming to win the hearts and minds of the nation's poor.

These actions were critical, but may have been less important than the simple fact that by this point a growing number of highland communities had grown weary of *Sendero*'s violence and bloodlust, and were increasingly happy to cooperate with government efforts to defeat the revolution. After 1984 it was *Sendero*, not the Army, which was more often accused of perpretrating indiscriminate killings and showing a complete disregard for the interests of Andean peasants. In the end *Sendero* was in a war as much against the peasants and urban poor as against the state.

By 1990 *Sendero* could be found actively terrorizing not just peasants, but all their rivals on the political left. The 1992 murder of community activist María Elena Moyano was a particularly powerful example of this practice. Machine gunned to death and then blown up with dynamite in front of her own children, Moyano was one of a number of urban leaders from the Lima slums who *Sendero* eliminated because they were insufficiently revolutionary (feminists were particular targets). Her death produced outrage, but by this time those individuals who had to face *Sendero* on a daily basis in the cities mostly ducked their heads to stay out of the line of fire, and hoped the nightmare would soon come to an end.

The most dramatic turning point in the battle came on September 12, 1992, when Fujimori announced that he had captured Presidente Gonzalo, who had been hiding in an apartment above a dance studio in Lima (he was betrayed by his psoriasis medication, which was found in the trash). Fujimori claimed, with some legitimacy, that by centralizing power in the hands of the executive and clearing away of all dissent from Congress and the judiciary, the *autogolpe* had allowed him to fight his war on the terrorists. That others, some of them clearly not terrorists but simply regime opponents, were caught up in the process was simply the price Peruvians had to pay to put an end to the scourge that was *Sendero*.

In succeeding years Fujimori would only grow more certain that Peruvians needed his strong hand to guide them through their remaining economic and political troubles. He wrote a new constitution that allowed him to be re-elected in 1995, and then did an end-run around that constitution to get himself re-elected in 2000. By then though, Peruvians were increasingly weary of his dubious practices. Caught up in a vote buying scandal in the aftermath of the election, he fled the country for exile in Japan in November 2000.

Peruvians then took a deep breath, and began to examine their recent past. Alejandro Toledo, who assumed the presidency in 2001, named a Truth and Reconciliation Commission, which began to look into *Sendero*'s war. They concluded that around half of the nearly 70,000 people who died in the conflict were killed by *Sendero*, the rest being the responsibility of the state, the *rondas*, and other private groups. In 2002, at the closure of the public hearings of Peru's Truth and Reconciliation Commission, Chairman Salomón Lerner Febres summed up his experience.

> The stories we have attentively heard, feeling sorrow and respect, create in us Peruvians the obligation of wondering what happened to us, how we arrived to those extremes of degradation that the victims have courageously and generously shown us with their narratives. I said degradation, and although this word may sound excessive, it is actually only a pale reflection of the acts we have been hearing about these days. We have spoken about crimes committed from an absolute position of power against unarmed and inadvertent victims. And if this had not been sufficient for the executioner, they were crimes committed under the cover of darkness and with malice aforethought, as the witnesses in these Hearings have told us repeatedly. Was not that already excessive? Apparently not. The violations had to be committed, besides, with rage and merciless-ness as if the others' suffering had become the main goal, a sick enjoyment motive for those executing these crimes, and for those who ordered them from comfortable and safe shelters or offices. The testimonies that have been presented to us coincide in pointing out this relish for cruelty, this desire to destroy the victims' dignity, starting with the use of language. The recurrence of insults, as if physical force were not sufficient, also reveals a disdain based on considerations of race, culture or poverty, and patently shows the devaluation of women. This vulgar language of executioners against unarmed victims reflects, in brief, the patterns of social alienation that, as we know, are still embedded in our country, and which are perhaps the greatest obstacles to achieving a fair and democratic society.[9]

Fujimori remained untouched by the findings of the commission until he attempted to return to Peru in 2006 in order to run, once more, for the presidency. Arrested in Chile and then extradited to Peru, during the following two years he faced trials for corruption, abuses of power, and for his role in the deaths of more than two dozen people killed by the *Grupo Colina*. He was convicted on several charges, and is currently serving a 25-year prison sentence.

The Documents: Scenes from the War

How does one tell the stories of the bloodbaths that engulfed so many Latin American societies between the 1960s and 1980s? For those given to Manichean visions of the world —the easy juxtapositions of good versus evil—it seems deceptively easy. You choose the good (usually an innocent victim, a student, an indigenous person, often a woman), and the evil (often some faceless but monstrous military figure), and tell how, without provocation the latter brutalized, tortured, and perhaps killed the former. It is a powerful story, and the audience, whether students in a lecture hall or readers of a text, is generally left silent, moved by the story, horrified and indignant.

During the 1980s a genre of Latin American writing called *testimonio* grew increasingly popular in North America as a means of relating these experiences. Rigoberta Menchú shocked audiences with the tales of her life, and particular the fates of her father, mother, and several brothers. Alicia Partnoy moved readers with her account of surviving torture by the Argentine military. Even Adolfo Scilingo, a member of the Argentine Navy and a torturer himself, managed to evoke a certain amount of sympathy by speaking truth to power. These texts evoke strong emotions, they are tragedies with sympathetic victims and monstrous perpetrators.[10]

There are, of course, problems to this approach. Beyond the troubling questions raised by the voyeuristic quality of these texts,[11] the simple notions of good and evil they convey offer few explanations of how otherwise normal people (people who today wander the streets of any number of Latin American cities) engaged in the inhuman acts they describe. This practice also tends to obscure other, very real things, such as the fact that some of the victims (many of whom also walk the streets today) threw bombs, robbed banks, and kidnapped their erstwhile enemies. These are, to borrow a term from Christopher Browning, *ordinary people*.[12] Even more, the Manichean nature of these texts can serve to reinforce a series of Northern stereotypes about the South (women as passive, indigenous peoples as mystical, non-political, Latin American men as violent *machos*).

Testimonios did help discredit the dictatorships, but as military rule fades into the past, we may be better served by telling a more complex story of the era. One way to begin this task involves an effort to understand just how the political and other differences that characterized these societies metastasized into a tendency to dehumanize one's adversaries. In Peru, where the animus and cognitive failures were so widely shared, we have an exceptionally good window into these practices. We have an enormous amount of evidence of the sympathies and sentiments that divided Peruvian society. These divisions were clearly rooted in the historical conflicts between coast and highlands and all the attendant cognitive failures (*Limeños* and Andean villagers each failed to see the other clearly), but as with other countries, Peru was also riven by conflicts between left and right, and conflicts within the left. Each of these struggles seemed all the more urgent in the context of an economic catastrophe.

We begin with an early and revealing example of the cognitive failures and deep anxieties that framed this epoch in Peruvian history. Document 9.1 is an excerpt from an essay published by the Peruvian novelist Mario Vargas Llosa in the *New York Times Magazine* in July 1983 (the entire essay can be found on the website). Vargas Llosa was improbably named as the head of a commission sent to investigate the murder of 8 journalists in the village of

Uchuraccay in the southern Peruvian Highlands in early 1983. This essay was based on the commission's findings. He reveals some troubling assumptions about Andean peasants here, rendering them as fundamentally primitive, unaware that they lived in a modern nation and thus unaccountable for their actions.

Vargas Llosa's observations were roundly criticized in Peru, in part because they were in fact untrue. Many peasants from the region had a great deal of experience living in coastal regions, and understood full well that Peruvian law did not allow them to execute outsiders. Later investigators would raise a series of questions about the massacre, insinuating that the military had been complicit in the murders, suggesting that the peasants were led to believe that the journalists were *senderistas* (their neighbors had, after all, just killed a number of *senderistas*.) Some even suggested that the locals may have thought the journalists were *pishtacos*. In any event, at this point the *comuneros* had good reason to fear outsiders. *Senderistas* would return to the region repeatedly in the coming years to carry out murderous reprisals, and during much of the decade both Uchuraccay and Huaychao (where the original murders took place) would be left deserted.

Document 9.2 is an excerpt from President Gonzalo's "Interview of the Century," given to the senderista paper *El Diario* in 1988 (the entire interview can be found on the website). If Vargas Llosa inflicted rhetorical violence on the peasants, and perhaps justified other forms of violence indirectly, Gonzalo celebrated actual violence—a war of annihilation. The text is quite chilling to read, but what is remarkable about it is that it resonated so deeply with a certain segment of the Peruvian left. We must wonder what it was (or is) that underpinned such millenarian thinking, why it was that middle-class university students and leftists (but by this point, relatively few peasants) would find this so appealing, why violence was so romanticized. We should also note that Gonzalo's love of violence is remarkably similar to the sentiments expressed by the torturers in Chile, Argentina, and elsewhere. They too described it as cleansing, as ritual. The nation is reborn in the bloodbath.

One of the curious things we see in juxtaposing Documents 9.1 and 9.2 is that both Vargas Llosa and Presidente Gonzalo had a superficial view of peasant and indigenous cultures. Both imagined that rural cultures needed to be remade, that in their present form they were either useless or dangerous. Both then, ultimately make peasants into components of a larger scheme, a larger war. Neither was destined to mourn too many peasant deaths, as their lives, as they were, offered little to the cause.

We see in Document 9.3 Fujimori's rationale for dismantling the Peruvian state on April 5, 1992. Some Peruvians note that his rhetoric in 1992 had a long history, and was not terribly unlike that of earlier *coups d'état*. It was certainly similar in tone and explanation to the Argentine and Chilean cases of the recent past. Something needs to be destroyed. The state and civil society are rotten to the core. A powerful, visionary figure will save the country, but he can only do so if freed from a bankrupt series of processes. Fujimori declared that he was not overthrowing a democratic system. He claimed he was paving the way for the establishment of a democratic state.

Document 9.4 leaves us with a cautionary tale about the extremes that Fujimori went to in his war against *Sendero*. When Fujimori was ultimately held to account for his response to *Sendero*, aside from charges of abuse of authority and the misappropriation of funds, he was charged with responsibility for four specific cases of human rights violations perpetrated by the *Grupo Colina*. Those incidents included the kidnappings of journalist Gustavo Gorriti

Figure 9.4 Family members of victims in the Cantuta massacre

Source: Courtesy of Reuters/Mariana Bazo

and businessman Samuel Dyer after the 1992 *autogolpe*. A third case involved the killings of 15 people in the Lima neighborhood of Barrios Altos in 1991. The document included below concerns the fourth incident, the massacre at Valle Nacional (Cantuta) University on July 18, 1992.

In the early morning hours of that day, hooded security officials entered the homes of several students and professors. The students were taken out of their dormitories, and forced into the fetal position, their faces pushed to the ground. One by one soldiers pulled their faces up by the hair, identifying students individually, and eventually separating nine from the group. They, along with one professor, were taken away, murdered, and secretly buried in mass graves on the property of the Lima water utility. Fujimori denies knowing about the killings. He denies knowing even that the *Grupo Colina* existed. He was nonetheless found guilty at trial for his role in the killings (Figure 9.4).

Document 9.1   Mario Vargas Llosa, "The Massacre," excerpt from "Inquest in the Andes: A Latin American Writer Explores the Political Lessons of a Peruvian Massacre," *New York Times Magazine*, July 31, 1983

Source: "Inquest in the Andes," published in the *New York Times Magazine*, July 31, 1983. Copyright © Mario Vargas Llosa, 1983.

The Massacre

How did the murder of the reporters take place? The Uchuraccayans refused to give us the details. We assumed the Indians came down the mountainsides that encircle the village and attacked suddenly, as the reporters approached, before anyone could speak. We supposed that they used sling-shots, which shoot stones so fast that they can hit a viscacha, the large, burrowing rodent of the pampas, running at full speed. (Proudly, they demonstrated that for us.) We were inclined to believe that there had been no dialogue—first, because the Iquichanos thought that the strangers were armed, and, second, because three of the journalists, Octavio Infante, Amador García and Félix Gavilán, spoke Quechua and could have tempered the hostility of their attackers.

But the facts turned out to be colder and crueler. They came to light two months later, when a patrol escorting the judge in charge of the separate judicial investigation, which is still going on, found a camera in a cave near Uchuraccay. Apparently, it had been uncovered by viscachas digging in the earth where the villagers had hidden it. It was a a Minolta, serial number 4202368, that had belonged to the young photographer from *El Observador*, Willy Retto, and it contained film which, when developed, provided a horrifying document.

It seems that Willy Retto had the presence of mind to take pictures during the moments just before the massacre, perhaps when the lives of some of his friends had already been taken. There were nine photographs; all were confiscated by the investigating judge. Somehow, three of the pictures found their way onto the pages of Ultima Hora; they were promptly reproduced by other papers. In one of these pictures, the hulking Jorge Sedano is on his knees next to the bags and cameras that someone, possibly Octavio Infante, has placed on the ground. In another picture, Felix Gavilán, the local correspondent with his radio program for the Indian peasants, has his arms raised. In the third picture, 22-year-old Jorge Luis Mendivil, with his teen-ager's face, is gesturing, as if asking everybody to calm down. From a reliable informant, I have learned that three other pictures—the last three pictures on the roll of film—show an Iquichano advancing threateningly on Willy Retto. The pictures prove that some words had been spoken but that talk did no good—that, although the Iquichanos saw the strangers were unarmed, they attacked them anyhow, convinced they were their enemies.

The massacre had magical and religious overtones, as well as political and social implications. The hideous wounds on the corpses were ritualistic. The eight bodies were buried in pairs, face down, the form of burial used for people the Iquichanos consider "devils"—people like the dancers of the *tijeras*, a folk dance, who are believed to make pacts with the Devil. They were buried outside the community limits to emphasize that they were strangers. (In the Andes, the Devil merges with the image of the stranger.) The bodies were especially mutilated around the mouth and eyes, in the belief that the victim should be deprived of his sight, so he cannot recognize his killers, and of his tongue, so he cannot denounce them. Their ankles were broken, so they could not come back for revenge. The villagers stripped the bodies; they washed the clothes and burned them in a purification ceremony known as *pichja*.

Knowing the circumstances does not excuse the crime, but it makes what happened more comprehensible. The violence stuns us because it is an anomaly in our ordinary lives. For the Iquichanos, that violence is the atmosphere they live in from the time they are born until the time they die. After our return from Uchuraccay, new tragedies confirmed that the Iquichanos' fear of reprisals by Sendero Luminoso was justified.

On April 3, four Senderista detachments, augmented by hundreds of peasants from a rival community, attacked Lucanamarca, 120 miles from Uchuraccay, and murdered 77 people in the village square, most of them with axes, machetes and stones. There were four children among the decapitated, mutilated bodies. On July 18, the guerrillas attacked Uchuraccay at dawn, in reprisal for the slaying of the five Senderistas there on Jan. 22. General Noel's office in Ayacucho said at least eight peasants were slaughtered—again in the village square—with bullets and axes. All indications were that the war in the Andes was continuing.

When our commission's hearing in Uchuraccay was over, and, overwhelmed by what we had seen and heard—the graves of the reporters were still open—we were getting ready to return to Ayacucho, a tiny woman from the community suddenly began to dance. She was quietly singing a song whose words we could not understand. She was an Indian as tiny as a child, but she had the wrinkled face of a very old woman, and the scarred cheeks and swollen lips of those who live exposed to the cold of the uplands. She was barefoot, and wore several brightly colored skirts and a hat with ribbons, and as she sang and danced she tapped us gently on the legs with brambles. Was she saying goodbye to us in an ancient ritual? Was she cursing us because we belonged to the strangers—Senderistas, "reporters," sinchis—who had brought new reasons for anguish and fear to their lives? Was she exorcising us?

For several weeks, I had been living in a state of extraordinary tension as I interviewed soldiers, politicians, policemen, peasants and reporters and reviewed dispatches, evidence and legal testimony, trying to establish what had happened. At night, I would often stay awake, attempting to determine the truth of the testimony and the hypotheses, or I had nightmares in which the certainties of the day became enigmas again. And as the story of the eight journalists unfolded—I had known two of them, and had been with Amador García just two days before his trip to Ayacucho—it seemed that another, even more terrible story about my own country was being revealed. But at no time had I felt as much sorrow as in Uchuraccay on that late afternoon, with its threatening clouds, watching the tiny woman who danced and tapped us with brambles, and who seemed to come from a Peru different from the one I live in, an ancient, archaic Peru that has survived in these sacred mountains despite centuries of isolation and adversity.

That frail, tiny woman had undoubtedly been one of the mob who threw rocks and swung sticks, for the Iquichano women are famous for being as warlike as the men. In the photographs from Willy Retto's camera, you can see them at the front of the crowd. It wasn't difficult to imagine the community of Uchuraccay transformed by fear and rage. We had a presentiment of it at the hearing, when, after too many uncomfortable questions, the passive assembly, led by the women, suddenly began to roar "Challa, challa!" ("Enough, enough!") and the air was filled with evil omens.

If the essential facts of the journalists' death have been clarified—who killed them, how and why—there are others that remain hidden in obscurity. What happened to Juan Argumedo? Why won't the Iquichanos take responsibility for his death? It may be that, in their minds, Juan Argumedo was a "neighbor"—someone from a rival area, but an area they had to coexist with for reasons of trade and travel—and a confession that they had killed him would be tantamount to a declaration of war on the valley farmers. If so, this precaution has failed: There have been several bloody confrontations between the Indians of Uchuraccay and the peasants of Chacabamba and another valley village.

Another unresolved question is the red flag. General Noel said the reporters were murdered because they walked into Uchuraccay with a Communist flag, and the villagers made the same statement to our commission. Willy Retto's photographs show no such flag. And why would the reporters carry a flag that could only mean danger for them? In all probability, the villagers, in realizing their mistake, invented the story to give greater credibility to their claim that they thought the strangers were Senderistas. The red flag they turned over to Lieutenant Bravo Reid of the Tambo patrol was, in all likelihood, the one they alleged had been flown over Iquicha by the Government representative at that village—the flag the Indians tied around his neck after bringing him to Uchuraccay.

Even more dramatic than the blood that flows through this story is the lack of understanding that made the blood flow. The reporters believed that, in the earlier incident at Huaychao, the Senderistas had been murdered by the sinchis and not the peasants. In Uchuraccay, the peasants killed some strangers because they thought the strangers were coming to kill them. It is possible that the journalists never knew why they were attacked. A wall of disinformation, prejudice and ideology separated one group from the other and made communication impossible.

Perhaps this story helps to clarify the reason for the mind-shattering violence that characterizes guerrilla warfare in Latin America. These guerrilla movements are not "peasant movements." They are born in the cities, among intellectuals and middle-class militants who, with their dogmatism and their rhetoric, are often as foreign and incomprehensible to the peasant masses as Sendero Luminoso is to the men and women of Uchuraccay. The outrages committed by those other strangers—the Government forces of counterinsurgency—tend to win peasant support for the guerrillas.

Put simply, the peasants are coerced by those who think they are the masters of history and absolute truth. The fact is that the struggle between the guerrillas and the armed forces is really a settling of accounts between privileged sectors of society, and the peasant masses are used cynically and brutally by those who say they want to "liberate" them. The peasants always suffer the greatest number of victims: At least 750 of them have been killed in Peru since the beginning of 1983.

The story of the eight journalists reveals how vulnerable democracy is in Latin America and how easily it dies under military or Marxist–Leninist dictatorship. It is difficult for people to defend a free press, elections and representative institutions when their circumstances do not allow them to understand, much less to benefit from, the achievements of democracy. Democracy will never be strong in our Latin American countries as long as it is the privilege of one sector of society and an incomprehensible abstraction for all the others. The double threat—the model of Gen. Augusto Pinochet in Chile and the model of Fidel Castro in Cuba—will continue to haunt democratic government as long as people in our countries kill for the reasons that the peasants of Uchuraccay killed.

Document 9.2 The Interview of the Century, 1988 (Excerpt)

Source: http://www.blythe.org/peru-pcp/docs_en/interv.htm#BM4.

El Diario: Chairman, let's talk about the people's war now. What does violence mean to you, Chairman Gonzalo?

Chairman Gonzalo: With regard to violence we start from the principle established by Chairman Mao Tsetung: violence, that is the need for revolutionary violence, is a universal law with no exception. Revolutionary violence is what allows us to resolve fundamental contradictions by means of an army, through people's war. Why do we start from Chairman Mao's thesis? Because we believe Mao reaffirmed Marxism on this question, establishing that there are no exceptions whatsoever to this law. What Marx held, that violence is the midwife of history, continues to be a totally valid and monumental contribution. Lenin expounded upon violence and spoke about Engels' panegyric praise of revolutionary violence, but it was the Chairman who told us that it was a universal law, without any exception. That's why we take his thesis as our starting point. This is an essential question of Marxism, because without revolutionary violence one class cannot replace another, an old order cannot be overthrown to create a new one—today a new order led by the proletariat through Communist Parties.

The problem of revolutionary violence is an issue that is more and more being put on the table for discussion, and therefore we communists and revolutionaries must reaffirm our principles. The problem of revolutionary violence is how to actually carry it out with people's war. The way we see this question is that when Chairman Mao Tsetung established the theory of people's war and put it into practice, he provided the proletariat with its military line, with a military theory and practice that is universally valid and therefore applicable everywhere in accordance with the concrete conditions.

We see the problem of war this way: war has two aspects, destructive and constructive. Construction is the principal aspect. Not to see it this way undermines the revolution—weakens it. On the other hand, from the moment the people take up arms to overthrow the old order, from that moment, the reaction seeks to crush, destroy and annihilate the struggle, and it uses all the means at its disposal, including genocide. We have seen this in our country; we are seeing it now, and will continue to see it even more until the outmoded Peruvian State is demolished.

As for the so-called dirty war, I would like to simply point out that they claim that the reactionary armed forces learned this dirty war from us. This accusation clearly expresses a lack of understanding of revolution, and of what a people's war is. The reaction, through its armed forces and other repressive forces, seeks to carry out their objective of sweeping us away, of eliminating us. Why? Because we want to do the same to them—sweep them away and eliminate them as a class. Mariátegui said that only by destroying, demolishing the old order could a new social order be brought into being. In the final analysis, we judge these problems in light of the basic principle of war established by Chairman Mao: the principle of annihilating the enemy's forces and preserving one's own forces. We know very well that the reaction has used, is using, and will continue to use genocide. On this we are absolutely clear. And consequently this raises the problem of the price we have to pay: in order to annihilate the enemy and to preserve, and even more to develop our own forces, we have to pay a price in war, a price in blood, the need to sacrifice a part for the triumph of the people's war.

As for terrorism, they claim we're terrorists. I would like to give the following answer so that everyone can think about it: has it or has it not been Yankee imperialism and particularly Reagan who has branded all revolutionary movements as terrorists, yes or no? This is how they attempt to discredit and isolate us in order to crush us. That is their dream. And it's not only Yankee imperialism and the other imperialist powers that combat so-called terrorism. So does social-imperialism and revisionism, and today Gorbachev himself proposes to unite with the struggle against terrorism. And it isn't by chance that at the VIIIth Congress of the Party of Labor of Albania Ramiz Alia dedicated himself to combatting terrorism as well with the pioneers of the people's revolutionary army! It is no longer a plot against some detested individual, no act of vengeance or desperation, no mere "intimidation"—no, it was a well thought-out and well prepared commencement of operations by a contingent of the revolutionary army. Fortunately, the time has passed when revolution was "made" by individual terrorists, because people were not revolutionary. The bomb has ceased to be the weapon of the solitary "bomb thrower," and is becoming an essential weapon of the people.

Lenin taught us that the times had changed, that the bomb had become a weapon of combat for our class, for the people, that what we're talking about is no longer a conspiracy, an isolated individual act, but the actions of a Party, with a plan, with a system, with an army. So, where is the imputed terrorism? It's pure slander.

Finally, we always have to remember that, especially in present-day war, it is precisely the reactionaries who use terrorism as one of their means of struggle, and it is, as has been proven repeatedly, one of the forms used on a daily basis by the armed forces of the Peruvian State. Considering all this, we can conclude that those whose reasoning is colored by desperation because the earth is trembling beneath their feet wish to charge us with terrorism in order to hide the people's war. But this people's war is so earth-shaking that they themselves admit that it is of national dimensions and that it has become the principal problem facing the Peruvian State. What terrorism could do that? None. And moreover, they can no longer deny that a Communist Party is leading the people's war. And at this time some of them are beginning to reconsider; we shouldn't be too hasty in writing anyone off. There are those who could come forward. Others, like Del Prado, never . . .

At the end of 1982, the armed forces came in. The CC had anticipated this for more than a year. It had studied the involvement of the armed forces, and concluded that it would increase until the army had substituted for the police, who would then assume a secondary role. This is how it has been, and given the situation it could not have been otherwise. We had prepared ourselves, but nevertheless, we had a second problem. The introduction of the armed forces had its consequences. They came in applying a policy of genocide from the beginning. They formed armed groups, called mesnadas, forcing the masses to join and putting them in front, using them as shields. This must be said clearly: here we see not only the policy of using masses against masses, an old reactionary policy already seen by Marx, but also a cowardly use of the masses, putting the masses in front of them. The armed forces have nothing to boast about—with good reason we have called them experts at defeat, and skilled at attacking the unarmed masses. These are the armed forces of Peru. Faced with this we convened an expanded session of the CC. It was a large meeting and it lasted a long time. It was one of the longest sessions we've ever had. That's when we established the Plan to Conquer Base Areas, and the People's Guerrilla Army was created to respond to a force that was obviously of a higher level than the police. It was there that we also raised, among other things, the problem of Front-State.

Thus arose the second problem, the problem of confronting the genocide, the genocide of 1983 and 1984. It is in the Party documents. It's not necessary to go into it a lot, but we do want to stress the fact that it was a vicious and merciless genocide. They thought that with this genocide "they would wipe us off the map." How real this was is shown by the fact that, by the end of 1984, they began to circulate among their officers documents concerning our annihilation. The struggle was intense, hard, those were complex and difficult times.

In the face of reactionary military actions and the use of mesnadas, we responded with a devastating action: Lucanamarca. Neither they nor we have forgotten it, to be sure, because they got an answer that they didn't imagine possible. More than 80 were annihilated, that is the truth. And we say openly that there were excesses, as was analyzed in 1983. But everything in life has two aspects. Our task was to deal a devastating blow in order to put them in check, to make them understand that it was not going to be so easy. On some occasions, like that one, it was the Central Leadership itself that planned the action and gave instructions. That's how it was. In that case, the principal thing is that we dealt them a devastating blow, and we checked them and they understood that they were dealing with a different kind of people's fighters, that we weren't the same as those they had fought before. This is what they understood. The excesses are the negative aspect. Understanding war, and basing ourselves on what Lenin said, taking Clausewitz into account, in war, the masses engaged in combat can go too far and express all their hatred, the deep feelings of class hatred, repudiation and condemnation that they have—that was the root of it. This has been explained by Lenin very clearly. Excesses can be committed. The problem is to go to a certain point and not beyond it, because if you go past that point you go off course. It's like an angle; it can be opened up to a certain point and no further. If we were to give the masses a lot of restrictions, requirements and prohibitions, it would mean that deep down we didn't want the waters to overflow. And what we needed was for the waters to overflow, to let the flood rage, because we know that when a river floods its banks it causes devastation, but then it returns to its riverbed. I repeat, this was explained clearly by Lenin, and this is how we understand those excesses. But, I insist, the main point was to make them understand that we were a hard nut to crack, and that we were ready for anything, anything.

Marx taught us: one does not play at insurrection, one does not play at revolution. But when one raises the banner of insurrection, when one takes up arms, there's no taking down the banner, it must be held high and never lowered until victory. This is what he taught us, no matter how much it costs us! Marx has armed us then, as Lenin has, and, principally Chairman Mao Tsetung taught us about the price we have to pay—what it means to annihilate in order to preserve, what it means to hold high the banner, come what may. And we say that in this way, with this determination, we overcame the sinister, vile, cowardly and vicious genocide. And we say this because someone—he who calls himself president—makes insinuations about barbarism, without blushing, when he is an aspiring Attila the Hun playing with other people's blood.

Have we gone through difficult times? Yes. But what has reality shown us? That if we persist, keep politics in command, follow our political strategy, follow our military strategy, if we have a clear and defined plan, then we will advance, and we are capable of facing any bloodbath. (We began to prepare for the bloodbath in 1981 because it had to come. Thus we were already prepared ideologically, that is principal.) All this brought about an increase in our forces, they multiplied. This was the result. It turned out as the Chairman had said: the reaction is dreaming when it tries to drown the revolution in blood. They should know they are nourishing it, and this is an inexorable law. So this reaffirms for us that we have to be more and more dedicated, firm, and resolute in our principles, and always have unwavering faith in the masses.

Thus we came out of it strengthened, with a larger Army, more People's Committees and Base Areas, and a larger Party, exactly the opposite of what they had imagined. We have already talked, I believe, of the bloody dreams of the reaction. They are nothing but that, bloody dreams that, in the final analysis, end up being nightmares. But I insist: by persisting in our principles and fighting with the support of the masses, mainly the poor peasants, we've been able to confront this situation. It is here that the heroism of which I have already spoken, the heroism of the masses, has been expressed.

Document 9.3 Fujimori's 1992 Declaration of the *Autogolpe*

Source: www.congreso.gob.pe/museo/mensajes/Mensaje-1992-1.pdf. Translated by
Robert Forstag and Patricia Rosas.

A Message to the Nation from the President of Peru, Alberto Fujimori, Engineer

April 5, 1992

My fellow Peruvians:

For the past 20 months, my government has proposed building a genuine democracy, a democracy that would effectively guarantee equal participation for all citizens. One in which there would be no place for special privileges or sinecures and one that would truly allow us to conquer, in the medium term, the problems of underdevelopment, extreme poverty, lack of opportunity, corruption, and violence.

Like many Peruvians, I thought that this might be the last chance for Peru to fulfill its destiny. The initial phase of my administration has seen some undeniable progress, which is a result of the discipline and order with which the nation's affairs have been managed and of the Peruvian people's responsible and self-sacrificial attitude. We can thus point to the reinsertion of our country into the international financial structure, the gradual reining in of hyperinflation, and a climate of increasing confidence and stability.

But today we can sense that something is impeding our continued march toward national reconstruction and progress. And the Peruvian people know what is holding us back.

They know that it is nothing other than the rotting of our government institutions. Chaos and corruption and a failure to identify with the most vital national interests on the part of some of our most important institutions, like the legislative and judicial branches, are tying the hands of the government when it comes to achieving our goals of national reconstruction and development. To the ineffectiveness of Congress and the corruption of the judiciary, we can add the obvious obstructionism and covert scheming of the political parties' top leaders as they try to undermine the efforts of the government and its citizens. Those leaders, an expression of traditional shady political machinations, are interested solely in blocking the economic measures that could lead to a recovery from our nation's bankruptcy, which they themselves have brought upon us.

Similarly, there are groups that are interested in seeing the Pacification Strategy fail because they do not have the courage to take a clear stand against terrorism. With utter disregard for the future of our nation, people who only yesterday were the bitterest of political rivals are now joining forces for the purpose of preventing the successful functioning of the government. The reason behind this unholy alliance is a shared interest in regaining lost political ground. In the struggle against drug trafficking, the Congress has shown itself to be weak and inconsistent. This is clearly seen in its position on legislation proposed by the Executive aimed at imposing sanctions on money laundering, abolishing banking secrecy, punishing the trafficking of goods obtained as a result of the illegal drug trade, and punishing public servants and officials engaged in the concealment of drug-trafficking activities. All of these measures, proposed by the government in Legislative Decree No. 736, were repealed by Congress with no explanation whatsoever and without considering that such action would leave the country powerless to impose the kinds of tough penalties necessary against those involved in the illegal drug trade.

The irresponsible and negative attitude displayed by legislators also shows a disdain for constitutional mandates, which are knowingly violated. This is the case with the enactment of Law No. 25397, the Law on Legislative Control of the President of the Republic's Regulatory Actions, which attempts to tie the president's hands, depriving him of powers essential for governing. This affects such important matters as economic policy and the fight against terrorism, by denying the President the authority to designate which areas are in states of emergency.

Without the least regard for the powers vested in the president by our Constitution, attempts have even been made to deny him the possibility of fully or partially complying with the Annual Budget Law. This demagogic and obstructionist excess has resulted in a very significant deficit in the budget, which may result in the reoccurrence of hyperinflation if urgent corrective measures are not taken. In an act that constitutes an affront to a country that is suffering severe economic hardship, Congress has grossly expanded its budget and improperly provided an extension of the *cédulas vivas*[13] to former congressional representatives. This action shows lawmakers' complete disregard for the complaints asking for austerity, efficiency, and seriousness in legislative matters—a complaint repeated on numerous occasions by ordinary citizens. Numerous times, congressional sessions could not proceed due to the chamber's lack of a quorum.

The irresponsibility, carelessness, and sloth of the so-called "Fathers of the Nation" have resulted in the tabling of many bills that were critical for the functioning of this country.

The people of Peru, the vast majority, have called for efficiently run institutions, committed to our nation's supreme interest, that would channel, focus, and harness the country's energies. Consequently, they have consistently rejected their Congressional representatives' irresponsible, unfruitful, anti-historical, and anti-national conduct, which lets the agenda of groups and party leaders prevail over those of Peru. The country wants a congress that addresses our major national challenges, free from the vices of political caciquismo and clientelism.

A justice system overcome by political sectarianism, venality, and complicit irresponsibility is a scandal that irreparably discredits democracy and the rule of law. The nation has grown weary of this state of affairs and wants solutions. It desires an effective and modern justice system, which would constitute a full guarantee for civic life. It does not want to see any more corrupt fiefdoms in places where irreproachable morality should be the order of the day.

Among other examples of how justice operates in this country, let it suffice to mention the inexplicable release of drug traffickers, or the egregiously partial treatment accorded to them, or the mass release of terrorists who not only have been convicted but who have confessed to their crimes. All are a misapplication of the standard of fairness. We must contrast that with the dubious slowness that characterizes proceedings against citizens with limited resources and the unusual degree of diligence in cases involving persons with power and influence. All of this makes a mockery of justice.

Corruption and political infiltration have permeated every level and every court in the judiciary. In Peru, justice has always been a commodity sold to the highest bidder. We are not denying that there are honest and upright judges and prosecutors. We need to rescue them by once and for all removing their corrupt colleagues. Regionalization represented a great hope for the peoples of Peru, but it was infected from the very beginning by the evils of the traditional political system. Thus, instead of representing a solution, regionalism is a problem with multiple facets because it has created regional "microcentralisms" and a new source of national frustration. Bloated bureaucracies, hungry for power and for government funds, have been installed in most of the regional governments, and each mirrors all of the vices and defects of the capital's old centralism.

There is nothing new in their ideas about how to spend the treasure of the nation and its people. Instead of privileging spending on necessary public works, they give priority to profligate spending that has no constructive purpose. We cannot allow this to continue.

Nobody believes that Peru can indefinitely postpone fundamental socioeconomic changes. Thus, now more than ever, the nation needs a profound transformation, not just a band-aid of partial reform. Peru cannot continue to let terrorism, drug trafficking, and corruption weaken it. We need to strengthen our resolve by radically altering the structures of our nation's institutions. We cannot wait three more years for citizens, committed to acting in the best interests of the people, to enter the congress. We also cannot wait even one more day to completely overhaul the nation's judiciary. The fate of our nation has hung in the balance during the past twenty months, and it will continue to hang in the balance in the future, for we have only just begun the task of rebuilding. The government is aware of the historic necessity of eliminating all obstacles that stand in the way of this process of reconstruction.

If the nation does not rebuild now—if it does not lay the foundations for national development—then there is no possible guarantee for the welfare of Peruvians as a civilized collectivity, as a Nation-State.

After rebuilding, our objective is to achieve a prosperous and democratic society. The current democratic formality is deceptive and false, and its institutions often serve the interests of the privileged groups.

It is true that the Constitution contemplates mechanisms for its own modification. But it is also true that, for this to happen, two consecutive first-session ordinary legislative sessions must convene, and this would mean that we would have to wait until nearly the end of the present presidential term to have the legal instruments needed for Peru's general rebuilding.[14] And this would happen only if Congress decides to approve the necessary modifications, including those that are contrary to its members' own interests, such as, for example, a reduction in pay compensation and a no-reelection rule.

What institution or mechanism will let us undertake all the profound changes that, in turn, will propel the nation forward? There can be no doubt that neither Congress nor the judiciary are agents of change. Instead, they are standing in the way of transformation and progress.

As President of the Republic, I have directly witnessed these irregularities, and I have felt that it is my responsibility to take emergency actions in the interest of hastening the process of national reconstruction. It is for this reason that I have decided to take the following extraordinary measures:

1. Temporary disbanding of the Congress of the Republic until the approval of a new organic structure for the nation's legislative branch, which a national referendum will approve.
2. Comprehensive reorganization of the judiciary, the National Council of the Judiciary, the Court of Constitutional Guarantees, and the Public Prosecutor's Office to ensure the honest and efficient administration of justice.
3. Restructuring of the Office of the General Comptroller of the Republic to ensure proper and timely oversight of the government, which will lead to imposing drastic sanctions on those responsible for the misappropriation of the State's resources.

As a citizen elected by a large majority of our nation's voters, I reaffirm that my only motive is my desire to have the Peruvian nation achieve prosperity and greatness. This will only be possible through a profound transformation of the State and its institutions, so that the latter become true engines for development and social justice.

Therefore, governmental continuity will temporarily occur through an Emergency and National Reconstruction Government, whose principal objectives are:

a. Modification of the current Constitution in order to reflect the creation of a new structure for both Congress and the judiciary, for the purpose of converting these branches of government into effective instruments for order and development. The former is to be transformed into a modern legislature, one which reflects the interests of the nation and which is subject to periodic renewal.
b. Radically inculcate morality in the judiciary and its affiliated institutions.
c. Modernize the government administration to adapt it for purposes of development and the best and most rationalized utilization of resources.
d. Pacify the country within a legal framework that imposes severe penalties on terrorists and drug traffickers. Doing this will guarantee a climate of peace and tranquility to make national and foreign investment possible.
e. Confront drug trafficking and associated illegal activities head on, and successfully eliminate isolated instances of immorality and corruption in law enforcement agencies and other institutions.
f. Admonitory punishment of all cases of immorality and corruption that involve government officials.
g. Promote a market economy within a legal framework that provides security and encourages efficiency and competitiveness in those participating in the economy.
h. Reorganize the educational system and adapt it to our development needs, foster a patriotic consciousness, and encourage the mass construction of schools. Doing this will generate employment at the same time.
i. Decentralize the powers of the Central Government by means of a regionalization

process that would reduce both the bureaucracy as well as the number of regional deputies.

j.   In the medium term, substantially increase the standard of living for the population as a whole, creating conditions for the comprehensive development of the human being. As long as this transitional situation lasts, we will suspend those Constitutional articles that are not compatible with these governmental objectives. Thus, congressional functions will be assumed by a Council of Ministers, which will have the authority to issue decree-laws.

In addition, as quickly as possible, we will create a commission tasked with comprehensively reorganizing the judiciary.

In addition, we will quickly form another commission, consisting of renowned jurists, to draft a constitutional reform bill for the previously indicated reason: to ensure that our Magna Carta meets our needs for development, modernization, and pacification of the nation. In due course, a national referendum will be held to pass that constitutional reform. Any real social change must revolve around the nation's youth, yet these young people must be imbued with a national spirit. We are a country of young people, and it will be the nation's youth who will determine our future. Young people are the most sensitive, idealistic, and honest component of our population. We must ensure that they do not fall prey to drugs, fanaticism, or frustration. Their energy will serve as the catalyzing agent for our nation's transformation.

The youth will understand that it is a matter of planting the seeds of a new nation and leaving behind the fetid ruins of the old order of corrupt politicians, judges, and officials who stand in the way of true democracy. Doing this will let the true interests of the nation guide the destiny of the Republic, rather than the pseudo-democratic formalities that do nothing but hinder our progress.

For Peru, there is only one path forward: national reconstruction. Nothing will change unless we ensure that this rebuilding happens and that the Peruvian people's will for transformation and quest for self-renewal not be undermined by sterile legislative debates or corrupt judges and government officials.

It is essential that the nation understand that the temporary and partial suspension of the present legal system does not constitute the negation of true democracy. On the contrary, this action constitutes the beginning of a search for a genuine transformation that will guarantee a legitimate and effective democracy and that will allow all Peruvians to become the builders of a Peru that is more just, more developed, and better respected within the family of nations.

As Commander-in-Chief of the Armed Forces and the National Police, I have undertaken to ensure that these institutions immediately take the steps required to guarantee compliance with these announced measures and to safeguard civil order and citizens' safety.

Goodnight.

Document 9.4   A Day in the Trial of the Century, by Carolina Huamán Oyague (Family Member of La Cantuta Victim)

Source: www.fujimoriontrial.org/?page_id=98.

It's difficult to describe the mix of feelings that overcome me today; almost 15 years and five months have passed since that morning when a premonition abruptly woke me and drove me to my sister's room. I looked for her, desperate and full of anxiety. I had never imagined all the horror that would come after. For me, the pain still feels like it is July 18, 1992. So many years have passed and today, finally, Fujimori is seated in the defendant's chair. Today, finally, the light at the end of the tunnel is no longer so faint; though hazy, I can read *Justice*. Some would hope that it is only a word, but it embodies a combination of actions and compromises that we decide to make.

Seated in this court room, I see the person who was principally responsible for the kidnapping, torture and murder of my sister. Today he is before a court, the time has come for him to be accountable and face justice. His mocking smile is no longer spontaneous, but feigned, in order to maintain his circus; his clowns try a thousand different scripts, but the show does not work anymore. The absence of his popular stage becomes more evident. Before the lack of arguments, the clowns remove their masks and act, like those who lack valid reasoning; they make themselves up and show themselves as they are, as they always were behind cameras ensnared by corruption. They are no longer accompanied by that false power with which, over all these years, they tried to bend us, incapable of understanding that power is not made by exercising force over others. Real power is internal; is able to create, to convert ideals into reality, and permits us to leave our Utopia because we are reality. The executioners could not destroy our ideals, despite such infamy. Even with the extreme to which they took us, we did not lose our capacity to bear fruit, to grow in the spirit. It has been our perseverance, and above all our immense love for our loved ones, that kept us from being defeated.

Day after day I listen attentively to the declarations of the defendant Fujimori, while multiple events come to my mind. With each answer, a train of images charges my memory. Today he wants us to believe that he was a neophyte, a victim of discrimination, a gift, a defender of human rights; saying that his information channels gave him mistaken facts. It sounds humorous, considering the control he exercised, that today he tries to erase our memory, but we remember the militia support for the coup d'état. We remember his famous, celebrated phrase "*dissolve.*" We remember the climate of impunity that he incited, giving orders and promoting laws that would impede us from reaching justice. So many times I was at my mother's side before some government institution, demanding justice, but they never heard our cries, much less stopped to see our tears. I remember their response to the horror that he called only "a simple excess . . . what sister are you talking about, that person does not exist, she fled with her boyfriend." Their tanks at the head of their victorious general to intimidate Congress, their accomplices closing the path to our mothers dressed in black, the delivery my sister's remains in a cardboard box, their forbidding her to be buried, the fraudulent sentences from the military, their midnight laws, the Cantuta Law, the threats my family received, the harassment and stigmatizing by their purchased press. I remember how he discredited the Armed Forces because in his government, there were no friendly soldiers, only fear of everyone in a uniform. He never thought about the human rights of Peruvians when he sent our soldiers to fight a futile war while he trafficked arms to the enemy with his partner, Montesinos.

The defendant Fujimori tries futilely to play dumb when they remind him of statistics, names, acts of horror, the halo of barbarity that his death squadron left; and five minutes later his egocentrism betrays him. Then he reminds us that he was in everything; in every village, in every activity that determined the events, reminding us that he was omnipresent and omnipotent. It is impossible for him to conceal his pride, but history teaches us that it is this ill-fated attitude that prints black pages in the memory of humanity and carries all those self-proclaimed saviors to failure.

So many sentiments converge within me during these times; sadness and impotence left by the malevolence of mankind, the absence of that which will never be filled. But there is also happiness and solidarity found in the gestures and expressions of beings who are incapable of being indifferent with their neighbors, who could not help but feel indignant, who were in that way our strength and a sign to keep going forward in the fight for justice, no longer just for our family members, but for all of the Cantutas that today are represented in this one trial.

The visualization of Alberto Kenya Fujimori and all that he represents converts everything in a whirlpool of emotions, images, memories, affronts without a mea culpa or even a simple apology. That's how my smile comes out easily upon the ludicrousness of his arguments. I wish tears did not run down my cheeks, but sometimes they come and it is impossible to stop them; they arrive along with all the vividness and with the hurt of seeing human beings like the former dictator Fujimori, capable of restoring human misery, incapable of seeing the magnitude of their mistaken acts, of the negative impact of their acts on others, self-involved and blinded by the pure ambition for power and money.

For Further Reading

Burt, Jo-Marie. "'Quien habla es terrorista': The Political Use of Fear in Fujimori's Peru," *Latin American Research Review* 41:3 (2006), 32–62.

Carey, Elaine. *Plaza of Sacrifices: Gender, Power, and Terror in 1968 Mexico*. Albuquerque: University of New Mexico Press, 2005.

Feitlowitz, Marguerite. *A Lexicon of Terror: Argentina and the Legacies of Torture*. New York: Oxford University Press, 1999.

Gorriti, Gustavo. *The Shining Path: A History of the Millenarian War in Peru*. Chapel Hill, University of North Carolina Press, 1999.

Grandin, Greg. *The Last Colonial Massacre: Latin America in the Cold War*. Chicago: University of Chicago Press, 2004.

Mayer, Enrique. "Peru in Deep Trouble: Mario Vargas Llosa's 'Inquest in the Andes' Reexamined," *Cultural Anthropology* 6:4 (1991), 466–504.

Menchú, Rigoberta and Elisabeth Burgos-Debray. *I, Rigoberta Menchú: An Indian Woman in Guatemala*. London: Verso, 1984.

Palmer, David Scott. "'Terror in the Name of Mao': Revolution and Response in Peru," *Perspectivas Latinoamericanas* 2 (2005), 88–109.

Partnoy, Alicia. *The Little School. Tales of Disappearance and Survival in Argentina.* San Francisco: Cleis Press, 1998; 2nd edn. 1986.

Payne, Leigh. *Unsettling Accounts: Neither Truth nor Reconciliation in Confessions of State Violence.* Durham, NC: Duke University Press, 2007.

Poole, Deborah and Gerardo Renique. *Peru: Time of Fear.* London: Latin America Bureau, 1992.

Smith, Gavin. "Pandora's History: Central Peruvian Peasants and the Re-covering of the Past," in Gerald Sider (ed.), *Between History and Histories: The Making of Silences and Commemorations.* Toronto, University of Toronto Press, 1997, pp. 80–97.

Starn, Orin. *Nighwatch: The Politics of Protest in the Andes.* Durham, NC: Duke University Press, 1999.

Stern, Steve. *Shining and Other Paths: War and Society in Peru, 1980–1995.* Durham, NC: Duke University Press, 1998.

Taylor Diana. *Disappearing Acts: Spectacles of Gender and Nationalism in Argentinas Dirty War.* Durham, NC: Duke University Press, 1997.

Verbitsky, Horacio. *Confessions of an Argentine Dirty Warrior: A Firsthand Account of Atrocity.* New York: The New Press, 2005.

April 30, 1977	1983	1980s	1980s	1991–1992	1993
Madres de la Plaza de Mayo begin marching in Buenos Aires, Argentina	Return to Democracy in Argentina	Rise of Medellín cartel in Colombia	Mexican Migration to the United States expands during successive economic crises	Tens of thousands of Haitians flee their country, seeking asylum in the United States	Women begin disappearing in Ciudad Juárez, Mexico

2007	2008
Mexicans in United States send $26 billion in remittances home	6,200 people die in drug related violence in Mexico

A Right to Have Rights in the New Democracies[1]

10

December 2, 1993	January 1, 1994	1996	2002	2003	2006
Pablo Escobar killed in Medellín Colombia	NAFTA comes into effect between Mexico, the United States, and Canada	Illegal Immigration Reform and Responsibility Act passed by U.S. Congress	Mexican government issues over 1,000,000 ID cards to undocumented Mexicans in the United States	Mothers of missing women of Juárez tour United States in search of support	Felipe Calderón elected President of Mexico, immediately declares war against the cartels

Almost every country in Latin America signed the Universal Declaration of Human Rights when it was adopted by the United Nations in 1948.[2] In the following forty years, every government in Latin America violated the human rights of its citizens, sometimes in horrifying ways. Some would argue that this does not represent a contradiction, but is a function of the fact that, in Latin America, the law has always been understood as an ideal, a theory, something that informs practice but determines nothing. After the dirty wars however, this explanation could no longer satisfy millions of people living in this part of the world. Having lived through the worst terror the region had ever seen, they insisted that it was time to produce a new kind of order in Latin America; one in which a right, if enshrined in the law, was something more than words on paper.

Rights, human and otherwise, are complex phenomena. They are for the most part held individually, and their violation is a crime against an individual. Traditionally this presented a conundrum for Latin Americans because the judicial system, the mechanism for ensuring individual rights, was not just weak, but was often complicit in the human rights violations perpetrated by authoritarian regimes. In the past one of the surest ways to invite the violation of one's rights was to complain to judicial authorities about the violation of one's (or others') rights. This danger was never more acute than during the dirty wars, when the courts for the most part acted as rubber-stamps for murderous regimes.

The dirty warriors openly condemned certain forms of subversion—such as communism and feminism—but took a more subtle approach to human rights. While systematically violating the rights of their citizens, they did it in secret, denying their actions, *disappearing*[3] dissidents while claiming that they had simply run away, or left the country. Yet in refusing to disavow human rights in principle (as have some regimes in recent years), these regimes unwittingly participated in their own undoing. They left open a small but important civic space in societies where political dissent was otherwise forbidden. Avoiding any identification with either the left or right, family members and victims of the violence took advantage of this opportunity, taking up a basic, human claim: that the state had no business kidnapping, torturing, and murdering its own citizens. In doing so they set in motion a series of processes that would revolutionize the practice of human rights in Latin America.

In demanding that their human rights be respected, victims of the dictatorships chose a language that is powerful both for its directness and for the way it seems to stand apart from political partisanship. Certain basic rights, that "all human beings are born free and equal" (Article 1 of the UN Declaration), that we all have the "right to life, liberty, and security of person" (Article 3), that "no one shall be subjected to torture or to cruel, inhuman or degrading treatment or punishment" (Article 5), or that "everyone has a right to freedom of thought, conscience and religion" (Article 18)[4] may have political implications, but they come as close to any statements in human history to the claim of universality. Human rights also transcend national boundaries, not simply because they are shared by all and their violation is a crime against humanity, but because human rights activists have been immensely successful in demonstrating the ways that human rights violations within one country often originate somewhere else (as in dirty warriors trained in the U.S. Army's School of the Americas).

We begin this chapter with the moment when the demand that human rights be respected began to gain traction in Latin America: in the Plaza de Mayo, Buenos Aires, in 1977. We then shift our attention to two of the critical human rights issues that have confronted citizens of the new democracies. The first is most easily phrased as the *right to security*, made most poignant by the waves of crime and violence that have plagued Latin America since the 1980s. Having passed out of an era characterized by states that routinely violated the rights of their citizens, Latin Americans must decide whether it is enough to simply end those atrocities, or if the state must also be an effective guarantor of rights. The second issue concerns *migrant rights*, which constitute one of the great unresolved questions that face our increasingly globalized economies. Migration, it seems, plays a key role in both North and Latin American societies, yet migrants today live in a netherworld, denied rights both at home and abroad. The value of our democracies as we move into the twenty-first century will be in part measured through their right to have rights.

Mothers, Sisters, Daughters

There is probably no better place to start the story of human rights in Latin America than with the *Madres de la Plaza de Mayo*.[5] After March 1976 the Argentine *junta* not only closed off all forms of political opposition, it also refused to release any information about the thousands of young people the military plucked from the streets and sequestered in its torture chambers. Government officials either stonewalled or ridiculed family members who came to their offices in search of information. It was then that a collection of mothers decided to occupy Argentina's most important public space. They confronted all physical threats stoically, never wavering from their single demand: the return of their children. This act—assuming the public face of grief and rage during a time when Argentines were largely silent—helped bring down one of the bloodiest dictatorships in Latin American history, a government that in less than a decade murdered perhaps 30,000 people.[6]

The women who started gathering in the Plaza de Mayo on April 30, 1977 were mostly working-class (Figure 10.1). Most had never worked outside of their homes, and had never before shown much interest in politics. Many had never voted in an election. We cannot say for certain, but some may have even supported the March 1976 military coup that began Argentina's *proceso*.[7] After all, at the time of the coup Argentines from all social classes believed that the country was verging on chaos, a problem many blamed on rebellious youths, feminists, and communists. Military rule promised a re-assertion of traditional family values, it promised that order and respect for authority would be restored. Working-class mothers were no more immune to the appeal of this claim than anyone else.

Then their children began to disappear. As mothers do everywhere, they went to the authorities. Sitting in government offices, waiting for answers from recalcitrant government officials, they slowly realized that it was not just their children who were missing, but the children of hundreds, maybe even thousands of other women. So, at a time when all forms of protest were prohibited, they decided to gather weekly in the Plaza de Mayo and publicly demand the return of their children.

At first the *junta* allowed the *Madres* to march relatively unmolested. They could barely imagine that these women represented a political threat. Soldiers told them they could not

Figure 10.1 The *Madres de la Plaza de Mayo*, 1977
Source: Courtesy of Associated Press Photo

sit in large groups in the plaza, and occasionally taunted them, but did not drive them from the square. This did not last. Within months the *junta* realized that these women were undermining the government's self-image, and the secret police began stalking the *Madres*, even kidnapping and killing a few. Soldiers blocked off the plaza, forcing the *Madres* to the margins, hoping they could contain the public relations damage. But they were too late. Members of the international press began to attend the demonstrations, writing sympathetic pieces about the *Madres* for their readers back home. With a growing national and international profile, the *Madres* could not be eliminated without making the regime an international pariah. They would not demobilize until they got their children back.

Whether they did so strategically or not, the *Madres* seized an opportunity afforded by the military *junta*'s blindness towards them, and occupied the public stage at a time when no one else could. In doing so, they were instrumental in bringing the attention of the western democracies to something that until then took place under a shroud of secrecy. Reports about body parts washing up on the beaches of Uruguay (the remains of victims tossed from airplanes over the South Atlantic) had been the subject of brief news stories, but there was nothing quite like the impression left by grieving family members, living memories of the disappeared. News coverage of their protests in turn prompted the first major Organization of American States (OAS) investigation of human rights abuses in Argentina in 1979.

As they lined up to testify at the OAS hearings, the *Madres* provided vivid evidence of how they had pushed the regime's human rights violations out of the shadows and onto center stage in Argentina. Political prisoners, the disappeared, were no longer simply statistics. They were somebody's child, grandchild, sister or brother, maybe even someone's mother or father. More importantly, the *Madres* were decent folk, people who were grieving a loss and did not deserve this fate. Had they been black, or indigenous, or communists, this might not have seemed like a tragedy of major proportions, especially at the height of the Cold War. But they were not. They were white, culturally conservative, mothers of the nation and loyal patriots. And a state that was murdering their children had gone too far.

This was a brilliant tactic, especially given the fact that many of these supposedly apolitical women had very political children. Their claim to human rights somehow made a universal claim for their children (that nobody should be kidnapped by the state) and a very particular claim for themselves (that they were particularly aggrieved because they, if not their children, were apolitical mothers). In doing so, they made themselves the victims of the disappearances, rendering the state's claim that their children were terrorists void.

This was not all that they accomplished. In transforming motherhood from a private matter into a public issue, they blurred the distinction between feminist and feminine politics. While they gained access to the public sphere because they were "traditional," the claims they made (respect for human rights) and the way they made them (sometimes going so far as to openly provoke the soldiers sent to rein them in) transformed the category they occupied. Prior to 1976 most members of the group never imagined joining a public protest, let alone openly confronting a government official. By the 1980s they would begin to protest in support of a wide variety of causes. Invariably adorned in their white headscarves, their motherly appearance belied the fact that they were one of the most openly bellicose groups in Argentine political life. Motherhood thus proved to be a flexible claim for the *Madres*, as it does for most women who enter politics. Here and elsewhere it would become the basis for demanding respect for an expanding repertoire of rights, including a right to personal safety for women and children (against all forms of public and private abuse), and rights to food, shelter, and basic sustenance.

Not all members of the *Madres* embraced the idea of widening their rights claims beyond finding their disappeared children. Advocates for a narrow focus believed their attentions would be divided and public sympathy would erode if the *Madres* enlarged their agenda. In 1986 a small faction split from the movement and took the name *Línea Fundadora* (Founding Line), claiming that the increasingly radical demands of the *Madres* were a betrayal of the movement's original goals. But by making this claim even these more conservative *Madres* revealed a deeply political sense of motherhood. Divisions in the *Madres* mostly followed class and regional lines. Middle-class *Madres* and those from the interior of the country were much more likely to take a conservative approach, to work cooperatively with the state and other human rights groups and remain narrowly focused on the fate of their children. They showed little interest in casting motherhood as a means to demand broader social change, in part because their politics tended to be conservative. Working-class *Madres*, typified by Hebe de Bonafini, actively expanded what were originally personal demands about their children into a broad agenda for reform based on their rights as mothers. Though this strategy has not always translated into widespread support (indeed, conservative women have been some of Bonafini's most ardent critics), this transition signaled the dawn of an era of dynamic and ideologically diverse women's organizing across the region.[8]

The *Madres* did not spawn women's rights movements across Latin America. Given their own internal ideological differences, it seems almost absurd to imagine that they could have done such a thing. While the *Madres* were women who came together to further a cause, we should not attempt to disentangle the cause from their identities as women; wives, mothers, and daughters. Women do not inexorably achieve some sort of feminist conscious-ness as a result of their participation in the public sphere. Instead, they foster limited transfor-mations of public life, making it in some ways easier for later generations of women to make their claims, whether it be for equal rights before the law, for an end to domestic violence and weak enforcement of sexual assault laws, for equal pay for equal work, for reproductive rights, or for the safety and well-being of their children. The complex legacies of the *Madres* thus include the active insertion of a previously silent group into the public sphere; it is simply not clear where that participation has led, or will lead.

One thing is clear. Mothers in many parts of Latin America continue to fear for the well being of their children. In some cases agents of the state remain complicit, as when police officers target poor children for murder in certain cities (Rio de Janeiro and Guatemala City have seen numerous public scandals around this practice). In others, the violence that threatens their children is tied to a general increase in violence and lax government responses. We see this most poignantly in a series of events that took place in Northern Mexico in recent years. During the 1990s, hundreds of young women in Cuidad Juárez, Mexico (many of them workers in the assembly plants that serve the U.S. market) were kidnapped, sexually assaulted, murdered, and dumped in the nearby desert. Mexican officials first ignored the crimes because of the ethnicity, class, and reputed professions of some victims (they were poor, dark, and some may have been sex workers), and botched the investigations by torturing suspects until they confessed. Twenty years earlier this strategy might have worked, but this time the families of the victims found new ways to get around the old barriers. They did not just complain to the police, they went to the media, in both Mexico and the United States.

In 2003 a group of mothers of the murdered women toured the United States, and one of its leaders, Norma Andrade, spoke before a sub-committee of the U.S. Congress. She condemned not just the perpetrators of the crimes, but a state that failed in the first instance to protect her child, and in the second instance to investigate the crime. When she returned to Mexico, government agents followed her home, and warned her and other mothers to keep quiet, to stop talking to the media, to stop embarrassing them. She refused, and within days reports that the government was harassing her were published in the Mexican and U.S. media.

After Andrade's pleas and the threats she received for making them received wide notice in the press, Mexican President Vicente Fox committed new resources to the investigation. In early 2004 he appointed prominent human rights lawyer María López Urbina to examine both the crimes and official malfeasance. After a short investigation she filed charges against 81 current and former state and local officials. Her prosecutions did not promise to end the killing spree, and the scope of her authority was quite limited, but the sheer number of charges filed against officials irrefutably exposed the Mexican state's failure to live up to a fundamental responsibility.

Moreover, thanks to the efforts of grieving mothers in Juárez, Mexicans are now familiar with the term *feminicide*, which denotes the murder of women because they are women. They are also increasingly aware that it is a national problem. While simply naming something and exposing it to public scrutiny does little to solve the problem of violence against women, it is a critical beginning. It forces a dirty secret into the open, where society can ignore it no longer.

Life, Liberty, and Security[9]

Violence is shaping up to be *the* critical issue in Latin America during the coming decades, and perhaps the greatest threat to the human rights of people in the region. Ideological struggles still produce violence in some places, though for the most part Latin Americans are less concerned about these Cold War relics than a new and ever-present danger: crime. Today a series of shadowy actors, including drug traffickers, urban gangs, paramilitary organizations, and government officials in the pay of criminal organizations are the notable actors in a region-wide crisis in human security. They are the product of changed circumstances, not just the return to democracy, but profound economic and demographic shifts in Latin America that date to the middle years of the twentieth century.

Latin American cities, already large by global standards in 1950, exploded in the latter half of the twentieth century. At first, urbanization was the product of concerted government efforts across the region. ISI policies promoted industrial development and good factory wages, while simultaneously discouraging small-scale cultivation in favor of capital intensive export agriculture. Small farmers in much of the region found it increasingly difficult to make a living in the countryside, and migrated in search of work, a better standard of living, and perhaps freedom from the restraints of small-town living. By the 1970s several urban centers in Latin America were being described as mega-cities, enormous urban complexes characterized by the massive growth of slums on their periphery. Today Lima, São Paulo, Buenos Aires, Bogotá, and Mexico City are among the largest cities in the world.[10]

In the early years of rapid urban expansion local governments extended social services to meet some of the needs of the new arrivals, building public housing, transportation networks, and schools, but a series of developments dating to the 1970s made it increasingly difficult for any state to care for the swelling urban population. The first was tied to the economic crises that plagued Latin American societies after the mid-1970s. Jobs evaporated, wages fell, and social services were curtailed or eliminated. For most people in the region the 1980s would become a "lost decade," characterized by eroding standards of living and negative economic growth.

Those without the means to either escape the crisis or weather the worst were left with a limited number of options in order to survive. Some migrated, first to other parts of Latin America and then abroad. Some turned to the informal economy, where one could work as a street peddler, buying and selling contraband, or working odd jobs that sometimes provided little more than could be gained from begging. Others gave up, sinking into personal nightmares of alcohol and drug abuse (inhalants, and particularly paint thinner and industrial glues became popular in the *misery belts*[11] that ringed the cities). Still others turned to a particularly perilous version of the informal economy, the trade in illicit drugs.

If you asked most Latin Americans in 1970, they would have insisted that the region did not have a drug problem, that illicit drugs were a problem of the First World. Statistics seemed to bear them out, as in Latin America the rates of cocaine, heroin, and marijuana use were much lower than in the United States and Western Europe. At the time it was relatively easy for the peasant cultivators of marijuana, opium poppies, and coca to imagine that they were simply farmers growing the most profitable crop they could. And if North Americans had a drug problem, why should they care?

During the 1960s and 1970s an expanding class of drug traffickers, based in places as diverse as Medellín Colombia, Santiago, Chile, Havana, Cuba, and Culiacán, Mexico, imagined themselves as entrepreneurs, moving merchandise to consumers who wanted it, and helping themselves and their societies in the process. At a time when the economy as a whole was worse than anyone could remember, they may have been the most important source of export revenues in the entire region.

It is no wonder then that the *narcotraficantes* were widely admired; they were Robin Hoods, taking the money and even vitality of those who oppressed Latin America and in turn re-vitalizing their own communities by building hospitals, schools, apartment buildings, and by supporting local teams, customs, and the devotion of local saints. Some even became national symbols of Latin American defiance of the United States. Colombian narco-trafficker Pablo Escobar successfully ran for the Colombian Congress in 1982 on a platform that included a provision that called for a ban on the extradition of drug traffickers to the United States.

Not coincidentally, it was also during this time that the Reagan administration in the United States stepped up its own war on drugs, shifting the government's attention from consumers to producers. Active interdiction in the drug trade became a precondition for U.S. aid and trade (Latin American countries by the 1980s had to be certified as good partners on an annual basis), raising the stakes of the trade considerably. Latin American states went to war with themselves, as those who favored eradicating the trade (or at least giving that appearance) battled corrupt government officials, growers, and traffickers. Traffickers responded by importing a growing arsenal of weapons from the United States in order to defend and expand their operations.

Even long simmering conflicts between leftist guerrillas and right-wing paramilitaries in Peru and Colombia were affected by the growing pressure to eradicate the trade, as both sides in these conflicts became actively involved in protecting growers, laboratories, and traffickers. Not to be outdone, military units stationed in these zones also took a piece of the action, leaving the rural civilian population completely vulnerable, and driving hundreds of thousands to flee the coca zones for the urban slums of cities like Bogota and Lima.

The police proved completely inadequate to the task of dealing with the crisis, at least in part because police forces across the region were riddled with officers who either actively participated in the trade or took bribes to look the other way. As a result, by the end of the 1980s the illegal drug trade was metastasizing into new and increasingly heinous forms of violence. Criminal gangs, armed with money and weapons from the trade, turned to kidnappings, extortion, and a booming street-level drug trade across Latin America in order to make money. Given these overlapping phenomena, it should be little wonder that Latin America today has the highest homicide rate of any region in the world (five times the world average, translating to 100,000 homicides in the region annually[12]). Homicides have doubled since the 1980s, property crimes have increased by a factor of three, and crime rates continue to rise, particularly in urban areas. Seventy-five percent of the world's kidnappings take place in Latin America. Arrests and convictions for these crimes are startlingly rare, in part because so few crimes are ever reported.[13] Victims rarely turn to the police, as public officials are often involved in the crimes. Among the poor especially, the police are more often seen as a menace than a solution to the violence.

Victims, bystanders, and criminal suspects generally have good reason to fear the police. Police agencies in Latin America have an exceptionally poor record of respecting civil rights. Even police agents who might be inclined to investigate crimes have few resources to do so, and partly because of this officials generally find easy targets to blame for criminal acts. For the most part this means focusing on young, impoverished males (who often tend to have darker skin than the elites) from marginal neighborhoods. For example, residents of Brazil's *favelas* (urban slums) are commonly blamed for the country's crime problems, and extra-judicial killings by the police of young black men from these communities are commonplace. Upwards of 1,000 people in Rio alone die at the hands of the police annually, in incidents usually explained as "acts of resistance followed by death." The term is strikingly similar to the phrase "shot while trying to escape" (the *ley fuga*), used elsewhere in Latin America to describe those summarily executed by the police.

These practices do generate rage in Latin America, where today more than ever before, citizens groups insist that the police should guarantee public safety. In July 2004 more than 350,000 protesters took to Mexico City's streets, demanding judicial and police reforms, particularly measures that would halt the epidemic of kidnappings that was plaguing the country. These and other efforts across the region have seen some success. Government transparency laws are now in place in several countries, and in some instances government officials have been held accountable for their crimes. Human rights groups now have extensive networks of activists who publicize judicial crimes to a global audience, further increasing the pressure for police accountability.

Still, at times the problem seems overwhelming. Reformers must not only change the culture of policing, they must increase salaries, protect police who come forward with charges against their fellow officers, and reform a judiciary that has no tradition of punishing malfeasance on the part of agents of the state. They must do this in the face of a long history of graft and lax investigative techniques, all the while facing the simple truth that their enemies are wealthy and threatening. Crime is profitable, and the traffickers have immense resources to either buy off new police agents or successfully intimidate them into silence. The military is a poor alternative, because it too is easily corrupted. Soldiers are generally even more poorly paid than the police (something like 100,000 troops have left the Mexican military to work for the traffickers in recent years). In any event, every time Felipe Calderón (Mexico) or Alvaro Uribe (Colombia) sends the troops into a community to eradicate crime, they risk an epidemic of human rights violations by troops with little experience respecting civil liberties.

In recent years Mexico has been particularly affected by an increase in violence, especially after President Felipe Calderón ratcheted up his war against the drug traffickers in 2007. Calderón sent more than 40,000 troops to the border to regain control of these regions from the cartels, in some cases displacing entire police forces in the process. The results were both inconclusive and costly. There were at least 6,200 drug related killings in Mexico in 2008, a period during which the government made some high profile seizures and arrests, but was clearly out-gunned by the cartels.

Again and again, Mexicans have been confronted with the capacity of the cartels to inflict pain, with police that are either ineffective or complicit, and with a federal state that seems unable to guarantee public safety; problems that seem to have intensified rather than diminished under Calderón. In early 2008 the Intelligence Chief for the Attorney General's Judicial Police resigned after he was accused of providing bullet-proof vests to members of the Sinaloa cartel. In August 2008 all 20 members of police force in Villa Ahumada in Chihuahua (80 miles south of El Paso) resigned after their police chief was murdered less than 24 hours into his tenure.

Calderón has faced a particularly strong challenge from the *zetas*, a group of former Special Forces soldiers who once worked against the drug cartels but are now major players in the drug trade. Taking advantage of the tendency of the Mexican press to focus on spectacular violence, the *zetas* have repeatedly earned national headlines by providing journalists with images of beheadings and other grisly murders. In February 2009 they killed retired General Mauro Enrique Tello Quiñones in Quintana Roo shortly after he was appointed to direct public security in Cancún. The police chief in Cancún was arrested in the investigation into the murder. Elsewhere during February 2009 Roberto Orduña, the army general assigned to lead the Ciudad Juárez police force, resigned his post after traffickers threatened to execute one police officer every 48 hours if he did not. The violence continued through the year, with repeated revelations of high-level corruption, threats against officials, and massacres.

It is possible that a resurgence of the old ruling party (the PRI) in the July 2009 mid-term elections may foretell an end to Calderón's drug war. While no major PRI politician openly advocates making peace with the traffickers, the party's history of tolerating the trade, along with a general desire for new policy directions, suggests Mexicans may be tired of being the victims in a battle that the state cannot win. Across Latin America we are now seeing pressure on politicians to decriminalize drugs, and in 2009 Mexican Congress even passed legislation that ends prosecution for possession of small quantities of most illicit drugs.[14] Whatever the results of these initiatives, they reflect the general sense on the part of Mexicans that the state as constituted cannot guarantee their security.

In the absence of states that can guarantee a right to human security, individuals are often left to their own devices. Those police officers who remain committed to the battle increasingly treat their beats as war zones, going about heavily armed, covered in body-armor (which they often pay for themselves), their faces hidden by masks that protect their identities. They do their best to move their families out of harm's way, often to the United States. Others will accept bribes or actively work for the cartels, as this option is often less fraught with danger than the alternative.

For the private individual, the choices confronted at this time are just as stark. Their cities become obstacle courses, filled with practices, places, and times deemed dangerous. Those with means can sequester themselves and their families in gated communities, such as the *countries* of greater Buenos Aires, or the high security apartment buildings of Santa Fé in Mexico City (ironically, this is also where many wealthier traffickers live). They can hire private security guards and arm themselves against potential threats such as kidnapping, armed robbery, and carjackings. Those with fewer means are left extremely vulnerable by the inability of the state to defend their rights, as they must travel on public transport and live in often-dangerous neighborhoods. Friends and neighbors in these communities may look out for one another, but for most, their best option for a more secure life is a life somewhere else.

Migrant Rights?

Following a precedent that has become tragically common in recent decades, in late 1991 thousands of Haitians took to leaky boats in order to escape political and economic chaos at home by making a new life in the United States. When they landed on the shores of Florida, the Haitians insisted that they were political refugees, fleeing the violent regime that had overthrown the democratically elected government of Jean-Bertrand Aristide in September 1991, and that if they were forced to return home, they would face persecution and almost certain death. As such, they were entitled to asylum in the United States, a right enshrined in both the Universal Declaration of Human Rights (Article 14) and a series of treaties signed in later years.[15] By early 1992 around 37,000 Haitians had fled their country, many of them with the goal of gaining asylum in the United States.[16]

The Bush administration did not welcome these claims. While 11,000 refugees were ultimately admitted to the United States, over the following four years most of the nearly 70,000 Haitian refugees intercepted at sea by the U.S. Coast Guard were forcibly returned to Haiti (some after a brief stay in Guantánamo Bay, Cuba). The Bush and later Clinton administrations argued that the vast majority of the refugees were fleeing economic conditions in Haiti, and not political persecution. While their circumstances were tragic, this did not entitle them to refugee status. In the end only 8.4 percent of claimants received refugee status. This success rate was lower than that of claimants from any other country in Latin America.

These Haitians were caught in one of the dilemmas that have faced migrants since the first people moved from one place to another. Migrants generally leave their homes for multiple reasons, including persecution (official and individual), economic necessity, warfare, population pressures and changing environmental circumstances. Nowadays most of these displaced people (as many as three million in Colombia, for example) are too poor, too disadvantaged to consider moving to another country. Most must try their luck in the slums that ring the region's metropolises, and have no hope of ever assembling either the funds or documentation it would take to apply for refugee status, let alone navigating their way through government bureaucracies that as a rule look for reasons to exclude applicants. Moreover, for most migrants the simple truth is that they are poor, and however much they might like to live in a society where they are not persecuted by police, guerrillas, paramilitaries, or others, they also desperately want an opportunity to earn a little money, to make a better life for themselves and their families.

This long-standing desire to escape local problems and embrace distant opportunities became an especially pronounced phenomenon in Latin America during the latter half of the twentieth century. Latin America has one of the most mobile populations in the world, and while much of that movement has been internal migration, today over 20 million Latin Americans live outside their country of birth.[17] The United States is the home to more of these people than any other country.

The recent waves of migration to the United States from Latin America began with the economic crises of the 1980s. Mexicans in particular sought to alleviate their suffering by looking for work in the United States, and during the 1980s established a pattern of migration that continues today. Almost half a million Mexicans migrate to the United States every year, and about 10.6 million people born in Mexico now live in that country.[18] Ironically, a significant number of contemporary migrants come from rural communities that suffered economic catastrophes with the introduction of the North American Free Trade Agreement in 1994. As peasant farmers, they simply did not have the means to make their plots of land viable in the new economy, and decided to sell their labor in the global market for the highest price it could fetch. Many of those migrants now travel to the United States annually to work in a series of agricultural harvests, and then return home to tend to their meager agricultural parcels and reconnect with their friends and families. They are circular migrants, tied to their communities of origin, and returning there frequently, but over time many also spend considerable periods of their adult lives working abroad.

Each migrant leaves Mexico for individual reasons, but the sheer numbers who have left turned this into a collective practice, with important implications for life on both sides of the border. Mexican migrants in the United States are crucial to a host of industries, including hotels and restaurants, construction, migrant agricultural labor, slaughterhouses, domestic service, and landscaping. Mexicans in the United States have produced significant communities not just in the Southwest, but also in the agricultural zones of the Midwest, Southeast, and Northwest, and in major cities like Chicago and New York. The money they pay in taxes represents important revenue streams for the government, in part because the Social Security Administration understands that the contributions they collect from these migrants will never be paid out as benefits. There is little credible evidence to suggest that the economic impact of these migrants has been anything but positive.

Migration has had a similarly striking impact in Mexico. Remittances (money sent home by migrants in the United States) edged over $20 billion in the early twenty-first century, peaking at $26 billion in 2007. They are the third largest source of foreign earnings in Mexico, behind only oil and manufactured goods. Today well over a million families in Mexico survive principally on the monies sent home by their relatives in the United States, and this money has in turn fueled building booms in communities across the country, as migrants have not only built homes for themselves, but churches, schools, hospitals, and other public facilities. Migrants also pay an increasingly important role in Mexican politics, contributing their votes and resources to politicians who promise to defend their interests.

Still, for their importance to both the United States and Mexico, undocumented migrants—or, if you will, illegal aliens—continue to live a precarious existence. Unlike the trade agreements that created a common market in Europe, NAFTA explicitly excluded the freedom to migrate, only offering that opportunity to a limited number of professionals (a category which explicitly excluded most Mexican migrants). This means that most migrants must violate U.S. law to enter the country, even though there is plenty of otherwise legal work awaiting them. There are today around 11 million undocumented immigrants in the United States. About 57 percent of these come from Mexico, and 24 percent from other Latin American Countries. Back home, these migrants often find it difficult to exercise their citizenship rights (migrants gained the right to vote in presidential elections only in 2006). They are regularly targeted for theft by customs officials, police, and criminals when they return home, and if they choose to send money home by wire transfer are often forced to pay exorbitant fees.

U.S. immigration policies have actually grown more draconian as the importance of these migrants to the U.S. economy has increased, largely as a result of efforts by American conservatives to placate nativist sentiment in the face of swelling migrant numbers. Long before the terrorist attacks of September 2001 the U.S. Congress was tightening immigration law (see, for example, the Illegal Immigration Reform and Responsibility Act of 1996). Border security similarly became a major political issue as early as the 1980s, played out through expansions in the Border Patrol, efforts to install high tech-surveillance systems, and the ever present demand that a fence be built along the border. These measures are invariably justified by suggesting that sinister migrants somehow threaten a law-abiding nation, in spite of the fact that there is no evidence to suggest that these migrants represent a criminal or political threat to the country (most studies suggests that illegal immigrants commit fewer crimes per capita than the native born).

Some have tried to defend the migrants. The Mexican government has repeatedly tried to protect the rights and interests of their citizens in the United States. Mexican politicians have demanded immigration reform in the United States, intervened in specific cases to insist that the rights of Mexican nationals to equal treatment before the law be respected, and since 2002 have successfully lobbied state and local governments (along with several banks) in the United States to accept ID cards (*Matrículas Consulares*) issued by Mexican Consulates to undocumented migrants as legal identification.[19] North American businessmen, many of whom fear that their companies would not survive without the undocumented laborers they employ, have also pushed for immigration reform that would allow Mexicans to enter the country as guest-workers; temporary laborers who promise to return to Mexico at the end of their contracts. Migrants themselves have organized demonstrations on several occasions (including protests attended by over a million demonstrators in May 2006), demanding both immigration reform and a respect for their basic human rights.

Together, these disparate groups are making claims for migrant rights. They insist that migrants are essential to both the communities they enter and the ones they leave, and that in treating them as criminals and denying them the same rights that others enjoy, we deprive them of a fundamental human right. In some ways this argument consists of a claim that the due process rights (for example, equal treatment before the law) of migrants are being systematically violated by the Border Patrol and Department of Homeland Security. Some advocates go further, insisting that we reconsider the very idea of the border as we understand it, and recognize that in a globally integrated world people should have as much right to move along international circuits as the goods they produce.

It is difficult to make this case for immigrant rights in a world where everyone's civil liberties have eroded in the face of terrorist threats. We can make an economic argument (they are necessary), a historical argument (the United States is the historical product of migration), even an argument based on the humane treatment of others. It does not really matter. Even legally admitted immigrants in the United States have been seeing their rights eroding for more than a decade, and there is little sympathy in the country for the plight of the undocumented immigrant. Right-wing politicians regularly link these migrants to criminality, even terrorism, arguing that as a whole they threaten homeland security. The very term used to describe them—*illegal* immigrants—implies as much.

It is a clever turn of phrase, in that it implies something illegitimate and criminal in its very essence, and thus throws any claim that the illegal immigrant should possess rights into doubt. As such, the term reminds us of the challenges that confront human rights activists in the contemporary world. For all its rhetorical power, absent any enforcement power the Universal Declaration of Human Rights is merely words on paper. Rights are the product of laws, and at this point in history those laws are national in scope. One's rights thus depend on the citizenship papers one carries. This helped make the case for rights quite clear for groups like the *Madres de la Plaza de Mayo*, and even for those who in recent years have publicly protested violent crime in their societies. The state violates the rights of its citizens if it murders them, or even if it fails to provide for basic human security. But what of the migrants, caught in limbo because while they are essential to both the sending and receiving society, they have few enforceable rights in either? Their crossings may be one of the dominant narratives of the twenty-first century. The type of story that will be remains to be seen.

The Document: Border Crossings

In 2004, the Mexican government published a pamphlet titled the *Migrant Guide* (Document 10.1).[20] It was one of the most unusual texts produced by any government in recent years. In effect, it offered advice to undocumented Mexican migrants on how to survive their journey, and how to deal with the Border Patrol if apprehended. U.S. officials were flabbergasted. How is it that the Mexican government, an erstwhile ally of the United States, would advise its citizens on how to break U.S. laws?

It is possible, even likely, that the booklet appeared because of a bureaucratic screw-up, that the officials who approved the publication had interests and desires contrary to those of their superiors. On the other hand, at the time of publication Mexican officials were feeling estranged from the Bush Administration, having pushed for major immigration reform in the United States but been completely rebuffed in the aftermath of the September 11, 2001 attacks. This would have been an ideal means to both annoy the U.S. government and demonstrate to the millions of Mexicans living in the United States that the Mexican government cared about their well being (even if it could do nothing to get them legal employment or jobs at home).

The pamphlet was in the form of a *historieta*, the comic books that for generations have been popular among poor Mexicans. Like other government publications for the poor, the *Migrant Guide* used the form to didactic ends, teaching the reader what they needed to know while attempting to keep their attention through the images. The *historieta* format also worked for other reasons. With its heroic migrants, threatening border guards, and warnings about the hidden dangers of life on the other side, the *Migrant Guide* fit well in a genre that typically relies on narratives of good versus of evil, of masculine men and sensual women.

More troubling was the larger message that the *Migrant Guide* conveyed through its very existence. By publishing the pamphlet, the Mexican government told the poor reader that since the government could not provide for their subsistence at home, they ought to migrate, and that this was the way to do it. The reader was advised that under certain circumstances they could turn to the Mexican consulates in the United States if they were in need, and they were informed of their rights, but for the most part the booklet reminded them that they lived in a dangerous world, and that they were on their own as they navigated those dangers. The book obliquely urges them to go on that perilous journey, because their remittances, if no longer their labor, were essential to the welfare of their country.

Document 10.1 *Migrant Guide* (2004)

Source: English translation from http://www.americanpatrol.com/AID_ABET/MEXICO/MexiBookTranslation.html.

INTRODUCCIÓN INTRODUCCIÓN

INTRODUCCIÓN

Estimado connacional:

Esta guía pretende aportarte algunos consejos prácticos que te pueden resultar de utilidad, en caso de que hayas tomado la difícil decisión de buscar nuevas oportunidades laborales fuera de tu país.

La manera segura de ingresar a otro país es con la previa obtención de tu pasaporte, que expiden las Delegaciones de la Secretaría de Relaciones Exteriores, y la visa, que solicitas ante la Embajada o Consulado del país a donde deseas viajar.

Sin embargo, en la práctica vemos muchos casos de mexicanos que intentan cruzar la frontera norte sin la documentación necesaria, a través de zonas de alto riesgo que implican enfrentar graves peligros, particularmente en áreas desérticas o ríos con fuertes y no siempre notorias corrientes de agua.

SRE 1

Introduction

Dear fellow citizen:

This guide tries to provide you with some practical advice that may be useful to you in case you have made the difficult decision to seek new work opportunities outside of your own country.

The safe way to enter another country is by first obtaining your passport, which is issued by the Delegations of the Secretariat of Foreign Relations, and your visa, which you request at the Embassy or Consulate of the country to where you wish to travel.

However, we actually see many cases of Mexicans who try to cross the northern border without the necessary documentation, crossing high-risk zones that are very dangerous, especially in desert areas or rivers with strong and not always noticeable currents.

INTRODUCCIÓN INTRODUCCIÓN

Con la lectura de esta guía, podrás enterarte también de algunas cuestiones básicas sobre las consecuencias legales de tu estancia en los Estados Unidos de América sin la documentación migratoria apropiada, así como sobre los derechos que tienes en ese país, una vez que te encuentres en él, independientemente de tu condición migratoria.

Ten en cuenta siempre que existen mecanismos para que puedas ingresar legalmente a los Estados Unidos de América.

En cualquier caso, si llegas a tener problemas o a enfrentar dificultades, recuerda que México cuenta con 45 Consulados en dicho país, cuyos datos también podrás encontrar en esta publicación.

Identifica tu Consulado y acércate a él.

2 SRE   SRE 3

As you read this guide you can also learn some basic questions about legal consequences of your stay in the United States of America without appropriate immigration documents, as well as the rights you have in that country once you are there, independent of your immigration status.

Always keep in mind that there are mechanisms for you to enter the United States of America legally.

In any case, if you encounter problems or difficulties, remember that Mexico has 45 Consulates at its disposal in that country, whose contact information you also can find in this publication. Identify your Consulate and go to it.

RIESGOS · RIESGOS

PELIGROS POR CRUZAR EN ZONAS DE ALTO RIESGO

Cruzar por el río puede ser muy riesgoso, sobre todo si cruzas solo y de noche.

La ropa gruesa aumenta su peso al mojarse y esto dificulta nadar o flotar.

4 SRE · SRE 5

Risks

Dangers of Crossing in High-Risk Zones

Crossing the river can be very risky, especially if you cross alone and at night.
Thick clothing weighs you down when it's wet and makes it hard to swim or float.

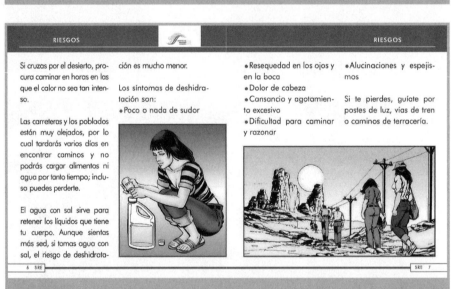

RIESGOS · RIESGOS

Si cruzas por el desierto, procura caminar en horas en las que el calor no sea tan intenso.

Las carreteras y los poblados están muy alejados, por lo cual tardarás varios días en encontrar caminos y no podrás cargar alimentos ni agua por tanto tiempo; incluso puedes perderte.

El agua con sal sirve para retener los líquidos que tiene tu cuerpo. Aunque sientas más sed, si tomas agua con sal, el riesgo de deshidratación es mucho menor.

Los síntomas de deshidratación son:
● Poco o nada de sudor
● Resequedad en los ojos y en la boca
● Dolor de cabeza
● Cansancio y agotamiento excesivo
● Dificultad para caminar y razonar
● Alucinaciones y espejismos

Si te pierdes, guíate por postes de luz, vías de tren o caminos de terracería.

6 SRE · SRE 7

If you cross in the desert, try to travel when the heat is not so intense.
Highways and towns are very far apart, so that it could take you several days to find roads and you will not be able to carry food or water for that long. You could even get lost.
Salted water helps you retain body fluids. Although you get more thirsty, if you drink salted water the risk of dehydration is lessened.
Dehydration symptoms are:

- Little or no perspiration
- Dryness of eyes and mouth
- Headache
- Fatigue and exhaustion
- Difficulty in walking and reasoning
- Hallucinations and mirages

If you get lost follow utility poles, railroad tracks, or furrows.

CUIDADO CON LOS "POLLEROS"   CUIDADO CON LOS "POLLEROS"

CUIDADO CON LOS "POLLEROS", "COYOTES" O "PATEROS"

Pueden engañarte asegurando que te cruzan en unas horas por montañas o desiertos. ¡Esto no es cierto!

Pueden arriesgar tu vida pasándote por ríos, canales de riego, zonas desérticas, vías de tren o carreteras rápidas. Esto ha ocasionado la muerte a cientos de personas.

Si decides recurrir a "polleros", "coyotes" o "pateros" para cruzar la frontera, considera las siguientes precauciones:

No lo pierdas de vista, recuerda que él es el único que conoce el terreno y, por lo tanto, el que

puede sacarte de ese lugar.

Desconfía de todo aquél que te ofrezca pasarte al "otro lado" y te pida que conduzcas un vehículo o que lleves o cargues un paquete por él. Regularmente esos

B SRE   SRE 09

Be Careful of Alien Smugglers

Be Careful of "Polleros," "Coyotes," or "Pateros" [Various Names for Alien Smugglers]

They can deceive you by assuring you they'll cross you [smuggle you across the border] at certain times over mountains or through deserts. This is not true! They can put your life in danger leading you through rivers, irrigation canals, desert areas, along railroad tracks, or freeways. This has caused the death of hundreds of people.

If you decide to use the services of a "pollero," "coyote," or "patero" to cross the border, consider the following precautions to take:

Don't let him out of your sight; remember that he's the only one that knows the terrain and therefore is the only one that can guide you safely.

Do not trust anyone who offers to cross you over to the "other side" and asks you to drive a vehicle or carry a package for him. Regularly those . . .

CUIDADO CON LOS "POLLEROS"   CUIDADO CON LOS "POLLEROS"

paquetes contienen drogas u otras sustancias prohibidas. Por esta razón, muchas personas han terminado en la cárcel.

Si transportas a otras personas puedes ser confundido con un "pollero" o "coyote", y te pueden acusar del delito de tráfico de personas o robo de vehículo.

No entregues a tus hijos menores a desconocidos que te ofrecen cruzarlos a Estados Unidos.

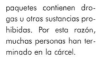

10 SRE   SRE 11

. . . packages contain drugs or other prohibited substances. For that reason many people have ended up in jail.

If you transport other people you can be confused with an alien smuggler and be accused of alien smuggling yourself or even vehicle theft.

Don't hand over your minor children to strangers that offer to cross them to the United States.

NO UTILICES DOCUMENTOS FALSOS O QUE NO TE PERTENEZCAN, NI TAMPOCO DECLARES FALSA NACIONALIDAD

Si intentas cruzar con documentos falsos o que pertenecen a otra persona, toma en cuenta lo siguiente:

Usar documentos falsos o de otra persona es un delito federal en Estados Unidos, por el que pue-des ser procesado penalmente y terminar en la cárcel; al igual que si declaras un nombre falso o decir que eres ciudadano de Estados Unidos, cuando no lo eres.

No mientas a los agentes estadounidenses de puertos o garitas.

12 SRE   SRE 13

Do Not Use False Documents

Do Not Use False Documents or Documents of Other People, Nor Declare a False Nationality

If you try to cross with documents that are false or that belong to someone else, keep the following in mind:

The use of documents that are false or that belong to someone else is a Federal crime in the United States, for which you can be criminally prosecuted and end up in jail; the same as if you give a false name or say you are a U.S. citizen when you are not.

Do not lie to U.S. border crossing or inspection booth agents.

SI ERES DETENIDO

No te resistas al arresto.

No agredas o insultes al oficial.

14 SRE

No arrojes piedras u objetos al oficial ni a las patrullas, pues esto se considera una provocación a los oficiales.

Si los oficiales se sienten agredidos, es probable que utilicen la fuerza para detenerte.

Alza lentamente tus manos para que vean que estás desarmado.

No lleves en las manos ningún objeto que pudiera ser considerado como arma, tales como: linternas, desarmadores, navajas, cuchillos o piedras.

If You Are Detained

Do not resist arrest.

Do not assault or insult the officer.

Do not throw stones or other objects at the officers nor at the patrol cars, because this is considered a form of provocation.

If the officers feel they've been assaulted they will probably use force to detain you.

Raise your hands slowly for them to see you're unarmed.

Do not carry or hold any objects that could be construed as weapons, such as: lanterns, screwdrivers, blades, knives, or stones.

No corras o trates de escapar.

No te escondas en lugares peligrosos.

No cruces carreteras de alta velocidad.

Es mejor que te detengan unas horas y seas repatriado a México, a que te pierdas en el desierto.

SI TE DETIENEN, ¡TIENES DERECHOS!

Proporciona tu nombre verdadero.

Si eres menor de edad y vienes acompañado por un adulto, dilo a la autoridad para que no los separen.

16 SRE   SRE 17

If You Are Detained / Your Rights

Don't run or try to escape.
    Don't hide in dangerous places.
    Don't cross freeways.
    It's better for you to be detained for a few hours and be repatriated to Mexico than to get lost in the desert.

If You Are Arrested, You Have Rights!

Give your true name.
    If you are a minor and are accompanied by an adult, tell the authorities so they do not separate you.

Tus derechos son:

Saber dónde te encuentras.

Pedir que te permitan comunicarte con un representante del Consulado de México más cercano, para que recibas apoyo.

No declarar o firmar documentos, sobre todo si están en inglés, sin la asesoría de un abogado defensor o representante del Consulado Mexicano.

Recibir atención médica si te encuentras lesionado o delicado de salud.

A ser respetado y tener un trato digno, sin importar tu calidad migratoria.

A que te trasladen de forma segura.

Tener agua y comida cada vez que lo necesites.

No estás obligado a proporcionar tu calidad migratoria al ser detenido.

18 SRE   SRE 19

Your Rights

Your rights are:
    To know where you are.
    To request to speak to the nearest Mexican Consulate representative in order to receive help.
    To not make statements or sign documents, especially if they are in English, without the aid of a defense attorney or Mexican Government Consulate representative.
    To receive medical attention if you are injured or in poor health.
    To receive respectful treatment regardless of your immigration status.
    To be transported safely.
    To have water and food when you need it.
    You are not obligated to disclose your immigration status when you are detained.

No ser golpeado o insultado.

No ser incomunicado.

En caso de que te quiten tus cosas, pide un comprobante para que puedas reclamarlos al momento de ser liberado.

Cualquier violación a estos derechos, es importante que lo informes a tu abogado o al representante del Consulado de México que te visite; o bien, a la Delegación más cercana de la Secretaría de Relaciones Exteriores en territorio mexicano.

Si quieres mayor información y vives en Texas, Estados Unidos o en Ciudad Acuña, Coahuila, sintoniza "La Poderosa" en el 1570 de AM

XERF 1570 AM
LA PODEROSA
Ciudad Acuña, Coahuila

20 SRE   SRE 21

To not be hit or insulted.
    To not be held incommunicado.
    In case they take away your personal effects, request a voucher in order to claim them when you are released.
    If there is any violation of these rights, it's important for you to inform your attorney or Mexican Consulate representative that visits you or even the nearest Delegation of the Secretariat of Foreign Relations within Mexico.
    If you want more information and you live in Texas or in Ciudad Acuña, Coahuila, tune in to "The Powerful Station" at AM 1570.

EN CASO DE SER DETENIDO

Si ya fuiste sentenciado por algún delito o te encuentras enfrentando un proceso criminal en alguna cárcel, tienes los siguientes derechos:

No ser discriminado por las autoridades policíacas, judiciales o penitenciarias.

Recibir visitas de funcionarios consulares y de tus familiares.

Recibir la asesoría legal correspondiente sin que se te condicione y sin que sea obstruida.

Si te encuentras enfrentando un proceso criminal y aún no te han sentenciado, pregunta a tu abogado o representante del Consulado, en qué consiste el "Acuerdo de Culpabilidad".

No te declares culpable sin antes consultar con tu abogado cuáles son las posibilidades de ganar tu caso en juicio.

Es importante que conozcas las leyes del estado de la Unión Americana donde vivas y trabajes, ya que las leyes en cada uno de ellos son diferentes. Toma en cuenta la siguiente información:

Si tomas no manejes, ya que si no tienes documentos podrás ser detenido y

deportado.

Si un residente legal es infraccionado más de dos veces por conducir en estado de ebriedad, podrá ser deportado.

No manejes sin licencia de conducir.

Respeta las señales de tránsito y usa el cinturón de seguridad.

No manejes sin seguro de auto ni aceptes manejar un vehículo desconocido.

22 SRE   SRE 23

If You Are Arrested / Detained

If you have already been sentenced for some crime or you are in jail facing criminal prosecution, you have the following rights:
    To not be discriminated against by the police, the courts, or prison authorities.
    To receive visits from consular officials and family members.
    To receive appropriate legal counsel without conditions or obstructions.
    If you are being criminally prosecuted and have not yet been sentenced, ask your attorney or consular representative what the "Plea Agreement" consists of.

. . . continued

Do not plead guilty without first consulting your attorney about the possibilities of winning your case if you go to trial.

It's important that you know the laws of the American state where you live and work, since each state's laws are different. Bear in mind the following information:

If you drink don't drive, since if you do not have papers you can be detained and deported.

If a legal resident is cited more than two times for drunk driving, he can be deported.

Do not drive without a driver's license.

Observe traffic signs and signals and use your seatbelt.

Do not drive without auto insurance nor drive an unknown vehicle.

EVITA

EVITA

No permitas que otras personas desconocidas suban a tu auto.

Si al conducir cometes alguna infracción de tránsito y eres detenido por la policía, coloca las manos sobre el volante y no bajes del auto hasta que te lo pida el oficial.

Evita llamar la atención, por lo menos mientras arreglas tu estancia o documentos para vivir en los Estados Unidos.

La mejor fórmula es no alterar tu rutina del trabajo a tu casa.

Evita las fiestas ruidosas, los vecinos pueden molestarse y llamar a la policía, y puedes ser arrestado.

Evita involucrarte en riñas.

Si acudes a un bar o centro nocturno y se inicia una riña, aléjate, ya que en la confusión puedes

ser arrestado aunque tú no hubieras hecho nada.

Evita la violencia familiar o doméstica. Al igual que en México, es un delito en Estados Unidos.

24 SRE

SRE 25

[Things to] Avoid

Do not pick up strangers.

If you commit some traffic violation and are detained by the police, place your hands on the steering wheel and do not get out of the car until the officer requests you to do so.

Avoid calling attention to yourself, at least while you are arranging your residence papers to live in the United States.

The best formula is not to alter your routine of going between work and home.

Avoid noisy parties because the neighbors can get upset and call the police, and you could be arrested.

Avoid fighting.

If you go to a bar or night club and a fight starts, leave immediately, since in the confusion you could be arrested even if you did not do anything wrong.

Avoid family or domestic violence. As in Mexico, it is a crime in the United States.

EVITA   EVITA

La violencia doméstica no son sólo golpes, también son amenazas, gritos o maltratos.

Si eres acusado de violencia doméstica en contra de tus hijos, pareja o alguna otra persona que viva contigo, podrías ir a la cárcel. Además, las autoridades de los Servicios de Protección al Menor - Child Protective Service (CPS), podrían quitarte a tus hijos.

No portes armas de fuego, armas blancas u otros objetos peligrosos.

Ten en cuenta que muchos mexicanos están muertos o en la cárcel por eso.

Si la policía entra a tu casa o departamento, no te resistas, pero solicita la "Orden de cateo" correspondiente. Es mejor cooperar, y pide comunicarte con el Consulado de México más cercano.

26 SRE   SRE 27

[Things To] Avoid

Domestic violence does not consist solely of hitting others but also can be threats, shouting, or mistreatment.

If you are accused of domestic violence against your children, your mate, or someone else who lives with you, you could go to jail. In addition, Child Protective Services authorities could take away your children.

Do not carry firearms, bladed weapons, or other dangerous objects.

Keep in mind that many Mexicans have died or are in prison because of these things.

If the police enter your house or apartment, do not resist, but ask to see a search warrant. It's better to cooperate with them and ask to speak to the nearest Mexican Consulate.

CONSULADOS   CONSULADOS

La Secretaría de Relaciones Exteriores cuenta con 45 representaciones consulares en el interior y en la frontera sur de Estados Unidos de América, las cuales tienen la función de auxiliarte. Recuerda: si has sido detenido o te encuentras cumpliendo alguna condena, tienes derecho a comunicarte con el Consulado de México más cercano. Lleva tu "Guía de Protección Consular", siempre contigo.

Acércate al Consulado...
Acércate a México.
¡Es tu casa, paisano!

-Secretaría de Relaciones Exteriores
-Dirección General de Protección y Asuntos Consulares.

CONSULADOS DE MÉXICO EN ESTADOS UNIDOS

Albuquerque	Atlanta
Tel. (505) 247-21-47	Tel. (404)266-22-33
Austin	Boston
Tel. (512) 478-23-00	Tel. (617) 426-41-81
Brownsville	Calexico
Tel. (956) 542-44-31	Tel. (760) 357-38-63
Chicago	Dallas
Tel. (312) 738-23-83	Tel. (214) 252-92-50
Del Río	Denver
Tel. (830) 775-23-52	Tel. (303) 331-11-10
Detroit	Douglas
Tel. (313) 964-45-15	Tel. (520) 364-31-07/42
Eagle Pass	El Paso
Tel. (830) 773-92-55	Tel. (915) 533-85-55
Filadelfia	Fresno
Tel. (215) 922-42-62	Tel. (559) 233-30-65
Houston	Indianápolis
Tel. (713) 271-68-00	Tel. (317)951-00-05
Kansas	Laredo
Tel. (816) 556-08-00	Tel. (956) 723-63-69
Las Vegas	Los Ángeles
Tel. (702) 383-06-23	Tel. (213) 351-68-00

28 SRE   SRE 29

Consulates

The Secretariat of Foreign Relations has 45 consular representatives within the U.S and on its southern border, which are designed to help you. Remember: if you have been detained or are serving a sentence, you have the right to speak with the nearest Mexican Consulate. Always carry your "Guide to Consular Protection" with you at all times.

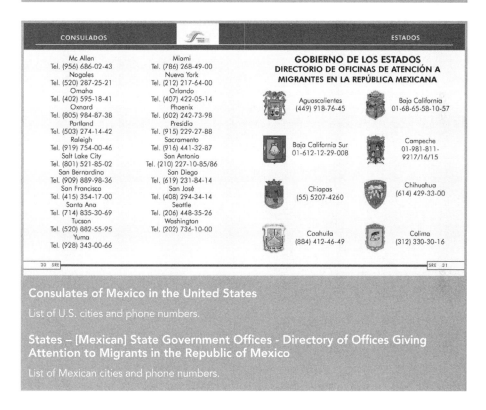

... continued

Get Near to the Consulate . . .
Embrace Mexico.
It's your home, fellow countryman!

- Secretariat of Foreign Relations
- General Administration of Protection and Consular Matters.

Consulates of Mexico in the United States

List of U.S. cities and phone numbers.

CONSULADOS		ESTADOS

Mc Allen	Miami	**GOBIERNO DE LOS ESTADOS**
Tel. (956) 686-02-43	Tel. (786) 268-49-00	**DIRECTORIO DE OFICINAS DE ATENCIÓN A**
Nogales	Nueva York	**MIGRANTES EN LA REPÚBLICA MEXICANA**
Tel. (520) 287-25-21	Tel. (212) 217-64-00	
Omaha	Orlando	Aguascalientes (449) 918-76-45 — Baja California 01-68-65-58-10-57
Tel. (402) 595-18-41	Tel. (407) 422-05-14	
Oxnard	Phoenix	
Tel. (805) 984-87-38	Tel. (602) 242-73-98	
Portland	Presidio	
Tel. (503) 274-14-42	Tel. (915) 229-27-88	
Raleigh	Sacramento	Baja California Sur 01-612-12-29-008 — Campeche 01-981-811-9217/16/15
Tel. (919) 754-00-46	Tel. (916) 441-32-87	
Salt Lake City	San Antonio	
Tel. (801) 521-85-02	Tel. (210) 227-10-85/86	
San Bernardino	San Diego	
Tel. (909) 889-98-36	Tel. (619) 231-84-14	Chiapas (55) 5207-4260 — Chihuahua (614) 429-33-00
San Francisco	San José	
Tel. (415) 354-17-00	Tel. (408) 294-34-14	
Santa Ana	Seattle	
Tel. (714) 835-30-69	Tel. (206) 448-35-26	
Tucson	Washington	Coahuila (884) 412-46-49 — Colima (312) 330-30-16
Tel. (520) 882-55-95	Tel. (202) 736-10-00	
Yuma		
Tel. (928) 343-00-66		

30 SRE   SRE 31

Consulates of Mexico in the United States

List of U.S. cities and phone numbers.

States – [Mexican] State Government Offices - Directory of Offices Giving Attention to Migrants in the Republic of Mexico

List of Mexican cities and phone numbers.

For Further Reading

Alvarez, Sonia E. *Engendering Democracy in Brazil: Women's Movements in Transition Politics*. Princeton: Princeton University Press, 1990.

Andreas, Peter. *Border Games: Policing the U.S.–Mexico Divide*. Ithaca: Cornell University Press, 2001.

Benhabib, Seyla. *The Rights of Others: Aliens, Residents, and Citizens*. Cambridge: Cambridge University Press, 2004.

Bergman, Marcelo S. "Crime and Citizen Security in Latin America: The Challenges for New Scholarship," *Latin American Research Review* 41:2 (2006), 213–27.

Brinks. Daniel M. *The Judicial Response to Police Killings in Latin America: Inequality and the Rule of Law*. New York: Cambridge University Press, 2008.

Cruz, José Miguel. "Police Abuse in Latin America," *AmericasBarometer Insights* 11 (2009), 1–8.

Frühling, Hugo and Joseph S. Tulchin (eds.). *Crime and Violence in Latin America: Citizen Security, Democracy, and the State.* Washington: Woodrow Wilson Center Press, 2003.

Haber, Stephen, Herbert S. Klein, Noel Maurer, and Kevin J. Middlebrook. *Mexico Since 1980.* Cambridge: Cambridge University Press, 2008.

Ignatieff, Michael. *Human Rights as Politics and Idolatry.* Princeton: Princeton University Press, 2001.

Jaquette, Jane. *The Women's Movement In Latin America: Participation and Democracy.* Boulder: Westview, 1994.

Kohen, Ari. *In Defense of Human Rights: A Non-Religious Grounding in a Pluralistic World.* New York: Routledge, 2007.

Martínez, Rubén. *Crossing Over: A Mexican Family on the Migrant Trail.* New York: Picador, 2002.

Nevins, Joseph. *Operation Gatekeeper: The Rise of the "Illegal Alien" and the Remaking of the U.S.–Mexico Boundary.* New York: Routledge, 2001.

O'Neil, Kevin, Kimberly Hamilton, and Demetrios Papademetriou. "Migration in the Americas," Paper Prepared for the Policy Analysis and Research Program of the Global Commission on International Migration, Washington, DC: September 2005.

Taylor, Diana. *Disappearing Acts: Spectacles of Gender and Nationalism in Argentina's "Dirty War."* Durham, NC: Duke University Press, 1997.

Tulchin, Joseph S. and Meg Ruthenburg (eds.) *Toward a Society under Law: Citizens and Their Police in Latin America.* Baltimore: Johns Hopkins University Press, 2006.

Velasco, Jose Luis. *Insurgency, Authoritarianism, and Drug Trafficking in Mexico's "Democratization."* New York: Routledge, 2004.

1982	1993	1994	1996	April 2000	2001
Electoral democracy re-established in Bolivia	Gonzalo Sánchez de Lozada elected president, undertakes free market economic reforms	The law of popular participation opens the way for greater municipal power and the election of more indigenous and peasant leaders	Privatization of YPFB, the national oil and gas company	Water War in Cochabamba	Santa Cruz autonomists publish a memorandum demanding greater decentralization of power

December 2007	May 2008	January 2009
Constituent Assembly proposes new constitution	Voters in Santa Cruz overwhelmingly vote for a referendum demanding autonomy	The new constitution is ratified with 61 percent of the vote

Bolivia's Left Turn   **11**

2002	September—October 2003	October 17, 2003	June 6, 2005	December 18, 2005	May 1, 2006
Sánchez de Lozada narrowly elected president to a second term. Evo Morales comes in second	Gas War	Sánchez de Lozada resigns after civil unrest. Carlos Mesa assumes presidency	Mesa resigns under threat of a general strike	Evo Morales elected President	Morales announces nationalization of the gas fields

"Bolivia is not for Beginners."[1]

Looking back from the start of the new millennium, it almost seems amusing that the American intellectual Francis Fukuyama earnestly proclaimed that the collapse of the Soviet Union signaled the "end to history."[2] Long gone are those halcyon days of global capitalism and freedom, replaced by climate change, terrorist threats, super viruses, and financial catastrophe. It is therefore unsurprising that the narrow political alternatives that seemed to confront Latin Americans with the end of the dirty wars broadened as new parties and philosophies emerged to confront the challenges the region faces. Among those new agents, we have seen a rebirth of the Latin American left, literally back from the dead. In recent years leftist leaders have been elected in Argentina, Bolivia, Brazil, Chile, Ecuador, Honduras, Nicaragua, Paraguay, Venezuela, and Uruguay.

This is not your grandparents' left, which tended to be overly concerned with doctrine and was vaguely hopeful for a revolution that the Soviet Union might one day lead. Today there is no global alliance, no leftist orthodoxies that inform a worldwide Stalinist, Trotskyite, or Maoist revolution. It is everywhere local, for the most part democratic (or at least reliant on democratic processes to come to power), and generally committed to using specific sources of national wealth for the public good while maintaining good standing in the global community. It is also a left that must compete for support within a political landscape that is more competitive than ever before. Leftist leaders once assumed that they *naturally* represented the poor and oppressed, that when marginalized peoples did not come to their support it was because they were ignorant or under the sway of their oppressors. Today they must contend with the fact that many of their erstwhile supporters, including women, the rural poor, indigenous peoples, and peoples of African origin are forming their own political movements with demands that do not always conform to a traditional right versus left party politics. In short, the ideological challenges that the resurgent left faces are much more complex than those faced by earlier, more doctrinaire, revolutionaries.

No country in Latin America embodies both the promise and challenges that face the current left more completely than contemporary Bolivia. As with other countries in the region, in recent years Bolivia has seen both a return to democracy and intense battles over questions of how poverty should be addressed. Also like other countries in the region, it is less clear that Bolivia is a poor country than that it is a deeply unequal society, where small numbers of people have historically monopolized the nation's mineral and agricultural wealth.

It is thus unsurprising that Bolivia has endured many battles over the country's greatest contemporary source of wealth—the vast natural gas deposits in the eastern lowlands—since the return to democratic rule. Though sometimes framed as a struggle between poor people and wealthy gas companies, this is also a regional battle, pitting people from the high Andean plateaus (the *altiplano*) in the west against their neighbors living in the country's eastern lowland departments. Racial overtones also intrude; Lowlanders see residents of the *altiplano* as indigenous, as foreigners who come to take their resources. Residents of the *altiplano* describe eastern lowlanders as phony Bolivians, foreign interlopers who have come to take *their* wealth.

Because self-determination (for both ethnic minorities and indigenous peoples) ranks high on the international agenda, these struggles have the potential to redraw the national map. Latin American leftists of a generation ago tended to reject self-determination, believing that ethnic and indigenous identities were false, that they obscured the true class interests of the poor. Such is not the case today, as the left in Bolivia has come to power in part because it embraced the language of indigenous autonomy. Indigenous peoples however, are not the only ones claiming autonomy these days. Eastern lowlanders have embraced the language of autonomy as aggressively as any other group, making an already complex and almost ungovernable country even more so. It seems that Bolivia's contemporary left turn could very well be the nation's undoing.

Revolution, Markets, and Democracy

As in most places, one could begin the story of Bolivia's recent past almost anywhere. If we start with the Spanish Conquest in the sixteenth century, we imply that the story is about a grievance that will not be addressed until indigenous peoples receive justice. If we start in the nineteenth century, when a weak and divided state lost its only access to the sea, our story might become a cautionary tale about the need for a strong central government. We will not tell either of those tales here. Instead we begin with another important moment in Bolivia's past, the 1952 Revolution. This starting point recalls a moment in which millions of Bolivians (miners, peasants, and the urban middle class in particular) came together to topple the oligarchy and create a more democratic, more equitable, and more united nation. Revolutionary governments expanded the electorate from around 200,000 voters to over a million, built schools across the country, and nationalized the tin mines (then Bolivia's greatest export). Perhaps most importantly, the agrarian reform introduced in 1953 broke up a century-old *hacienda* system in the *altiplano*, distributing land to peasants, while clearing the way for the growth of commercial agriculture in the Amazonian lowlands.

The 1952 Revolution thus transformed Bolivia, though in unexpected ways. In the *altiplano*, land reform and the nationalization of the tin mines were politically popular, but proved to be an economic catastrophe. The mines, already in decline, never produced the wealth that the Bolivian state needed. The break-up of the *haciendas* turned semi-productive estates into wastelands, as agricultural credit, aid, and marketing never materialized to promote economic development in these regions. Moreover, investment in the countryside became virtually impossible, as *campesino* unions blocked the entry of outside investors into the rural economy for fear of losing their land to the old bosses. There is little exaggeration to the claim that by the early 1970s the only profitable agriculture in these regions was tied to growing coca. Some portion of the crop was chewed or brewed into teas in Bolivia, but the majority of the coca was exported, processed into cocaine, and sold in the United States.

In the lowlands, the opposite happened. After 1952 the *media luna* (half moon, for the shape of the region comprised of the Departments of Santa Cruz, Tarija, Beni, and Pando) boomed. In Santa Cruz in particular, landowners took advantage of policies adopted by the *Movimiento Nacionalista Revolucionario* (Nationalist Revolutionary Movement—MNR) government to create a new agro-export industry focused on sugar, cotton, soybeans, and other crops. Just as the great estates of the *altiplano* disappeared, they established massive farms, often at the expense of local indigenous groups. Elites in La Paz barely seemed to notice the fraud and compulsion that went along with these land acquisitions, as by the 1960s Santa Cruz represented a disproportionately large share of the national economy.

The divergent tendencies between the *media luna* and the *altiplano* were not checked either by the military coup that felled the MNR in 1964 or by the 18 years of military rule that followed. By 1964 Bolivia was facing problems that were common to many Latin American societies during the Cold War. A system that relied on clientelism and crony capitalism to maintain order was increasingly sinking under the weight of economic stagnation, but until things truly fell apart, the solution was simply more social spending, more efforts to bail out or nationalize inefficient industries, and more attempts to buy worker complaisance with better wages and benefits.[3] These practices produced an increasingly fragmented Bolivian economy during the years of military rule; desperate poverty in the *altiplano*, new shanty-towns on the edges of cities like La Paz, Cochabamba, and Santa Cruz de la Sierra where rural migrants worked in the informal sector, an emerging illicit coca economy in the temperate valleys (often tolerated by well compensated members of the armed forces), and an export economy in Santa Cruz that was largely disconnected from the rest.

When the military relinquished power to the popularly elected *Unidad Democrática y Popular* (Democratic and Popular Unity—UDP) government in 1982, they left behind the trifecta of Latin America's lost decade, soaring government debt, out of control inflation, and negative economic growth for the country as a whole. A Cuban-style revolution was not the popular choice in Bolivia, which left few options for solving these problems, most of which involved turning to Bolivia's foreign creditors and trading partners for help. And if this was the only option, the Bolivian government would need to take an economics lesson from the International Monetary Fund (IMF).

IMF economists believed that the problems that confronted Bolivia and other Latin American nations were the result of over-regulation of the economy, a bloated public sector (i.e. government owned companies), and barriers to trade and investment. They were only willing to re-negotiate the debt and open new lines of credit if their clients deregulated, cut spending, and opened their economies. Invariably this meant two dreaded practices: austerity measures and shock treatments. The former involved dramatic reductions in government spending. The latter required the rapid elimination of a series of government controls over the economy (i.e. price controls, subsidies, tariffs, and wage guarantees), often causing extreme short-term hardship with the promise of long-term benefit. As evidence of their wisdom they pointed to Chile, which had undergone its own painful restructuring in the 1970s and was now the most prosperous economy in the region. At this point, few economists anywhere had the evidence to challenge such a claim.

In an effort to meet some of these demands the UDP government devalued the currency and raised prices for food and fuel. When miners and peasants protested these measures, the government increased wages, thus negating their own efforts. It was not until Victor Paz Estensorro took power in 1985 that substantial market reforms were implemented. Paz Estensorro cut government spending, reduced the debt, improved tax collection, opened markets to investment, and lowered tariff barriers. Still, he stayed away from the most polarizing IMF demand: that the government sell state owned enterprises. This would wait until his finance minister, Gonzalo Sánchez de Lozada (popularly known as Goni), was elected president in 1993. During his first presidency (1993–7) Goni privatized telecommunications, electricity, air and rail transportation, and oil and gas. Critics claimed the national patrimony was sold for a song (often to well connected insiders). Proponents argued that privatization promised companies that would either prosper or fail on their own, benefiting Bolivians generally. Foreign investment also promised to reinvigorate services that were virtually crumbling (if at a profit to investors), and provide technology and capital inputs to industries that were desperately in need of them.

Hydrocarbons were a particularly important target for privatization. A single company dominated this sector of the economy, the national oil and gas company *Yacimientos Petrolíferos Fiscales Bolivianos* (YPFB), yet the company was desperately under-capitalized, unprofitable, and lacked the infrastructure needed to explore for and exploit new gas reserves. Goni's 1996 hydrocarbons law aimed to resolve this problem by attracting foreign investment under a scheme that reduced royalty rates in Bolivian gas fields from 50 percent to 18 percent, and eased restrictions on investments in the gas industry. Three years later Hugo Banzer sold off YPFB's remaining assets, offering private investors a pre-existing inventory of refineries, pipelines, and storage facilities from which they could develop the industry.

Figure 11.1 Map of Bolivia's departments

Source: Courtesy of: http://www.lib.utexas.edu/maps/americas/bolivia_admin_2006.jpg

Geological surveys in the lowland regions of Bolivia had long suggested that the region had vast untapped gas reserves, and with the privatization of YPFB and the reduction in royalty rates three foreign companies, Total (France), Reposol YPF (Spain), and Petrobras (Brazil) moved quickly to invest in Bolivia. Finding that Bolivia's reserves were even larger than previously thought, and exploiting them at a time of soaring prices (prices increased by 500 percent between 1995 and 2005), they made enormous profits while expanding gas production by 65 percent. Much of that gas left the country for energy-hungry markets in Argentina and Brazil, carried by a privately built $2.2 billion pipeline that opened in 1999.

This was a grand success, and yet it was perhaps too grand, especially in a country where so many people live in desperate poverty. While government revenue from gas rose, the 10 percent increase in revenues (about $150 million per year) seemed paltry compared to the profits made by the energy companies. Even more galling to many residents of the *altiplano* was the fact that the region of Bolivia that benefited most from this windfall was Santa Cruz (Figure 11.1).

The Commodity Wars and the Popular Coup

Far away from the gas fields of Santa Cruz, Bolivia was undergoing another series of transformations during the 1990s, also largely due to Goni's reforms. In 1994 he signed a Law of Popular Participation, which was designed to increase participation in the then fairly exclusive Bolivian political system by decentralizing government authority and opening up a large number of local political offices to popular election. Suddenly the poor, marginalized outsiders who lacked access to money, influence, or an ability to ascend within national political parties could run for local offices, and build larger networks that they could use as springboards to higher office.

Within a decade, more than a third of the mayoralties in Bolivia were held by individuals who openly identified as indigenous, a remarkable shift in the ethnic make-up of power in the country. Just as importantly however, the new law created a platform for a generation of leaders who previously had no legal means to challenge the system. Some were former Marxist revolutionaries, like Álvaro García Linera and Felipe Quispe, leaders who had been the guerrillas of an earlier generation but encountered new opportunities to mobilize legally within the new system. Others, like Evo Morales, the leader of a coca growers movement from the Chapare region, came from sectors that had been economically dynamic but politically marginalized, and seized on the opening to build regional and later national movements.

By the late 1990s Quispe, García Linera, Morales, and others could find increasingly sympathetic audiences in the poor, marginalized slums that ringed cities like Cochabamba and La Paz. Watching their own standards of living erode while others grew rich from the privatization of the national patrimony (particularly water and gas), many poor Bolivians seethed with resentment. They could, and would take out their anger at the ballot box, but at this point the urban and rural poor were not content to simply wait for the next election. Using the power of the crowd to make the country ungovernable, they launched the era of the popular coup.

Bolivians got their first real taste of the resurgent power of popular groups during a conflict over rate increases implemented by the foreign owned water utility Aguas de Tunari in Cochabamba in April 2000. Though protests against the rate increases were first organized by middle-class residents of the city, the protestors chose a target and developed a symbolic repertoire that struck a nerve in the surrounding valley. The image of a foreign company making excessive profits from something that was so essential to life—so impregnated with symbolic importance—provided a powerful rallying cry. Thousands joined the protest from around the region, setting up roadblocks that brought life in the valley to a standstill. Aguas de Tunari was quickly forced to capitulate to the demands of the protesters.

After Cochabamba, roadblocks rapidly emerged as a key currency in Bolivian politics. Often organized by members of the *Confederación Sindical Unica de Trabajadores Campesinos de Bolivia* (Bolivian Confederation of Rural Workers—CSUTCB), roadblocks paralyzed La Paz from June to September 2001 during protests over a variety of government policies (Figure 11.2). More followed between January and April 2002 after the government outlawed the sale of coca grown in the Chapare region.[4] In February 2003, when a newly re-elected Goni increased income and gasoline taxes at the behest of the IMF, he faced not only renewed roadblocks, but a police mutiny and riots that left 32 people dead. None of this however, would compare to the gas war of September 2003.

First, we begin with the back-story. As gas production and global prices skyrocketed after 1999, many economists, government officials, and businessmen argued that Bolivia should begin to export its gas to the United States, where liquefied gas extracted in Bolivia could fetch four times the price it received in Brazil or Argentina (the country's two largest export markets). In 2001, a consortium made up of Repsol-YPF, British Gas, and BP/Bridas announced plans to export 168 million cubic meters of gas in liquid form over 20 years to North America. In 2002 President Jorge Quiroga signaled his approval of the plan, which called for private interests to build a pipeline to Mejillones in Chile at a cost of $6 billion, where gas would be liquefied and shipped. Investors argued that this was the most cost

Figure 11.2   El Alto road block
Source: Courtesy of Reuters/David Mercado

effective and thus most profitable way to ship the gas to the U.S. market. The only drawback was that in order to do this, the Bolivian gas had to be shipped to Chile.

This was a hard sell back in Bolivia. Chile was the country that had stolen Bolivia's access to the sea, albeit more than a century ago. Bolivians generally view this loss as one of the great tragedies in their history, and as a source of many of the problems that have haunted them since that time. What was more, that gas would leave the country in unprocessed form, and all the benefits associated with processing the gas into liquid form, or adding further value, would accrue to foreigners (many of whom would be Chilean). It was an image that the opposition was able to exploit to maximum advantage.

In September 2003, while Goni stalled on making a final decision on the project, popular anger overtook him. Protesters took to the streets of Cochabamba and La Paz on September 19 demanding that the government defend gas as a national patrimony. The following day police killed six Aymara-speaking protesters in the town of Warisata, leading to further protests and eventually a general strike on September 29. Roadblocks went up across the country.

The most important roadblocks went up in El Alto, the poor city that rises above La Paz, which at the time was largely dominated by Felipe Quispe. Fifty years ago El Alto was a tiny community on the margins of La Paz, a poor shanty-town of around 3,000 inhabitants who worked menial jobs in the city. Today it has nearly 900,000 residents, and is the larger of the two. El Alto is deeply linked to La Paz; each day 100,000 people travel between the two cities, mostly for work. It is also the home of the gas refineries that keep its sister city running, the critical highways that lead to the capital, and it is home to the international airport, but these structural linkages betray a stratified geography. Above la Ceja (the marker between the two cities) the city is self-identified as Aymara, below it lie the *criollos*, and to cross the line is to enter a world where outsiders feel unwelcome.

As the explosive growth of El Alto since the 1950s suggests, most people here trace their origins in the community to the crises in the countryside that followed the 1952 Revolution (Figure 11.3). Many thousands of residents of El Alto come from the *altiplano* and return regularly, using wages earned in the informal sector in the city to supplement the meager incomes they earn from peasant agriculture (70 percent of workforce in El Alto is in the informal sector). Their ties to rural areas provide them with a sense that they belong to a specific and disadvantaged ethnic community, and this sensibility acts as a powerful glue for protest movements in what is already a highly organized community (there are over 400 community associations in El Alto).

El Alto was able to suffocate La Paz in early October 2003, evoking long dormant fears of race war in Bolivia among residents of the capital. Facing severe fuel and food shortages in the capital, on October 12 Goni declared martial law in El Alto. Violent clashes in the aftermath of the decree left 16 dead, and Goni in an untenable position. On October 13 he suspended the gas project. A few days later he resigned and left the country, leaving Vice-President Carlos Mesa in power. This assured a truce, but at a cost of 63 lives.

Mesa would fare little better as president. Ninety-four percent of voters approved a referendum in favor of nationalizing hydrocarbons in 2004, but Mesa took no action. Indeed, he refused to sign a law that would have raised taxes on the profits of the gas companies. Other measures, such as Mesa's decision to raise gasoline prices only further antagonized popular groups. Protests and roadblocks became an everyday occurrence. Facing strikes from *cocaleros*,[5] peasants, miners, indigenous rights activists, and others, he resigned in June 2005.

Figure 11.3 Marchers from El Alto

Source: Courtesy of AP Photo/Dado Galdieri

El Alto emerged as the new locus of national power during these protests. No government could govern the country if it did not first control El Alto. This seemed to play into Felipe Quispe's aspirations for national power, but Quispe found it difficult to build a national following out of the protests that accompanied the ousters of Goni and Mesa. Instead it was his rival Evo Morales who turned the outrage in El Alto to his advantage.

During the protests Quispe positioned himself as an Aymara nationalist, committed to the preservation and reinvigoration of specific Aymara cultural traditions. He used starkly racial language to describe his non-indigenous enemies, and inflamed audiences on more than one occasion by suggesting he would like to drive all non-indigenous people out of Bolivia.[6] By contrast, Morales evoked a more romantic version of a communal indigenous community as a socialist antidote to the ravages of global capitalism. Quispe demonstrated that he was about place—El Alto and Aymara communities in the *altiplano*. Morales advocated a pan-indigenous identity that linked all Bolivians. In this sense, Morales' rhetoric had echoes of the 1952 Revolution (which advocated a nationalist working-class struggle against capitalist oppressors) but instead of appealing to an outdated sense of class solidarity, he appealed to a sense that all Bolivians are somehow indigenous.

Morales struck the right note at the right time. Nowadays a growing number of Bolivians, even though they might not have done so in the past, identify as indigenous. Whereas in years past the category "indigenous" was largely reserved for those who did not speak Spanish, lived in clearly identified indigenous communities, and practiced customary law, today a significant portion of the 63 percent of Bolivians who self-identify as indigenous are urban, Spanish speaking, literate, and cosmopolitan. While in rural Bolivia the term *indigena* remains a racial slur, among the urban poor and intellectuals it has become an important self-identifier. One often finds people chewing coca in the jazz bars in the capital, invoking Andean deities that their forebears long ago discarded, and learning the languages of their grandparents.

Morales, who was born in an Aymara-speaking region but migrated to a Quechua speaking region as a child, and who does not seem to speak any indigenous language very well, was well positioned to represent this constituency in recent elections. He came in a close second to Goni in the presidential elections of 2002 (winning 21 percent to Goni's 23 percent), and in 2005 his *Movimiento al Socialismo* (Movement towards Socialism—MAS) political party dominated the elections. In December 2005 he was elected president with 53.7 percent of the popular vote. The MAS also won a majority in the Congress. Residents of El Alto voted overwhelmingly for the MAS.[7]

The MAS in Power

Morales' narrow margin of victory in 2005 revealed a country that was deeply divided, both ideologically and regionally. The MAS was barely a political party. Rather, it was a collection of powerful personalities; Morales, the former *cocalero*, stood in contrast to his Vice President, the professorial Álvaro García Linera, whose love of words and foreign affectations gave him intellectual gravitas but prompted his enemies to dismiss him as a homosexual. Others, such as David Choquehuanca, Morales' choice for foreign minister, generated applause in some sectors but mockery in others by declaring Aymara the language of Bolivian diplomacy. That said, residents in El Alto and union members were only marginally interested in these issues. They wanted real change, now.

Knowing that the next roadblocks may go up in response to his policies, Morales opted for a no-holds-barred approach to reform. He immediately decreed a new hydrocarbons law that substantially increased the taxes and royalties charged to foreign companies, and established Bolivian ownership over the fields.[8] On May 1, 2006 (Labor Day in the socialist world), soldiers accompanied by Morales occupied the gas fields, while MAS operatives hung banners from refineries and gas stations around the country proclaiming the fields the "property of the Bolivian people." Explaining the decision, García Linera proclaimed that after earning only $180 million in royalties and tax revenues from natural gas in 2005, government revenues from the gas fields would increase to more than $2 billion in just three years.

This, of course, was just the beginning of the reform process. Morales aspired not just to reclaim gas for Bolivians, but to reorganize the political and judicial systems, further empowering the poor and largely indigenous majority that was his base. For this he needed a constituent assembly to rewrite the constitution. This represented a special sort of challenge, because constitutional reforms historically required the support of two-thirds of voters, and Morales had the support of barely more than half the electorate. The solution: empanel a constituent assembly that could approve a new constitution with a simple majority. It was the only way to ensure radical reform in a deeply divided society, and while it no doubt would generate more division rather than less, Morales announced an assembly that would be governed by simple majority rule in June 2006.

The fix was in from the very beginning. Morales controlled enough votes in the assembly (about 54 percent) to get what he wanted, and the opposition was sufficiently incensed that they walked out on the process. MAS delegates paid them little heed, dismissing their opponents as traitors to the nation.

The constitution that the rump assembly passed in December 2007 had a number of provisions that would please MAS supporters and anger their enemies. The presidency was strengthened, and re-election legalized. Indigenous peoples were granted greater political, cultural, and legal autonomy. Bolivia's Departments were also granted greater autonomy, though the means by which autonomy was granted (by increasing regional and municipal power) would undermine the political power of Morales' opponents. Lastly, the new constitution promised a major land reform, outlawing estates of larger than 5,000 hectares. This provision was aimed squarely at the *media luna*, as this was the only region of the country with estates that large.

On December 15, 2007 the governments of Santa Cruz, Tarija, Beni, and Pando declared that they would no longer take orders from the central government, and set in motion plans to have their own referendums on autonomy. Santa Cruz acted first, announcing its vote for May 4, 2008. Morales fought back, first by scheduling a national vote on the new constitution for the same day, and later by convincing the Supreme Electoral Tribunal to announce that the timing for the vote did not meet the standards of Bolivian law. The *Cruceños* pushed ahead anyway, and so did Morales, who tried to discredit the vote by having his supporters in Plan 3000, the poor *barrio* on the outskirts of the city of Santa Cruz de la Sierra, burn ballot boxes, set up roadblocks, and attack autonomy supporters on referendum day.

More than 80 percent of those who cast votes in Santa Cruz on May 4 opted for a form of autonomy that would effectively make their department an independent state. Thousands gathered in the department capital that evening to celebrate what they viewed as a repudiation of *altiplano* colonialism, waving *Cruceño* flags instead of the Bolivian emblem. Governor Rubén Costas declared to the assembled that this was a victory for democracy. A few hundred miles away, in Cochabamba and La Paz, thousands more gathered to condemn the vote, their leaders declaring it a travesty against democracy.

On national television Morales told Bolivians that the vote was illegal, unconstitutional, and would be ignored. His words only exacerbated the crisis. During the following months other referendums followed, some favoring autonomy in the *media luna*,[9] and others demonstrating Morales' growing popularity in the highlands (he won a national vote on his policies in August with 67.76 percent of ballots cast). The battles became violent in August and September when federal efforts to divert more revenue from natural gas into government programs sparked protests in the *media luna*, leaving more than 30 people dead. Each side in the conflict committed a range of atrocities, but for the moment it was Morales—fresh off his referendum victory and in control of the military—who had the upper hand. Accusing the governors of the *media luna* of "conspiring against us with a fascist, racist coup," he sent the military into the region and deposed and arrested Pando governor Leopoldo Fernández on September 16, charging him with genocide.

Both sides ultimately made limited concessions in order to end the violence, which seemed to be pushing the country into civil war. On October 20 Morales agreed with the governors of the *media luna* to hold a referendum on the constitution on January 25, 2009, in return for his promise not to run for re-election in 2014. The constitution was passed in January 2009 with 61.43 percent of the vote. The "No" vote won handily throughout the *media luna*. Morales was re-elected with 63 percent of the vote the following December.

Autonomies

Having adopted a constitution that goes further in supporting indigenous autonomy than any other in the Americas, Bolivians today find themselves at the center of a series of global debates over self-determination. Recent years have seen two distinct types of movements for self-determination across the planet, one type centering on the claim that ethnic minorities, long the victims of discrimination at the hands of national majorities, have a right to their own states, and the other based in the claim that indigenous peoples are distinct nations with distinct customs, and should be respected as such. Though they seem like similar demands, the recent history of Bolivia reminds us that they are not entirely alike.

Bolivia's current conflicts are rooted in both types of claims. In Santa Cruz the case for autonomy has been popular because residents of this region really do imagine themselves as members of a distinct national community. *Cruceños* generally call themselves *cambas*, and for most of Bolivia's history they have lived pretty much unaffected by the Bolivian state. In their life-ways and traditions *cambas* did not identify with other Bolivians. They were more oriented towards the world beyond Bolivia's borders than to their neighbors in the *altiplano*. They saw themselves as cosmopolitan, while residents of the *altiplano* generally viewed the world beyond their home regions with distrust. *Cambas* considered themselves individualists, while they saw the Aymara and Quechua of the *altiplano* as communal, backwards, and poor.

To be sure, much of this difference was written in the language of race. *Camba* is a racial category, defining the region as *mestizo* in contrast to the indigenousness of the highlands.[10] The 63 percent of residents of Santa Cruz who identify as *cambas* privilege lighter skin, using phenotypical differences as a short-hand for the difference between *Cruceño* and highlander. Female beauty is intensely racialized in the *media luna*, with Andean features equated with ugliness. Moreover, the racialization of the category was exacerbated by the waves of immigrants who were attracted to Santa Cruz' dynamic agro-export economy after the 1950s. Newcomers from the United States, Brazil, and Europe moved to Santa Cruz by the thousands to take advantage of the boom, acquiring land cheaply (and often under dubious circumstances), and making Santa Cruz a society that was still more distinct from the rest of Bolivia. Whiteness came to be associated with an entrepreneurial, pioneer spirit, whereas indigeneity became a mark of some form of dependence: on a union, on an employer, and most of all, on the state.

It seems quite clear that the hardening of *camba* nationalism coincided with a growing fear in Santa Cruz that pressures from the *altiplano* were about to intrude on their lives. People here viewed the water war, gas war, and 2005 presidential election with alarm, as each incident empowered groups that seemed intent on extending the power of the *altiplano*'s government into the *media luna*.[11] Nowadays movements like the *Nación Camba* (Camba Nation—a large nationalist group, said to have 40,000 members), the *Comité Pro-Santa Cruz* (Pro-Santa Cruz Committee—a businessmen's association), and the *Unión Juventud Cruceña* (Cruceña Youth Union—violent and ultranationalist enforcers, said to act on behalf of the Committee), can claim without hyperbole that their way of life is threatened by powerful enemies. Their use of a language often linked to indigenous struggles for self-determination—condemning colonialism, asserting their nationhood—may be galling to indigenous peoples in the *altiplano*, but it is not without merit. *Cruceño* claims to a regional identity are in fact rooted in history, geography, and culture. They are a distinct society, and inasmuch as outsiders today want to dominate the region, they can legitimately claim to be an oppressed nationality. Of course, *camba* claims about their own oppression avoid mention of the indigenous peoples of Santa Cruz—of the fact, for instance, that much of their prosperity came at the expense of the indigenous peoples of Santa Cruz.[12]

About 37 percent of people living in Santa Cruz consider themselves indigenous. Within this category however, there is a significant cleavage between those who are originally from Santa Cruz, who number 16.57 percent of the department's population, and those who trace their origins to the *altiplano*. Like the *cambas*, the original, mostly Amazonian indigenous groups in the region tend to view the migrants from the *altiplano* with hostility, as interlopers who came here to take their land, resources, jobs, and wealth. As the results of the May 2008 referendum remind us, they no more support the MAS than they do the *cambas*, and have instead for the most part created their own organizations demanding that their communities and lands be respected by all outsiders. Local Guaraní groups have formed their own Bolivian Landless Peasant Movement, and occupied fields belonging to BP and Repsol on their own accord, claiming that the multinationals were taking their land and destroying their communities.

Unlike the *cambas*, who base their claim to self-determination in a universal notion of human rights, indigenous *Cruceños* and other advocates of indigenous autonomy in Bolivia claim that the very notion of universal human rights is part of the problem. Human rights are invested in individuals, whereas indigenous rights movements insist in rights that are invested in the community. They demand respect for their distinct culture, their customary practices. Indigenous rights movements claim that western political and legal systems are alien to indigenous communities. Customary law (*usos y costumbres*), means allowing justice, governance, and property rights to be adjudicated at the local level according to local tradition.

While *camba* claims went unanswered, these rights were codified in the new constitution. This was a cause for celebration for some, and alarm for others. Critics wonder what we are to make of the fact that customary law sometimes involves punishments that could be considered torture, and the lack of judicial oversight of community justice. What are we to think when indigenous authorities expel dissidents, confiscate their land and other property in violation of national laws, or kill their political opponents? Or that those political opponents often lack recourse to due process? As citizens, indigenous peoples in countries where customary laws are enforced are sometimes entitled to protection from two competing systems of rights. If the national constitution outlaws capital punishment, but custom allows it, whose law should prevail? Under the new Bolivian Constitution the answer to this question is unclear. While the Constitution prohibits capital punishments even in indigenous communities, communal authorities have executed dozens of individuals in recent years without facing any sanction from the Bolivian state.

There is evidence from Bolivia that communal justice has clearly entailed the denial of basic human rights. Article 189 of the new constitution gives communal justice equal footing with ordinary judicial authority, and communal justice is not subject to judicial review. What this means in practice is that acts which would otherwise be considered egregious cannot be punished through the Bolivian courts. Moreover, since indigenous Bolivians cannot opt out of the system of community justice, they are left without access to their nation's justice system. Even if this is a broadly popular measure, it offers chilling prospects to dissidents within indigenous communities.

It seems extremely unlikely that the state will prosecute the individuals who in 2004 kidnapped, tortured, and then burned Benjamin Altamirano to death. Residents of Ayo Ayo, where he was the former mayor, accused him of misconduct, and this was evidence enough for local authorities. His death was part of a wave of lynchings, lashings, and crucifixions that the perpetrators generally defend as customary practice. Moreover, these same local authorities also punish women differently than men for the same crimes. Men generally receive minor punishments for adultery, while women are sometimes killed; this representing only the most egregious example of gender inequality within traditional systems of justice. Local leaders may claim that they are simply enforcing their cultural norms, but their victims often disagree.

Cultural norms are slippery things; remade constantly like all cultural practices, they can just as easily be used to reinforce the power of an exclusive clique as defend some community-wide practice. This is because culture is not a simple or self-evident thing, but a series of dynamic practices that are called a culture because some expert, interlocutor, or authority has the power to name them as such. For instance, in communities in various parts of Latin America, the murder or expulsion of political or religious dissidents has a long history as a customary practice. While community leaders portray these acts as efforts to defend communal unity, dissidents point out that the unity community leaders are often defending functions principally to their own benefit; that dissidence may be more a threat to their personal power than to the well-being of the community. No community is without its conflicts, and the assumption that indigenous leaders always act in the interests of the community as a whole is absurd, a fiction perpetrated by those who prefer a romantic indigenous symbol to living people. Bolivia's new constitution offers no way out of this dilemma, and in fact seems to deepen it. While no Latin American state has ever done a particularly good job of defending the citizenship or human rights of its indigenous peoples, the current project here and elsewhere seems to abandon that responsibility altogether.

Towards an Uncertain Future

In Evo Morales' nightmare scenario, hardcore Aymara nationalists, led by individuals like Felipe Quispe, decide to work with the *camba* nationalists, each supporting the other's claim to full autonomy in order to dismantle the Bolivian state and possess the wealth that lies in their respective subsoils (the current constitution reserves the entire subsoil for the nation). This idea may seem far-fetched, but there are activists in Bolivia's indigenous rights movement who now insist that the vast lithium[13] deposits in the highlands ought to be local, not national patrimonies. The claim that it is their land and therefore their lithium may gain more international sympathy because of the traditional poverty of Aymara communities, but it is not substantively different from the demands coming from Santa Cruz.

Morales' claim, that the subsoil should benefit everyone, resonates on the left, but there is little historical evidence that this kind of project has the capacity to end inequality in Latin America or elsewhere. Other countries have nationalized hydrocarbons and minerals, only to see decidedly mixed results. Mexico's 1938 oil nationalism benefited industrialists, government bureaucrats, and workers at the giant firm created to run the industry (PEMEX), but over its long history nationalized oil has offered only meager benefits for other Mexicans, and often served to reinforce anti-democratic practices. *Petróleos de Venezuela* (PDVSA), created in 1976, was so broadly loathed that the image of whisky-swilling, orgy-loving company executives helped get Hugo Chávez elected president in 1998. Even under Chávez the company has a spotty record when it comes to ameliorating inequality. In Chile, the nationalized copper company was for several decades a key source of revenue for an authoritarian state that saw the gap between rich and poor grow. In each case, critics argue that if these resources were in private hands, the social and political benefits derived from them would be greater.[14]

Bolivia, which nationalized its own tin mining sector in 1952, has a similarly dismal record of using natural resources to promote social welfare. And things are likely to grow more difficult. Fearing for the safety of their capital, foreign companies essentially stopped investing in Bolivian gas after 2002. The government has done little to make up for the shortfall in investment, and critics claim that since the nationalization YPFB has been largely character-ized by mismanagement, inefficiency, and corruption. That said, Bolivia seemed to withstand the 2008–9 global economic crisis better than most of its neighbors, as revenues from pre-negotiated gas contracts bolstered government spending and contributed to a period of economic growth even as most other economies in the region were contracting. Whether or not these short-term benefits can be translated into long-term strategies for development is anyone's guess, but most economists (who admittedly do not tend to favor high levels of government control over the economy) are not particularly optimistic about Bolivia's prospects. They point out that today, more than ever, Bolivians depend on a series of volatile export commodities, and that the nationalization of gas has only deepened their dependence on the global economy.

The Documents: Santa Cruz Versus Bolivia

Regional identities have played a powerful role in Latin American history. The *caudillos* who ruled much of the region in the aftermath of independence reflected and ultimately rein-scribed those identities. Later on, powerful centralizing governments tried to erase regional loyalties, to little avail. Into the twenty-first century regional boundaries continue to be racial-ized. Residents of Central Mexico tend to think of themselves as *mestizo* and the south of their country as Indian. The whites of São Paulo imagine northeasterners as black. Dominicans describe their black neighbors (even those born in the Dominican Republic) as Haitian.

These divisions are imagined, but as Benedict Anderson would say, they are not "imagi-nary."[15] They remain relevant to political and cultural conflicts across the region, and are particularly important in contemporary Bolivia.

For these reasons, we choose a series of documents in this chapter to address what remains the most controversial issue in the country today: Santa Cruz' demand for autonomy. While indigenous autonomy and the political orientations of the Bolivian state will certainly remain the subject of political battles for some time to come, no issue threatens the very existence of the country more than the unrelenting demand on the part of some Cruceños for the radical decentralization (if not elimination) of central state power. Absent a flood of migration to the region that changes its demographics significantly, these demands seem destined to persist.

The documents below approach the question of Cruceño autonomy from a number of perspectives. Document 11.1 is the 2001 Memorandum of the *Nación Camba*, which introduces readers to the ways in which autonomist claims are rooted in a sense of history. Cruceños are often vilified in the national and international press, but this document represents the most broadly supported and least easily condemned expression of Cruceño politics. If they are indeed a distinct people, with their own history, and a long experience of being dominated by outsiders, why indeed would *camba* claims to nationhood be any different than Paraguayan, Uruguayan, or Irish?

Document 11.2, written by Walter Chávez and Bolivian Álvaro García Linera in early 2005, seeks to repudiate these claims by arguing that the *camba* rebellion was directed by a small business elite against the actual interests of both Bolivians and Cruceños. One might be tempted to simply use this text to reject the former, or reject this text by sympathizing with the former, but there may be a better way to read both. We should perhaps read them for the ways they represent distinct and opposing viewpoints, but also for the ways that these texts talk past one another as much as they engage one another. Is this a dialogue, or two distinct monologues directed not at each other, but elsewhere?

Document 11.3, published online on a website known as the *Bolpress* immediately after Evo Morales won the recall election in August 2008, is a further example of the extent to which participants in these dramas are talking past, rather than to one another. The *Bolpress* has been operating since the end of the gas war in 2003, and acts as a strident defender of the MAS's socialist project for the Bolivian future. Like many internet phenomena it is part blog, part news organization, and unrelenting in promoting its political point of view. *Bolpress* is also widely read; the site claims more than 65 million visitors since it was launched in 2003. This makes it a potent example of the dawn of an era in which journalism openly defines itself as a form of advocacy—where readers choose their news based on their political views, and where the opinion of the largely unknown blogger is often as valuable as the work of a seasoned journalist. The quality of that information, however, is open to debate.[16]

The piece we read from the *Bolpress* was written by the *Comisión Organica Consejos Pro-Bolivia—Europa* (the Organic European Commission of the Pro-Bolivia Council), a group 12 of Bolivians living in Europe. One cannot know just how organized they are from their submission to the Bolpress, but one supposes that twelve people living in several countries across Europe do not represent much of a physical threat to Cruceños. They do however reveal the underlying threat of violence that is ever present in this conflict, and the powerful identification with these issues that Bolivians preserve even as they move abroad. Of course, the *cambas* also have friends who weigh in from abroad to support them. Their supporters include business interests, anti-communists, ethnic nationalists, and, if we are to believe Evo Morales, Eastern European assassins.

Document 11.4 takes us to the night that the new constitution was ratified by referendum in January 2009. In it we hear the much-maligned Branko Marinkovic speak in Santa Cruz, offering his own rendering of both the referendum and of Cruceño interests. Marinkovic, who is one of the wealthiest men in the country (he is said to own 300,000 hectares of land), is the object of more vitriol than almost anyone else in Santa Cruz. In attacks he is compared to the Serbian Slobodan Milosevic. Though born in Bolivia to Croatian immigrant parents, official news agencies regularly refer to him as a Croat, and imply that, among other things, he is a Nazi-sympathizer who wants to Balkanize Bolivia in the same way that Croats contributed to the Balkanization of Yugoslavia. He is also accused of becoming one of Bolivia's richest men principally by seizing lands from Guarayo Indians.

Some readers might find his invocation of a capitalist strategy to alleviate poverty cynical, and to be sure, there is plenty of cynicism on all sides in contemporary Bolivia. Still, we miss something quite significant if we simply dismiss his words. Speaking on behalf of the region that has been the engine of the Bolivian economy in recent years, Marinkovic identifies Cruceño values—a love of hard work, an entrepreneurial spirit—as critical to lifting Bolivia out of poverty. Should Evo Morales' socialism fail to produce a more prosperous and equitable society, it is likely that more and more Bolivians will find themselves in agreement with Marinkovic's words, if not the man himself. At the very least, he challenges his enemies to show that socialism can lift the country out of poverty. It is a tall order.

Our last document comes from Tuffi Aré, the editor and chief of the newspaper *El Deber*, the leading paper in Santa Cruz. Published the day following the 2009 Constitutional Referendum, Document 11.5 is as close as we come to rendering a simple truth: the conflict over autonomy was not resolved with the new constitution. We are left with more questions than answers.

Document 11.1 *Memorandum*, a Declaration from the *Nación Camba*, February 14, 2001

Source: http://www.nacioncamba.net/documentos/MEMORANDUM.htm. Translated by Patricia Rosas.

Introduction

Beginning with the 1904 Memorandum, the people of Santa Cruz changed their thinking about their demands, focusing on two concrete regional issues: the railway, as a means to merge with the rest of Bolivia, and the opening of an Andean market. Subsequently, struggles over petroleum royalties, the restoration of democracy, and the law on administrative decentralization would be added to the list. Decades later, these objectives would be partially achieved. Today's reality calls for new proposals.

At the end of the 20th century, the Santa Cruz of today and of the future is being handed challenging social, economic, political, and environmental issues, which the endemic crisis of the State, founded in 1825, cannot and will not solve.

Facing the accelerated processes of Latin American integration and the globalizing dynamics that tend to homogenize the world, today more than ever, it is necessary to have an ideological instrument that affirms our self-esteem as a differentiated collectivity and that publicly redefines our identity as a people-nation.

Our Strategic Objectives in the 21st Century

Thus, on November 21, 1816, our liberating flags fell, crushed by the colonial barrage in the fields of Pari. Today, on the same date 184 years after that military defeat, the Nación Camba Autonomy Movement was founded as an expression of our region-nation and to follow in the footsteps of that heroic deed.

Now facing the 21st century, this Movement takes upon itself the task of consolidating six basic fundamental objectives, which this memorandum explains:

1. Democracy

The reestablishment of democracy in Bolivia offered the possibility that people, exercising their right to vote, would be able to transform the State. However, experience has clearly and objectively shown that this mutilated democracy has only served—with a few honorable exceptions—to strengthen the Business-State, with its sinecures and centralist and distant character.

The most recent constitutional reform was insufficient, and it amounted to a shameful backsliding that has reinforced internal and external dependence, bureaucracy, and the colonialism of the State. The political, economic, and institutional model imposed on the country has enormously increased regional disequilibria, inequality, corruption, and social marginalization.

The national political parties' monopoly over public representation annulled the regional initiatives and leadership and has created a logic of toadying and authoritarianism, among other things.

We urgently need to radicalize democracy in order to transform the nature of a fiercely unitarian State, dependent and servile. We must construct of a State of autonomous departments and/or nations, in order to perfect state institutions and to democratize power in the State's national, departmental, and municipal agencies.

2. Self-determination

Supported by the right of national self-determination, and with the possibility of realizing constitutional reforms that would lead to a materialization of these achievements, we proclaim the need to convert Santa Cruz into an AUTONOMOUS REGION, with its own government and protected by a special statute for self-government that would be the expression of CRUCEÑO POWER, as a formal and legal recognition of our NATION-STATE.

3. Identity

The national identity of the Cruceños and, in general, that of the Chaco-Amazonian and Valley peoples arises from the place that our geography and our culture occupies in the concerto of the peoples of Latin America and the world.

Our identity—which is the basis for our development and the result of our shared history, language, and the legacy of our heroes and ancestors—defines the personality of this cultural nation, which declares its right to be different. But as part of its national essence, it also confirms its integrationist calling, its ethnic democracy, and its cultural pluralism.

Faced with a systematic denial of our cultural identity on the part of the colonialist State, some of the media, the presence of other cultures, and globalization, we affirm that the Camba national identity and Cruceños nationalism must be part of our essence, the detonator of economic and social development, and the binding substance of our will to be free.

4. Natural Resources, Territory, and Power

Cruceño natural resources are inalienable property of the Camba nation. This natural and historical right is anchored in the fact that our province existed before the creation of the Bolivian Nation-State, and it was reinforced by the legal principle of "Uti Possidetis," which has been recognized since the founding of Santa Cruz in 1561, a right that the Republican oligarchy that usurped power from us in 1825 has trampled on.

We understand our extensive territory as a shared fatherland for all Camba peoples. It is indivisible, and it extends as far as our culture does. It constitutes the material basis for our NATIONAL POWER. Its exploitation must be reasonable, shared, and technologically sustainable.

As we are not anyone's colony, we emphatically reject any policy that under a label of "colonization" predatorily involves unconsulted human settlements, whether these be Bolivian or foreign and/or that conspires against the internal and external geopolitical equilibrium.

Our forest reserves and protected areas are untouchable.

5. Integration

With the understanding that isolated communities are not viable, the Cruceño project for the 21st century must be based on an intelligent and equitable process of continental integration. Up until now, the Bolivian market has fulfilled its role as a recipient of a small part of what we produce. However, it is insufficient, and demand tends to run out, due to that market's own structural limitations.

Cruceño development for the century that is beginning must be based on a broad market, which is beginning to take shape through subregional agreements in South America.

Our national viability necessarily resides in our physical integration with the continent and the rest of the world. We must attain the comparative advantages of our enviable geographic location, by playing a fundamental role as a geopolitical nexus for the South American continent in furtherance of a shared market, which will be forged by 2005 as a result of the FTAA and MERCOSUR, agreements to which Bolivia is a signatory.

6. A New Accord with the Bolivian State

The factual conditions that create our current reality have changed. Santa Cruz in the third millennium is not the Santa Cruz of the beginning of the 20th century. We are owners of more than a third of the country, and we make up almost two million of its inhabitants. We have a Gross Domestic Product (GDP) that is one-third of the national total, and our Human Development Index (HDI) is the highest of any in Bolivia. Nevertheless, we feel neither satisfied nor realized.

In 1825, they annexed us to Bolivia because of our institutional, demographic, and economic weakness. Today, we are in a situation in which we can demand—not only egalitarian treatment, of equal to equal, with the state power—but we can also impose a political and economic management model that fits with our own idiosyncrasy and our own vision of the future. A self-governing model, with executive, legislative, and judicial capacities, constitutes the MINIMUM BASIS for negotiation of a NEW ACCORD with the Bolivian State.

We must deepen democracy, attain national self-determination, confirm our collective identity, defend and protect our natural resources, promote continental integration, and formulate a new accord with the Bolivian State. This is the foundation on which we will erect the structures of a new nationalism that will be the expression of Cruceño civilization.

Santa Cruz de la Sierra, February 14, 2001, in the 21st century.

Document 11.2 Walter Chávez and Álvaro García Linera, "From the Diesel-Price-Hike Protests to the Struggle for Autonomy: The Camba Rebellion." La Paz, *El Juguete Rabioso*, January 23, 2005

Source: *El Juguete Rabioso*, January 23, 2005. Translated by Patricia Rosas.

The protests against the hike in the price of diesel connected with a long memory, with the struggles for autonomy by the people of Santa Cruz. But the renaissance of this hard-core regionalism, fundamentally indicates a certain weakness in the Eastern elite, which has abandoned a national hegemonic project.

Walter Chávez/Álvaro García Linera

The Eastern political crisis has bubbled over. Meanwhile, in the West, analysts, journalists, and politicians continue to act from a centralist point of view. Despite the evidence, they continue to spread the belief that these are "minority groups," "mere business interests," "and "an oligarchy that pays people to go into the streets." However, an even more pathetic case may have been the statement by the Prefect Carlos Hugo Molina, a Cruceño, who declared to the entire country that it was a matter of "addicts." A day after this outburst, Santa Cruz university students threw the prefect out of his office, obliging him to move his workplace to an undisclosed location.

History is never lineal. It spreads out through bends and folds, shaping an enormous fresco in which some dots connect with others in a manner that is, at times, quite random. An apparently minor conflict—the diesel price hike demanded by the International

Monetary Fund (see page 11 of this issue, and *La Razón*, December 29, 2004)—led to civic protests that directly connected with the long Cruceño memory, with the autonomist memory.

At the beginning, the strategy of the government of Carlos Mesa was "to let the movement wear itself out," believing that "Carnival will deactivate the conflict." And, indeed, in the West, people believe that the greatest drive for the Cruceños are festivals, Carnival, and beauty pageants. But events unfolded in a different way. From the protests over diesel, things went—little by little—to the continuation of the so-called "June Agenda." Thus, the mass concentration of that time—a town meeting in which 100,000 people participated—found its counterpart in the "diesel anti-price-hike" street mobilization. This civic insurrection blockades the streets and immobilizes the central government as the protestors took control of the places in which state institutions make decisions—the Prefectures, Internal Revenue offices, the airport, etc.—without the police being able to do anything about it.

On Thursday, the 21st, the newspaper *La Razón* reported that the government of Carlos Mesa was still betting on "letting the protest wear itself out over the weekend." Meanwhile, the movement continued on a natural course to radicalization, to such a degree that the demands for autonomy—shared by other regions in Bolivia and taking on secessionist overtones—seemed very similar to those of the 1924 "separationist" movement. At that time, a group of Cruceños rebelled, arguing that "among the peoples of Bolivia, Santa Cruz, with its interests the most snubbed, has especially suffered the (centralist) tyranny." In 1924, President Bautista Saavedra had no other choice than to send in a military contingent to subjugate the rebels, but today, things are very different.

In last Friday's town meeting, the civic leader Rubén Costas announced that Cruceños are moving toward "the formation of the first provisional autonomous government for the Department of Santa Cruz de la Sierra." He justified that by arguing that Cruceños "account for a little more than 25 percent of the Bolivian population, but we generate almost half of all the national taxes, and we shoulder the burden for a large part of the economy." While that was occurring, the government in La Paz was entirely silent.

In an earlier issue of *El Juguete Rabioso* ("La ofensiva camba" [The Camba Offensive], no. 116) we were already warning that the Bolivian West was basing its dynamics on the so-called "October Agenda," but that both the government of Carlos Mesa and part of the social movement—especially the MAS, which had acted as a sly ally of Mesa— had, for all intents and purposes, sabotaged that agenda. In this way, they blocked the popular hope for a rapid nationalization of the hydrocarbon industry and for a Constituent Assembly that might have been held in the near term.

The plebeian indigenous social movements that defeated Gonzalo Sánchez de Lozada in 2003 had created a historical opening for those things to happen. During the October insurrection, they had pulverized the power of the parties (traditionalists and, indeed, centralists) as well as that of the business elite that cohabitated with the central State. However, facing that disruption, the reformist/neoliberal government of Carlos Mesa and the passivity of the MAS acted as brakes on this process and the opening, which this historical opportunity for radical change in national politics offered, was being filled by another group, the Santa Cruz autonomy movement.

The truth is that a business, conservative, and landholding elite dominates and is the driving force behind the Santa Cruz autonomy movement. It is always this way: only the strong sectors are capable of establishing hegemonies. The interesting thing about this case is that those business elites have been able to persuade the Cruceño proletariat, Colla immigrants, workers, and housewives to mobilize, making them active agents for the elite's ideas. They achieved this by connecting current circumstances with the long historical memory, with the memory of the autonomy movement that, in the strictest sense, is now older than a century.

On assuming the presidency, Carlos Mesa chose to surround himself with leftovers, officials from the traditional political parties, particularly Goni's people [followers of Gonzalo Sánchez de Lozada]. Consequently, at a moment of change, he ran things conservatively, in that he wanted to relativize the changes and decelerate the march of time. Perhaps the situation that is occurring today in Santa Cruz is the result of these historic incoherencies.

Six Hypotheses about the Current Situation in the Political Crisis

1.   The State crisis that began five years ago has made the neoliberal (partisan and ideological) hegemony, established in 1985, weaken and retreat. However, this has left the new national leadership irresolute. On one hand, the conservative ideas of the established order have retrenched and been reinforced in the eastern and southern parts of the country (Santa Cruz, Beni, and Tarija). Meanwhile, progressive and modernizing ideas and projects have advanced and been accepted by the leadership in the western parts of the country. However, none of these political projects has managed to radiate out or spread itself throughout the country as the national project and that has created a regionalization of leadership.

     This has led to the emergence of a "centrist" type of government that seeks to accommodate itself between these two polarities. It tries to articulate a reformist neoliberal project that could maintain the general structure of the economic policies that have been in place for the last 19 years, while incorporating some elements of the demands and criticisms from the popular, indigenous end of the spectrum.

     This neoliberal reformism manages to broaden its social base to the degree that the polarities restrain its positions, but that base narrows to the degree that the polarized positions radicalize the reformist actions. Although it seeks to attenuate the conflicts, this neoliberal reformism is incapable of resolving the crisis of national leadership, of hegemony. That leads to a situation in which both the conservative business pole and the more militarized popular or indigenous sector, which is seeking radical solutions to its demands, are dissatisfied with the centrist government's measures. This leads to an increasing political orphanhood for this reformist center.

2.   Clearly, Santa Cruz is experiencing a bourgeoisie uprising, a business-regional revolt against the government. Led by the regional business community, it involves a series of direct protests, mobilizations, and actions that rally the business

sector around certain objectives. The notable thing is that society has responded positively to this call. Regional labor and popular sectors support it, making it possible to speak of an active presence of a hegemony, of a regional entrepreneurial leadership. In contrast, in western Bolivia, the popular and indigenous social movements have constructed a shared, generalized explanation for scarcity, the lack of jobs, discrimination, and crisis, by blaming it all on the "neoliberal model." In eastern Bolivia, the same problems that cut across the subaltern sectors are instead blamed on "centralism," which is an ideology and vision of the world held by the business elites. This makes it possible to understand the autonomous movement's leadership and social base, which, certainly, has to do with the popular sector's thin social fabric, lack of ideology, and so forth.

The Santa Cruz Elite Displaced by State Power

3. The regional elites' rebellion against the government has to do with the increase in the price of diesel, which affects agro-industrial production costs. It has to do with the government's formal errors in making agreements. But, fundamentally, it has to do with the fact that in the last 16 months, since October 2003, the Cruceño business elite has lost its grip on a good part of the political duties that it uninterruptedly controlled for 19 years.

   Since 1985, regardless of whether it was under an MNR, ADM, or MIR government, the Santa Cruz elite occupied ministerial positions that were key for defining the country's economic policy. They held leadership positions in the principal political parties; and they controlled areas of decision making in Parliament. This gave them direct influence over the definition of public policy, which favored their empowerment as a modern-day business faction. In its own way, the Cruceño bourgeoisie for 30 years—but particularly in the last 15—has done what historically in the Republic all dominant business people have done: they used their political power to broaden, expand, and protect businesses' economic capitalization.

   Their displacement from the seat of power initially came with the resignation of Sánchez de Lozada, who had created a series of ties to the Santa Cruz business community, based on loyalty and support, which continued until the final moments before he left for his "self-exile" in October 2003.

   The second step in this loss of power came with the political weakening of the parties (MNR and MIR) in which the business community had controlled the structures of influence and decision making.

   The third step was their loss of control over the government power apparatus, which came about when members of the Santa Cruz intellectual and civic elite, which is distant from the region's economic elite, were appointed to ministerial posts by President Mesa.

   The final step in this loss of government power was the outcome of the municipal elections, which ended up with the parties traditionally at the center of national politics (MNR, MIR, ADN) weakened and almost excluded from the political decision-making spheres.

It was only a matter of time before a corporatist-style business offensive was launched, which was their last ditch effort at interest aggregation (the Civic Committee and business associations). The objective was to recover posts in the power structure that is no longer under their direct and personal control. The diesel price hike was a pretext to mobilize, channel, and direct social unrest in the defense of business interests. The current business-regional revolt is, consequently, an open fight to control the power of the State, to control everything or a substantial part (the issue of land, tax regimens, the economic model), and to control the decision-making mechanisms managing public resources. The fact that a regional business elite is involved and that the armed forces, for the moment, have a neutral or distant attitude towards the demands of the business class (due to the separatist insinuations made at certain times by Cruceño civic leaders) limits the possibility for a complete changeover in the structure of power that would favor the Cruceños. Nevertheless, the strength that they demonstrate may force a gradual transition toward reassuming the influence that they had before October 2003.

4.   Because of the characteristics of this fight for government power, because of what these business sectors were defending and continue to defend, and because of the manner in which they have accumulated economic power in recent years, this struggle is also about redirecting the country, by stopping the set of political and economic reforms that are underway as a result of the popular-indigenous pressure in western Bolivia. A continuation of those reforms could directly affect the business class's mechanisms of economic power (a Constitutional Convention that would modify the system of landholding, a nationalization of the hydrocarbon industry that would end the anticipated regional petroleum royalties, and so forth). Consequently, this fight for power is also a resistance to the continuation of the so-called "October Agenda" that came out of the urban-rural rebellion of October 2003.

Autonomy: A Regional Retreat

5.   However, this struggle for the control of the government's decision-making structures does not take the form of a "national" struggle for the generalized total control of the State. The Cruceño business class instead is demanding a series of proposals, of calls aimed at mobilizing the rest of the country, expressing the interests of other social sectors, not just the eastern region's interests. For the elite in Santa Cruz, this is impossible since they champion and defend a future for the country (free market, foreign investment, racism, and so forth) that was thoroughly defeated throughout western Bolivia in October 2003. The Santa Cruz vision is a tired ideology that is in retreat, at least temporarily. Consequently, through its demand for autonomy, the Santa Cruz business class has committed itself to regionalizing its political struggle.

Strictly speaking, the demand for autonomy by the Cruceño business class is consequently presented as a defensive struggle, as a withdrawal into their primary sphere of influence (Santa Cruz) and, with that, the abandonment of the struggle for a national hegemony, which they feel is impossible. The fight for the autonomy of Santa Cruz is thus the political withdrawal from what the Cruceño elite previously controlled (the "national" state apparatuses), and the verification of regional limitations for a bourgeoisie that is unwilling to attempt to lead the country—politically, economically, or culturally.

They retreat to their regional dominion to fight for control, shared with the oil company, of the existing gas surpluses. Converted into the central banner of the business elites, Cruceño autonomy is consequently the struggle for political power in its fragmented, regionalized, and partial aspect, and a materialization of the abandonment of the struggle for general "national" power in Bolivia. Their victory, if they achieve it, will not solve the lack of national hegemony, of leadership, and of a vision that could be shared by most of society. It will radicalize the regionalization of the class fight, of political leadership, and of national projects, increasing secessionist tendencies that have always latently nested in the political behavior of social subjects in both eastern and western Bolivia.

6.   In the current circumstances, one way of stopping this process of corporatist reconstruction of the business and conservative forces that were displaced in October [2003] would be the deepening of "de-neoliberal" reforms that began with the water war and the indigenous uprisings and that the Mesa government's moderation has recently undermined. If it does not want to find itself removed from power, the government must accelerate economic and political reforms with the objective of winning broad popular support, in both the West as well is the East, which could neutralize and isolate the conservative forces. The government's irresolute and ambiguous attitude is contributing to the right-wing business interests advancing more rapidly than the interests of the left-wing indigenous actors.

Another option would be an immediate reinforcing and broadening of the social movements' popular-indigenous hegemony, through a strategy of broad-based alliances. They must focus on a program to radicalize the reforms and to create a cohesive social mobilization of all their segments, both radical and moderate.

Document 11.3 "Santa Cruz Belongs to All Bolivians," *Bolpress*, August 24, 2008.

Source: http://www.bolpress.com/art.php?Cod=2008082402. Translated by Patricia Rosas.

Organized in Pro-Bolivia Councils (CPBs) and in solidarity networks and organizations, some of us, as Bolivians residing in Europe, again congratulate, and express our admiration for, the heroic Bolivian people for their resounding vote in the Recall Referendum. They said YES to continuing with irreversible change and NO to the quartering of our homeland. They said YES to Brother President Evo Morales Ayma and NO to two corrupt prefects, thus weakening the influence of the "waning quarter."

The media's abundant, calumnious propaganda aimed at misinforming and defaming the current government in order to topple it and the Cruceño youth brigades' paramilitary racial violence have made them the victims of their own venom. The people responded, with 67.41 percent voting in favor of the government policy that was imposed on 97 of Bolivia's 112 provinces. Moreover, we can add to that the catastrophic division in the ranks of the neoliberal right, which has thus broken the purported "catastrophic stalemate."

Another result of the Recall Referendum was the unmasking of the alleged conflicts between the East and West. In reality, this is a continuation of the popular mandate for structural changes in the political system and of the decaying of the neoliberal economic model. The ever-more-aware popular vote affirmed the recuperation of our natural resources, lands, and territories; an equitable distribution of wealth; development for the entire country; and greater democratic participation. These just aspirations were opposed, above all, by the pseudo-Civic Committee of Santa Cruz. It is led by Rubén Costas, Marinkovic, and Dabdub, who think that they own Santa Cruz, who publicly affirm their fascist and racist ideology, the final objective of which is the division of Bolivia so that they can continue exploiting the Cambas [eastern Bolivians], the Collas [western Bolivians], and other ethnicities. The oligarchs, desperate after the "civic strike," resorted to blocking roads and the shipment of meat to the West, subversive activities that are no different than Banzer's fascist military coup on August 21, 1971, which began in the city of Santa Cruz.

During the Recall Referendum, the crossover vote, which also occurred in Santa Cruz, showed that the oligarchs manipulated the aspirations for autonomy, but the Santa Cruz people will not accept a new butchering of its territory. Santa Cruz belongs to all Bolivians, men and women alike. In coordination with our embassies, we Bolivians residing in Europe and other places organized demonstrations and symbolic voting in the August 10 referendum. Currently, we sponsor public lectures by Citizen Gerardo García, vice president of the MAS-IPSP in Switzerland. In the European Social Forum that will be held in Malmo, Sweden, from September 17–20 of this year, we have secured the participation of Citizen Margarita Terán, a member of the Constitutional Convention, and Grover Cardozo, head of the ABI [Agencia Boliviana de Información or Bolivian Information Agency]. With greater commitment and results, we will continue to support our people and our government as well as the Coordinating Office for Social Movements in order to consolidate the process of change and the passage of the State's New Political Constitution, drafted by the great Constitutional Convention.

Decolonization, Identity, Dignity, Unity, and Sovereignty!
For the Right to Vote for All Bolivians Living Abroad!!

Document 11.4 Speech by the President of the Pro-Santa Cruz Committee, Branko Marinkovic, in the Plaza "*24 de Septiembre*," Santa Cruz de la Sierra, January 25, 2009.

Source: http://www.ernestojustiniano.org/2009/01/discurso-del-presidente-del-comite-pro-santa-cruz-branko-marinkovic-en-la-plaza-24-de-septiembre/. Translated by Patricia Rosas.

Today, January 25, 2009, is a date that our children are going to remember. Today the NO vote won in Santa Cruz, in Beni, in Tarija, in Pando, _and_ CHUQUISACA.

Moreover, today, in each department in Bolivia, many Bolivians made history, saying NO to the MAS Constitution.

Today the Bolivians have said NO to poverty, because the Bolivian people know that the day we conquer poverty, we will have constructed a free _and_ democratic country.

That is why conquering poverty is the mission of the autonomous movement. Conquering poverty is a priority for those who today voted NO.

Those of us seeking autonomy want to conquer the poverty that leaves thousands of families jobless each year.

We want to conquer the poverty that foists low wages on the Bolivian people. Poverty that does not let our children have the health care and education that they deserve. This poverty affects everyone, members of the MAS and the pro-autonomy supporters alike. This poverty beats down everyone, in neighborhoods and in the provinces.

We want to overcome the poverty that lets dictators hold power forever. We want to conquer that poverty. And to conquer that poverty, today we have voted NO to the MAS Constitution.

And how does autonomy propose to conquer poverty?

Autonomy offers new opportunities for everyone.

What opportunities are we talking about?

I am talking about the opportunity of holding down a good job. A secure job, in industry, in agriculture.

I am talking about respectable employment and wages; I'm not talking about patronage jobs. I am talking about opportunities like a respectable wage, which autonomy in Santa Cruz encouraged.

Opportunities, because the man who has these opportunities has a future for his family.

Today we have voted NO, because we believe that all Bolivians deserve better opportunities. Mothers and fathers of families deserve the opportunity to ensure that their children advance. The youth. My indigenous brothers. Businessmen. Laborers. People in transportation. Workers in health care, in education, and in services. All deserve new opportunities.

On this historic night, to the people who support autonomy and to those who voted NO, I also want to explain what our road will be in our fight, from here onward.

Tonight the autonomy movement has won in Santa Cruz, in Beni, in Pando, and in Tarija. And the MAS Constitution has lost in Santa Cruz, in Beni, in Pando, in Tarija, _and_ in CHUQUISACA.

That is why nobody can deny that Bolivia has two visions. And that is why nobody can deny that we need a pact for unity and coexistence between these two visions.

We, the autonomists, demand that the MAS sign an agreement that recognizes the autonomy for which we have voted. We voted in 2005 to elect an autonomous prefect and we won. We voted in 2006 to put autonomy in the new Constitution and we won. We voted in 2008 to have a statute mandating autonomy and we won. We voted in 2008 to ratify our new autonomist prefect and we won again. And we just voted today, January 25, 2009, to protect our autonomy and to say NO to the MAS Constitution, NO to the Constitution that does not recognize autonomy and that strips us of our resources.

But the response of MAS to this pro-autonomist vote that has won five times in a row, one after another, has been to deny us autonomy.

Today, after having prevailed over the MAS Constitution in Santa Cruz, in Beni, in Pando, and Tarija, we demand a pact in which MAS recognizes our autonomy.

Those of us who today have voted for autonomy, we are departments, entire towns, neighborhoods, and entire provinces, we are workers, indigenous people, professionals, and more than anything else, we are Bolivians. And the government must recognize our vote.

Here in Santa Cruz, we demand that the MAS recognize us as the people we are. People with our own identity.

We demand that we be recognized as an industrious people, a people made up of Bolivians, Bolivians of all origins: Bolivian men and Bolivian women, who only want to work day in and day out in order to ensure that their households advance.

We demand that the MAS recognize us as a population that has its own way of being and thinking.

We want them to recognize us because, even though we may not be members of the MAS, we are Bolivian men and women who deserve recognition.

We want to them to recognize us and stop imprisoning us for thinking differently.

That they not persecute us. That they do not exile us. That they do not insult us.

That they do not carry our resources off to the centralizing authorities in La Paz.

That they do not bring the Venezuelan military to suppress us. That they not treat us like enemies. They should treat us as their brothers, which we are. Treat us as an industrious people, a mature population that knows how to decide its own future.

From here on, our fight, our struggle is to make the MAS government recognize that we have chosen a distinct road from that of the socialism of Hugo Chávez. In other words, we have chosen autonomy and freedom as a way of life. It is not moral nor is it possible to impose a Constitution on people who have rejected it.

Compatriots: we need a country where we all coexist in peace. And for that, we propose a pact between the two visions for Bolivia. An accord that recognizes the culture, the identity, and the faith of the autonomist departments, while also being a path that recognizes the culture, the identity, and the faith of the departments that voted for the socialism of the MAS.

We have two great visions, and together we must construct a great Bolivia.

We face a great stalemate. On one hand, we have the MAS Constitution that does not recognize autonomy, and it takes our resources off to the centralizing authorities in

La Paz. On the other hand, we have Santa Cruz, Beni, Pando, Tarija, and Chuquisca, departments that have won the right to autonomy.

Facing this NATIONAL stalemate, the only solution for moving forward is a MAJOR NATIONAL PACT.

It is in the hands of President Evo Morales Ayma to make that pact a reality, an accord that is the only way to guarantee peaceful and democratic coexistence for all Bolivians.

Finally, I want to thank the people of Santa Cruz. And the people of Santa Cruz—let me make clear—are all Bolivians, men and women, who live and work in Santa Cruz.

Thank you our indigenous brothers. Thank you the workers.

Thanks to the mothers and fathers of families.

Thanks to the students.

Thanks to the people in the rural areas and in the cities.

Thanks to the committee and to all its institutions that never doubted and that patriotically launched the NO campaign.

Thank you to everyone. Thanks to Bolivia. Thank you, Potosí. Thank you, Oruro.

Thank you, La Paz. Thank you, El Alto. Thank you, Cochabamba. Thank you, Chuquisaca.

Thank you, courageous Sabina [Cuellar].

Thanks to all for this clear and decisive vote against poverty. Thank you for this clear and decisive vote in favor of autonomy.

And from the bottom of my heart, I give thanks to God.

Viva Santa Cruz! Viva autonomy! Viva freedom!

Document 11.5 Tuffí Aré, "A Reading of Yes and No," *El Deber*, January 26, 2009

Source: http://www.eldeber.com.bo/2009/2009-01-26/vernotaahora.php?id=0901252 22824. Translated by Patricia Rosas.

The government's celebration over the triumph of the YES campaign is justified, but it should also be moderated. Only this past Sunday, the 25th, the people did approve the new Political Constitution of the State (PCS), an event that guarantees the continuity of Juan Evo Morales Ayma's political project.

The Yes campaign won, but a large part of the country also voted for the No campaign. Certainly, the referendum's outcome strengthens Morales' mandate. The question is whether the Yes victory will mean that the text of the Constitution can put an end, once and for all, to the problems of governability that persist in the country and resolve the structural crisis that has lasted for several years. At the beginning of the Yes campaign, Morales hoped to win about 80 percent support for the new PCS.

As the referendum neared, he had to moderate his expectations and hope for 65 percent, that is, support close to what he achieved last August in order to remain in power. Two months ago, the president bragged that he had defeated the opposition and had made them sign their capitulation. But this triumphalism led him to make errors that were visible in his campaign. And in the home stretch, it was more his errors of officialdom than the opposition's virtues that forced him to moderate his expectations of an overwhelming vote in favor of the Constitution. Despite everything, we cannot deny the victory of the Yes campaign.

We must also recognize the still-intact counterweight of the power in Santa Cruz, Beni, Tarija, and Pando. Moreover, it is evident that there are two visions for the country that have not rendered themselves compatible in a single Constitution. This leads us to conclude that the alleged national accord is, as yet, just a presentment, and that Bolivia is a very complex nation, difficult to govern. How should we read yesterday's results? The first is that most of the country supports the MAS project, but Evo Morales' party is still far from reaching total supremacy, an absolute territorial hegemony.

It is also unclear if the opposition appreciates that the stalemate with officialdom persists. The adversaries of Morales must undertake a mature self-criticism and redefine their strategies in order to propose to the country as a whole an inclusive development project, which would win over everyone. The polarization is scarcely continuing in Chuquisaca, where the capital, Sucre, continues being confronted by its provinces' vision. In the high plateau, the MAS vision continues being hegemonic.

It is true that in the urban worlds of the departments of La Paz, Oruro, and Potosí, a call for an alternative project to the one offered by Morales is beginning to appear. The MAS continues to control Cochabamba, above all, for the power that the Chapare Province lends it, since officialdom continues to be contested in the center of this department. So far, no surprises. It is in Pando, however, where we begin to find an interesting variant in the national political map. There, the government made its worst misstep of the entire campaign.

An assumption was made that having military control over the long-suffering Pando population was not only going to repeat the MAS success of the August recall referendum but that a Yes victory would be a cinch to achieve there. But just the opposite happened. The reliance on repression in the end seemed to inspire the Pandinos to rebel. *Voto bronca* (punishment voting)? Probably. As for Santa Cruz, it is worth taking note that the opposition retains its hegemonic position, but this time it has had to resign itself to losing control of three or four provinces, such as Ichilo, Caballero, Ñuflo de Chávez, and Obispo Santistevan.

Nevertheless, the polarization attempted by the government is still distanced from the Santa Cruz region. Finally, in Tarija, the prefectural ranks seem to have been divided in ways similar to the virtual technical stalemate of the recall vote. The cause? It is a mystery.

With one difficult political stage closing, another even more complex one opens. The opposition has not recognized the triumph of the government, and it is resisting the imposition of the Constitution in places where the No campaign won.

Morales celebrates and overemphasizes that the victory of the Yes campaign gives the Constitution sufficient legitimacy for its absolute observance. For now, we will have to hope that the two sides are sincere when they say they want to reach a national accord to implement the Constitution without tensions.

For Further Reading

Albro, Robert. "Bolivia's 'Evo Phenomenon': From Identity to What?," *Journal of Latin American Anthropology* 11:2 (2006), 408–28.

Brysk, Alison. *From Tribal Village to Global Village: Indian Rights and International Relations in Latin America*. Stanford: Stanford University Press, 2000.

Canessa, Andrew. "Contesting Hybridity: Evangelistas and Kataristas in Highland Bolivia," *Journal of Latin American Studies* 32:1 (2000), 115–44.

Canessa, Andrew. "Todos somos indígenas: Towards a New Language of Indigeneity," *Bulletin of Latin American Research* 25:2 (2006), 241–63.

Corrales, Javier. "In Search of a Theory of Polarization: Lessons from Venezuela, 1999–2005," *European Review of Latin American and Caribbean Studies*, 79 (2005), 105–18.

Dunkerley, James. "Evo Morales, the 'Two Bolivias,' and the Third Bolivian Revolution," *Journal of Latin American Studies* 39:1 (2007), 133–66.

Ellner, Steven B. "Venezuela: Defying Globalization's Logic," *NACLA Report on the Americas* 39:2 (2005), 20–4.

García Linera, Álvaro. "State Crisis and Popular Power," *New Left Review* 37 (2006), 73–85

Gustafson, Bret. "Spectacles of Autonomy and Crisis: Or, What Bulls and Beauty Queens Have to Do with Regionalism in Eastern Bolivia," *Journal of Latin American Anthropology* 11:2 (2006), 351–79.

Gustafson, Bret. *New Languages of the State: Indigenous Resurgence and the Politics of Knowledge in Bolivia*. Durham, NC: Duke University Press, 2009

Lucero, José Antonio. *Struggles of Voice: The Politics of Indigenous Representation in the Andes*. Pittsburgh: University of Pittsburgh Press, 2008.

Parker, Dick. "Chávez and the Search for an Alternative to Neoliberalism," *Latin American Perspectives* 32:2 (2005), 39–50.

Roberts, Bryan R. and Alejandro Portes. "Coping with the Free Market City: Collective Action in Six Latin American Cities at the end of the Twentieth Century," *Latin American Research Review* 41:2 (2006), 57–83.

Salman, Ton. "The Jammed Democracy: Bolivia's Troubled Political Learning Process," *Bulletin of Latin American Research* 25:2 (2006), 163–82.

Steiglitz, Joseph. *Globalization and Its Discontents*. New York: Norton, 2003.

Veltmeyer, Henry and Petras, James F. "Bolivia and the Political Dynamics of Change," *European Review of Latin American and Caribbean Studies*, 83 (2007), 105–19.

Yashar, Deborah J. *Contesting Citizenship in Latin America: The Rise of Indigenous Movements and the Postliberal Challenge*. Cambridge: Cambridge University Press, 2005.

Epilogue

The ending is critical to most stories. A good ending helps the narrative feel finished, helps it to make sense to the reader. For their part, histories tend to end with commonly accepted turning points, affirming to the reader that the end of the era means the end of the text. It is easier this way, as our stories have predetermined beginnings and conclusions. Histories of the colonial period usually stop at independence. Stories of specific processes (revolution, emancipation, industrialization) are likewise framed by what any given author determines to be the end of that process.[1] Even texts that bring us into the present do this, as history by definition concludes with the current day. When compelling, these endings have the power to give the past a finished quality, and to constitute a place and its people. We might describe a place called Latin America because we have imagined a Latin American past.

It is my hope that this text has made that task quite difficult. Instead of a history of Latin America, the reader was introduced to eleven distinct Latin American pasts, each in some ways incommensurable with the others. We might see whispers of a common Latin American past in the way Evo Morales' current claims about indigeneity evoke memories of earlier struggles over race and citizenship, or in the ways that economic growth and progress remain as important in the region today as they did a century ago. Still, it is likely that these similarities are better understood as an invitation to dialogue about linkages, continuities, and discontinuities than as evidence of that elusive thing we would call Latin America.

What would that dialogue look like? We may begin by wondering why we need a concept of Latin America at all. Would the histories of this region be more compelling if they were simply local, national, or framed by some larger concept, such as the post–colonial world? Would we be better served by a frame of reference that made the inequality between rich and poor nations the center of our narrative? Or is the method we have adopted here the best practice because it relies on a variety of approaches to the past and ultimately generates multiple histories?

Ideologues on both the left and the right do not tend to favor this tendency, because it undermines their desire to use the past as a morality tale, as a justification for their current agenda. Romantics too tend to eschew this approach, as their desire to find the essence of the thing—the quintessential Latin American novel, for instance—is made impossible if we suggest that they create the fiction that is Latin America through their search for its essence. We have chosen it, however, for one simple reason. This text does not aim to produce a vision of Latin America that fits into the fantastic imaginings of readers. It instead complicates that fiction by interrogating it at every point, and substituting a narrative that relies on a sense of complexity, contingency, and at times, acceptance that there are things about the past that we cannot know.

Throughout the histories in this text we see individuals working to shape the worlds they live in. Like people everywhere, they are invariably constrained by their pasts, their present circumstances, and the limits of what they believe to be possible. In making an effort to understand these people on their own terms and develop a more nuanced view of the worlds they lived in, it becomes much more difficult to either insert them into a morality play or stand in judgment of their failures and shortcomings. And it is only then that we begin to acquire some actual knowledge of the history of the region we study.

Glossary

Agrarista (agrarian) Those who demand land be distributed to peasants. Term used principally in Mexico.

Altiplano A region of high mountain plateaus. Term used in the Andes.

Austerity measures Fiscal policies implemented to reduce government debt and spending relative to GDP, usually at the behest of the International Monetary Fund.

Authoritarian government System where the will of leaders tends to override civil society.

Banana republic Central American and Caribbean nations where a dependence on just a few commodity exports makes the country extremely vulnerable to external pressures.

Baroque catholicism A tradition in which elaborate symbolism and ornate decorative practices were used to project the authority of the Catholic Church.

Bourbon reforms A general term describing economic and political reforms undertaken by the House of Bourbon, which came to power in Spain after the end of Habsburg rule in 1700. Overall, changes undertaken during the course of 80 years were intended to improve defense, make administration more efficient, and generate more revenue for the crown.

Cabildo A town council.

Cariocas Residents of Rio de Janeiro.

Carnivalesque Describes moments of social inversion, when marginalized and oppressed groups symbolically place themselves on top of society, subverting the social order.

Castas Colonial term describing people of mixed racial (and cultural) origins.

Caste system Colonial system that enforced social position through caste status.

Caudillo (caudillismo) Military strongmen.

Clientelism A political system in which political networks work principally to dole out political favors to friends and allies of office holders (distributing the spoils provided by the state).

Cocalero A peasant coca grower. Term used in Bolivia.

Cold War The period from 1948 to 1989 characterized by global competition between the United States and U.S.S.R. Regions like Latin America were the settings for numerous proxy battles.

Compadrazgo   A notion of fictive kinship, in which god-parents and close friends effectively become family members.

Comunero   Peasants with a strong connection to community and long history of resistance against outsiders. Term used in the Andes.

Conservatives   A nineteenth-century term describing groups that sought to maintain colonial-era political, social, and cultural hierarchies. Conservatives generally believed the end of the old order would produce chaos.

Corporatism   Systems in which one participates in political and social life as a member of a corporate group (as a member of an indigenous community, a union, or a professional association, for instance).

Coup d'état   The overthrow of a government by a small elite, usually led by members of the military.

Criollos   Persons of European origin born in the Americas.

Crony capitalism   An economic and political system where businessmen rely on close connections with the state to prosper, and where those without such connections are deeply disadvantaged.

Debt peonage   A labor practice in which workers are tied to their employer through debt, and generally cannot leave that employer until debts are paid.

Dependency theory   An economic theory that posits that poor regions remain impoverished because of asymmetrical relations with more prosperous regions.

Descamisados   Literally "shirtless ones," Eva Perón's term for her supporters.

Dirty wars –   Refers to conflicts (1960s–1990s) that involved state-sponsored violence meted out against largely unarmed groups identified as "subversives." Torture, summary execution, and forced exile were relatively common strategies for silencing regime opponents.

Enganche labor   A labor contracting system, common in plantation agriculture, in which workers sign a contract (often under duress) and are forced to work until the contract ends.

Estancia (estancieros)   Large rural estates. Term used commonly in Argentina.

Favela   Urban slums. Term used in Brazil.

Feminicide   The murder of women because they are women.

Finca (finqueros)   A rural estate, sometimes a plantation. Term used in Southern Mexico, Central America, and parts of South America.

Gamonalismo   The Andean system in which large landowners exploit and dominate the indigenous and other poor peoples on their estates.

Golpe de Estado   The overthrow of a government by a small elite, usually led by members of the military.

Gross Domestic Product (GDP)   The value of all goods and services produced in a given country during a single year.

Haciendas (hacendados)   Large rural estates. Term used in Mexico.

Hegemony   The domination of one group over another. Hegemony suggests that domination is not simply a function of military influence, but of cultural and social practices as well. The concept imagines that systems of domination are contested and negotiated, and not simply coercive.

Historietas   Graphic novels (comic books).

Import Substitution Industrialization (ISI) An economic policy, popular from the 1930s to the 1960s, that promoted industrial growth by supplanting imports with domestically produced manufactures.

Junta A small group of military leaders (sometimes including some civilians) who dominate the state, often in the aftermath of a coup.

Kataristas A political tendency in the Andes that emerged during the 1960s, which sought to empower a radicalized indigenous peasantry in part through the defense of indigenous cultures.

Latifundia A system in which large agricultural estates rely on workforces that are tied to or dependent on the estates.

Ley fuga "Shot while trying to escape." A policing practice in which criminal suspects are executed without first being tried and convicted.

Liberals (liberalism) Nineteenth-century term describing those who favored some array of individual rights, free market capitalism, and limited democracy. Liberals opposed monarchy and special privileges (*fueros*) for the monarchy, the aristocracy, Indian villages, the church, and the military.

Libertos Former slaves.

Limpieza de sangre "Cleanliness of the Blood." Term used to denote the amount of European blood in any given individual, which in turn played an important role in personal prestige during the colonial and later periods.

Machista A term used to describe contexts in which characteristics considered to be aggressively heterosexual and masculine are valued.

Manichean Practices and belief systems that tend to divide the world into extremes of good and evil.

Manumission The act of freeing an individual slave.

Maoists Aficionados of Mao Zedong. Maoists advocate a revolution in which peasant guerrillas overwhelm the cities.

Marshall Plan Plan by the U.S. government to speed the reconstruction of Europe at the end of the Second World War through aid and investment.

Mass politics Political movements based in the widespread mobilization of popular groups through mass communication techniques.

Media luna The eastern lowland departments of Bolivia.

Mestizo A person with both European and indigenous ancestry. It may denote race, but is principally a cultural signifier.

Millennarianism Popular movements that coalesce around the belief that a major transformation in the world is pending. Millennarian movements are generally informed by a deep religious sensibility that in turn spurs dramatic political acts.

Misery belts The impoverished, often ad hoc communities of rural migrants that emerged on the fringes of Latin America's largest cities, beginning in the 1960s. Rural migrants continue to move to these communities, but they are now the home to multiple generations of the urban poor.

Monocrop economy An economy that is dependent on the export of a very limited number of commodities.

Mulatto A person of African and European ancestry.

Narcotraficante Individuals who earn income in the illicit drug trade.

Neo-liberalism   Sometimes called neo-conservatism, describes the belief (increasingly popular after 1970) that governments needed to reduce spending, regulation, and taxes, and promote foreign trade and investment.

Oligarchy   Political or economic system in which power rests in the hands of a small elite.

Orientalism   The practice of representing non-Western cultures as irreconcilably different from those of Western Europe and the United States, and implying that this difference indicates inferiority.

Peninsular   An individual born in the Iberian peninsula.

Plantations   Agricultural estates in semi-tropical and tropical environments that cultivate a limited number of high value commodities.

Populism   Political practices in which leaders appeal for support from a broad community of supporters, defined as the folk, citizens, or the people, usually with the aid of mass communication.

Porteño   A resident of Buenos Aires.

Positivism   A nineteenth-century ideology, informed by the writings of Herbert Spencer and Auguste Comte, which posited that society needed to be governed by scientific principles rather than democratic practices. "Order and Progress" was a key positivist claim.

Radionovelas   Radio soap operas.

Relics   In Catholic tradition, the physical remnants of a deceased saint, venerated as a representation of that saint.

Rentier states   A state that derives most of its incomes from rents (i.e. royalties from mineral concessions and hydrocarbons), making it less reliant on other forms of taxation. Political theorists suggest that, because they do not rely on a broad citizenry for tax revenue, rentier states tend to be less democratic.

Rondas campesinas   Peasant self-defense committees, which played a critical role in the Peruvian civil conflict of the 1980s and 1990s.

Samba   A popular Brazilian musical form, rooted in a mixture of African and European traditions.

Serrano   A person from the high desert regions of Northern Mexico. Used to describe the followers of Pancho Villa in Mexico's 1910 Revolution.

Shock treatments   The sudden imposition of economic austerity measures (i.e. cuts in government spending), meant to "shock" the economy into health.

Tango   An Argentine music and dance form, originally popular among poor residents of Buenos Aires.

Testimonio   A literary practice that emerged during the 1980s, which relies on the testimony of persons who self-identify as members of marginalized or oppressed groups (e.g. indigenous peoples, women, victims of torture).

The Two Republics   The Spanish colonial practice of attempting to divide the population into two distinct communities, *indios* and *españoles*.

Usos y costumbres **(customary law)**   A right claimed by many contemporary indigenous groups, to preserve their customary governance, judicial, and other practices.

Vanguard   A small, committed elite, which endeavors to shape a mass of followers to reflect its ideals.

Notes

Introduction: Latin America's Useable Past

1 The former is the cities largest urban park, and the latter is Mexico City's historical central square.
2 These last designations are typically reserved for persons born in the United States, but they can nonetheless be found sometimes in the media describing Mexicans.
3 This is a somewhat obscene descriptor for people from Mexico City, commonly used in other parts of the country.
4 For our purposes, Latin America comprises Mexico, Central America, the Caribbean, and South America. For an excellent in-depth discussion of this question, see Marshall Eakin, "Does Latin America Have a Common History" (a pdf is available on the website). Students are also encouraged to read Benedict Anderson's *Imagined Communities* (London and New York: Verso, 1983).
5 The term often used to describe this phenomenon is orientalism.
6 This narrative suggests that Mexicans share a common culture built on the trauma imposed on indigenous cultures by the Spanish Conquest in 1521. It constitutes a chapter in his epic work, *The Labyrinth of Solitude* (New York: Grove, 1961). Claudio Lomnitz' *Exits from The Labyrinth* (Berkeley: California University Press, 1993) represents one of the most interesting critiques of this tradition.
7 See, for instance, Bernard Goldberg, *Bias: A CBS Insider Exposes How the Media Distort the News* (New York: Perennial, 2003).

1 Independence Narratives, Past and Present

1 "Schoolhouse Rocks, Shot Heard Round the World," by Bob Dorough, 1976. See http://www.youtube.com/watch?v=7VQA5NDNkUM.
2 A good place to start on Sáenz is Sarah Chambers, "Republican Friendship: Manuela Saenz Writes Women into the Nation, 1835–1856," *Hispanic American Historical Review* 81: 2, 2001, 225–57.
3 A free womb law declared that children born to slaves would be free.
4 The full letter was nearly eight thousand words long, and can be found in Spanish on the website.
5 Translated by Lewis Bertrand in *Selected Writings of Bolívar* (New York: The Colonial Press Inc., 1951).
6 http://www.guyana.org/Speeches/ishmael_bolivar.html.

2   *Caudillos* versus the Nation State

1   "[T]hey do things differently there." From *The Go-Between* (London: H. Hamilton, 1953).
2   This is a system of government where power is controlled by a small number of elites.
3   The term for the owners of large estates varies from region to region. They and their estates are variously known by the terms hacendados/haciendas, finqueros/fincas, estancieros/estancias, latifundistas/latifundia.
4   Protecturia de indígenas.
5   Mestizo is a common term in Latin America, indicating a person with both European and Indigenous ancestry. It is often used as a racial category, but is also used as a cultural category, with no reference to physical ancestry.
6   The term denotes people of mixed racial origins.
7   Facundo was a real caudillo, but the text was indirectly aimed at Rosas.
8   Shumway, 206 (see "For Further Reading").
9   This term describes persons from Buenos Aires.
10   These are owners of large estates, or estancias.
11   Translator's note: The political party that opposed Rosas.
12   Translator's note: In 1820, Juan Manuel de Rosas, leader of the Federalist Party, was given the title of "Restorer of the Laws" by the legislature when he reestablished the Federalists' legal government.
13   Translator's note: Refers to the British and other fair-haired, light-skinned foreigners, with a pejorative connotation.
14   Translator's note: Crested caracara (*Polyborus plancus*), a bird of prey common to Argentina and belonging to the falcon family.
15   Translator's note: The Day of Sorrows was the Friday before Good Friday. Vatican Council II decided to remove it from the liturgical calendar since it duplicated the feast day of Our Lady of Sorrows, September 15.
16   Translator's note: Reference to the 1833 Revolution of the Restorers, which defeated the governor, Juan Ramón Balcarce, and established Juan Manuel de Rosas' dominion over the province of Buenos Aires.
17   Translator's note: Rosas' personal army of henchmen.
18   Translator's note: A rectangular piece of fabric or leather wrapped around the back and front of the waist, passed between the legs over the trousers, worn for warmth and protection by farmhands, gauchos, and, in general, by the humbler elements of society, the prosperous preferring to wear the traditional short Spanish trousers called *calzón corto español*.
19   Translator's note: Azul was located south of the province of Buenos Aires.
20   Translator's note: *Matasiete* = Killed seven. In Lunfardo, *matahambre* means "a dead man"; "matahambre" or "matambre" is also a typical Argentine dish that translates as "rolled flank steak."
21   Translator's note: "Franciscan Saint and Patron of the Blacks and Mulattos of Buenos Aires," in Evelyn Picon Garfield and Iván A. Schulman, *Las literaturas hispánicas: introducción a su estudio* (Detroit: Wayne State University Press, 1991, 146).
22   Spanish: "verga." According to literary critics Burgos and Salessi, *El Matadero*, the term refers to the use of sodomy as a form of torture employed by the Federalists. In the story, the "verga" is clearly a whip, specifically an *arreador*, used by cowboys, herders, and carters, also called "verga de toro" because the skin of a bull's penis was used to cover its wooden handle (*Diccionario Argentino*,1910). In English: "pizzle": a whip made from a bull's penis.

3   Race and Citizenship in the New Republics

1   Debt peonage tied workers to agricultural estates because the workers were extended a loan (sometimes involuntarily) and then required to work for a specific employer until the loan was

paid off. They would often accrue more debt while working, and thus become caught in a cycle of debt.
2 At the time Africans made up 40 percent of the island's population.
3 People with African and European ancestry.
4 Partly due to these pressures, Britain would proclaim emancipation in 1834 for its 668,000 slaves. A system of forced apprenticeships would be abandoned amidst strikes and protests four years later.
5 A resident of São Paulo.
6 A resident of the northeast.
7 Capoeira is an Afro-Brazilian form of dance that invokes self-defense as a part of its form.
8 Notable exceptions include Francisco Manzano, Olaudah Equiano, and Miguel Barnet's controversial (auto)biography of the runaway Cuban slave, Esteban Montejo.

4 The Export Boom as *Modernity*

1 Friedman was the Nobel Prize winning University of Chicago economist who became one of the most important advocates of Free Market Capitalism For Latin America during the 1960s–1980s.
2 Clorinda Matto de Turner believed that the largely vegetarian diet consumed by Indians caused their brains to swell, and urged that more meat be introduced into their diets. She was not alone in describing what others called the "tragedy of meat," and in trying to introduce miracle cures to Indian backwardness (Manuel Gamio, the *father* of Mexican anthropology, later tried to introduce a tortilla made from one-third soy).
3 GDP measures the value of all goods and services produced in the national economy in a single year.
4 This analysis is drawn from Victor Bulmer Thomas.
5 In Mexico a series of domestic measures, including the privatization of land (which put land and labor on the market), and the suppression of alcabalas (taxes that placed barriers to internal trade), produced a growth rate of 2.3 percent per year 1877–1910, doubling per capita income.
6 An excellent example of this can be found in Greg Grandin, "Can the Subaltern Be Seen? Photography and the Affects of Nationalism," *Hispanic American Historical Review* 84:1 (2004), 83–111.
7 In this, they were unlike about one-third of the students in the school, who fled.

5 Signs of Crisis in a Gilded Age

1 See his book, *Hybrid Cultures: Strategies for Entering and Leaving Modernity* (Minneapolis: University of Minnesota Press, 1995).
2 Dario did pen other poems that were far more sympathetic to the United States, including "Salutación del águila."
3 Millennial movements generally mix deep religious devotion, a sense that the end of the world as we know it is at hand, and rebellion. Mexico had its own millennial movements, including Tomochic in 1892.
4 Those groups that showed their strength most forcefully through the use of arms would generally also be the most successful in demanding land from the revolutionary state.
5 Miners were of course a distinct part of this group, and in some regions factories were built in rural areas. Plantation agriculture, which tended to be highly mechanized and specialized, could also be included. Miners and rural workers did take part in various labor movements. Several important strikes during this era took place at mines (e.g. Cananea, Mexico, 1906).
6 In all, two million immigrants came to Argentina between 1870 and 1910, mostly from Spain and Italy. The rural working class remained largely Argentine born, but the working proletariat was largely foreign born.

7 In 1914 there were only 110,000 Jews in Argentina, out of a total national population of 7.9 million.

6 Commerce, Coercion, and America's Empire

1 We use the term "American" here to describe the United States. There has been considerable debate among scholars about its merit in recent years. Some have substituted North American or some other term because they find the very term imperialistic (we leave aside how Mexicans and Canadians feel about the use of North American in this context). I use the term for two reasons. Firstly, it is how citizens of the United States call themselves. Secondly, Latin Americans generally know what it means, and very few of them use the term to refer to themselves.

2 See his book, *Capitalism and Slavery* (Chapel Hill: University of North Carolina Press, 1944).

3 The plantations they left in their wakes suffered from reduced biodiversity, and were not easily turned to other forms of agriculture.

4 Víctor Raúl Haya de la Torre famously identified Central America as the critical testing ground for U.S. imperialism in Latin America (see an excerpt from 1929's *A donde va indoamericana* on the website (2nd edn., Santiago de Chile: Ercilla, 1935). Others in this camp included Augusto Sandino, C. L. R. James (author of *The Black Jacobins*), and Fidel Castro.

5 The plan also empowered local peasant committees to oversee their lands, shifting power from the central government to marginalized groups.

6 The domino theory, which proposed that weak regimes would fall to communism when influenced by Communist neighbors, eventually seriously weakening the United States, was first articulated by George Kennan in a 1947 article in Foreign Affairs. It was a guiding theory of U.S. cold war politics, and part of the rationale behind both U.S. policy in Latin America and the Vietnam War.

7 Allen Dulles had once served on the Board of Trustees of the UFCO, and John Foster Dulles served as legal counsel to the Firm before joining the administration. Both held UFCO stock.

8 In the aftermath UFCO agreed to new taxes on profits of 30 percent (up from 10 percent in 1953). A total of 250,000 acres of land were returned to the company, but the UFCO did agree to give up 100,000 for a land reform, and the United States gave $80 million in aid. After PBSUCCESS the Eisenhower administration allowed an anti-trust suit against UFCO to proceed that weakened the company, which ultimately rebranded itself as Chiquita Bananas.

9 Bartenders at the Hotel Nacional in Cuba even invented a drink named after Mary Pickford.

10 The conglomerate was founded in 1902, as a joint venture between the Imperial Tobacco Company and James Duke's American Tobacco Company.

11 The film debuted in Mexico City in December 1944, and in the United States in 1945.

12 The film actually debuted in Rio de Janeiro in 1942, and was released in the United States in 1943.

13 Sandino wrote a notable letter to Hipólito Yrigoyen in 1929, called his "Plan for Realizing Bolívar's Dream."

14 Sandino was killed in 1934, but the movement that overthrew the U.S.-backed Somoza regime in 1979 was named for him.

7 Power to the People

1 Daryle Williams, *Culture Wars in Brazil*, p. 87.

2 Radio Nacional began as a commercial station and was taken over by the government in 1940, but continued as a commercial venture, featuring music and radionovelas.

3 There is some question as to the authenticity of the note. Quoted in Levine, 150-2 (see "For Further Reading").

4 Levine, p. 138.

5 Literally, "A Peronist Day." The phrase was used among Perón's supporters for decades to describe a good day.
6 See Chapter 5.
7 As with translations of slang generally, in order to maintain the form and meaning, this translation is not literal. For the Spanish, see the website, or www.todotango.com.
8 Clientelism involves politicians acting as personal agents for their constituents, providing favors and benefits in return for support. The Radical Party used this strategy to gain votes in working-class neighborhoods consistently during the 1910s and 1920s.
9 This is the term used in Latin America to describe military governments characterized by a committee of officers rather than one dominant leader.
10 Some ten thousand people died in the earthquake, which remains the greatest national disaster in Argentine history.
11 It was originally called the Fundación Maria Eva Duarte de Perón.

8   A Decade of Revolution in Cuba

1 For a recent example of this, see Sean Penn, "Conversations with Chávez and Castro," in the *Nation*, November 25, 2008, and Roger Cohen "The End of the Cuban Revolution," in the *New York Times*, December 5, 2008.
2 That thirty years later doves again landed on Castro during a speech commemorating the Revolution is used by partisans to either remind their adversaries of his mythical powers, or suggest that he was simply a slick manipulator.
3 "Hasta la victoria, siempre" is perhaps the most important revolutionary slogan.
4 This is the measure economists use for describing inequality. Zero would be perfect equality. Most Western European nations have Gini coefficients of around 0.3; Latin American nations, where we see some of the greatest inequality on the planet, average around 0.5.
5 In the 15 years after Kennedy announced that all Cuban exiles would be granted immediate asylum in the U.S., 700,000 Cubans took advantage of this offer. Dentists, doctors, and technicions fled the island (20,000 out of 85,000 professionals) leaving the islands schools, hospitals, factories, and administration without expertise, but also open to control from revolutionary cadres.
6 Pilar López Gonzales was a protagonist in Oscar Lewis and his research team's study of life in revolutionary Cuba, the three–volume *Living the Revolution* (Oscar Lewis, Ruth M. Lewis, and Susan M. Rigdon, *Four Women: Living the Revolution: An Oral History of Contemporary Cuba*, Champaign: University of Illinois Press, 1977).
7 Small farms also generally provided little tax revenue, as small farmers were good at avoiding taxes.
8 *Junta Central de Planificación*.
9 See, for example, Lino Novás Calvo's *Manera de Contar* (New York: Las Americas Publishing Co., 1970).
10 Readers who wish to see other interviews will find them on the website.

9   Peru in an Age of Terror

1 Maoists are communists who pattern their idea of revolution after the Chinese Revolution and Chairman Mao Zedong. They tend to be exceptionally doctrinaire and vanguardist, and follow a strategy of fomenting a rural revolution among peasants that is intended to surround and ultimately choke off the cities.
2 Literally, he overthrew himself. The term *golpe de estado* is the Spanish equivalent of the French *coup d'état*.

3 The 1984 report for the Conadep can be found in English at: http://web.archive.org/web/20031004074316/nuncamas.org/english/library/nevagain/nevagain_001.htm. A link should be included on the website. The Rettig commission report can be found at: http://www.usip.org/library/tc/doc/reports/chile/chile_1993_toc.html.

4 Look no further than Werner Herzog's 1972 film, *Aguirre: Wrath of God*, to understand how this narrative can explain all types of modern holocausts.

5 ISI relied on high tariffs, subsidized inputs to industry (in several countries government monopolies in oil, steel, electricity, and transportation reduced production costs), and a labor force made compliant by a mix of wages and social spending (free education through university, health care, pensions, subsidized transport), along with occasional repression.

6 A classic example of this complaint can be seen in Carolina Maria de Jesus' *Child of the Dark* (New York: Penguin, 1962) which is based on diaries she wrote between 1955 and 1960.

7 It was named for a phrase used by José Carlos Mariátegui to describe the prospects of a Marxist revolution.

8 Some beneficiaries also chafed under the seemingly arbitrary and overly bureaucratic nature of the government's programs.

9 www.cverdad.org.pe/ingles/informacion/discursos/en_apublicas08.php.

10 In Scilingo's case, he generated sympathy through his tale of following orders, of remorse, and of unfair treatment at the hands of civilian authorities. See Menchú's *I, Rigoberta Menchú*, Partnoy's *The Little School*, and Verbitstky's *Confessions of an Argentine Dirty Warrior*. These texts are in "For Further Reading," this chapter.

11 Diana Taylor argues this persuasively in *Disappearing Acts*: see "For Further Reading," this chapter.

12 Christopher R. Browning, *Ordinary Men: Reserve Police Battalion 101 and the Final Solution in Poland* (New York: Harper, 1993).

13 Translator's note: Pensions paid to former congressional members at the level of current congressional pay.

14 Translator's note: The first session of the Peruvian legislature is between July and December, so the text (para que ello suceda se necesitan dos primeras legislaturas ordinarias consecutivas) means that the reforms would have to be approved during two consecutive July–December sessions, in other words, as much as a year and a half could pass before the reforms would be approved (April 1992 to December 1993).

10   A Right to Have Rights in the New Democracies

1 This concept has been much discussed in recent years: see, for example, Werner Hamacher, "The Right to Have Rights (Four-and-a-Half Remarks)," *South Atlantic Quarterly* 103: 2–3, 2004, 343–56; and Neil Harvey, *The Chiapas Rebellion* (Durham, NC: Duke, 1998).

2 See the Declaration at http://www.un.org/en/documents/udhr/.

3 During the dirty war the term "to be disappeared" indicated that state security forces had kidnapped a person.

4 There are 30 articles in all.

5 Mothers of the Plaza de Mayo. This plaza is in the center of Buenos Aires, across from the presidential palace.

6 Tallies vary, from a low of around 9,000 to as many as 30,000.

7 The Argentine *junta* referred to its dirty war as *el proceso*—or The Process of National Reorganization.

8 This ranges from protests and political organizing, to soup kitchens and the creation of micro-credit organizations. The latter (banks that administer tiny loans to women who might want to engage in a small scale business) have provided loans to over 40 million Latin Americans since they began operating in the 1980s. Today more than 400 micro-finance agencies give out loans that average less than $1,000, but are critical to the small businesses that provide an income to about 40 percent of Latin Americans.

9 From Article 3 of the Universal Declaration of Human Rights.
10 Today Mexico City has around 18 million residents. São Paulo has 17.7 million, Buenos Aires 12.4 million, Rio 10.5 million, Lima 7.5 million, and Bogotá 6.8 million.
11 This term describes the impoverished communities that literally ring many contemporary Latin American cities. These communities are relatively recent phenomena, produced originally by rural migration to the cities.
12 The country with the highest rate is Venezuela, with 65 per 100,000 people annually.
13 Across the region only about 10 percent of crimes result in an arrest, and half of those lead to a conviction. Ninety percent of Mexicans do not report crimes committed against them.
14 Decriminalization has also proceeded in Argentina and Brazil.
15 These include the UN Convention Relating to the Status of Refugees (1951) and the Protocol Relating to the Status of Refugees (1967).
16 By the end of the decade nearly a million Haitians would also flee to the Dominican Republic.
17 I include people from the Caribbean in this total.
18 There are 17.5 million people with Mexican ancestry living in the United States.
19 They are called the *Matricula Consular de Alta Seguridad* (MCAS). Several million were issued.
20 Over 1.5 million copies were distributed in Mexican border states in 2004–5.

11 Bolvia's Left Turn

1 See the *Economist*, July 17, 2004.
2 His essay "The End of History?" was published in the journal *The National Interest* in 1989. It was later expanded into a 1992 book (*The End of History and the Last Man*, New York: Penguin, 1992).
3 Clientelism is a political practice that functions primarily through support networks in which loyalty is exchanged for material benefits. Tammany Hall was a quintessential clientelistic system. Crony capitalism is a system in which well connected capitalists use their influence with the state to pass laws in their interest, often supporting inefficient or corrupt industries.
4 Millions of Bolivians consume coca in one form or another regularly, and consider it medicinal when not simply made into a powerful drug like cocaine.
5 Cocaleros are peasant farmers who grow coca. Some of their coca is consumed domestically, its leaves chewed, brewed into a tea or in some other form, as has been done for centuries. Some coca is also processed into cocaine, much of which is exported to the United States.
6 In this, he comes from a political tradition that emerged in the 1970s that called themselves "kataristas" after the eighteenth-century Aymara peasant rebel, Tupac Katari.
7 The MAS got only 64,425 votes in the national elections in 1999, mostly from in and around Cochabamba.
8 Under the old law the government charged an 18 percent royalty on gas production. With the new law, the old royalty was supplemented with a 32 percent tax at some wellheads and 64 percent at others (bringing the total to 82 percent in some of the largest fields). A newly nationalized YPFB also claimed a 51 percent ownership stake in all wells under the new law.
9 Beni and Pando held theirs on June 1, 2008.
10 Some 62.5 percent call themselves *camba*.
11 A rentier state depends on rents generated by a monopoly on natural resources for revenue instead of taxes on income. Rentier states tend to be poor at promoting economic growth and authoritarian.
12 They are mostly Guaraní, Ayoreo, Chiquitano, and Guarayo.
13 These deposits may fuel the next generation of electric cars.
14 This is a contested claim, but it is possible that private sector ownership would produce better wages, more tax revenue, and better economic growth, and that a government that was less dependent on rents from a single industry and more reliant on the electorate for tax income would be more democratic. Critics invoke a theory of the rentier state to make this argument.
15 See Benedict Anderson, *Imagined Communities: Reflections on the Origin and spread of Nationalism* (London and New York: Verso, 1983).

16 Bolivia has an active blogging community. See voces bolivianas (http://vocesbolivianas.org/) on this.

Epilogue

1 These endings are invariably the subject of historiographical and political debate. The end points of the Mexican Revolution and Industrial Revolution, for example, have long been disputed.

Index